CHILDHOOD, MEMORY, AND THE NATION
YOUNG LIVES UNDER NAZISM IN
CONTEMPORARY GERMAN CULTURE

LEGENDA

LEGENDA is the Modern Humanities Research Association's book imprint for new research in the Humanities. Founded in 1995 by Malcolm Bowie and others within the University of Oxford, Legenda has always been a collaborative publishing enterprise, directly governed by scholars. The Modern Humanities Research Association (MHRA) joined this collaboration in 1998, became half-owner in 2004, in partnership with Maney Publishing and then Routledge, and has since 2016 been sole owner. Titles range from medieval texts to contemporary cinema and form a widely comparative view of the modern humanities, including works on Arabic, Catalan, English, French, German, Greek, Italian, Portuguese, Russian, Spanish, and Yiddish literature. Editorial boards and committees of more than 60 leading academic specialists work in collaboration with bodies such as the Society for French Studies, the British Comparative Literature Association and the Association of Hispanists of Great Britain & Ireland.

The MHRA encourages and promotes advanced study and research in the field of the modern humanities, especially modern European languages and literature, including English, and also cinema. It aims to break down the barriers between scholars working in different disciplines and to maintain the unity of humanistic scholarship. The Association fulfils this purpose through the publication of journals, bibliographies, monographs, critical editions, and the MHRA Style Guide, and by making grants in support of research. Membership is open to all who work in the Humanities, whether independent or in a University post, and the participation of younger colleagues entering the field is especially welcomed.

ALSO PUBLISHED BY THE ASSOCIATION

Critical Texts
Tudor and Stuart Translations • New Translations • European Translations
MHRA Library of Medieval Welsh Literature

MHRA Bibliographies
Publications of the Modern Humanities Research Association

The Annual Bibliography of English Language & Literature
Austrian Studies
Modern Language Review
Portuguese Studies
The Slavonic and East European Review
Working Papers in the Humanities
The Yearbook of English Studies

www.mhra.org.uk
www.legendabooks.com

GERMANIC LITERATURES

Editorial Committee
Chair: Professor Ritchie Robertson (University of Oxford)
Dr Barbara Burns (Glasgow University)
Professor Jane Fenoulhet (University College London)
Professor Anne Fuchs (University College Dublin)
Dr Jakob Stougaard-Nielsen (University College London)
Professor Annette Volfing (University of Oxford)
Professor Susanne Kord (University College London)
Professor John Zilcosky (University of Toronto)

Germanic Literatures includes monographs and essay collections on literature originally written not only in German, but also in Dutch and the Scandinavian languages. Within the German-speaking area, it seeks also to publish studies of other national literatures such as those of Austria and Switzerland. The chronological scope of the series extends from the early Middle Ages down to the present day.

APPEARING IN THIS SERIES

11. *E.T.A. Hoffmann's Orient*, by Joanna Neilly
12. *Structures of Subjugation in Dutch Literature*, by Judit Gera
13. *Isak Dinesen Reading Søren Kierkegaard:
On Christianity, Seduction, Gender, and Repetition*, by Mads Bunch
14. *Yvan Goll: The Thwarted Pursuit of the Whole*, by Robert Vilain
15. *Foreign Parts: German and Austrian Actors on the British Stage 1933–1960*, by Richard Dove
16. *Paul Celan's Unfinished Poetics*, by Thomas C. Connolly
17. *Encounters with Albion: Britain and the British in Texts by Jewish Refugees from Nazism*, by Anthony Grenville
18. *The Law of Poetry: Studies in Hölderlin's Poetics*, by Charles Lewis
19. *Georg Hermann: A Writer's Life*, by John Craig-Sharples
20. *Alfred Döblin: Monsters, Cyborgs and Berliners 1900–1933*, by Robert Craig
21. *Confrontational Readings: Literary Neo-Avant-Gardes in Dutch and German*, edited by Inge Arteel, Lars Bernaerts and Olivier Couder
22. *Poetry, Painting, Park: Goethe and Claude Lorrain*, by Franz R. Kempf
23. *Childhood, Memory, and the Nation: Young Lives under Nazism in Contemporary German Culture*, by Alexandra Lloyd

Managing Editor
Dr Graham Nelson, 41 Wellington Square, Oxford OX1 2JF, UK
www.legendabooks.com

Childhood, Memory, and the Nation

*Young Lives under Nazism in
Contemporary German Culture*

ALEXANDRA LLOYD

Germanic Literatures 23
Modern Humanities Research Association
2020

Published by Legenda
an imprint of the Modern Humanities Research Association
Salisbury House, Station Road, Cambridge CB1 2LA

ISBN 978-1-78188-536-9 (HB)
ISBN 978-1-78188-540-6 (PB)

First published 2020

All rights reserved. No part of this publication may be reproduced or disseminated or transmitted in any form or by any means, electronic, mechanical, photocopying, recording or otherwise, or stored in any retrieval system, or otherwise used in any manner whatsoever without written permission of the copyright owner, except in accordance with the provisions of the Copyright, Designs and Patents Act 1988, or under the terms of a licence permitting restricted copying issued in the UK by the Copyright Licensing Agency Ltd, Saffron House, 6–10 Kirby Street, London EC1N 8TS, *England, or in the USA by the Copyright Clearance Center, 222 Rosewood Drive, Danvers MA 01923. Application for the written permission of the copyright owner to reproduce any part of this publication must be made by email to legenda@mhra.org.uk.*

Disclaimer: Statements of fact and opinion contained in this book are those of the author and not of the editors or the Modern Humanities Research Association. The publisher makes no representation, express or implied, in respect of the accuracy of the material in this book and cannot accept any legal responsibility or liability for any errors or omissions that may be made.

Trademark notice: Product or corporate names may be trademarks or registered trademarks, and are used only for identification and explanation without intent to infringe.

© *Modern Humanities Research Association 2020*

Copy-Editor: Dr Alastair Matthews

CONTENTS

❖

	Acknowledgements	ix
	List of Figures	x
	Introduction	1
1	Children's Lives under Nazism and Contemporary Cultural Memory	15
	Growing Up in the Third Reich, 1933–45	15
	Remembering the Third Reich in the Berlin Republic	19
	Cultural Memory and Emotionally Experienced History	22
	Childhood and the Emotionalization of the Past	28
2	The Alibi of Youth? Writing a National Socialist Childhood	41
	Introduction: Patterns of Childhood	41
	Writing the Childhood of the Self: The Truth of Feelings	44
	Taking Stock: *Zwischenbilanz: Eine Jugend in Berlin* (1992)	45
	A Defence of Childhood: *Ein springender Brunnen* (1998)	52
	Grass's Onions: *Beim Häuten der Zwiebel* (2006)	59
	Conclusion	66
3	Seen, but Not Heard: Memories of Child Holocaust Survivors	77
	Introduction: A Silent Legacy?	77
	Jewish Children as Objects and Agents: Post-War Perspectives	79
	'Für ein Kind war das anders' [For a child it was different]: *weiter leben: Eine Jugend* (1992)	82
	'Ich bin ein Lebensschmuggler' [I am a smuggler of life]: *Die Absonderung* (1991)	90
	Childhood's Games: *Erwachsenenspiele* (1997)	96
	Conclusion	102
4	Imagined Childhoods: Writing Fictional Lives	111
	Introduction	111
	Negative Revelations: *Austerlitz* (2001)	112
	Imagined Authenticity: *Bruchstücke* (1995)	119
	Through the Looking Glass: *Reise im August* (1992)	126
	Conclusion: The Ethics of Memory and Problems of Authenticity	131
5	The Fascination of Fascism in Contemporary Film	139
	Introduction	139
	'Das glaubt dir kein Mensch' [Nobody will believe you]: *Hitlerjunge Salomon* (1990)	140
	Hitler's Elite: *NaPolA: Elite für den Führer* (2005)	145
	Authenticating Discourses in Contemporary Film	153
	Coming to Terms with the Past: *Lore* (2012)	158
	Conclusion	162
	Conclusion	171
	References	181
	Index	203

ACKNOWLEDGEMENTS

This book began life as my doctoral thesis, completed at the University of Oxford and generously funded by the Arts and Humanities Research Council. I am very grateful to the many librarians, curators, academics, and staff both in Germany and in the UK who helped me during the course of my research. I owe the greatest debt of gratitude to my supervisor, Karen Leeder, whose skill and patience not only ensured the success of the project but extended even beyond its timely completion. In preparing the manuscript for publication I have benefited from the support of colleagues, especially those at St Edmund Hall where 'hall spirit' and the encouragement of fellow modern linguists Wes Williams, Andrew Kahn, and Jake Wadham, proved invaluable. I am grateful too to the many students I have taught (and from whom I have learnt in return) for their insightful questions and enthusiasm for the topic. I would like to thank Ritchie Robertson and the anonymous peer-reviewer for their extremely helpful feedback on earlier drafts, as well as Alastair Matthews for his careful copyediting, and Graham Nelson for his quiet but persistent encouragement to get the book into print. Finally, I wish to thank my family and friends for their love and support, especially Daniel. *Deo gratias*!

A.L., Oxford, June 2020

LIST OF FIGURES

FIG. 1.1. '"Schule unterm Hakenkreuz" und Neuanfang nach 1945' ['School Life beneath the Swastika' and New Beginnings after 1945] in the permanent exhibition at the Hamburg School Museum

FIG. 1.2. 'Puppenhaus — Deutschland, nach 1933' [Doll's House — Germany, after 1933] in the permanent exhibition at the Deutsches Historisches Museum, Berlin

FIG. 1.3. Wallpaper detail from the doll's house at the Deutsches Historisches Museum, Berlin

FIG. 3.1. Frank Meisler's sculpture *Züge in das Leben — Züge in den Tod* [Trains to Life — Trains to Death], Berlin

FIG. 5.1. Solly and Isaak set off into their future (*Hitlerjunge Salomon*, 01:44:53)

FIG. 5.2. The NaPolA school at Allenstein (*NaPolA*, 41:48)

FIG. 5.3. Friedrich (Max Riemelt) leaves the NaPolA (*NaPolA*, 01:44:16)

FIG. 5.4. Friedrich (Max Riemelt) surveys his new uniform (*NaPolA*, 00:16:28)

FIG. 5.5. Solly (Marco Hofschneider) practises the Nazi salute (*Hitlerjunge Salomon*, 01:02:48)

FIG. 5.6. Solomon Perel (as himself) in the final sequence of *Hitlerjunge Salomon* (01:45:27)

FIG. 5.7. Lore and her siblings journey into the forest (*Lore*, 00:25:08)

FIG. 5.8. Lore smashes her grandmother's porcelain figurines (*Lore*, 01:39:27)

INTRODUCTION

Childhood, Memory, and the Nation

Between January 1981 and August 1982, the *Frankfurter Allgemeine Zeitung* [Frankfurt General Newspaper] published a series of accounts in which writers recalled their childhood and adolescence in the Third Reich. Their reminiscences documented a range of experiences, from Hitler Youth membership to racial persecution. The texts were subsequently published as an anthology, *Meine Schulzeit im Dritten Reich: Erinnerungen deutscher Schriftsteller* [My Schooldays in the Third Reich: German Writers Remember] (1982). The critic Marcel Reich-Ranicki provided a foreword to the collection in which he raised questions about memory work and the contemporary view of the past:

> Wie war es eigentlich damals, als überall Hakenkreuzfahnen wehten und die SA marschierte 'in ruhig festem Schritt?' Über die historischen Fakten sind wir informiert. An wissenschaftlichen Werken mangelt es nicht. Unentwegt werden wir mit Dokumenten aus der Zeit des 'Dritten Reiches' versorgt, mit Fakten und Daten jeglicher Art beliefert. Was sich auf der Ebene, auf der Geschichte entschieden wird, abgespielt hat, ist ungefähr bekannt. Und doch: Wer ist schon sicher, er sei hinreichend unterrichtet? Viele von uns befürchten, überinformiert und trotzdem unwissend zu sein.[1]

> [What was it really like back then, when swastika flags were flying everywhere and the SA marched with 'calm and steady step'? We are informed of the historical facts. There is no shortage of academic works. We are endlessly provided with a steady stream of documents from the period of the Third Reich, and supplied with facts and dates of all kinds. Everyone knows more or less what happened, at the level at which history is written. And yet: who can truly say he has been sufficiently well taught? Many of us fear that we are overinformed and yet, at the same time, ignorant.][2]

Reich-Ranicki suggested that the wealth of documentary accounts of Nazism was obscuring individuals' understanding of past events and what it was like to experience them. Although his comments pertain to the (West) German memory culture of the early 1980s, they are still highly pertinent today, some decades later. Ever since the end of the Second World War, the Third Reich has remained entrenched in German public and private memory, as the boom in first-hand accounts, scholarly studies, and public debates attests.

Post-reunification public discourse has been dominated by the complex and often contentious issue of German identity in the Berlin Republic. The sudden and unforeseen collapse of the GDR and the rapid reunification of the two German states with their contrasting political and ideological systems radically changed politics, society, and culture. It also changed the memorial culture of Germany, creating a new context in which to approach the past and its legacy in the present. In addition, important moments of national remembering, such as significant anniversaries of the end of the Second World War, have given an added impetus to the interest in Third Reich history. We have seen this both on the part of those who lived through this time, and of those who, coming after, attempt to make sense of what was and remains a defining period of the German past. The post-reunification era has also been shaped by a series of public engagements with the subject of Nazism: what Anne Fuchs and Mary Cosgrove term 'memory contests'.[3] These are defined as 'highly dynamic public engagements with the past that are triggered by an event that is perceived as a massive disturbance of a community's self-understanding'.[4] Such debates deal with opposing interpretations of the past, and are vital to the way individuals and national communities understand themselves. The frequency and intensity of such debates demonstrate the centrality of the legacy of National Socialism and its representation to contemporary Germany. The kinds of 'memory contests' which Fuchs and Cosgrove identify have overwhelmingly involved members of the generation born in the 1920s and 1930s. These include the revelations that Christa Wolf had been an *inoffizielle Mitarbeiterin* [unofficial collaborator] for the Stasi; Martin Walser's controversial speech upon receiving the Friedenspreis des Deutschen Buchhandels [Peace Prize of the German Book Trade] in October 1998, in which he spoke of Auschwitz as a 'Moralkeule' [moral cudgel], and the ensuing public debate with the German Jewish leader Ignatz Bubis; and the exposure of Binjamin Wilkomirski's *Bruchstücke: Aus einer Kindheit 1939–1948* [Fragments: Memories of a Childhood, 1939–1948] (1995) as a fake Holocaust memoir. Thus, in the 1990s and 2000s, at a time when newly reunified Germany seemed to be turning towards its future, public debates and discourse were dominated by the memories of those who had grown up under Nazism.

When Joseph Ratzinger (b. 1927) was elected pope in April 2005, the *Bild* newspaper carried the headline 'Wir sind Papst' [We are the pope], evoking the slogans of the road to reunification, 'Wir sind das Volk' [We are the people] and 'Wir sind ein Volk' [We are one people]. Pope Benedict XVI's inauguration was a decisive moment for reunified Germany's national identity: for the first time in nearly 1,000 years, the Roman Catholic Church had a German leader. Strikingly, though perhaps not surprisingly, a certain amount of press and public commentary focused on Benedict's early biography, including his membership of the Hitler Youth and his wartime service.[5] The new Pope's formative experiences under Nazism overshadowed the start of his pontificate. The following year, Günter Grass revealed that he had been a member not only of the Hitler Youth, a fact of his biography that was well known by that point, but also of an SS Panzer division. This caused what amounted to no less than a national scandal: criticism was directed towards Grass in part because of his SS service, but more so because he had remained silent about it for so long, all the while apparently acting as the 'conscience of the nation'.[6] The belatedness of his confession, rather than its substance, proved to be the greatest source of controversy and outrage.[7]

As members of the generation who grew up under Nazism, both Grass and Ratzinger carried with them a legacy that they could not simply shake off, and an experience of growing up, the memory of which bound the private to the political, muddying childhood with the evil of the most notorious regime in the West in modern times. Members of this generation, who came to maturity around the end of the Second World War, were indelibly marked by their childhood and adolescent experiences. 1945 represented a moment of rupture, a kind of biographical caesura, when the carpet was ripped from beneath their feet and they realized that all they had believed in, all they had been sold by the state as true and good, was in fact a deception. For those who, unlike Grass and Ratzinger, were actively persecuted by the regime, primarily because of their Jewish heritage and identity, childhood was disrupted, attacked, and cut short entirely. The few that survived experienced 1945 as a moment of liberation, but it by no means provided a 'happy ending'. Family members, friends, and communities had perished, and life was dominated by loss: of loved ones, homeland, language, and identity.

Since reunification, there has been a growing awareness that the rising generations have no first-hand experience of the National Socialist period, and that the last of the generation of eyewitnesses that experienced Nazism will soon be gone, and with them the immediacy of first-hand memory. Recognition of these shifts in collective memory has resulted in the frequent publication and popularity of autobiographical accounts of the period, particularly by former Hitler Youth members and war children. In visual and museum culture too, the narratives of individuals' experiences in the Third Reich have gained currency, particularly those by people who were children and adolescents at the time. The historian Norbert Frei dubbed the years 1995–2005 the 'Dekade der Zeitzeugen' [decade of witnesses],[8] as more and more accounts of apparently neglected aspects of Third Reich history were shared. Such accounts of what it was like to live through this time raise important aesthetic and ethical questions about the representability of history, legitimacy and authenticity, and the politics of memory.

This book is concerned with representations of childhood and adolescence in the Third Reich within post-reunification German cultural memory, focusing particularly on autobiographical writing, fictional accounts, and film. I examine the different ways in which writers and filmmakers depict the experience of growing up under Nazism, asking how they navigate the limits of representation, how individuals explore and transmit the events of their lives, and how representation functions at the intersection of childhood, memory, and identity. The works under discussion aim above all to depict individual experience, and in doing so, evoke a plurality of childhoods and modes of remembrance. Like Fuchs and Cosgrove's 'memory contests', which 'reflect a pluralistic memory culture which does not enshrine a particular normative understanding of the past',[9] these accounts of childhood under Nazism are part of a broader discourse of origins and identity. Indeed, we can understand recent cultural memories of childhood in the Third Reich as a direct reflection of the shift away from what Aleida Assmann has termed a 'normative framework' of memory and memorial practices,[10] towards a pluralistic approach in which constructions of the past incorporate a wide spectrum of experience that individuals can engage with critically. In this way, they are crucial to our understanding of contemporary cultural and collective memory and national self-understanding, in particular the complex figuring of German identity in the decades since reunification. These works, which span a range of media and genres, shed light on the politics of memory in the Berlin Republic, but they also provoke discussions about the aesthetic and ethical limitations and possibilities inherent in writing about childhood under dictatorship.

Chapter 1 provides a historical and theoretical background to the subsequent analysis of texts and films by considering the range of cultural memories of childhood under Nazism since reunification. It addresses the interest in this topic and the ways in which it has been portrayed. I analyse the key categories that underpin the readings that follow, using examples from contemporary museum displays and exhibitions. The way museums present stories and the material culture of the past, especially as they pertain to childhood and youth under Nazism, can tell us a great deal about the issues and challenges posed by that topic within cultural memory. Here, I outline theories within memory studies that are essential for the analyses in subsequent chapters: 'cultural memory' as theorized by Aleida Assmann and Jan Assmann, Marianne Hirsch's frequently deployed concept of 'postmemory', and Alison Landsberg's 'prosthetic memory'. In addition, I set out my own understanding of what in German has come to be encapsulated in the term 'gefühlte Geschichte' [emotionally experienced history].[11] This approach to historical representation is ubiquitous in post-reunification culture and provides a useful way to draw together the diverse texts that speak of and to the experience of growing up under Nazism. I also examine tropes of childhood here, particularly the child's presumed otherness, innocence, vulnerability, and, most importantly for this study, its association with authenticity. While writers and filmmakers engage with these ideas, in many cases they challenge and subvert them.

The following chapters provide close readings of primary texts that are situated within the broader context of contemporary German memory politics. Some have received significant scholarly attention, and others have not, or have not *yet*. The material is organized according to the medium and subject of storytelling, and in this way, the study foregrounds issues related to genre, questions of authenticity and legitimacy, and the various possibilities of authentic and mediated forms of representing the past.[12] Several different schemes for organizing the material suggested themselves, since inevitably questions of memory, narrative, authenticity, and agency are prominent in all the texts discussed. By bringing together multiple works within each chapter, I am able to read them both as individual contributions to the debates at hand, and in dialogue with each other. This is especially important given the way cultural memory has been theorized, and given how many of the writers and filmmakers discussed in this volume intersect, communicate with each other, and refer to each other's works.

Chapter 2 considers autobiographical accounts by three former members of the Hitler Youth: Günter de Bruyn in *Zwischenbilanz: Eine Jugend in Berlin* [Taking Stock: A Berlin Childhood] (1992), Martin Walser in *Ein springender Brunnen* [A

Gushing Fountain] (1998), and Günter Grass in *Beim Häuten der Zwiebel* [Peeling the Onion] (2006). These authors share many similar formative experiences, and their accounts express similar concerns, above all with the aesthetic and ethical problems of autobiographical writing about their own generation's childhood experiences. The authors speak with the authority not just of the eyewitness but also of prominent public intellectuals from both sides of the formerly divided Germany. In this way, their accounts function both as a description of private experience, and as a way of speaking on behalf of others. They explore well-established tensions between the private and political, and between history and memory, as well as asking fundamental questions about the way personal history should or can be written.

In Chapter 3, I examine autobiographical works by Jewish writers who produced accounts in German about their formative years under Nazism: *weiter leben: Eine Jugend* [Still Alive: A Holocaust Girlhood Remembered] (1992) by Ruth Klüger, *Die Absonderung* [Seclusion] (1991) by Georges-Arthur Goldschmidt, and *Erwachsenenspiele: Erinnerungen* [Games for Grown-Ups: Memories] (1997) by Günter Kunert. In these texts, we encounter a challenge to the Romantic symbolism of the Jewish child victim of the Holocaust as found in post-war discourse. The authors achieve this by showing the child protagonist's journey to adulthood and emphasizing their agency, and by questioning tropes showing the child as innocent and unknowing. While Klüger, Goldschmidt, and Kunert never deny the victim status of Jewish children during the Holocaust, they nevertheless unsettle the idea of passive victimhood through the depiction of their younger selves. They also assert the *breadth* of experience and suffering and its manifold effects on those who survived as children, thus countering the overwhelmingly symbolic reception of this cohort within post-war cultural memory.

Chapter 4 explores fictional portrayals of childhood under Nazism. With the transition from communicative to cultural memory, eyewitness accounts give way to more free-ranging approaches. This chapter examines three texts in which writers have imagined and fictionalized the Jewish child's experience of the Holocaust. In W. G. Sebald's *Austerlitz* (2001), the protagonist's childhood is pieced together through memory and in photographic images which further complicate his relationship with the child he used to be. Binjamin Wilkomirski's now-notorious false Holocaust memoir, *Bruchstücke: Aus einer Kindheit 1939–1948*, presses the analogy between memory and the photograph into service to prove the veracity of its contents.[13] Three years after its publication, the narrative was exposed as a fabrication, as a mixture of historical events that happened to other people and authorial invention. Nevertheless, it continues to be credited with providing an account infused with emotional authenticity, and I examine here such continuing claims made on this extremely problematic work's behalf, the direct result of the narrative strategies used to create the child's voice and experience in the text. In *Reise im August* [The Final Journey] (1992), Gudrun Pausewang offers an imagined account of a Jewish child's journey to Auschwitz, primarily for young-adult readers. The text raises questions about the aesthetic creation of the child's voice and invites a consideration of the process of writing such a narrative when the author herself, at the time when her fictional protagonist undertook her final journey, was a member of the female wing of the Hitler Youth. These texts provoke discussion about the ethics of memory, representational practices, and the complex issue of legitimacy in writing about the past.

Finally, in Chapter 5, I examine three films which foreground the fascination of fascism for the young, and the painful process of coming to terms with that particular past from a postmemory perspective. I discuss Agnieszka Holland's *Hitlerjunge Salomon* [Europa Europa] (1990) and Dennis Gansel's *NaPolA: Elite für den Führer* [Before the Fall] (2004), both films that assert personal experience and its emotional effects by focusing on the development of young male protagonists. Despite their vastly different formal and thematic approaches, both demonstrate the appeal of Nazism to the young, and in doing so attempt to show how such indoctrination was possible. I then consider Cate Shortland's *Lore* (2012), which focuses on a female protagonist at the end of the war, and her confrontation with the results of her indoctrination at the hands of the state. I examine these films in light of the idea that, as the 'organic memory' of the Third Reich increasingly disappears, German cinema will become the most important site on which history is disseminated.

Setting the Study in Context

With its focus on textual analysis and reception, this study is situated at the intersection of thriving research fields encompassing history, literature, film, memory studies, and childhood studies. Scholarly engagement with the memory and representation of the Third Reich in contemporary culture has become what Chloe Paver has termed a 'moving target'.[14] New subjects for study appear continuously, and with them new and varied critical approaches and perspectives. Several critical works have focused on family stories and generation novels ('Generationenromane'), genres that have gained extraordinary popularity from the 1990s onwards. In *Phantoms of War in Contemporary German Literature, Films and Discourse: The Politics of Memory* (2008), Anne Fuchs views the surge in 'experiential representations of the war experience and its long after-life in post-war memory' as an 'agitated legacy' that continues to shape post-reunification German identity.[15] Fuchs points to the tenor of regret in family stories, while also positing a more hopeful conclusion: that the widespread interest in such narratives in Germany is not just a cynical marketing ploy but rather indicates 'the transitional discourse of a threshold culture that is about to redefine its cultural identity'.[16] Family stories and generational novels are characterized by efforts at empathy and understanding,[17] and, in Friederike Eigler's view, provide a valuable space in which to explore issues of history and identity.[18] The 'Generationenroman' has been examined as a vehicle for reconstructing family stories and secrets, especially from the National Socialist period, and as a site in which the 'heroization' of the first generation takes place. In *Rekonstruktion und Entheroisierung: Paradigmen des 'Generationenromans' in der deutschsprachigen Gegenwartsliteratur* [Reconstruction and De-Heroization: Paradigms of the Generation Novel in Contemporary German Literature] (2013),[19] Julian Reidy proposes another category, 'postheroisch' [post-heroic], where the protagonist is ambivalent about their place in family history.[20]

Another important and related topic is the representation of women's experiences in the Third Reich, including those who grew up in the 1930s and 1940s. Katherine Stone's recent study, *Women and National Socialism in Postwar German Literature: Gender, Memory, and Subjectivity* (2017),[21] builds on a significant body of work examining women's writing about the National Socialist past from first-, second-, and third-generation authors.[22] Stone suggests that there are challenges to the myth that women were less culpable than men in the Third Reich, but that it is also perpetuated as a trope of 'the innocent and potentially redemptive German woman'.[23] This can also be viewed within the broader post-reunification discourse about German wartime suffering and victimhood, which especially dominated discussions of the past in the early 2000s. This also provides an important context for the present study.[24] Writing in 2005, Norbert Frei suggested that in the years since reunification, Hitler and National Socialism dominated cultural memory. This is encapsulated in the phrase 'Soviel Hitler war nie' [There has never been so much Hitler]. In *Die Erfindung der Erinnerung: Deutsche Kriegskindheiten im Gedächtnis der Gegenwart* [The Invention of Memory: German Wartime Childhoods in Contemporary Memory], the sociologist Michael Heinlein proposes a reformulation of Frei's phrase: 'Soviel *Kriegskindheit* war nie' [There has never been so much wartime childhood].[25] In Heinlein's view, memories and representations of the former war children, those born in Germany in the 1930s and early 1940s, have been ubiquitous in contemporary culture. Such accounts of the war 'from below' have indeed proliferated in the past three decades across a wide range of media and genres, as well as in political discourse.

Several other studies have sought to examine the dominant discourses in post-reunification German culture, taking a wide-ranging approach and bringing together multiple representations and perspectives, including the legacy not only of fascism but also of other difficult histories, including German division and terrorism in 1970s West Germany.[26] A number of central concerns emerge from this body of research: how have the conditions of reunification affected German memory culture and national identity? What ethical questions are raised by modes of historical representation? How does the increasing historical distance from the period of Nazism shape aesthetic approaches to that past? What is the future of memory, especially as the number of eyewitnesses dwindles and eventually disappears?[27] A number of autobiographical works and life writing about the National Socialist period have provoked, and responded to, such questions. Most recently, in *Nationalsozialismus und Shoah im autobiographischen Roman: Poetologie des Erinnerns bei Ruth Klüger, Martin Walser, Georg Heller und Günter Grass* [National Socialism and the Shoah in the Autobiographical Novel: Poetics of Memory in Ruth Klüger, Martin Walser, Georg Heller, and Günter Grass] (2016), Dorothea Kliche-Behnke examines the poetics of memory in four works by authors who belong to the generation that grew up in the Third Reich. Focusing on the writers' 'Konzept von Erinnerung' [concept of memory], Kliche-Behnke examines the narrative strategies used to engage with the authors' past in autobiographical form. Although these works are selected as prominent examples of a much larger corpus of autobiographical writing about childhood in the Third Reich, the author's interest lies in the way these texts navigate the generic possibilities and limitations of 'autobiography' and 'fiction', rather than in what they offer with regard to the experience and theme of childhood. Stuart Taberner's *Aging and Old-Age Style in Günter Grass, Ruth Klüger, Christa Wolf, and Martin Walser* (2013) examines a similar set of authors, focusing on the way they conduct narrative life review, 'a form of storytelling which selects from the remembered past, reworks events, and narrates meaning'.[28] Focusing on four writers as case studies, Taberner addresses a number of more general literary questions, for example: how does a writer at the end of their life review the preceding events? What conventions are associated with old-age style, and how do writers confirm, subvert, or reject them? Despite being about old age rather than childhood, Taberner's study provides a useful model in his focus on the way writers construct, perform, and inscribe their own biography into literature. Nadine Jessica Schmidt focuses on literary authenticity in various modes of autobiographical writing in *Konstruktionen literarischer Authentizität in autobiographischem Erzählen* [Constructions of Literary Authenticity in Autobiographical Writing] (2013).[29] Her analysis of works by Klüger, Grass, and Wolf demonstrates the diversity of approaches to literary authenticity, which cannot be reduced to a simple dichotomy between the staging of 'Wahrhaftigkeit' [truthfulness] or 'Gefühlswertes' [emotional value].[30] The case of Wilkomirski's *Bruchstücke* provides a counter-example of how 'ein autobiographischer Fälschungsmodus' [falsely-autobiographical mode] can be received as particularly 'authentic'.[31] As I will go on to argue in Chapter 4, this reception is also the direct result of Wilkomirski's deployment of a child's voice and perspective, which perform an authenticating function. In *Zerstörte Kindheit: Literarische Autobiografien zur Shoah* [Childhood Destroyed: Literary Autobiographies of the Shoah] (2001), Eva Lezzi examines autobiographies of childhood by German-Jewish writers, or writers with a German-Jewish background, originally written in German, Dutch, Swedish, and French. She argues that it is precisely through writing that the authors are able to depict the experience of persecution as children, and its effect on their lives.[32]

The decades since reunification have also seen an increased interest within historical research about childhood and education in the Third Reich, and children's experience of, and perspectives on, the Second World War. Nicholas Stargardt's ground-breaking book *Witnesses of War: Children's Lives under the Nazis* (2005) set the standard for studies of modern childhood and conflict, focusing on children's material culture as a primary source. Stargardt's child-centric approach, which gives space to the voices of children themselves, rather than speaking solely on their behalf, is part of a broader shift within history as a discipline that values children's accounts and material culture as sources worthy of study.[33] Michael H. Kater's *Hitler Youth* (2004) traces the history of the Nazi youth groups, their role during wartime, and those who dissented, such as the 'Swingjugend' [Swing Youth]. He questions the complicity of former Hitler Youth members, asking at what point they can be considered to have become culpable for their actions. While for Kater their complicity is not in question, their 'moral guilt' must be measured according to their age, their position within the hierarchy of 'Nazi governance', and the extent to which they participated in criminal acts.[34] A number of studies have also examined the fate of Jewish children in the Third Reich, revealing the diversity of experience of those who were systematically persecuted and annihilated.[35]

One of the great strengths of the research into representations of childhood in the Third Reich has lain in its interdisciplinary and transnational approaches. Viktoria Hertling's edited volume *Mit den Augen eines Kindes: Children in the Holocaust, Children in Exile, Children under Fascism* (1998) bridges the gap between history and literary studies, taking a wide-ranging approach which incorporates analysis of fiction, film, autobiography, and testimony, as well as considering persecuted children alongside those who were deemed 'acceptable' by the regime and socialized under Nazism.[36] Gillian Lathey's *The Impossible Legacy: Identity and Purpose in Autobiographical Children's Literature Set in the Third Reich and the Second World War* (1999) provides a comparative study of autobiographical texts about wartime childhood experiences by German, Jewish, and British authors for a child or adolescent readership. Similarly, Hamida Bosmajian's *Sparing the Child: Grief and the Unspeakable in Youth Literature about Nazism and the Holocaust* (2002) focuses almost exclusively on texts written for children by authors who experienced the Third Reich as children and adolescents. Bosmajian explores children's texts that have either a Holocaust survivor or a former member of the Hitler Youth as a protagonist. These critical works focus on aesthetic questions, such as how writers can (re)create the language of the child, and on the didactic question of how the events of the Second World War and the Holocaust should be depicted for a juvenile readership. Bill Niven has observed that sometimes those who research Germany's 'problematic' history and memory 'fall into the trap of imagining that it is the only country which has such a past to face'.[37] *Kriegs- und Nachkriegskindheiten: Studien zur literarischen Erinnerungskultur für junge Leser* [War and Post-War Childhoods: Studies on Literary Memory Culture for Young Readers], edited by Gabriele von Glasenapp and Hans Heino Ewers (2008) is representative of studies which avoid this pitfall, taking into account works published across Europe, as well as in Israel, the US, Japan, and South Korea. This facilitates an extraordinarily broad view of the experience of childhood in wartime.

Critical interest in literary depictions of childhood under Nazism for adult readers has focused primarily on the narrative construction of the child's perspective as a narrative device, which provides many varied ways to approach difficult subjects. In contrast to its identificatory function in children's and young-adult literature,[38] in texts for adult readers it often affords a defamiliarizing perspective. Monika Spielmann's *Aus den Augen des Kindes: Die Kinderperspektive in deutschsprachigen Romanen seit 1945* [Through the Eyes of a Child: The Child's Perspective in German-Language Novels since 1945] (2002) looks at a range of post-war texts which are not specifically focused on the Third Reich but are narrated from a child's perspective. For Spielmann, the child's perspective fulfils four main functions: it acts as a point of identification for the reader, as a means of exploring the psychological origins of the adult that the child will become, as a means of autobiographical engagement with childhood, and as a means with which to critique society.[39] In *Mit den Augen des Kindes: Narrative Inszenierungen des kindlichen Blicks im 20. Jahrhundert* [With the Eyes of the Child: Narrative Stagings of the Child's View in the Twentieth Century] (2009), Mechthild Barth takes a comparative approach, focusing in particular on works by Boris Pasternak, Imre Kertész, Salman Rushdie, and Georges-Arthur Goldschmidt, and examining in detail the history and development of the child's perspective as a literary device and its function. Barth argues that, in addition to the defamiliarizing that comes with the child's perspective and its invitation to the reader to see with fresh eyes, it demands from the reader 'eine stärkere Partizipation im Kommunikationsgefüge Text' [a greater participation in the communicative structure of the text].[40] Sue Vice examines a range of texts for adult readers that depict Jewish children caught up in the Holocaust, including those by former child survivors, in *Children Writing the Holocaust* (2004). She identifies two main ways in which child's-eye views of the Holocaust are distinctive: first, in the narrative features (such as defamiliarization), and second, in that their accounts are markedly different from those by adults. Similarly, in *Kinderblick auf die Shoah: Formen der Erinnerung bei Ilse Aichinger, Hubert Fichte und Danilo Kiš* [A Child's View of the Shoah: Forms of Memory in Ilse Aichinger, Hubert Fichte and Danilo Kiš] (1999), Tanja Hetzer examines the function of the child's perspective in three post-war texts by writers who experienced persecution. The Jewish child is seen as an 'unbeteiligter Beobachter' [impartial observer],[41] and Hetzer argues that the child's perspective, often unqualified by the voice and retrospective knowledge of the adult writer, is used to create a more authentic sense of fear, as the child is unable to make sense of the events it observes. This in turn engages the reader, who, unsettled by the discrepancy between their own historical knowledge and the child narrator's lack of understanding, becomes more invested in the object of narration.[42] Hetzer views this as a contrast to the role of the child's perspective in literary accounts of non-Jewish children in the Third Reich, which she considers reflect the desire to assume a position of historical innocence.

Debbie Pinfold's *The Child's View of the Third Reich in German Literature: The Eye among the Blind* (2001) examines a rich corpus of post-war German-language texts set between 1933 and 1945 which use a child as narrator and/or focalizer. She argues that the child is one of several traditional outsider figures who can be utilized as part of a defamiliarization technique, enabling the reader to engage in new ways with the object of narration. The audience or reader is able to see with 'fresh eyes' as the child observes the perverted moral and political system of Nazism in a detached and therefore shocking way. Writers also criticize the regime retrospectively by depicting the corruption of the child by the state. More recently, Nora Maguire's *Childness and the Writing of the German Past: Tropes of Childhood in Contemporary German Literature* (2014) explores literary constructions of childhood, in particular Romantic tropes associated with the child and how these come to be utilized in post-1990 literary texts. Maguire builds on and extends Pinfold's study by focusing on post-reunification texts and by broadening the theoretical framework to consider not only the 'defamiliarizing potential of the child's perspective',[43] but also the figuring of literary children as both the 'agents' and 'objects' of narrative.[44] Deploying the term 'childness'[45] — which incorporates narratological and thematic aspects — enables her to address a problem frequently found in studies of literary children, namely 'the conflation of '"childhood" as an empirical state and "childhood" as a socio-cultural construct'.[46] This critical framework takes account of the way childhood is depicted, but also looks at broader issues, including tropes and myths, depictions of childhood memory, and reader response. Maguire confirms that post-1990 German writers are still 'deeply saturated with the Romantic myth of childhood', as Pinfold had previously argued about the post-war period.[47] Maguire concludes that the 'innocence myth' is alive and well in German literature today;[48] while I agree with this, I also want to argue that, in post-reunification culture, there *are* attempts to challenge, if not totally to debunk, that myth. Indeed, the filmmakers and writers discussed in this study explore and, in some cases, question traditional notions of, and myths about, the experience of childhood in the Third Reich as they have been perpetuated in literary and cinematic narratives since 1945.

The present work builds on this significant body of research by taking a sustained and detailed look at the way the experience of childhood and youth under Nazism finds expression in a wide range of literary and filmic material. Childhood has long been conceptually linked with origins; by focusing on the post-reunification period, this book asks how such narratives of growing up contribute to cultural memory and identity formation in the new context of the Berlin Republic. It goes beyond existing studies by broadening its focus beyond the aestheticizing of the child and its 'view from below' to examine attempts at representing experiences of childhood rooted in a specific historical context. How are *real* childhoods conceptualized in art? What narrative strategies (beyond the child's perspective or its figuring as innocent) are used to convey children's experiences? Where do these originate and how are they received? By examining a range of accounts of growing up in the Third Reich, the study is set within a material, visual, and literary context. In this way, it takes account of the way literature and film contribute to, and in many cases, challenge, prevailing discourses, and the way private experience is mediated in different ways. Its view is deliberately broad so as to provide a fuller picture of the way this historical experience continues to shape individual and national identity in the present, a phenomenon which has far-reaching implications for the way we understand contemporary Germany, seventy-five years after the war's end.

Notes to the Introduction

1. Marcel Reich-Ranicki, 'Vorwort', in *Meine Schulzeit im Dritten Reich: Erinnerungen deutscher Schriftsteller*, ed. by Marcel Reich-Ranicki (Cologne: Kiepenheuer & Witsch, 1982), pp. 9–12 (p. 9). The book contains contributions from seventeen authors, born between 1917 and 1929.
2. My translation. Throughout this book, translations of quotations and book titles are taken from published English versions where available. All other translations are my own.

3. Anne Fuchs and Mary Cosgrove, 'Introduction', in *German Memory Contests: The Quest for Identity in Literature, Film, and Discourse since 1990*, ed. by Anne Fuchs, Mary Cosgrove, and Georg Grote (Rochester, NY: Camden House, 2006), pp. 1–21 (p. 2).
4. Ibid.
5. He writes candidly about his childhood and youth in Joseph Ratzinger, *Aus meinem Leben: Erinnerungen, 1927–1977* (Stuttgart: DVA, 1998).
6. Fritz Stern, *Five Germanys I Have Known: A History & Memoir* (New York: Farrar Straus Giroux, 2006), p. 242. See also Frank Brunssen, 'A Moral Authority? Günter Grass as the Conscience of the German Nation', *Journal of Contemporary European Studies*, 15 (2007), 565–84.
7. See Anne Fuchs, '"Ehrlich, du lügst wie gedruckt": Günter Grass's Autobiographical Confession and the Changing Territory of Germany's Memory Culture', *German Life and Letters*, 60 (2007), 261–75 (pp. 264–65).
8. Norbert Frei, *1945 und wir: Das Dritte Reich im Bewußtsein der Deutschen* (Munich: Beck, 2005), p. 24.
9. Fuchs and Cosgrove, p. 2.
10. Aleida Assmann, *Shadows of Trauma: Memory and the Politics of Postwar Identity*, trans. by Sarah Clift (New York: Fordham University Press, 2016), p. 173.
11. I use Fuchs's translation of 'gefühlte Geschichte' here: Anne Fuchs, *Phantoms of War in Contemporary German Literature, Films and Discourse: The Politics of Memory* (Basingstoke: Palgrave Macmillan, 2008), p. 6.
12. Given the wealth of material on this subject, this study cannot hope to be exhaustive, and many texts that provided useful background might have been included more prominently. Examples include Dieter Forte, *Der Junge mit den blutigen Schuhen* (Frankfurt a.M.: Fischer, 1995); Ulla Berkéwicz, *Engel sind schwarz und weiß* (Frankfurt a.M.: Suhrkamp, 1994 [1992]); Joachim Fest, *Ich nicht: Erinnerungen an eine Kindheit und Jugend* (Reinbek: Rowohlt, 2008); Ludwig Harig, *Weh dem, der aus der Reihe tanzt* (Munich: Hanser, 1990); Marcel Beyer, *Flughunde* (Frankfurt a.M.: Suhrkamp, 1996).
13. Binjamin Wilkomirski is the name under which *Bruchstücke* was originally published. Subsequent investigations revealed that the author's birth-name was Bruno Grosjean, and that he was later adopted by a family named Doesseker. For ease of reference, I refer to the author of the text as Wilkomirski, as is common practice in critical literature on the subject.
14. Chloe Paver, *Refractions of the Third Reich in German and Austrian Fiction and Film* (Oxford: Oxford University Press, 2007), p. 1.
15. Fuchs, *Phantoms of War*, p. 1.
16. Ibid., p. 204.
17. See Ariane Eichenberg, *Familie — Ich — Nation: Narrative Analysen zeitgenössischer Generationenromane* (Göttingen: V&R unipress, 2009), p. 18.
18. Friederike Eigler, *Gedächtnis und Geschichte in Generationenromanen seit der Wende* (Berlin: Schmidt, 2005), p. 24.
19. Julian Reidy, *Rekonstruktion und Entheroisierung: Paradigmen des 'Generationenromans' in der deutschsprachigen Gegenwartsliteratur* (Bielefeld: Aisthesis, 2013), p. 40; see also the rather robust literature review, pp. 14–39.
20. Julian Reidy, 'Die Unmöglichkeit der Erinnerung: Arno Geigers "Es geht uns gut" als Persiflage des Generationenromans der Gegenwartsliteratur', *German Studies Review*, 36 (2013), 79–102 (pp. 82–83).
21. Katherine Stone, *Women and National Socialism in Postwar German Literature: Gender, Memory, and Subjectivity* (Rochester, NY: Camden House, 2017).
22. See esp. Barbara Kosta, *Recasting Autobiography: Women's Counterfictions in Contemporary German Literature and Film* (Ithaca: Cornell University Press, 1994); Joanne Sayner, *Women without a Past? German Autobiographical Writings and Fascism* (Amsterdam: Rodopi, 2007); Elaine Martin, *Gender, Patriarchy and Fascism in the Third Reich: The Response of Women Writers* (Detroit: Wayne State University Press, 1993). See also Caroline Schaumann, *Memory Matters: Generational Responses to Germany's Nazi Past in Recent Women's Literature* (Berlin: de Gruyter, 2008).
23. Stone, p. 139. Particularly valuable is her discussion of the position of such narratives within post-reunification literary and filmic trends; see pp. 142–54.

24. Bill Niven, ed., *Germans as Victims: Remembering the Past in Contemporary Germany* (Basingstoke: Palgrave Macmillan, 2006); Helmut Schmitz, ed., *A Nation of Victims? Representations of German Wartime Suffering from 1945 to the Present* (Amsterdam: Rodopi, 2007); Stuart Taberner and Karina Berger, eds, *Germans as Victims in the Literary Fiction of the Berlin Republic* (Rochester, NY: Camden House, 2009).
25. Michael Heinlein, *Die Erfindung der Erinnerung: Deutsche Kriegskindheiten im Gedächtnis der Gegenwart* (Bielefeld: transcript, 2010), p. 9. Heinlein cites Frei, *1945 und wir*, p. 7.
26. See esp. Fabrizio Cambi, ed., *Gedächtnis und Identität: Die deutsche Literatur nach der Vereinigung* (Würzburg: Königshausen & Neumann, 2008); Christina Guenther and Beth Griech-Polelle, eds, *Trajectories of Memory: Intergenerational Representations of the Holocaust in History and the Arts* (Newcastle upon Tyne: Cambridge Scholars Publishing, 2008); Helmut Schmitz, ed., *German Culture and the Uncomfortable Past: Representations of National Socialism in Contemporary Germanic Literature* (Aldershot: Ashgate, 2001); Torben Fischer, Philipp Hammermeister, and Sven Kramer, eds, *Der Nationalsozialismus und die Shoah in der deutschsprachigen Gegenwartsliteratur* (Amsterdam: Rodopi, 2014); Judith Klinger and Gerhard Wolf, eds, *Gedächtnis und kultureller Wandel: Erinnerndes Schreiben, Perspektiven und Kontroversen* (Tübingen: Niemeyer, 2009); Barbara Beßlich, Katharina Grätz, and Olaf Hildebrand, eds, *Wende des Erinnerns? Geschichtskonstruktionen in der deutschen Literatur nach 1989* (Berlin: Schmidt, 2006); Laurel Cohen-Pfister and Dagmar Weinroeder-Skinner, eds, *Victims and Perpetrators: 1933–1945 — Representing the Past in Post-Unification Culture* (Berlin: de Gruyter, 2006).
27. Amir Eshel, *Futurity: Contemporary Literature and the Quest for the Past* (Chicago: University of Chicago Press, 2013), sets out what he terms a 'hermeneutics of futurity' (p. 253), arguing that we can expand our reading of a diverse body of writing, including works published in post-war Germany, by examining the way texts about traumatic pasts take a future-oriented stance. See also Richard Crownshaw, Jane Kilby, and Antony Rowland, eds, *The Future of Memory* (New York: Berghahn, 2010).
28. Stuart Taberner, *Aging and Old-Age Style in Günter Grass, Ruth Klüger, Christa Wolf, and Martin Walser* (Rochester, NY: Camden House, 2013), p. 20.
29. See also Klinger and Wolf, eds; Owen Evans, *Mapping the Contours of Oppression: Subjectivity, Truth and Fiction in Recent German Autobiographical Treatments of Totalitarianism* (Amsterdam: Rodopi, 2006).
30. Nadine Jessica Schmidt, *Konstruktionen literarischer Authentizität in autobiographischem Erzählen* (Göttingen: V&R unipress, 2014), p. 267.
31. Ibid.
32. Eva Lezzi, *Zerstörte Kindheit: Literarische Autobiografien zur Shoah* (Cologne: Böhlau, 2001), p. 8.
33. On the historiography of childhood, see Hugh Cunningham, *Children and Childhood in Western Society since 1500*, 2nd edn (Harlow: Pearson Longman, 2005), pp. 3–15.
34. See also Lisa Pine, *Education in Nazi Germany* (Oxford and New York: Berg, 2010).
35. See Debórah Dwork, *Children with a Star: Jewish Youth in Nazi Europe* (Newhaven and London: Yale University Press, 1991); Patricia Heberer, *Children during the Holocaust* (Lanham, MD: AltaMira Press in association with the United States Holocaust Memorial Museum, 2011); George Eisen, *Children and Play in the Holocaust: Games among the Shadows* (Amherst: University of Massachusetts Press, 1988).
36. See also Barbara Bauer and Waltraud Strickhausen, eds, *'Für ein Kind war das anders': Traumatische Erfahrungen jüdischer Kinder und Jugendlicher im nationalsozialistischen Deutschland* (Berlin: Metropol, 1999), which considers the subject of trauma in accounts by, and about, children in the Holocaust, and Andrea Reiter, ed., *Children of the Holocaust* (London: Vallentine Mitchell, 2006), which examines contemporary and retrospective accounts of childhood in the Holocaust.
37. Bill Niven, 'German Victimhood Discourse in Comparative Perspective', in *Dynamics of Memory and Identity in Contemporary Europe*, ed. by Eric Langenbacher, Bill Niven, and Ruth Wittlinger (New York: Berghahn, 2012), pp. 180–95 (p. 180).
38. See Regina Hofmann, *Der kindliche Ich-Erzähler in der modernen Kinderliteratur: Eine erzähltheoretische Analyse mit Blick auf aktuelle Kinderromane* (Frankfurt a.M.: Lang, 2010). Hofmann underlines the proximity of the child narrator to both the content of narration and to the reader. This results in heightened emotionality (p. 254).

39. For a summary of these arguments, see Monika Spielmann, *Aus den Augen des Kindes: Die Kinderperspektive in deutschsprachigen Romanen seit 1945* (Innsbruck: Universität Innsbruck, 2002), pp. 202–29.
40. Mechthild Barth, *Mit den Augen des Kindes: Narrative Inszenierungen des kindlichen Blicks im 20. Jahrhundert* (Heidelberg: Winter, 2009), p. 233.
41. Tanja Hetzer, *Kinderblick auf die Shoah: Formen der Erinnerung bei Ilse Aichinger, Hubert Fichte und Danilo Kiš* (Würzburg: Königshausen & Neumann, 1999), p. 10. See also Andrea Reiter, 'Die Funktion der Kinderperspektive in der Darstellung des Holocausts', in *'Für ein Kind war das anders'*, ed. by Bauer and Strickhausen, pp. 215–29.
42. Hetzer, p. 135.
43. Nora Maguire, *Childness and the Writing of the German Past: Tropes of Childhood in Contemporary German Literature* (Berne: Lang, 2014), p. 7.
44. Ibid., p. 8.
45. After Peter Hollindale, *Signs of Childness in Children's Books* (Stroud: Thimble Press, 1997).
46. Maguire, p. 1.
47. Debbie Pinfold, *The Child's View of the Third Reich in German Literature: The Eye among the Blind* (Oxford: Clarendon Press, 2001), p. 158.
48. Maguire, p. 167.

CHAPTER 1

Children's Lives under Nazism and Contemporary Cultural Memory

Growing Up in the Third Reich, 1933–45

One of the most striking features of the generation that grew up in the Third Reich is the great diversity of their experiences as children and adolescents. In subsequent chapters, I am going to focus on individual texts and films that explore and portray childhood experiences under Nazism from a variety of perspectives. To lay the foundations for this, I want to consider in broad terms the kinds of experiences children had between 1933 and 1945. The regime targeted children in an unprecedented way — either to mould those it deemed 'acceptable' to best serve its cause, or to eliminate those it deemed 'unacceptable' on grounds of race and disability.

As a movement, National Socialism made use of the energy and positive potential of the young, colonizing childhood at home, at school, and in leisure time. The Hitler Youth emerged from, and eventually replaced, the multiple youth organizations which had existed during the Weimar Republic,[1] and the 'Gesetz über die Hitlerjugend' [Hitler Youth Law], promulgated in December 1936, made membership compulsory for all Germans aged between ten and eighteen. The text of the law itself communicated the importance of youth to National Socialist policies and aims: 'von der Jugend hängt die Zukunft des deutschen Volkes ab. Die gesamte deutsche Jugend muß deshalb auf ihre zukünftigen Pflichten vorbereitet werden' [the future of the German people depends upon its young people. For this reason, all German youths must be prepared for their future duties].[2] The Hitler Youth augmented the National Socialist education programme, which was intended to prepare the young for their future as members of the 'Thousand Year Reich'.

The principal division between the individual organizations which made up the Hitler Youth was by gender: the *Deutsches Jungvolk* [German Youth] and *Hitlerjugend* [Hitler Youth] (HJ) for boys; the *Jungmädelbund* [Young Girls' League] and *Bund deutscher Mädel* [League of German Girls] (BDM) for girls. The socialization of girls and young women during the Third Reich was largely similar to that of their male contemporaries, and as Michael H. Kater suggests, there was 'little planning from above to account for gender difference'.[3] Indeed, the sense of equality between girls and boys it engendered was arguably part of the reason for the popularity of the BDM.[4] Although these similarities did exist, the different divisions expected different things of their members. BDM activities, in line with National Socialist ideology and the perceived needs of the regime, emphasized the importance of each girl's duty to become a mother and a bearer of German culture.[5] Boys in the Hitler Youth were to leave culture to the girls, and become 'bearers of the new Reich'.[6] Thus, where the girls were, to a large extent, prepared in the skills of motherhood and home-making, the boys were trained in military skills.[7] Germany had been taken by political means: she was now to be shaped anew, and this German culture 'properly' expressed.

The school was another primary locus of indoctrination. With the process of *Gleichschaltung* [co-ordination] in 1933, the education syllabus was altered to include and to emphasize subjects relating to racial, national, and political ideas; by 1938, official texts had been introduced to focus on these subjects more systematically. The intention was, as Robert B. Kane writes, 'to inculcate the regime's nationalist spirit and racial principles into the school-age population, bolstering the work of the HJ'.[8] Education was intended to strengthen obedience to the Party line. The system sought to deprive children of free will and agency, discouraging any kind of curiosity, dissent, or critical evaluation.[9] The educational system was further altered to include the establishment of a series of elite schools: the *Nationalpolitische Erziehungsanstalten* [National Political Institutes of Education] (NaPolAs), the *Adolf-Hitler-Schulen* [Adolf Hitler Schools], and the *Ordensburgen* [Order Castles].[10] At these elite educational institutions, pupils were instructed in National Socialist ideology and prepared for their future role as members of a privileged class, much more so than their contemporaries in ordinary schools. Lisa Pine's study of education in Nazi Germany shows that such schools 'represented a microcosm of the Nazi *Weltanschauung* by fostering the leadership principle, promoting competitiveness and emphasising life as a struggle and survival of the "fittest"'.[11] The schools became a kind of 'Reich in miniature', a training ground for future leaders and politicians. Not content with exerting control over the young within the education system, and over their extra-curricular activities, the National Socialist regime sought to exercise influence from birth, and even beforehand. The SS-run *Lebensborn* [Fountain of Life] programme exhorted young women and adolescent girls to 'schenk dem Führer ein Kind' [have a baby for the Führer].[12] Children who fitted the regime's racial requirements became a commodity, to be born under the Party's control, educated under its supervision, ordered by its programme in their free time, and thus equipped, according to their background, to be its servants, members, and leaders.

Not all children in the Third Reich were deemed worthy of this widespread and far-reaching 'nurture' and 'education', and those whom the regime deemed 'unacceptable' inevitably received vastly different treatment. Children defined as Jewish were excluded from educational establishments, in the same way that Jewish adults were being debarred from all areas of public life.[13] The 'Gesetz gegen die Überfüllung deutscher Schulen und Hochschulen' [Law against Overcrowding in German Schools and Universities] in April 1933 set a cap on the total number of

Jewish pupils at 1.5 per cent of the total enrolment figures.[14] When the threat of Nazism to Jewish citizens became increasingly urgent following the November pogroms of 1938, or Kristallnacht [Night of Broken Glass], many children were taken, or sent, out of Germany, either to friends and relatives, or with the Refugee Children's Movement and the Kindertransports. This formalized programme, run by the Central British Fund for German Jewry, facilitated the emigration of ten thousand children and teenagers from Central and Eastern Europe to the United Kingdom between 1938 and 1939.[15] Those who could not leave were concealed in various ways: some were masked by false identities and fictional origins; others were kept hidden from sight.[16] The majority were deported to the network of ghettos and camps, where they were unlikely to survive. If they were not sent to the gas chambers, they might be able to survive within the adult population, but they were faced with harsh labour, inhumane conditions, and the constant threat of punishment, disease, and death. Jewish children who survived the war represent the exception. In all, it is estimated that 1.5 million children and adolescents died as a result of Nazi persecution,[17] in ghettos and concentration camps, and as forced labourers.[18] As Sue Vice has observed, 'children were included in the Nazis' racial murder because they not only represented the threat of future revenge for their parents' death, but were themselves the next Jewish generation'.[19] The Nazis' definition of 'unacceptability' also extended beyond race.[20] From 1938 onwards, five thousand children classed as individuals with 'cognitive or developmental impairment, severe physical disability, or incurable mental illness', dubbed 'lebensunwertes Leben' [life unworthy of life], were killed as part of a child euthanasia programme.[21]

In the aftermath of the war, the profound effects of these diverse conditions on those who had grown up under Nazism and during wartime were revealed. The scale and impact of Nazi indoctrination was reflected in the practical, but also ideological, difficulties faced by the occupying powers. The high death toll resulting from the war meant that many families were incomplete or fragmented: by 1945, 250,000 German children had lost both parents, and over a million had lost their fathers.[22] International humanitarian efforts were launched across Europe in order to reunite families, and to rehouse children. Attention was also directed to the proportion of children who had been socialized under Nazism. As part of the programme of denazification ('Entnazifizierung'), which was designed to eradicate National Socialist thought and ideology from political, economic, cultural, and intellectual life, individuals' relationships to the Nazi party were scrutinized. This process was also considered for those aged under eighteen. Jaimey Fisher has shown that denazifying the young proved highly problematic: the extent to which they could be deemed 'adult agents' was by no means clear-cut. This only exacerbated the complex question of guilt and culpability.[23] In the years after the war, the thorny issue of German guilt, as well as the moral or political agency of minors, began to be addressed. The Hitler Youth had participated in the Second World War, and their efforts, both on the Home Front and as soldiers, undeniably prolonged the conflict. Yet, as was argued at the time, their age complicated the question of complicity. A statement had been issued by the anti-fascist youth committee in Chemnitz in July 1945, declaring all Germans, including the youth, complicit ('mitschuldig') in Nazi crimes.[24] However, in early 1947 a 'youth amnesty' was enacted in the Soviet occupation zone, exempting many young people from the denazification process.[25] German youths — which included anyone up to the age of twenty-six at the war's end — were pronounced 'too young to be held accountable for Nazism'.[26] A similar youth amnesty was introduced in the US zone in August 1946 and in the British and French zones in May 1947.[27] This is striking because, in declaring these juveniles innocent, there was an inherent suggestion that they might have been guilty, or at least culpable. The Soviet amnesty at least recognized that these young people had been too young to vote for the National Socialists up to 1933. On this reading, they were not culpable because they had had no opportunity to speak of to exercise real choices. Despite such legal and political rulings, these former Hitler Youth members were faced with the need to reassess the regime in which they had been raised, including its values, ideals, and doctrines, and their own part in it.[28] The philologist and diarist Viktor Klemperer, himself the object of persecution during the Third Reich, expressed their peculiar condition succinctly:

> dieser Generation ist das Denken und Fühlen vom Abc an vergiftet worden, sie hat nie etwas anderes gelernt, gesehen, in sich eingeatmet als Nazismus; sie ist von sich aus vollkommen unschuldig, und ist doch ganz eingetaucht in die Erbsünde des Nazismus und ganz durchtränkt von ihr.[29]
>
> [this generation's thoughts and feelings have been poisoned from their ABC onwards, they have never learned, seen, or breathed in anything but Nazism; they are in themselves completely innocent, and yet totally immersed in the original sin of Nazism and completely saturated by it.]

The members of this generation expressed feelings of bewilderment and betrayal but lacked the necessary time and methods to work through such emotions. To have been saturated by Nazism, but declared innocent of its crimes, proved a crisis of identity that would haunt them for decades to come. As the author Gudrun Pausewang wrote in the afterword to a collection of short stories and autobiographical pieces, *Ich war dabei: Geschichten gegen das Vergessen* [I Was There: Stories against Forgetting] (2004): 'Nach dem Kriegsende erkennen zu müssen, wie schmählich das NS-Regime unseren jugendlichen Idealismus benutzt und missbraucht hatte, tat weh. [...] Die Nazizeit hinterließ uns, ihren Kindern, ein schweres Erbe' [After the war ended, it hurt to have to recognize how shamefully the National Socialist regime had used and abused our youthful idealism. [...] The Nazi period left us, its children, a difficult legacy].[30]

After 1945, Jewish children initially represented one of the smallest groups of displaced young people, since those who had been too young to work had perished. Those few who survived had to come to terms with their experiences, or at least attempt to do so. The historian Heide Fehrenbach suggests that only four options were available for Jewish children who had been in hiding: they could continue to live with the family that had hidden them, attempt to find surviving relatives, be rehoused with another family, or be sent to a Jewish orphanage.[31] Thus, 1945 might have represented a liberation from the oppression of Nazism, but it did not provide immediate safety or an end to their suffering. In a study of Holocaust survivors in post-war Germany, Margarete Myers Feinstein describes their situation and the challenge which it posed:

> traumatized by feelings of abandonment and tremendous loss, hungry to make up for lost years of experiences and education, desperate for the comfort of family, and yet often fiercely independent, child survivors represented a tremendous challenge to the adults who would care for them and seek to ease their transition to life in normalcy.[32]

The consequences of National Socialist policies during the Third Reich, as well as the events of the Second World War, were far-reaching and profound, leaving an indelible mark on all those who grew up during this period, albeit in very different ways.

Following the war, the extent to which such experiences might be discussed or commemorated publicly depended on geographical location. As Germany was divided and that division cemented with the founding of the two states in 1949, two distinct memory cultures ('Erinnerungskulturen') emerged, along with two 'official cultures of commemoration'.[33] The founding myth of the GDR was one of anti-fascist resistance, which, to put it simply, claimed that because fascism was essentially a capitalist phenomenon, there could be no continuity between National Socialism and the East German state. As Sara Jones has argued, this myth 'not only drew a line between the GDR and the past (Weimar Republic and Third Reich), but also separated East Germany and the West, which was accused of not having truly broken with its Nazi past'.[34] In the Federal Republic, a process of 'Vergangenheitsbewältigung' [coming to terms with the past] placed emphasis on atrocities committed by Germans during the Third Reich, emphasizing their role as perpetrators of the Holocaust and focusing on (collective) guilt and contrition. These divergent memory cultures naturally affected the way in which childhood memories were disseminated, particularly those that thematized suffering.

Remembering the Third Reich in the Berlin Republic

Following reunification, the advancing age of the last eyewitnesses to Nazism, namely those who grew up in the regime, has intensified the dissemination of their stories and interest in what they have to say. This is reflected in the steady outpouring of memoirs, novels, anthologies of oral testimony, sociological studies, films, and museum exhibitions about those who grew up in the Third Reich, both within Germany and abroad. Guido Knopp's multiple ZDF series, begun in the 1990s, including *Hitlers Kinder* [Hitler's Children], first broadcast in March 2001, shed light on aspects of Third Reich history.[35] Indeed, a discourse of taboo-breaking and never-before-heard tales has dominated cultural memory since reunification. This has included the education system and the elite educational establishments;[36] the *Lebensborn* programme, the state-supported project to produce racially 'outstanding' children;[37] and, most prominently, accounts of civilian children's experiences during the Second World War. The generation of war children was, it seemed, beginning to tell their stories publicly for the first time. Motivation came partly from their age and stage, and from widely publicized images of refugees fleeing Kosovo in the late 1990s (the first conflict in which the German armed forces had taken part since the end of the Second World War), which drew the public's attention to the suffering of children displaced by national conflict.

Several studies about those who experienced the Second World War as children and adolescents were published, most famously Sabine Bode's *Die vergessene Generation: Die Kriegskinder brechen ihr Schweigen* [The Forgotten Generation: The War Children Break their Silence] (2005).[38] With their emphasis on 'breaking the silence' and giving a voice to the voiceless, texts such as Bode's contributed to a wider discourse of taboo-breaking in post-reunification Germany with regard to public discussion of Germans as victims of the Second World War. This was part of a shift that occurred in the late 1990s and early 2000s, away from a focus on the crimes and atrocities committed by Germans, to the widespread suffering and sense of victimhood of civilians in the war. Publications such as W. G. Sebald's *Luftkrieg und Literatur* [On the Natural History of Destruction] (1999), Jörg Friedrich's *Der Brand: Deutschland im Bombenkrieg 1940–1945* [The Fire: The Bombing of Germany, 1940–1945] (2002), and Günter Grass's *Im Krebsgang* [Crabwalk] (2002) precipitated a change in public discussions about German wartime suffering. These were accompanied by a number of books and television series on the flight and expulsions of Germans from the Eastern territories, the Allied bombing of German cities, and the rape of German women by Soviet soldiers.[39] While this attention to German victimhood initially ran the risk of being seen as a way of relativizing Nazi crimes, the result of this ongoing discourse has been a climate in which, as Stuart Taberner and Paul Cooke observe, the presentation of German wartime suffering is 'typically seen not as a descent into revisionism [...] but as the final stage in Germany's coming to terms with its past and an indication of the country's new normality'.[40] Aleida Assmann describes this as follows:

> Nachdem die jüdische Opfererfahrung im Gedächtnis der Deutschen verankert ist, können andere Leidensgeschichten in dieses Bild mit eingezeichnet werden, ohne das ganze Gefüge zu verschieben. Die Traumata der deutschen Zivilbevölkerung habe in dem Maße Platz neben den Traumata der Holocaustopfer, in dem sich ein Bewusstsein historischer Zusammenhänge etabliert.[41]

> [Once the Jewish experience of victimhood is rooted in German memory, other histories of suffering can be included in the picture without having to reorient or shift the entire framework. The traumas suffered by the German civilian population can only gain a position alongside traumas suffered by the victims of the Holocaust after an awareness of historical connections has been established.][42]

In Assmann's view, one set of experiences of suffering does not cancel out or 'trump' the other. Both can exist contemporaneously. She views this shift as part of a 'broadening of perspective' which does not seek to unseat the centrality of the Holocaust and acknowledgement of German perpetratorship to the framework of memory at a national level, but to allow a space within social memory for the transmission and exchange of memories of German suffering.[43]

It is vital to understand this phenomenon within the context of discussions during the previous decade. The 1990s had seen a discourse about the part played by 'ordinary' Germans in the Third Reich, as exemplified by Daniel Jonah Goldhagen's *Hitler's Willing Executioners* (1996), published in German in the same year, which provoked widespread debate in the German media and led many to reassess their parents' or grandparents' complicity in Nazi atrocities. Similarly, the infamous 'Wehrmachtausstellung' [*Wehrmacht* exhibition], displayed first between 1995 and 1999 and in a revised format between 2001 and 2004, focused on war crimes committed by the *Wehrmacht* on the Eastern Front from 1941 to 1944. Although mired in controversy (it had to be suspended due to multiple labelling inaccuracies), the exhibition radically altered the widely held, unblemished view of the *Wehrmacht*, demonstrating that it had worked in close collaboration with the SS (*Schutzstaffel*) and SD (*Sicherheitsdienst*) in providing infrastructure for, and in some cases participating in, the killing of prisoners-of-war, Jews, and other civilians.[44] At the same time, works such as Bernhard Schlink's *Der Vorleser* [The Reader] (1995) sought to demythologize the view of the perpetrators through a more complex portrayal of the moral issues involved.

The broad interest in stories that had (apparently) never been told suggests the need to reassess what is apparently *known* about historical events. The generational shift that has seen those who grew up in the Third Reich become grandparents has instigated a change in interlocutors, so that children are no longer accusing their parents but grandparents are answering their grandchildren's questions. A body of literature has emerged which is dominated by accounts from the perspective of those born after the end of the Third Reich. Such stories are structured around intergenerational communication, as individuals, taught in history classes about the events of their grandparents' lifetime, now seek to discern their own place within the historical narrative. These family stories and generation novels commonly focus on private, familial experiences of Nazism.[45] In contrast to the more accusatory stance taken in the 'Väterliteratur' [fathers' literature] genre of the 1970s and 1980s, which Schmitz describes as a kind of 'tribunalisation of family relationships',[46] recent family novels are often characterized by attempts at empathy. Younger generations seek to understand their grandparents' actions. Where 'tribunalisation' *is* depicted, this is frequently intended to show its inadequacies.[47] Aleida Assmann argues, along the same lines, that 'Väterliteratur' is characterized by 'a breach' but family novels are about 'continuity'.[48] The passage of time, and the caesura of reunification, have driven and shaped this turn. Consequently, the testimony of 'what it was like' to live through this period is gaining currency, as are efforts to depict such testimony accessibly: in literature, film, and museum exhibitions, particularly given that these eyewitnesses will soon no longer be able to communicate their own stories anew.

Cultural Memory and Emotionally Experienced History

The present study explores how experiences of childhood under Nazism contribute to the cultural memory of the period since reunification.[49] Here, I want to set out some of the key theories of memory that form a backdrop to the later close readings: cultural memory, postmemory, prosthetic memory, and 'gefühlte Geschichte' [emotionally experienced history].

Jan and Aleida Assmann introduced the notion of cultural memory in the 1980s, building on and refining Maurice Halbwachs's 'mémoire collective' [collective memory]. The Assmanns tease out three 'memory frameworks', or dimensions of memory: personal, or individual, memory; social, or collective, memory; and cultural memory. Personal, or individual, memories are 'indispensable because they are the stuff out of which individual experiences, interpersonal relations, the sense of responsibility, and the image of our own identity are made'.[50] Yet they also incorporate more than our own individual experiences. They necessarily interact with collective memories of the past. Communicative, or social, memory can be understood as intergenerational, conveyed by oral means, over a period of around three generations or about eighty years.[51] It is 'non-institutional' and 'lives in everyday interaction and communication'.[52] Dietrich Harth, outlining Jan Assmann's theory of cultural memory, puts this succinctly: 'every culture connects every one of its individual subjects on the basis of shared norms (rules) and stories (memories; *Erinnerungen*) to the experience of a commonly inhabited meaningful world'.[53] Cultural memory is created and sustained by representations in literature, film, museum exhibitions, memorials, and commemorative acts. These things are both the media by which cultural memory is perpetuated, and in themselves shape it. Aleida Assmann argues that, while individual and collective memory are 'embodied' and 'cling to and abide with human beings and their embodied interaction', cultural memory is 'mediated'.[54] This latter aspect is important and has been emphasized particularly by Astrid Erll, who foregrounds the mediality of cultural memory. It has the power to 'shape the collective imagination of the past in a way that is truly fascinating for the literary scholar (and somewhat alarming for the historian)'.[55] It is also essential to view cultural memory as part of a dynamic process of remembering and forgetting which enables individuals and collectives to navigate their relationship to the past.[56] As Erll and Rigney argue:

> The very concept of *cultural* memory is itself premised on the idea that memory can only become collective as part of a continuous process whereby memories are shared with the help of symbolic artefacts that mediate between individuals and, in the process, create communality across both space and time.[57]

An essential question for the present study is the extent to which it is possible for representations of the past to challenge dominant discourses within cultural memory. Aleida Assmann argues that individuals' memories are heterogeneous because they are 'multiperspektivisch' [multiperspectival],[58] and when they are 'taken up in representations' (the 'Ebene der Repräsentationen') they become 'homogenized'.[59] Conflicting memories necessarily coexist in society; 'on the level of public discourse and national identity, however, the question arises as to how one can integrate divergent and even contradictory memories into a generally acceptable framework'.[60] In Germany, there is a 'Norm des nationalen Gedächtnisrahmens' [normative framework for national memory],[61] which is the memory of the Holocaust and the acknowledgement of guilt and responsibility for the crimes of the regime. All other memories have to be integrated into this framework.[62] As we will see in the case studies that follow, texts that challenge these 'homogenized' representations upset the status quo.

Within post-reunification cultural memory, we have seen a turn towards 'emotional' accounts of history, in contrast to documentary descriptions, and a greater focus on the memories of individuals who lived through the period. In his study of post-1990 approaches to the Third Reich, Bill Niven writes:

> there is much to suggest that, while the period of National Socialism is a deeply 'political' era, [...] post-unification literary treatment does what it can to depoliticize it, in other words to 'return' the perspective to those who experienced the Third Reich and take it 'out of the hands' of the post-war evaluation and adjudication [...]. There is a search for the 'authentic' voice, unmediated by the political correctness of post-war responses to National Socialism.[63]

Here, Niven uses 'authentic' to describe accounts that move away from what he views as the moral strictures of post-war perspectives. In this context, authenticity also comes to mean something approaching an inner truth — not 'Wahrhaftigkeit' [truthfulness], but a deeper truth about the past. Indeed, this has become a signature of post-*Wende* cultural representations of the Third Reich. The German term that has emerged to encapsulate such an approach, 'gefühlte Geschichte', emphasizes both the emotional response such representations engender, and its sense of proximity and embodiment: it is history that you feel. Representations within this mode of emotionally experienced history offer a chance to encounter not only what happened but also *how it felt* to be there. Responses focus on experience rather than 'factual knowledge', or what Schmitz terms a 'shift both in historiographical and popular discourse from a history of "hard facts" to "story", human interest and emotionalisation'.[64] This, he suggests, is part of a decentralization of historiography: a move away from 'master narratives' to a 'pluralisation of historical narratives' and an 'increasingly emotionalised and individualised approach'.[65]

The term 'gefühlte Geschichte' was also used by the sociologist Harald Welzer, who led a now much-discussed study of intergenerational communication in contemporary Germany, published as *Opa war kein Nazi: Nationalsozialismus und Holocaust im Familiengedächtnis* [Grandpa Wasn't a Nazi: National Socialism and the Holocaust in Familial Memory] (2002). Welzer attributes the popularity of publications such as Grass's *Im Krebsgang* and Friedrich's *Der Brand* in part to the fact that they are closer to the 'gefühlte Geschichte der Bundesbürger' [citizens' emotionally experienced history], telling stories of German suffering rather than of Nazi crimes.[66] Here, 'gefühlte Geschichte' comprises the stories of individuals told within families and communities, but which do not necessarily represent 'official', public accounts of history. Furthermore, narratives that are situated within the framework of emotional history both give an account of, and appeal to, emotions: 'sie sprechen die Gefühle an' [they appeal to emotions].[67] As I will argue, narratives of childhood, whether autobiographical or fictional, are frequently considered to evoke precisely this kind of emotionally experienced history because of generally held ideas about, and associations with, this period of life.

We can also understand 'gefühlte Geschichte' in relation to two important and relatively recent concepts within the field of memory studies. First, Marianne Hirsch's 'postmemory', a term originally intended to describe the relationship between children of Holocaust survivors and their parents' memories.[68] Hirsch explains:

> 'Postmemory' describes the relationship that the 'generation after' bears to the personal, collective, and cultural trauma of those who came before — to experiences they 'remember' only by means of the stories, images, and behaviours among which they grew up. But these experiences were transmitted to them so deeply and affectively as to *seem* to constitute memories in their own right. Postmemory's connection to the past is thus actually mediated not by recall but by imaginative investment, projection, and creation. [...] These events happened in the past, but their effects continue into the present.[69]

Hirsch legitimizes the idea that those coming after can feel profoundly affected by the suffering of previous generations, but emphasizes that this is not the same experience as the original trauma: postmemory is 'not an identity position, but a space of remembrance'.[70] As Hirsch writes, 'it is a question of adopting the traumatic experiences [...] of others as experiences one might oneself have had, and of ascribing them into one's own life story'.[71] The application of the term has by now expanded far beyond Hirsch's original usage, and has been criticized on the grounds that the empathy Hirsch calls for can easily become a form of appropriation.[72] Kathy Behrendt concludes that 'postmemory' is most useful 'when it is restricted to cases in which there is close and relatively unfettered access to the victim's past on behalf of the post-rememberer'.[73] There is necessarily a work of empathy and imagination — a kind of subjunctive thinking, of what might have been — but it risks over-identification and, at worst, the appropriation of one individual's trauma by another who did not experience it.[74]

A second form of culturally mediated memory is Alison Landsberg's 'prosthetic memory'. Landsberg argues that memory can function like a prosthesis, whereby it becomes possible to '*experience* an event or a past without having actually lived through it'.[75] Memory is gained vicariously through encounters with visual and digital media that display historical events. An individual watching a film or visiting a museum can have an emotional and embodied memorial connection to the past. Landsberg explains:

> This new form of memory, which I call *prosthetic memory*, emerges at the interface between a person and a historical narrative about the past, at an experiential site such as a movie theater or museum. In this moment of contact, an experience occurs through which the person sutures himself or herself into a larger history

> [...] In the process that I am describing, the person does not simply apprehend a historical narrative, but takes on a more personal, deeply felt memory of a past event through which he or she did not live. The resulting prosthetic memory has the ability to shape that person's subjectivity and politics.[76]

The 'memories' that such encounters create 'are derived from engagement with a mediated representation'.[77] As with postmemory, there are inherent dangers in this approach, because this kind of memory, acquired through exposure to mass-market material, could result in the (unwitting) direction of individuals' apprehension of the past. It does not necessarily encourage the kind of plurality of memory for which critics like Aleida Assmann in the German context have so persuasively argued. Equally, Landsberg's emphasis on the central role in prosthetic memory work of 'identification' with the victims of trauma and suffering[78] risks, at an extreme, appropriation. Despite these reservations, however, I find Landsberg's theory particularly persuasive in its acknowledgement of the artificial nature of this kind of memory work, though I agree with Susannah Radstone, who has argued that, in its arguments about cinema, it neglects to take account of theories of spectatorship by conceiving of viewers as passive spectators.[79]

I want now to consider an example of how such embodied, or emotional, histories play out by using an example from the space of the museum. By preserving and exhibiting the paraphernalia of Nazism, the museum is an important site in which visitors can encounter representations of this historical period, and it makes an important contribution to cultural memory.[80] Pierre Nora identifies the museum, among other sites, as a 'lieu de mémoire' [site of memory], 'which by dint of human will or the work of time has become a symbolic element of the memorial heritage of any community'.[81] When there are no longer communities of memory ('milieux de mémoire'), memory becomes the province of sites ('lieux') and commemorative practices.[82] The Hamburger Schulmuseum [Hamburg School Museum] exhibits an assortment of artistically reconstructed German schoolrooms from different historical periods, including the Third Reich.[83] The permanent 'hands-on' exhibition seeks to put the visitor in the position of the historical child, both through links that can be drawn with their own school experiences and through engagement with the exhibition space. This is particularly apt given that the exhibition is intended primarily for young people. In the section of the exhibition entitled '"Schule unterm Hakenkreuz" und Neuanfang nach 1945' ['School Life beneath the Swastika' and New Beginnings after 1945], period objects are displayed in glass cases, on the walls, and even underfoot: the visitor is literally surrounded by objects from the past. To view the objects exhibited within the floor space, the visitor is required to bend down and, in this way, is placed effectively in the position of the child, temporarily looking back up into the schoolroom from this new, childlike perspective. A similar effect is achieved through the use of school desks, which contain a variety of objects such as books and toy soldiers, and at which the visitor can sit. The overall effect is heightened by the presence of a white papier-mâché figure of a child at one of the desks; sounds of children come from the real primary school next door.

Fig. 1.1. '"Schule unterm Hakenkreuz" und Neuanfang nach 1945'
['School Life beneath the Swastika' and New Beginnings after 1945]
in the permanent exhibition at the Hamburg School Museum. Photograph by
the author. Reproduced by kind permission of the Hamburg School Museum.

The display includes a series of original school textbooks of the period available for the visitor to hold and read. Here, the tangible link to the past which the books provide contributes further to the overall endeavour of the exhibition to bring the past 'to life' for a contemporary audience. In this exhibition space, the notion of 'gefühlte Geschichte' takes on a concrete function: the multi-sensory experience offered by the museum enables the visitor to 'experience' the past, through tangible means. This has something to do with the material quality of objects from the past. In their introduction to *Das historische Museum* [The Historical Museum] (1991), Gottfried Korff and Martin Roth write:

> das museale Objekt ist ein authentisches Objekt. Damit ist es Dokument und Zeuge. Doch weil Authentizität mehr meint als Echtheit und Originalität, kommt beim musealen Objekt neben dem Zeugnischarakter noch eine andere Dimension ins Spiel. Und zwar ist dies die sinnliche Anmutungsqualität, die Ausgangspunkt für die faszinierende Wirkung der Objektwelten des Museums ist.[84]
>
> [the museum object is an authentic object. It is therefore both a document and a witness. Yet because authenticity means more than simply being genuine and

original, another dimension comes into play with the museum object besides its character of witnessing. This is the sensory impression it creates, which is the starting point of the fascinating effect of that world of objects which constitutes the museum.]

Here, it is not only the provenance of the object that creates its aura of authenticity, but also its 'sinnliche Anmutungsqualität' [sensory impression]: its status as a link to the past. This doorway into the past is, for Korff and Roth, at the heart of the visitor's fascination with the museum. Museum objects come to be seen as 'unmediated anchors to the past'.[85] This sense of tangibility is, of course, heightened in interactive or 'hands-on' museums where objects can actually be handled rather than simply observed behind glass or Perspex. This places the museum visitor, albeit it in an artificial way, in the position of the original user of the object. It is perhaps fitting that the German term 'Sachzeuge' [artefact] is so close to the word for an eyewitness, 'Zeitzeuge'. In its quasi-personification of the historical object, the term encapsulates well ideas about material culture's 'truth-value'.

The experience of childhood under Nazism seems to offer the essence of everyday life as it was lived, the 'Alltag im Faschismus' [everyday world under fascism],[86] which can be viewed as an acute form of a wider concern with accounts of the past. In addition, such accounts seem to respond directly to the desire to secure some kind of narrative of 'authentic experience': 'authentic' both in terms of being 'first-hand' and in possessing an 'experiential' quality in contrast to purely factual material on the topic. This is something that Axel Bangert identifies in his analysis of filmic representations of the Third Reich since reunification, *The Nazi Past in Contemporary German Film: Viewing Experiences of Intimacy and Immersion* (2014). Bangert argues that since 1990, cinema and television have become primary sites of cultural memory with a particular focus on 'the experiential dimension of the Nazi past', encompassing intimate and immersive experiences of the Third Reich on screen.[87] This emphasis on subjectivity accords with the broader turn towards emotional history taken in the post-reunification period in literature and visual culture that treats the Nazi period. It accords with the etymology of the German word 'Erinnerung' [memory], which Gerhard Richter takes to be drawn from the phrase 'er innert' [he interiorizes].[88] This, he argues (drawing on Derrida), 'bespeaks a kind of interiorizing or incorporative memory, a memory that emphasizes an experiential relation of the self to the object of its mnemonic act'.[89] This contemporary demand for authenticity may surprise us. When the cultural theorist looks at a photograph, they are aware of the constructedness of its form, and of the elusiveness of the 'authenticity' it promises. Yet how often do we see the historical referentiality of photographs invoked? Or we might take historical films: we know they are fictional adaptations of historical events, yet so often in reviews and critical discussions they are measured against their historical accuracy (or lack of it). The elusiveness and impossibility of the term 'authenticity', picked over by critics and academics, is not reflected in the demand for it from the public. As Andrea Reiter observes: 'whereas cultural theorists are sceptical about authenticity, there is in general a renewed yearning for it among "ordinary" people'.[90] This, she observes, explains the overwhelmingly positive reception of works like Wilkomirski's *Bruchstücke*, which, as I will argue, offers a flawed authenticity. Finally, we might consider the extent to which 'authenticity' can be understood to signify the connection between the creator of an artistic work and their own experience. For example, Schmitz points to the 'increasing impossibility of "authenticity" in relation to the past' as we become ever more removed from the historical events in question.[91]

Childhood and the Emotionalization of the Past

Post-reunification representations of growing up in the Third Reich offer, or appear to offer, just such an emotionally experienced history. Childhood, rooted both in a literal and poetic sense in the private sphere, seems to offer a more personal view of history, not fettered by public rhetoric and adult concerns, but rather accessing and representing the most direct experience of Nazism and the Second World War. This is certainly the result of modern Western ideas about children and childhood which have developed particularly since Romanticism. I want briefly to outline some of the most influential theories of childhood and its meanings here, since the analysis in subsequent chapters hinges on the ways in which this collection of ideas is pressed into service and interpreted.[92]

First, the child is innately 'different'. Children are part of the adult world, but simultaneously separate and separated from it by reason of their age. In the modern Western treatment of children, this situates them in different social spaces, such as the nursery and the school. As part of this 'difference', the child is viewed as being linked to the natural world. The child is deemed to have a special kind of nature which, from Romanticism to the twenty-first century, has been associated with a kind of inner self and with the individual's personal history.[93] Sigmund Freud's work sought the origin of the adult individual in their childhood. As a result, early childhood experience came to be regarded more widely as a place which could be searched for the roots of the personality and character of the adult which the child had become. Thus, childhood can be used effectively to suggest a desire or search for origins, for both individual and collective identity. This is manifested in the established literary and cinematic trope of childhood as a physical space or location, a prelapsarian Garden of Eden, the time before the Fall.

The belief in children's innate innocence can also be traced to Romanticism. Jean-Jacques Rousseau's novel *Émile* (1762) is widely considered to have radically changed perceptions of childhood by suggesting that the child arrived in the world in a state of innocence which was then gradually corrupted.[94] The novel had a particular impact in Germany, where it was available in translation within a year of its original publication and, as Pinfold has shown, it 'had a profound influence on contemporary German writers who were deeply affected by the idea of the child's original innocence'.[95] Rousseau argued that humankind was essentially good, and that this goodness was to be found in the child in a primal condition. By educating children according to 'natural' principles, these qualities could be properly nurtured. From this perspective, innocence is the child's essential quality, where innocence

Fig. 1.2. 'Puppenhaus — Deutschland, nach 1933' [Doll's House — Germany, after 1933] in the permanent exhibition at the Deutsches Historisches Museum, Berlin. Photograph by the author. Reproduced by kind permission of the DHM.

is constructed around a kind of naivety and initial incorruptibility. Education and knowledge, as well as sexuality, are corrupting influences which 'spoil' the child's natural innocence. This suggests not only innocence in the sense of being free from sin or corruption, but also the idea of innocence as ignorance. In modern Western cultures, children's ignorance is used as a means with which to preserve the state of childhood, and if children acquire what is viewed as premature knowledge of sex and death, then the taboo is broken. Of course, from a psychologist's point of view this privileging of innocence can result in a potentially harmful denial of childhood sexuality.[96] The innocence of childhood must be the most difficult association from which to break free.

We can see ideas such as these at work in another example from the museum. The Deutsches Historisches Museum [German Historical Museum] (DHM) in Berlin displays the history of the German lands from the first century BC to the fall of the Berlin Wall and reunification.[97] Its permanent exhibition includes several objects associated with childhood in the context of Nazi social policy and the Second World War. First, there is a doll's house produced after 1933, made up of three rooms: a bedroom, living room, and kitchen. While the first two rooms resemble a nineteenth-century domestic scene, with floral wallpaper and Biedermeier furniture, the kitchen is decorated with wallpaper bearing a pattern depicting Hitler

Fig. 1.3. Wallpaper detail from the doll's house at the Deutsches Historisches Museum, Berlin. Photograph by the author. Reproduced by kind permission of the DHM.

Youth and BDM members engaged in a range of outdoor activities.[98] A photograph of Hitler and Mussolini hangs on the wall. The exhibition also includes other such coded objects: board games of the period ('Wir fahren gegen Engelend' [We're Moving against England] and '*Adler* Luftkampfspiel' [*Adler* Air Battle Game]), and toy figures of soldiers and other military or elite figures.

Chloe Paver has argued that toys and dolls decorated with National Socialist insignia can be made to speak of corruption and loss of innocence, and of the all-pervasive reach of the totalitarian state. An object like the doll's house enhances 'the impression of the extraordinary reach of National Socialist ideology into the smallest and most private corners of 1930s Germany'.[99] Indeed, a doll's house could be expected to conform to the Romantic idealization of childhood as a world of naivety, innocence, and a close affinity with nature. The innocence represented by the doll's house is shown to be corrupted by National Socialism. In her study of the material culture of childhood exhibited in museums, Sharon Brookshaw proposes a distinction between the material culture of *childhood* and that of *children*. Those items and objects created by adults for children should be categorized as the material culture of childhood; the material culture of children should cover items which children make for themselves or use in different ways than adults envisaged.[100] In this way, children can be seen as autonomous creators of their own material culture, and as the recipients of adults' designs for them. The doll's house displayed in the DHM reinforces an idea of German non-Jewish youth as the passive receivers of National Socialist indoctrination through its display of objects saturated by Nazi symbols and produced by adults for their use.

In recent years, historians of childhood have sought to highlight children's agency, viewing them as individuals who, even in small ways, make decisions and choices. As Colin Heywood argues in his history of childhood: 'children must be seen as active in determining their own lives and the lives of those around them'.[101] Agency is 'influenced by the belief in one's effectiveness in performing specific tasks, which is termed *self-efficacy*, as well as by one's actual skill'.[102] This shift in the discipline is evident, for example, in one of the earliest studies of children after 1945, Dorothy Macardle's *Children of Europe*, published in 1949. The author calls German children 'Hitler's first victims', describing them as having been 'hammered and twisted, like iron on the anvil, into weapons for his ends'.[103] Macardle's reading suggests the malleability of children, emphasizing what is taken to be their essential passiveness. Stargardt has since countered this kind of idea, arguing that the prevailing rhetoric used to discuss war children results in an image of them as 'the objects rather than the subjects of history'.[104] Their status as agents should be neither underestimated nor understated. The historian Hugh Cunningham has observed that 'it is in many ways easier to write a history of childhood than of children'.[105] This is undoubtedly due to the deeply entrenched, and often fiercely guarded, 'truths' about childhood which pervade Western culture.

Perhaps most crucially for the present study, childhood has become synonymous with a measure of authenticity. 'Authenticity' has many shades of meaning, from stark adherence to facts, to a less rigid concept of a quality of truthfulness, what we might term 'inner' or 'symbolic truth'.[106] It is the latter which is most commonly associated with the child, which, as Kate Douglas writes, 'has long been a cultural symbol of authenticity'.[107] This has two principal modes of expression. First, authenticity means presenting an account which is rooted in private experience. In the West today, where it seems nothing can be done without it being recorded and shared on digital platforms, it is impossible to argue that childhood represents a 'private' world no longer accessible to remembering adults. Yet, since the Romantic annexation of childhood as a concept, it has been idealistically viewed as a space sheltered and secluded from the adult world.

Second, critics have frequently pointed to the inherent truth-value of writing about childhood. In a study of childhood autobiographies, Werner Brettschneider suggests that childhood becomes a guarantor of authenticity when it is the subject of an autobiographical account.[108] Similarly, in her study of childhood autobiographies, Marianne Gullestad argues that 'childhood reminiscences, in particular, can be true without being historically accurate'.[109] She undertakes to challenge the dichotomy between 'truth and authenticity' and 'literary constructedness', arguing that 'it is often through literary or imaginary means that a narrator can construct an approximately authentic account of experiences from the point of view of the child in the narrated past'.[110] Thus, autobiographical writing about childhood might reveal an inner truth about an individual, even if this does not correspond to past events. It is the nature of childhood, its special qualities and perceived universality, which makes this possible.

Richard N. Coe's study of childhood autobiography takes a slightly more nuanced view, asserting that the author who recalls and recreates their childhood in literary form 'refashions accuracy in the direction of truth'. He argues that the truth is, in any case, out of reach forever:

> at best, it can be reevoked through art in a new form, conjured up by way of symbols, images and impressions, and endowed retrospectively with a pattern and a significance which it can rarely, if ever, have possessed at the time, when the later-circumscribed facticity of the past was dissolved into the shapeless and elusive fluidity of the present.[111]

In Coe's view, autobiographical writing about childhood cannot reveal the truth of the past but will necessarily be informed by present concerns. The past is shaped by the present. As such, the past as it is re-presented will exist in a newly crafted form. According to this reading, the truth of the past is rooted in the truth of the individual and of identity.

We also find this trend in writing about cinema, as I will explore in detail in Chapter 5. Here, an example will suffice. Roberto Benigni's much-debated film *La vita è bella* [Life is Beautiful] (1997) combined fairy tale and make-believe to portray a Jewish family's internment in a concentration camp. The author and Holocaust survivor Imre Kertész described the film as authentic: 'der Geist, die Seele dieses Films sind authentisch, dieser Film berührt uns mit der Kraft des ältesten Zaubers, des Märchens' [the spirit, the soul of this film are authentic; this film touches us with the power of the oldest magic, the fairy tale].[112] For Kertész, who had survived Auschwitz and Buchenwald,[113] the film's historical authenticity lies not in its material details, but rather in its special quality of authenticity, by which he means the appeal it makes to the audience's emotions, enabling them to engage with the events and characters. This effect is heightened through the evocation of the fairy tale and its associations with childhood. This is an idea that appears repeatedly in critical literature on cultural representations of childhood and which is a central focus of the present study. While such an interpretation of the truth-value of childhood accounts clearly has great potential, it also needs to be treated with care. As I will explore in Chapter 4, Binjamin Wilkomirski's false Holocaust memoir *Bruchstücke* raised precisely this ethical question about authenticity, legitimacy, and historical representation.

Yet precisely because of this intimate association with 'inner' or 'poetic' truth, children are recognized as a powerful tool with which to engage an audience or reader. They are invested with symbolic capital. Furthermore, images of, and narratives about children are deemed to invite an emotional response. As Patricia Holland outlines in her study of photographic representations of children, 'they are a signal for a release of emotions'.[114] While this quality creates opportunities for memory work and engagement with the suffering of others, the image of the suffering child may well also elicit a purely emotional response, with the effect that ethical and emotional judgements are substituted with an uncritical response. Such catharsis arguably results in a lack of political or social action. This approach, of course, is not without potential problems, and these will be signalled and explored throughout the study. As we have seen repeatedly in recent times, with the wars in Afghanistan and Syria, and with the European refugee crisis, images of dead and wounded children have provoked widespread shock and outrage, but this does not automatically result in material change.[115]

Richard Flynn writes that 'our tendency to view childhood as an idea or ideal makes it difficult for us to see childhood as lived experience'.[116] Indeed, such tropes of childhood neglect an important aspect of its lived reality: namely that, unless this childhood is cut short, children *grow up*. In the same way, narratives of childhood also frequently include the journey from childhood to adulthood. Indeed, the term 'growing up', in German 'heranwachsen', denotes both a sense of journey, of movement and trajectory, as well as a delineation between adulthood and everything that may be considered pre-adulthood. It is commonly understood as a stage on the way to adulthood, the 'not-yet-ness of adulthood'.[117] This may mean that children reach the legal age of majority during the course of the narrative, or that by its close they have reached a new level of maturity or understanding which would indicate that they are somehow no longer children. In doing so, such narratives thematize the liminal period between the two: adolescence. Like childhood, adolescence eludes clear definitions and has a range of connotations. However, it is most strongly associated with development and change. Derived from the French ethnographer Arnold van Gennep's theory of rites of passage, and the cultural anthropologist Victor Turner's development of the theory,[118] liminality has come to be associated with adolescence in contemporary culture. Adolescents become ambiguous, no longer children but not yet adults, but at the same time, they are hybrid, embodying both transgressive potential and childlike vulnerability. This inherent ambiguity has led Western societies to see youths as polarized, as having the potential to be both 'goodies and hoodies'.[119] Erik Erikson described adolescence as a period during which the individual moves from one stable identity (childhood) to another (adulthood), and that an 'identity crisis' of some form, even a muted one, is a universal aspect of development from childhood to adulthood.[120] To speak of childhood, then, is necessarily to include a consideration of the transition out of childhood into adulthood, which occurs through this transitional process of adolescence.

As I will demonstrate in subsequent chapters, the writers and filmmakers in this study inevitably draw on tropes of childhood, either pressing them into service or challenging them through their narratives. Children and adolescents are important vehicles with which to negotiate complex and difficult issues, because, as Pinfold argues, the child is 'rich in potential meanings and extends an open invitation to writers with very different agendas'.[121] Children can embody hope for the future, the evils of society, fears, promises, desires, and nostalgic innocence for a lost past. Furthermore, writers and filmmakers looking back at their own formative years can frame their experiences within these diverse associations. Of course, all the works I go on to analyse provide retrospective accounts of childhood, from the perspective of hindsight, and in this way, they comment as much about the conditions and needs of the present as they do about the past.

Notes to Chapter 1

1. Detlev Peukert, *The Weimar Republic: The Crisis of Classical Modernity*, trans. by Richard Deveson (London: Penguin, 1993), pp. 89–93.
2. 'Gesetz über die Hitlerjugend', cited in *Deutschlands Aufstieg zur Großmacht 1936*, ed. by Axel Friedrichs (Berlin: Junker und Dünnhaupt, 1939), pp. 328–29.
3. Michael H. Kater, *Hitler Youth* (London: Harvard University Press, 2004), p. 73. See also Dagmar Reese, 'The BDM Generation: A Female Generation in Transition from Dictatorship to Democracy', in *Generations in Conflict: Youth Revolt and Generation Formation in Germany 1770–1968*, ed. by Mark Roseman (Cambridge: Cambridge University Press, 1995), pp. 227–47; Pine, *Education in Nazi Germany*, pp. 117–37; Lisa Pine, 'Creating Conformity: The Training of Girls in the Bund Deutscher Mädel', *European History Quarterly*, 33 (2003), 367–85; Kater, pp. 70–113.
4. Pine, *Education in Nazi Germany*, p. 120.
5. Ibid., p. 121.
6. Kater, p. 15.
7. See Kater, pp. 28–42; Pine, *Education in Nazi Germany*, pp. 95–117.
8. Robert B. Kane, *Disobedience and Conspiracy in the German Army 1918–1945* (London: McFarland, 2002), p. 107.
9. See Matthias von Hellfeld and Arno Klönne, *Die betrogene Generation: Jugend im Faschismus* (Cologne: Pahl-Rugenstein, 1985), p. 345.
10. Pine, *Education in Nazi Germany*, pp. 71–72.
11. Ibid., p. 72.
12. Richard Grunberger, *The 12-Year Reich: A Social History of Nazi Germany, 1933–1945* (New York: Holt, Rinehart and Winston, 1971), p. 246. See also Volker Koop, *'Dem Führer ein Kind schenken': Die SS-Organisation Lebensborn e.V.* (Cologne: Böhlau, 2007).
13. On the situation of Jewish children in Europe before, during, and after the war, see Simone Gigliotti and Monica Tempian, eds, *The Young Victims of the Nazi Regime: Migration, the Holocaust and Postwar Displacement* (London: Bloomsbury Academic, 2016), esp. Part 2 ('The Holocaust: Ghetto and Camp Battlegrounds: Imprisonment, Activism and Forced Labour').
14. Marion Kaplan, 'The School Lives of Jewish Children and Youth in the Third Reich', *Jewish History*, 11 (1997), 41–52 (p. 41).
15. There has been a good deal of new historical research into the Kindertransports recently, especially to coincide with the eightieth anniversary of the programme's inception in 1938. See esp. Jennifer Craig-Norton, *The Kindertransport: Contesting Memory* (Bloomington: Indiana University Press, 2019), which challenges the celebratory account of the Kindertransports in popular memory, and Andrea Hammel and Bea Lewkowicz, eds, *The Kindertransport to Britain 1938/39: New Perspectives* (Amsterdam: Rodopi, 2012), which examines the Kindertransports and their legacy from a wide variety of perspectives. See also Simone Gigliotti, *The Train Journey: Transit, Captivity, and Witnessing in the Holocaust* (New York: Berghahn, 2009); Vera K. Fast, *Children's Exodus: A History of the Kindertransport* (London: I. B. Tauris, 2011).
16. Howard Greenfeld, *The Hidden Children* (New York: Ticknor & Fields, 1993), p. 3.
17. Robert Krell, 'Child Survivors of the Holocaust: The Elderly Children and their Adult Lives', in *And Life is Changed Forever: Holocaust Childhoods Remembered*, ed. by Martin Ira Glassner and Robert Krell (Michigan: Wayne State University Press, 2006), pp. 1–17 (p. 1).
18. Patricia Heberer, *Children during the Holocaust* (Lanham, MD: AltaMira Press in association with the United States Holocaust Memorial Museum, 2011), p. 228.
19. Sue Vice, *Children Writing the Holocaust* (Basingstoke: Palgrave Macmillan, 2004), p. 3.
20. Although I focus here on Jewish victims, it is important to remember that other groups were persecuted on racial grounds. See e.g. Tina Campt, *Other Germans: Black Germans and the Politics*

of Race, Gender, and Memory in the Third Reich (Ann Arbor: University of Michigan Press, 2004); Anton Weiss-Wendt, ed., *The Nazi Genocide of the Roma: Reassessment and Commemoration* (New York: Berghahn, 2013).
21. See Patricia Heberer, 'The Nazi "Euthanasia" Program', in *The Routledge History of the Holocaust*, ed. by Jonathan C. Friedman (Abingdon and New York: Routledge, 2011), pp. 137–48 (p. 138).
22. Nicholas Stargardt, *Witnesses of War: Children's Lives under the Nazis* (London: Cape, 2005), p. 342.
23. Jaimey Fisher, *Disciplining Germany: Youth, Reeducation, and Reconstruction after the Second World War* (Detroit: Wayne State University Press, 2007), p. 240.
24. Alan McDougall, 'A Duty to Forget? The "Hitler Youth Generation" and the Transition from Nazism to Communism in Postwar East Germany, c. 1945–49', *German History*, 26 (2008), 24–46 (p. 30).
25. Ibid., pp. 30–31.
26. Fisher, p. 240.
27. Kater, p. 253.
28. On the condition of former Hitler Youth members after 1945, see A. Dirk Moses, *German Intellectuals and the Nazi Past* (Cambridge: Cambridge University Press, 2007), p. 57.
29. Viktor Klemperer, *Kultur: Erwägungen nach dem Zusammenbruch des Nazismus* (Berlin: Neues Leben, 1946), p. 54.
30. Gudrun Pausewang, *Ich war dabei: Geschichten gegen das Vergessen* (Frankfurt a.M.: Fischer, 2015), p. 154.
31. Heide Fehrenbach, 'War Orphans and Post-Fascist Families: Kinship and Belonging after 1945', in *Histories of the Aftermath: The Legacies of the Second World War in Europe*, ed. by Frank Biess and Robert G. Moeller (New York and Oxford: Berghahn, 2010), pp. 175–96 (p. 179).
32. Margarete Myers Feinstein, *Holocaust Survivors in Postwar Germany: 1945–1957* (Cambridge and New York: Cambridge University Press, 2010), p. 159.
33. Silke Arnold-de Simine, *Memory Traces: 1989 and the Question of German Cultural Identity* (Oxford and New York: Lang, 2005), p. 7.
34. Sara Jones, *Complicity, Censorship and Criticism: Negotiating Space in the GDR Literary Sphere* (Berlin and New York: de Gruyter, 2011), p. 9.
35. Rainald Grebe's satirical song *Guido Knopp* captures something of the ubiquity and influence of the Knopp narratives: 'Guido Knopp ist ein Historiker [...] Er wohnt im deutschen Fernsehen | Er wurde dort geboren [...] Er ist mein Gedächtnis | Was ist weiß, hab ich von ihm' [Guido Knopp is a historian [...] He lives on German television | He was born there [...] He is my memory | Everything I know comes from him] (Rainald Grebe, *Guido Knopp* <http://www.youtube.com/watch?v=fKoXjpn5mgo> [accessed 1 July 2019]).
36. See Christian Schneider, Cordelia Stillke, and Bernd Leinweber, *Das Erbe der Napola: Versuch einer Generationengeschichte des Nationalsozialismus* (Hamburg: Hamburger Edition, 1996); Hans Günther Zempelin, *Des Teufels Kadett: Napola-Schüler von 1936 bis 1943: Gespräch mit einem Freund* (Frankfurt a.M.: Fischer, 2000); Johannes Leeb, *'Wir waren Hitlers Eliteschüler': Ehemalige Zöglinge der NS-Ausleseschulen brechen ihr Schweigen* (Hamburg: Rasch und Röhring, 1998).
37. On literary representations of the *Lebensborn* programme after reunification, see Karina Berger, 'Children of the Lebensborn: The Search for Identity in Selected Literary Texts of the Berlin Republic', *Focus on German Studies*, 15 (2008), 105–20.
38. See also Hilke Lorenz, *Kriegskinder: Schicksal einer Generation* (Munich: List, 2003); Yury Winterberg and Sonya Winterberg, *Kriegskinder: Erinnerungen einer Generation* (Berlin: Rotbuch, 2009). Increasingly, not only the war children themselves but also their children and grandchildren came into focus; see Anne-Ev Ustorf, *Wir Kinder der Kriegskinder: Die Generation im Schatten des Zweiten Weltkriegs* (Freiburg: Herder, 2008), and Sabine Bode, *Kriegsenkel: Die Erben der vergessenen Generation* (Stuttgart: Klett-Cotta, 2009), which explore the far-reaching intergenerational trauma of a wartime childhood among those born after 1945.
39. E.g. Guido Knopp, *Die große Flucht: Das Schicksal der Vertriebenen* (Munich: Econ, 2001), and the accompanying ZDF series which first aired in 2001; *Dresden*, dir. by Roland Suso Richter (ZDF, 2006). The extent to which such works can be viewed as taboo-breaking has been

widely debated. I agree with those who argue that narratives of German wartime suffering *had* appeared earlier, for example during the 1950s; however, it is clear that the particular post-reunification context created a space for such narratives to enter the public sphere in a way that was unprecedented.

40. Stuart Taberner and Paul Cooke, 'Introduction', in *German Culture, Politics, and Literature into the Twenty-First Century: Beyond Normalization*, ed. by Stuart Taberner and Paul Cooke (Rochester, NY, and Woodbridge: Camden House, 2006), pp. 1–17 (p. 8).
41. Aleida Assmann, *Der lange Schatten der Vergangenheit: Erinnerungskultur und Geschichtspolitik* (Munich: Beck, 2006), p. 188.
42. A. Assmann, *Shadows of Trauma*, p. 159.
43. Ibid., p. 173.
44. For a full account of this, see Chloe Paver, ' "Ein Stück langweiliger als die Wehrmachtsausstellung, aber dafür repräsentativer": The Exhibition Fotofeldpost as Riposte to the Wehrmacht Exhibition', in *German Memory Contests*, ed. by Fuchs, Cosgrove, and Grote, pp. 107–25.
45. See Eigler, *Gedächtnis und Geschichte*, pp. 29–37.
46. Helmut Schmitz, *On their Own Terms: The Legacy of National Socialism in Post-1990 German Fiction* (Birmingham: Birmingham University Press, 2004), p. 60.
47. See e.g. Günter Grass, *Im Krebsgang* (Munich: dtv, 2002), and Tanja Dückers, *Himmelskörper* (Berlin: Aufbau Taschenbuch Verlag, 2004), in which the accusatory approach of the post-war generation is shown to have a negative effect on their relationship to the past and, consequently, the present.
48. Aleida Assmann, 'Limits of Understanding: Generational Identities in Recent German Memory Literature', in *Victims and Perpetrators*, ed. by Cohen-Pfister and Weinroeder-Skinner, pp. 29–48 (p. 33). Reidy, *Rekonstruktion und Entheroisierung*, pp. 23–35, vehemently contests this reading, arguing that there is a greater continuity between 'Väterliteratur' and the family novel than scholars have hitherto shown.
49. For an excellent overview of key concepts in German memory studies, see Dorothea Kliche-Behnke, *Nationalsozialismus und Shoah im autobiographischen Roman: Poetologie des Erinnerns bei Ruth Klüger, Martin Walser, Georg Heller und Günter Grass* (Berlin: de Gruyter, 2016), pp. 10–25. On the term 'cultural memory', see also Eigler, *Gedächtnis und Geschichte*, pp. 41–48.
50. Aleida Assmann, 'Memory, Individual and Collective', in *The Oxford Handbook of Contextual Political Analysis*, ed. by Robert E. Goodin and Charles Tilly (Oxford: Oxford University Press, 2006), pp. 210–27 (p. 212). Assmann also discusses a fourth category here, 'political memory'; see pp. 215–20. For a succinct overview of the Assmanns' theory of cultural memory, see Eigler, *Gedächtnis und Geschichte*, pp. 41–48.
51. Jan Assmann, *Kultur und Gedächtnis* (Frankfurt a.M.: Suhrkamp, 1988), pp. 9–19. See also Jan Assmann, 'Communicative and Cultural Memory', in *A Companion to Cultural Memory Studies*, ed. by Astrid Erll and Ansgar Nünning (Berlin and New York: de Gruyter, 2008), pp. 109–18.
52. J. Assmann, 'Communicative and Cultural Memory', p. 111.
53. Dietrich Harth, 'The Invention of Cultural Memory', in *A Companion to Cultural Memory Studies*, ed. by Erll and Nünning, pp. 85–96.
54. A. Assmann, 'Memory, Individual and Collective', p. 215.
55. Astrid Erll, 'Literature, Film, and the Mediality of Cultural Memory', in *A Companion to Cultural Memory Studies*, ed. by Erll and Nünning, pp. 389–99 (p. 389).
56. Astrid Erll and Ann Rigney, 'Introduction: Cultural Memory and its Dynamics', in *Mediation, Remediation, and the Dynamics of Cultural Memory*, ed. by Astrid Erll and Ann Rigney (New York: de Gruyter, 2009), pp. 1–15 (pp. 1–2).
57. Erll and Rigney, p. 1.
58. A. Assmann, *Schatten der Vergangenheit*, p. 202; my translation here.
59. A. Assmann, *Schatten der Vergangenheit*, p. 202; A. Assmann, *Shadows of Trauma*, p. 172.
60. A. Assmann, *Shadows of Trauma*, p. 172.
61. A. Assmann, *Schatten der Vergangenheit*, p. 203; my translation here.
62. A. Assmann, *Shadows of Trauma*, p. 173.
63. Bill Niven, 'Literary Portrayals of National Socialism in Post-Unification German Literature', in *German Culture and the Uncomfortable Past*, ed. by Schmitz, pp. 11–29 (p. 15).

64. Helmut Schmitz, 'Introduction', in *A Nation of Victims?*, ed. by Schmitz, pp. 1–31 (p. 5).
65. Ibid., p. 6.
66. Harald Welzer, 'Schön unscharf: Über die Konjunktur der Familien- und Generationenromane', *Mittelweg*, 36 (2004), 53–64 (p. 53).
67. See also Harald Welzer, 'Im Gedächtniswohnzimmer: Warum sind Bücher über die eigene Familiengeschichte so erfolgreich? Ein Zeit-Gespräch mit dem Sozialpsychologen Harald Welzer über das private Erinnern', *Die Zeit*, 25 March 2004 <http://www.zeit.de/2004/14/st-welzer> [accessed 1 July 2019]. Norbert Frei, too, in 'Gefühlte Geschichte', *Die Zeit*, 21 October 2004 <http://www.zeit.de/2004/44/kriegsende> [accessed 1 July 2019], points to the example of Grass's *Im Krebsgang*, which he sees as representative of publications that call for a more understanding approach to the experiences and plight of individuals, and empathy for German victims of the war.
68. See Marianne Hirsch, 'Family Pictures: *Maus*, Mourning, and Post-Memory', *Discourse*, 15.2 (1992), 3–29.
69. Marianne Hirsch, *The Generation of Postmemory: Writing and Visual Culture after the Holocaust* (New York and Chichester: Columbia University Press, 2012), p. 5.
70. Marianne Hirsch, 'Projected Memory: Holocaust Photographs in Personal and Public Fantasy', in *Acts of Memory: Cultural Recall in the Present*, ed. by Mieke Bal, Jonathan V. Crewe, and Leo Spitzer (Hanover: Dartmouth College; Hanover and London: University Press of New England, 1999), pp. 3–24 (p. 9).
71. Marianne Hirsch, 'Surviving Images: Holocaust Photographs and the Work of Postmemory', *The Yale Journal of Criticism*, 14.1 (2001), 5–37 (p. 10). On postmemory in relation to trauma theory, see Fuchs, *Phantoms of War*, pp. 47–52.
72. For an insightful critique of Hirsch's concept, see Kathy Behrendt, 'Hirsch, Sebald, and the Uses and Limits of Postmemory', in *The Memory Effect: The Remediation of Memory in Literature and Film*, ed. by Russell J. A. Kilbourn and Eleanor Ty (Waterloo: Wilfrid Laurier University Press, 2013), pp. 51–71.
73. Behrendt, p. 65.
74. Such as in the, albeit extreme, case of Binjamin Wilkomirski.
75. Alison Landsberg, *Prosthetic Memory: The Transformation of American Remembrance in the Age of Mass Culture* (New York: Columbia University Press, 2004), p. 48.
76. Ibid., p. 2.
77. Ibid., p. 20.
78. See ibid., pp. 123–25.
79. Susannah Radstone, 'Cinema and Memory', in *Memory: Histories, Theories, Debates*, ed. by Susannah Radstone and Bill Schwarz (New York: Fordham University Press, 2010), pp. 325–43 (p. 335). Landsberg's treatment of the museum context is more persuasive in recognizing the active role of museum visitors.
80. Some of this discussion has previously appeared in Alexandra Lloyd, '"Institutionalized Stories": Childhood and National Socialism in Contemporary German Museum Displays', in *Post-War Literature and Institutions*, ed. by Seán M. Williams and W. Daniel Wilson (= special issue of *Oxford German Studies*, 43 (2014)), pp. 89–105.
81. Pierre Nora, *Realms of Memory: Rethinking the French Past*, trans. by Arthur Goldhammer (New York: Columbia University Press, 1996), p. xvii.
82. See also Pierre Nora, 'Between Memory and History: Les Lieux de Mémoire', *Representations*, 26 (1989), 7–24.
83. Hamburger Schulmuseum <http://www.hamburgerschulmuseum.de> [accessed 1 July 2019].
84. Gottfried Korff and Martin Roth, 'Einleitung', in *Das historische Museum: Labor, Schaubühne, Identitätsfabrik*, ed. by Gottfried Korff and Martin Roth (Frankfurt a.M.: Campus, 1991), pp. 9–41 (p. 17).
85. Janet Marstine, 'Introduction', in *New Museum Theory and Practice: An Introduction*, ed. by Janet Marstine (Oxford: Blackwell, 2006), pp. 1–37 (p. 2).
86. Helmut Schmitz, 'Soundscapes of the Third Reich: Marcel Beyer's *Flughunde*', in *German Culture and the Uncomfortable Past*, ed. by Schmitz, pp. 119–41 (p. 121).

87. Axel Bangert, *The Nazi Past in Contemporary German Film: Viewing Experiences of Intimacy and Immersion* (Rochester, NY: Camden House, 2014), p. 2.
88. Duden's etymology (<https://www.duden.de/rechtschreibung/erinnern>) [accessed 29 November 2019]) suggests that the word comes from the Old High German 'innarōn', meaning 'machen, dass jemand einer Sache innewird' [to become internally aware or certain of something external].
89. Gerhard Richter, 'Acts of Memory and Mourning: Derrida and the Fictions of Anteriority', in *Memory*, ed. by Radstone and Schwarz, pp. 150–61 (p. 157).
90. Andrea Reiter, 'Memory and Authenticity: The Case of Binjamin Wilkomirski', in *The Memory of Catastrophe*, ed. by Peter Gray and Kendrick Oliver (Manchester: Manchester University Press, 2004), pp. 132–46 (pp. 135–36).
91. Helmut Schmitz, 'Introduction', in *German Culture and the Uncomfortable Past*, ed. by Schmitz, pp. 1–11 (p. 9).
92. For an overview of the child figure in German literature, including tropes associated with childhood, see Pinfold, *Child's View*, pp. 9–25.
93. Carolyn Steedman, *Strange Dislocations: Childhood and the Idea of Human Interiority, 1780–1930* (London: Virago, 1995), pp. 4–5.
94. Jean-Jacques Rousseau, *Émile; or, On Education*, trans. by Allan Bloom (New York: Basic Books, 1979). For a detailed discussion, see Peter Coveney, *The Image of Childhood: The Individual and Society* (Harmondsworth: Penguin, 1967), pp. 37–51.
95. Pinfold, *Child's View*, p. 11.
96. See Mary Jane Kehily and Heather Montgomery, 'Innocence and Experience: A Historical Approach to Childhood and Sexuality', in *An Introduction to Childhood Studies*, ed. by Mary Jane Kehily (New York: Open University Press, 2004), pp. 57–75 (p. 68).
97. On the role and design of the Deutsches Historisches Museum, see Rosmarie Beier-de Haan, 'Re-Staging Histories and Identities', in *A Companion to Museum Studies*, ed. by Sharon MacDonald (Oxford: Blackwell, 2010), pp. 186–98 (pp. 189–90).
98. It is not clear whether this wallpaper came with the doll's house as sold, whether it was an accessory for doll's houses available in shops, or whether it was home-made. See Alexandra Lloyd, 'Dolls and Play: Material Culture and Memories of Girlhoods in Germany, 1933–1945', in *Deconstructing Dolls: The Many Meanings of Girls' Toys and Play*, ed. by Miriam Forman-Brunell and Jennifer Whitney (New York: Lang, 2015), pp. 37–63; Alexandra Lloyd, ' "Institutionalized Stories": Childhood and National Socialism in Contemporary German Museum Displays', in *Post-War Literature and Institutions*, ed. by Seán M. Williams and W. Daniel Wilson (= special issue of *Oxford German Studies*, 43 (2014)), pp. 89–105.
99. Chloe Paver, ' "You Shall Know Them by their Objects": Material Culture and its Impact in Museum Displays about National Socialism', in *Cultural Impact in the German Context: Models of Transmission, Reception and Influence*, ed. by Rebecca Braun and Lyn Marven (Rochester, NY: Camden House, 2010), pp. 169–87 (p. 172); on Nazi-coded objects in the exhibition space, see pp. 171–75.
100. Sharon Brookshaw, 'The Material Culture of Children and Childhood: Understanding Childhood Objects in the Museum Context', *Journal of Material Culture*, 14 (2009), 365–83 (p. 381).
101. Colin Heywood, *A History of Childhood*, 2nd edn (Cambridge: Polity Press, 2017), p. 5.
102. Barry J. Zimmerman and Timothy J. Cleary, 'Adolescents' Development of Personal Agency: The Role of Self-Efficacy Beliefs and Self-Regulatory Skill', in *Self-Efficacy Beliefs of Adolescents*, ed. by Frank Pajares and Timothy C. Urdan (Greenwich, CT: IAP, 2006), pp. 45–71 (p. 45).
103. Dorothy Macardle, *Children of Europe: A Study of the Children of Liberated Countries: Their War-Time Experiences, their Reactions, and their Needs, with a Note on Germany* (London: Gollancz, 1949), p. 19.
104. Stargardt, p. 10.
105. Cunningham, p. 2.
106. Richard N. Coe, *When the Grass Was Taller: Autobiography and the Experience of Childhood* (London: Yale University Press, 1984), p. 2.

107. Kate Douglas, *Contesting Childhood: Autobiography, Trauma, and Memory* (New Brunswick: Rutgers University Press, 2010), p. 45.
108. Werner Brettschneider, *'Kindheitsmuster': Kindheit als Thema autobiographischer Dichtung* (Berlin: Schmidt, 1982), p. 5.
109. Marianne Gullestad, 'Modernity, Self, and Childhood in the Analysis of Life Stories', in *Imagined Childhoods: Self and Society in Autobiographical Accounts*, ed. by Marianne Gullestad (Oslo and Oxford: Scandinavian University Press, 1996), pp. 1–41 (p. 24).
110. Ibid., p. 24.
111. Coe, p. 3.
112. Imre Kertész, 'Wem gehört Auschwitz?', *Die Zeit*, 19 November 1998 <http://www.zeit.de/1998/48/Wem_gehoert_Auschwitz_> [accessed 1 July 2019].
113. The autobiographical Imre Kertész, *Fateless*, trans. by Tom Wilkinson (London: Vintage, 2006), first published in 1975, tells the story of a fifteen-year-old boy from Budapest deported to Auschwitz.
114. Patricia Holland, *Picturing Childhood: The Myth of the Child in Popular Imagery* (London: I. B. Tauris, 2006), p. 15.
115. See, in particular, discussions around the death of Aylan [Alan] Kurdi: Helena Smith, 'Shocking Images of Drowned Syrian Boy Show Tragic Plight of Refugees', *The Guardian*, 2 September 2015 <http://www.theguardian.com/world/2015/sep/02/shocking-image-of-drowned-syrian-boy-shows-tragic-plight-of-refugees> [accessed 1 July 2019]; Josie Ensor, 'Photo of my Dead Son has Changed Nothing', *The Telegraph*, 3 September 2016 <http://www.telegraph.co.uk/news/2016/09/01/photo-of-my-dead-son-has-changed-nothing-says-father-of-drowned> [accessed 1 July 2019]. See also (beyond Europe) Patrick Timmons, 'Shocking Photo of Drowned Father and Daughter Highlights Migrants' Border Peril', *The Guardian*, 26 June 2019 <http://www.theguardian.com/us-news/2019/jun/25/photo-drowned-migrant-daughter-rio-grande-us-mexico-border> [accessed 1 July 2019].
116. 'Richard Flynn, '"Infant Sight": Romanticism, Childhood, and Postmodern Poetry', in *Literature and the Child: Romantic Continuations, Postmodern Contestations*, ed. by James Holt McGavran (Iowa City: University of Iowa Press, 1999), pp. 105–30 (p. 105).
117. David Archard, *Children: Rights and Childhood* (London: Routledge, 2004), p. 44.
118. See Arnold van Gennep, *The Rites of Passage*, trans. by Monika B. Vizedom and Gabrielle L. Caffee (London: Routledge and Kegan Paul, 1977), p. 21; Victor Turner, *The Ritual Process: Structure and Anti-Structure* (London: Routledge & Kegan Paul, 1969); Victor Turner, *Dramas, Fields, and Metaphors: Symbolic Action in Human Society* (Ithaca and London: Cornell University Press, 1974).
119. Jon Anderson, *Understanding Cultural Geography: Places and Traces*, 2nd edn (London: Routledge, 2015), p. 132.
120. See Erik H. Erikson, *Identity: Youth and Crisis* (New York: Norton, 1968).
121. Pinfold, *Child's View*, p. 9.

CHAPTER 2

The Alibi of Youth?
Writing a National Socialist Childhood

Introduction: Patterns of Childhood

Since reunification, several autobiographical accounts of growing up in the Third Reich have appeared in print, including individual memoirs, collections of oral testimony, and what Helmut Schmitz has termed 'literary memoirs and "ordinary memoirs"'.[1] The challenge facing members of this generation is twofold: first, to negotiate the tension between their private memories and experiences and their retrospective knowledge of the historical facts of the Third Reich, and second to reconcile society's expectation that childhood be a happy, carefree period with their knowledge that this was a time of suffering and persecution for many.

Fifteen years before reunification, a very early attempt at confronting the shame and guilt of a Nazi childhood came in Christa Wolf's *Kindheitsmuster* [Patterns of Childhood] (1976).[2] Wolf's text, published in East Germany in the dying breaths of Erich Honecker's liberalized cultural policy, came as a sharp contrast to the GDR's anti-fascist foundation myth, and influenced both East and West German approaches to the National Socialist past.[3] Wolf was motivated to write by what she saw as an unacknowledged continuity between Nazism and the GDR. Arguing that East Germany had consigned fascism and its legacy to the West, she wrote:

> *Kindheitsmuster* unternahm den Versuch, den Alltag von damals und den von heute zu beschreiben, um zu zeigen: das sind doch die gleichen Personen, die damals lebten und die heute auch noch leben. [...] Vor und nach der Stunde Null existieren die gleichen Leute.[4]
>
> [*Patterns of Childhood* undertook to try to describe everyday life in those days and to show that those who lived then and are still alive today are the same people. [...] The same people exist before and after the zero hour.]

Through its complex and radical aesthetics, *Kindheitsmuster* charts the narrator's quest to locate her child-self, exploring her fractured sense of identity and the intermingling of the private and the political. Wolf's autobiographically informed text was highly self-critical: it rejected the approach which Helmut Kohl would later come to characterize as 'die Gnade der späten Geburt' [the grace of a late birth].[5] Indeed, in her acceptance speech on receiving the Geschwister-Scholl-Preis in 1987, Wolf stated: 'nie habe ich etwas wie "Gnade" über den späten Zeitpunkt meiner

Geburt, etwas wie Entlassensein aus der Verantwortung empfinden können' [I have never been able to feel anything like 'grace' for having been born late or a sense of having been released from responsibility].[6] *Kindheitsmuster* clearly struck a chord with members of Wolf's generation. She found herself overwhelmed by the positive responses it received, in particular from those who found a resonance with their own experiences under Hitler which had not been acknowledged within official narratives of the past: 'wie ich aus Briefen und Gesprächen weiß, haben viele Leute bei diesem Buch die nackte Alltagsbeschreibung als das wichtigste genommen, als eine Bestätigung ihrer eigenen Erlebnisse' [as I know from letters and conversations, for many people the unvarnished description of everyday life in the book was the most important thing they took away from it, it was a confirmation of their own experiences].[7] Wolf argued that coming of age in the Third Reich was a formative experience that continued to shape her generation's adult life, but that the GDR was not permitting those who had undergone it to admit and confront that truth. It should, she contended, be acknowledged: 'solange Menschen leben, die diese Kindheit hatten, die diese Jahre als Kinder oder junge Menschen erlebt haben, ist das alles in ihnen' [as long as people are alive who had this childhood, who experienced these years as children or young people, it stays with them].[8] Her private exploration of childhood made a very public statement, a memory contest that challenged the status quo and East Germany's official memory of the past.

Several autobiographical accounts were published on both sides of the Wall in the 1970s and 1980s, influenced in some cases by Wolf's work. First-time writers as well as published authors and public intellectuals confronted their childhood and its legacy, motivated in part by the passing of time to write about their formative years.[9] Kater ascribes this belatedness to 'the trauma of their knowledge, about the rule of force and the intolerance engendered by a totalitarian dictatorship'.[10] These autobiographical texts range in tone from the overtly self-critical to the defensive, and are often characterized by a sense of conflict between 'official' narratives of history and private memories and experiences. There is a significant gap between the adults looking back on their childhood, and the children they once were, expressed by literary means through the use of the third-person singular or the use of a pseudonym to refer to themselves. Wolf put this succinctly when discussing the autobiographical nature of *Kindheitsmuster*:

> Aber es gibt doch — das ist eine der Eigentümlichkeiten meiner Biographie, aber vielleicht geht es anderen in meinem Alter auch so — ein Fremdheitsgefühl gegenüber dieser Zeit. Seit einem nicht auf den Tag genau, aber doch auf eine Zeitspanne genau anzugebenden Moment ist man nicht mehr diese Person, habe ich nicht mehr das Gefühl, daß ich das war, die das gedacht, gesagt oder getan hat.[11]

> [There is, and this is perhaps one of the peculiarities of my life story, though others of my age may have had the same experience, a sense of alienation from this period. From a definite moment, which one cannot trace to the exact day but certainly to the exact period, one is no longer the same person. I no longer feel that it was I who had thought, said or done those things.][12]

Frequently, authors express regret for their lack of curiosity during those days as it caused them to acquiesce with National Socialist doctrines and ignore the suffering of others. They also express their difficulty in reconciling their childhood memories with their retrospective knowledge of the extent of National Socialist crimes, and the ensuing sense of shame. They posit that their childhood memory has been colonized by adult knowledge gained after the fall of the Third Reich. Indeed, this knowledge hampers the possibility of a nostalgic view of personal childhood. Gullestad writes that 'in modern autobiographical narratives there is generally a feeling of loss. [...] One's own childhood is gone, as well as the historical conditions associated with it'.[13] The Third Reich context inevitably compounds this. While members of the generation who grew up under the banner of Nazism may mourn the passing of their childhood, it is more problematic for them to mourn the historical conditions in which they lived. Retrospective knowledge of Nazi crimes makes it difficult to view childhood during this era with the kind of 'legitimate' sense of nostalgia permitted in writing about other, 'normal' childhoods. Aspects of this may well be specific to the Third Reich context, though there may be commonalities with those growing up under conditions of oppression and dictatorship more generally.

What emerges from this body of autobiographical writing is the sense of a broadly common experience in the period of the Nazi dictatorship. However, as a generation, these individuals were not characterized as much by their collective experience, as by their condition at the end of the Second World War. As Mark Roseman argues, it is 'the particular psychological position of the Hitler Youth generation *after defeat* that gives it such a distinct profile'.[14] They had witnessed the failure of National Socialism, the defeat of the Germany army, the destruction of their homes, towns, and cities, and the loss of family and friends. As Viktor Klemperer observed astutely, they were caught in a grey zone between having been implicated in Nazism and being ultimately free from guilt for its crimes by virtue of their youth. In a reframing of Kohl's 'Gnade der späten Geburt', the author Eva Zeller (b. 1923), in her autobiographical novel *Solange ich denken kann: Roman einer Jugend* (1981), wrote of her childish ignorance of the *Kirchenkampf* [church struggles]: 'Zum erstenmal kann ich hier mein hieb- und stichfestes Alibi Jugend ins Feld führen' [For the first time I can invoke my watertight alibi of youth].[15] Zeller suggests that her generation's youth at the time of Nazism provides the alibi: they are widely considered to have been too young to understand the consequences of that in which they were participating and by implication too young to be held accountable. It is an idea with which other texts considered in this study engage.

In this chapter, I examine three autobiographical accounts of growing up under Nazism published since reunification: Günter de Bruyn's *Zwischenbilanz: Eine Jugend in Berlin* (1992), Martin Walser's *Ein springender Brunnen* (1998), and Günter Grass's *Beim Häuten der Zwiebel* (2006). De Bruyn, Walser, and Grass were all born in the 1920s, and they share many similar formative experiences: all three were brought up as Catholics, pupils in the Nazi education system, and members of the Hitler Youth; participated in the *Arbeitsdienst* [compulsory labour service] and the military; and were prisoners of war. Yet their respective approaches to writing childhood differ significantly, as they negotiate the impulse to represent the self authentically while responding to the demands and expectations of contemporary memory politics.

Writing the Childhood of the Self: The Truth of Feelings

As a literary genre, autobiography has long been considered to invoke a tacit understanding between reader and author that the text will contain a quality of authenticity.[16] As the theorist Paul John Eakin writes, 'telling the truth [...] is surely the most familiar of the rules we associate with autobiographical discourse'.[17] Readers are motivated by an interest in being privy to the personal lives of people they consider public figures, or the desire to attain a private perspective on historical events. Similarly, the motivation for *writing* autobiographically stems from a fascination with the self and a desire for self-knowledge. Roy Pascal views this as a kind of 'Selbstbesinnung' [taking stock of oneself],[18] and emphasizes the author's desire 'to give the truth about' themself.[19] An important distinction emerges between the truth of a life as it was lived and the deeper truth of the individual and his or her identity, the elusive 'truth of feelings'.[20]

Of the works widely considered as embodying the 'great tradition' of autobiographical writing,[21] Rousseau's *Confessions* (1782) constitutes the first great autobiography that treated the author's worldly, rather than spiritual life. Rousseau's definition of 'truth' in autobiographical writing was a kind of 'truthfulness', 'the non-verifiable *intention* of honesty on the part of the author', as Linda Anderson puts it. She writes that 'truth, therefore, can never be established once and for all, but can only be presented in terms of the constant reiteration of avowals and disclaimers by Rousseau himself'.[22] Coe sees the truth of feelings as an important element of autobiographical writing about childhood. He argues that authors are 'concerned first and foremost with telling a truth about themselves which shall be as complete, as authentic, and as absolute as possible'.[23] This is what Goethe calls for in *Aus meinem Leben: Dichtung und Wahrheit* [Autobiography: Truth and Fiction Relating to my Life] (1808–1831).[24] While he endeavours to give an accurate account of the events of the past, Goethe is equally, if not more, concerned with the literary reshaping of these events. He strives to depict the 'Grundwahre' [fundamental truth] of his life, by which is meant the truth of lived experience as it is expressed through imaginative, poetic language.

Writers' fascination with their own formative years stems partly from the idea of childhood as the source of identity. Autobiographical writing about childhood becomes, therefore, an exploratory endeavour, in which the writer seeks to discover as much for themself as they seek to reveal to the reader. Coe argues that while all autobiography is assertion — '*This* is what I was; *that* is what I did' — in the autobiography of childhood, the mode of assertion tends to be secondary to the mode of interrogation: '*How* did I come to be like that? *Why* was I impelled to do this?'.[25] The author Eva Zeller likens this kind of writing to an archaeological dig: '[es] wird zu einem archäologischen Unternehmen; man gräbt und wühlt in der Vergangenheit, man trainiert sein Gedächtnis und staunt, was es freigibt, und ahnt kaum, was es verdrängt' [it becomes an archaeological endeavour; you dig and scrabble about in the past, you exercise your memory and marvel at what it sets free and hardly notice what it blocks out].²⁶

The works discussed in this chapter address the interaction between individual and collective historical experience, demonstrating how their authors' own private experiences of childhood were, and continue to be, affected by Nazism. In his autobiography *Zwischenbilanz* (1992), de Bruyn provides a representation of the past in which he offers the 'Wahrheit der Kunst' [truth of art].²⁷ He structures his account as a dual narrative, interweaving memories of his childhood and what he knows of its historical context. In *Ein springender Brunnen* (1998), Walser fervently defends the right to preserve and present his own childhood memories without reference to the Holocaust. He makes a claim for the historical innocence of his childhood, and by extension that of members of his generation, by writing almost exclusively from the child's apparently limited perspective. Finally, in his memoir *Beim Häuten der Zwiebel*, Grass problematizes each 'path' into the past, first describing its luring promise of factuality and authenticity, only to demonstrate the absences and constructedness contained within each of these. He draws attention to the problematic nature of memory, and his feelings of guilt and shame for not having resisted, or having questioned, Nazism.

As individuals, and as members of this generation, de Bruyn, Grass, and Walser face the challenge of reconciling their memories of childhood with their retrospective knowledge of the extent of National Socialist crimes. They express the difficulty of recalling and re-presenting their childhood experience during this pernicious historical period, and of incorporating that experience into their adult lives, particularly after reunification. They offer different modes of approaching this historical experience and writing about it. By giving autobiographical, or autobiographically inflected, accounts about growing up under Nazism, all three authors contribute to public debates about how to remember this period in the Berlin Republic. Their different approaches to writing childhood reflect their very individual styles and attitudes towards literature and philosophy, as well as demonstrating the complex and often contested sites of memory politics in contemporary Germany.

Taking Stock: *Zwischenbilanz: Eine Jugend in Berlin* (1992)

Günter de Bruyn's *Zwischenbilanz*²⁸ was one of a number of autobiographies published in the early 1990s in which authors previously resident in the GDR recounted their experiences both of Nazism and East German Socialism.²⁹ De Bruyn had been a moderately well-known author in the GDR, but his reputation and 'literary standing' received a boost in the years following reunification, thanks in part to the success of *Zwischenbilanz*, and also to the eagerly anticipated second volume of his autobiography, *Vierzig Jahre: Ein Lebensbericht* [Forty Years: A Life Story] (1996).³⁰ *Zwischenbilanz* spans de Bruyn's first twenty-three years, from his birth in Berlin in 1926 to the formal division of Germany in 1949. He recalls his childhood and youth in Berlin-Britz und Neukölln, time spent in an evacuation camp (*Kinderlandverschickungslager*) in Kattowitz (Katowice), service as an anti-aircraft auxiliary (*Flakhelfer*), compulsory labour service (*Arbeitsdienst*), and, at the end of the war, military action as a soldier in the *Wehrmacht*. In his account, de Bruyn interweaves personal experiences and private memories with the collective, historical experience of Nazism, and the retrospective awareness of its crimes.

As a narrative of childhood in the Third Reich, *Zwischenbilanz* is untypical of autobiographical accounts of the period in that the author does not particularly express contrition for his own part in National Socialism. As Dennis Tate has observed, de Bruyn establishes himself as an outsider and, as a result, his narrative 'shows no reason why he should feel shame about anything he did in the years up to 1945'.[31] Throughout his childhood, he was protected from Nazi indoctrination by his parents and was instead influenced primarily by his family and by the Catholic Church. He recalls that it was only later, and to a limited extent, that he was influenced by the Nazi education system through attendance at school, and never by his time in the Hitler Youth (*Zwischenbilanz*, p. 87). His parents' protective efforts ensured this: for example, his mother regularly provided him with excuses to keep him back from the *Jungvolk* and later the Hitler Youth. The world of his childhood is characterized by 'Toleranz und Freizügigkeit' [tolerance and liberality].[32] He writes: 'die Seelenruhe meiner frühen Kindheit beruhte zum Teil auf Unwissenheit. Durch Verschweigen glaubten meine Eltern bei Hitlers Machtantritt die heile Welt des Sechsjährigen erhalten zu können' [the tranquillity of my early childhood was based to an extent on ignorance. My parents believed that by remaining silent when Hitler came to power, they could preserve their six-year-old's idyllic world] (*Zwischenbilanz*, p. 53). His parents' attempt to preserve the untroubled world of childhood also reveals a facet of adult attitudes to children: a child may be unaware of what information or opinions they may safely pass on to whom, and this ignorance could itself be dangerous. Thus, de Bruyn's parents withhold all information from him, ensuring nothing can be inadvertently passed on and interpreted by others as anti-fascist comment. The preservation of his innocence is not wholly altruistic, for it also serves to protect their subversion.

This 'heile Welt' of childhood is twice shattered, however, and on both occasions, it is when adult realities impinge on the child's consciousness. The first occasion is when de Bruyn finds a series of letters, poems, and also a novel that his father wrote and sent to de Bruyn's mother during a period of imprisonment during the First World War. The novel is overtly sexual, and de Bruyn recalls his shock upon reading it at the age of seventeen. It is at this moment that the innocence of childhood is penetrated: 'die heile Kindheitswelt brach mir entzwei' [the idyllic childhood world shattered] (*Zwischenbilanz*, p. 14). A second point of disruption comes, marking the definitive end of his childhood. He describes the destruction of his family home in Berlin in a bombing raid, recounting how he and his brother played in the ruins: 'unter dem schneebedeckten Schutthügel ließ sich das Haus, in dem ich geboren und aufgewachsen war, nicht mehr erkennen. Meine Kindheit war nun wohl wirklich zu Ende. Ich war 17 Jahre und zwei Monate alt' [the house in which I was born, in which I grew up, was no longer recognizable beneath the snow-covered heap of rubble. My childhood was now truly over. I was seventeen years and two months old] (*Zwischenbilanz*, p. 165). The chapter in which this takes place is entitled 'Das Puppenhaus' [The Doll's House]. Here, the apparently innocuous child's toy becomes the symbol of the destroyed house, the site of de Bruyn's childhood. Just as the bombs have destroyed the house beyond repair, so his childhood ends and there is no going back.

In his theoretical work on autobiography, *Das erzählte Ich: Über Wahrheit und Dichtung in der Autobiographie* [The Narrated Self: On Truth and Poetry in Autobiography] (1995), de Bruyn argues that, in autobiographical writing about childhood, the retrospective view of the remembering adult is, and should be, present: 'der Standort des Kindes, der nur Kurzsicht erlaubt, wird benannt und beschrieben, aber nicht eingenommen. Der Erzähler von heute weiß mehr als das Kind damals, und wenn es nötig ist, sagt er es auch' [the child's standpoint, permitting only a short-term perspective, is named and described, but not occupied. The present-day narrator knows more than the child did then, and, if it is necessary to do so, he says as much].[33] For de Bruyn, it appears always to be necessary: the child's viewpoint is never unqualified or unmediated. Writing, then, from the 'sicheren Hafen des Alters' [safe haven of old age],[34] de Bruyn can evaluate his own youthful part in National Socialism, interweaving his private experience with historical knowledge. De Bruyn reflects on his perception of events as a child. For example, he describes his response to the outbreak of war as disappointment, rather than fear, and he amusingly comments that 'nicht einmal die Schule fiel aus' [we didn't even have a day off school] (*Zwischenbilanz*, p. 101). However, rather than trying to give the illusion of the child's perspective, de Bruyn encases this comment within the perspective of the remembering adult. For example, he writes: 'zu den deutschen Katastrophenjahren 1933 und 1939 werden Verbindungslinien zwischen dem, was ich als Kind wußte, und dem, was wirklich geschah, gezogen' [when it comes to Germany's years of catastrophe between 1933 and 1939, lines of connection are drawn between what I knew as a child and what really happened].[35] He explores the extent to which history has impinged upon the child's life, citing the simultaneous appointment of Goebbels as Gauleiter of the NSDAP in his hometown of Berlin and his own birth: 'einen Zusammenhang bekommt das in der Rückschau erst' [a connection is only visible with hindsight] (*Zwischenbilanz*, p. 23). De Bruyn's account of his childhood and adolescence is one in which history and memory interweave, though this is consciously the result of hindsight. He comments: 'alles, was mit mir und um mich geschah [wurde] nur in bezug auf mich selbst registriert. Die eigne Verwobenheit ins Historische, die in der Rückschau interessiert, wurde nur am Rande bemerkt' [I only registered what happened to me and around me in as much as it affected me. The interweaving of my experience into history, which becomes interesting with hindsight, was only perceptible on the margins] (*Zwischenbilanz*, p. 134). Similarly, he later comments that 'die Weltgeschichte aber trat an diesem Abend [...] an' [that evening [...] world history reported for duty] (*Zwischenbilanz*, p. 53).

A significant moment in de Bruyn's childhood is a trip to the cinema to see the 1931 film adaptation of Erich Kästner's *Emil und die Detektive* [Emil and the Detectives], which coincidentally took place on the day that Hitler took power (*Zwischenbilanz*, pp. 46–52). De Bruyn describes his young, naive belief in the triumph of good over evil. Despite the film's happy ending, the young de Bruyn is in tears at the fact that 'ein Traum [ging] zu Ende' [a dream was ending] (*Zwischenbilanz*, p. 53). In an interview with Uwe Wittstock, de Bruyn comments on this scene:

> ich habe die Erinnerung an diesen Kinobesuch auch deshalb ziemlich zu Anfang meiner *Zwischenbilanz* geschildert, weil das Buch natürlich den Reifeprozeß des jungen Menschen beschreiben soll, der ich einmal gewesen bin. Dieser naive Glaube an den Sieg des Guten wird dann später durch Lebenstatsachen korrigiert. Nebenbei: Die Szene im Kino endet damit, daß ich die Angst schildere, die ich als Kind hatte, aus dem schönen Traum zu erwachen, den mir der Film vermittelte. Offenbar hat auch das Kind, das ich war, zumindest geahnt, daß die Welt nicht so schön und gerecht ist wie dieser Film.[36]

> [I depicted this visit to the cinema relatively early on in my book *Zwischenbilanz*, because the book is naturally intended to show the coming of age of the young person who I once was. This naive faith in the triumph of good is then corrected by the facts of life. Incidentally, the scene in the cinema ends with the fear I felt as a child of waking from this beautiful dream which the film had conveyed to me. Clearly, the child that I was had at least grasped that the world is not as beautiful and fair as it is in that film.]

This comment reveals much of de Bruyn's approach towards childhood, and specifically his own childhood. The child naively believes in the triumph of good over evil, yet his tears at the end of the film, and his suggestion that he had begun to suspect the naivety of this view, afford the child more than a simplistic innocence. It is also significant that de Bruyn raises the idea of authenticity in this passage, commenting that cinema was 'das bewegte Bild, das vorgab, Wirklichkeit zu zeigen' [the moving picture that purported to show reality] (*Zwischenbilanz*, p. 52).

Indeed, authenticity is central to de Bruyn's autobiographical project. He explicitly situates his own autobiography within the tradition of autobiographical writing and theory.[37] He explores the tension between 'truth' and 'fiction' in autobiographical writing, particularly through the allusion in the text's title to the Goethean dialectic of 'Dichtung' [poetry] and 'Wahrheit' [truth]. De Bruyn conforms to Goethe's notion that an author's collected works serve as 'eine große Konfession' [a great confession],[38] and had accordingly attempted to write about his wartime experiences in his fictional works, for example in *Der Hohlweg* (1963).[39] However, he felt he failed to do justice to his intentions and chose a more overtly autobiographical form in *Zwischenbilanz*. In *Das erzählte Ich*, he describes his motivation to write about his experiences: his relief at having survived the war gave him a sense of duty to write a 'wahrheitsgetreuer Bericht darüber, [...] wie es gewesen war' [faithful report about [...] what it was like].[40] Yet, at the same time, de Bruyn questions the possibility of presenting an accurate picture of 'how it really was'. He writes: 'ich lernte [...], daß man Wirklichkeit durch Erzählen nur schattenhaft wiederbelebt' [I learned that telling a story can only bring back shadows of the truth] (*Zwischenbilanz*, p. 29). For de Bruyn, accurate historical representation is problematic, and he implicitly rejects Brettschneider's comment that the Goethean combination of 'Dichtung' and 'Wahrheit' is essentially the 'Wahrheit des Kindes' [truth of the child].[41] Conversely, de Bruyn considers literature, or rather fiction, to be truly successful only when it is underpinned by authentic experience. As he comments in an interview with Chris Lewis, 'ich habe [...] gemerkt, daß die Literatur immer nur dann wahrhaftig wird, wenn irgendwas Selbsterlebtes dahintersteht' [I have [...] noticed that literature only becomes authentic when some personal experience is behind it].[42]

In the opening paragraph of *Zwischenbilanz*, de Bruyn plays on the Rousseauian concept of autobiographical truth, promising the reader that he will tell the truth, but not the whole truth: 'der berufsmäßige Lügner übt, die Wahrheit zu sagen. Er verspricht, was er sagt, ehrlich zu sagen; alles zu sagen, verspricht er nicht' [the professional liar practises telling the truth. He promises that what he says will be truthful; he does not promise to tell the whole truth] (*Zwischenbilanz*, p. 7). It alludes to Rousseau's assertion that as an autobiographer, he had to confess everything: 'I must leave nothing unsaid.'[43] Yet, in a playful subversion of Rousseau's formulation, de Bruyn asserts the veracity of his account by stressing that, though the material he chooses to share will be limited, it will, at least, be accurate. In addition, by referring to the writer of fiction as a 'liar', he establishes the autobiographer as the harbinger of truth. Like Zeller and her notion of the autobiographical excavation, de Bruyn takes on a quasi-academic approach to his own life, describing himself as a 'Historiker meiner selbst' [historian of my self] (*Zwischenbilanz*, p. 134). Yet de Bruyn promises the reader that he will strive for truth, whilst at the same time recognizing that this will be a complex task.

For de Bruyn, the tension between authenticity and constructedness is a necessary one, which lends autobiography its particular interest:

> das Besondere der Autobiographie besteht ja nicht darin, daß hier derjenige ein Leben beschreibt, der am meisten über es weiß, sondern darin, daß hier jemand sich so beschreibt, wie er sich selbst sieht und beurteilt. Interessanter als die mitgeteilten Fakten über eine Person ist die Art, wie sie von dieser Person mitgeteilt werden. Objektivität, die auch nicht möglich wäre, wird gar nicht verlangt.[44]
>
> [the special thing about autobiography is not that the writer describes a life about which he himself knows the most, but rather that the writer describes how he sees and judges himself. More interesting than the facts about a person that are communicated is the way in which they are communicated by that person. Objectivity, which would in any case be impossible, is not even required.]

De Bruyn contends that, though history and biography necessarily cannot convey the total reality of a situation, part of the truth resides in the mediation of that reality as expressed by the writer. Autobiography, for him, becomes 'die Wahrheit der Kunst'.[45] As he comments in *Das erzählte Ich*:

> mit der Wahrheit der Autobiographie verhält es sich ähnlich wie mit der der Geschichte. Deren Inhalt ist nicht unbedingt das, was geschah, sondern das, was wir durch die Geschichtsschreibung von ihr wissen [...]. Nicht die Wirklichkeit der Vergangenheit können wir von ihnen [Geschichtsschreiber] erfahren, sondern die Vorstellung von Vergangenheit, die sie sich gemacht haben.[46]

> [the truth of autobiography is similar to that of history. Its contents are not necessarily what happened, but what we know of it through the writing of history [...]. We cannot experience the reality of the past from them [historians], but rather the idea of the past which they have created.]

De Bruyn offers the reader an account of the past through the lens of the present, acknowledging that it is the result of memory and of the writing process. It is necessarily part of an imaginative endeavour.

De Bruyn provides an example of this in his use of the material he himself possesses from the period, having a significant archive of documents, photographs, and diaries at his disposal.[47] On the one hand, these written documents perform a positive function: 'andere [Erinnerungen], die verschüttet waren, wurden durch das Lesen wieder freigelegt' [other [memories] that were buried have been set free through reading] (*Zwischenbilanz*, p. 110). On the other hand, they form a barrier to the past, as memory and documentary source do not concur. He explains:

> würde der Leser von heute den Schreiber von damals nicht so genau in Erinnerung haben, könnte er in ihm ein fröhliches, unbeschwertes Kind vermuten, das sich problemlos in die Zwangsgemeinschaft fügt, die Lager- und Klassen-Hierarchien fraglos akzeptiert. (*Zwischenbilanz*, pp. 110–11)

> [if today's reader did not have the writer from back then so clearly in his memory, he could presume he was a happy, carefree child that submitted easily to the forced coexistence and accepted unquestioningly the camp and class hierarchies.]

The diary, despite its documentary status, cannot give an accurate account of history. Like memory, it fails to record the entirety of the past, retaining merely a fragment of it. For example, in response to an entry on the subject of an argument, he comments: 'auf die Frage, was ich damals über den Streit dachte, gibt das Tagebuch keine Antwort' [as to the question of what I thought about the argument at the time, the diary gives no answer].

De Bruyn frequently switches between the first-person and the third-person singular narrative voice to emphasise his separation from his child-self. In the closing chapters of *Zwischenbilanz*, de Bruyn articulates this: the past and present identities merge through the exclusive use of the first person to narrate this section. He views this in retrospect as a way of coping with his part in Nazism. In his essay 'Fremd im eigenen Land' [Foreign in one's Own Country], he explains that, when he was forced into uniform, 'es hatte bei mir eine Trennung des Ich vom erzwungenen äußeren Leben zur Folge, eine Art Schizophrenie, die mich schützte, aber auch krank machte' [as a consequence, I experienced a separation of myself as a subject from the enforced external world, a kind of schizophrenia which protected me but also made me ill].[48] Thus, the division he sees between his adult self and the child he used to be may have deeper roots and be part of a division he made to protect himself from his involvement in the structures of the Nazi regime.

Nevertheless, de Bruyn presents a largely positive depiction of his childhood and, while his adolescence is at times troubled, he is not plagued by the shame of having been a committed believer in National Socialism, as were many of his contemporaries who have dealt with the subject in literary form. On the contrary, he asserts his innocence of the crimes of Nazism, and his subsequent lack of guilt. He argues that for him, and many of his generation, a discussion of guilt is inappropriate. De Bruyn writes: '[wir] fühlten [...] uns mehr oder weniger mit Schuld beladen und glaubten den Emigranten und Widerstandskämpfern gegenüber zu Ehrfurcht verpflichtet zu sein: in diesem Punkt war man moralisch erpreßbar' [[we] felt [...] more or less laden with guilt and believed we were obliged to venerate the emigrants and the resistance fighters: on this point one was susceptible to moral blackmail] (*Zwischenbilanz*, p. 374). De Bruyn here suggests that he feels to some extent bound by the enforced sense of collective guilt that, as an individual, he does not share.[49] He claims that, although all those who were children in the Third Reich were affected by Nazi propaganda and ideology, they did not, contrary to expectations, all become 'fanatische Nazis' [fanatical Nazis] (*Zwischenbilanz*, p. 143).

More than one critic has viewed this lack of self-questioning as a shortcoming of de Bruyn's text. In her article comparing *Zwischenbilanz* with Wolf's *Kindheitsmuster*, Renate Rechtien argues that, although de Bruyn claims the pursuit of truth as his primary endeavour, he lapses into sentimentality and romanticism on occasion.[50] Similarly, Tate argues that, although de Bruyn's account of his lack of susceptibility to fascist doctrine is plausible and justified (given his upbringing), his claim to have known nothing about the fate of the Jews in 1945 is problematic 'in the context of the whole post-Holocaust analysis of the complicity of "ordinary" Germans'.[51] In an episode of ZDF's *Das literarische Quartett* programme, Werner Fuld described the innocence de Bruyn claims as 'vorgestellte Dummheit' [imagined ignorance], which, he argued, led to the book's success because 'es bietet ein Alibi' [it offers an alibi].[52] *Zwischenbilanz* offers no reflection on the impact that this knowledge, once gained, had on de Bruyn at any later stage. De Bruyn does, however, offer a critical view of the way this news was received by others. When asked by a German woman whether he believes the BBC's reports about the mass murder of Jews, he replies in the affirmative. The woman, clearly distressed, asks in return: 'Aber der Führer habe doch sicher davon nichts gewußt?' [But surely the Führer didn't know anything about that?] (*Zwischenbilanz*, p. 245).

De Bruyn's method of mingling personal and collective historical experience throughout *Zwischenbilanz* cannot be characterized as unreflective. By taking this approach, the re-presentation of the child's experience growing up does not seek to relativize the crimes of Nazism, nor does it really depict Germans as victims of Nazism. As Owen Evans argues, it is primarily designed to demonstrate the interaction between the private and public spheres:

> despite describing how the family's privateness is sullied by history, de Bruyn seeks neither to exonerate himself nor to make an issue of how members of his family were victimised. He underlines, instead, the extent to which the private sphere can distract attention from events outside.[53]

In this way, de Bruyn offers a worm's-eye view of the past, creating 'aus dem Einzelfall so etwas wie eine Geschichtsschreibung von unten' [from an individual example something like an account of history from below].[54] In the apparently idyllic world of his childhood, de Bruyn is shielded from Nazi ideology, but he acknowledges that this shielding, which could continue into the present, is no longer defensible. The result is an account of a childhood that is contextualized within the retrospective acknowledgement and understanding of events beyond the view of the author's younger self.

A Defence of Childhood: *Ein springender Brunnen* (1998)

Walser's 1998 autobiographical novel *Ein springender Brunnen* tells the coming-of-age tale of a boy named Johann, born in 1927 in the Swabian village of Wasserburg on Lake Constance. While critics have debated how best to categorize Walser's text, it is without doubt highly autobiographical: Walser's own middle name is Johannes, and we know from paratextual information that the circumstances of the protagonist are extremely similar to those of the author.[55] Furthermore, some versions of the book's dust jacket feature a photograph of the young Walser, corresponding to the photograph of Johann described in the opening chapter of the novel.[56] The text consists of a chronological account of the protagonist's childhood, divided into sections by three reflective, theoretical chapters all entitled 'Vergangenheit als Gegenwart' [The Past as Present]. We see Johann at three points in his young life: in 1932, at pre-school age; in 1937, at the age of his First Holy Communion; and in 1944/45, in the *Wehrmacht*. The narrative ends as Johann, now aged eighteen, returns to Wasserburg having been interned as a prisoner of war.

The text has received an extraordinary amount of critical attention. Maguire helpfully summarizes critical responses to the text as those which focus on the interplay between *Ein springender Brunnen* and Walser's political affiliations and positioning, those which focus principally on the text itself (rather than the paratextual debates and controversies), those which see it as uncritical, and those which highlight Walser's use of 'irony and reflexivity'.[57] Like de Bruyn, Walser emphasizes the minimal impact that National Socialism had on his formative years, partly due to the family's geographical location, and partly because of his interest in literature, which he used as a means of protecting himself from the influences of National Socialist ideology and doctrine. In a similar way to de Bruyn, Walser's text does not conform to the model established by earlier autobiographical accounts of childhood in the Third Reich in which, as Lathey argues, 'childhood's joys are rarely celebrated' and 'all attempts to reconstruct the childhood self are ultimately judged against the magnitude of the holocaust'.[58] This is what Walser seeks to avoid. Indeed, in contrast to de Bruyn's admission that he might have contextualized his recollections more but declined to do so, Walser asserts his right to depict his childhood experiences without contextualizing them within his retrospective knowledge of the crimes of Nazism. Walser wants to depict the National Socialist period as his young protagonist perceived it at the time, rather than through the lens of a retrospective commentary. It was this approach, with its apparent omission of any mention of Auschwitz, which caused a furore following Walser's speech on receipt of the Friedenspreis des Deutschen Buchhandels for *Ein springender Brunnen*, in which he contested the historical memory of the Holocaust in contemporary Germany.[59]

In a speech given ten years earlier, in autumn 1988 at the Munich Kammerspiele, Walser expressed the need to alleviate the difficulty, frequently articulated by members of his generation, of reconciling personal memories of Nazism with retrospective knowledge of Nazi crimes. He argued:

> Das erworbene Wissen über die mordende Diktatur ist eins, meine Erinnerung ist ein anderes. Allerdings nur so lange, als ich diese Erinnerung für mich behalte. Sobald ich jemanden daran teilhaben lassen möchte, merke ich, daß ich die Unschuld der Erinnerung nicht vermitteln kann. [...] Ich müßte also so reden, wie man heute über diese Zeit redet. Also bliebe nichts übrig als ein heute Redender. Einer mehr, der über damals redet, als sei er damals schon der Heutige gewesen. [...] Die meisten Darstellungen der Vergangenheit sind deshalb Auskünfte über die Gegenwart.[60]

> [The knowledge I have acquired about the murderous dictatorship is one thing, my memory is another. To be sure, that's the case only as long as I keep the memory to myself. As soon as I want to share it with someone else, I notice that I cannot convey the innocence of the memory. [...] I would thus have to speak in the way one speaks about those times today. So all that would remain would be a person of today speaking. Just another one speaking about those times as if he were then the person he is today. [...] That's why most depictions of the past are really information about the present.][61]

This is the essential tension he enacts in and through *Ein springender Brunnen*. He seeks to capture an 'authentic', unmediated account of his childhood under Nazism as it was, without having to conform to contemporary political debates about the way in which the past ought to be remembered or retrospective knowledge which, he asserts, he could not have known about at the time.

Walser's interest in the theme of childhood is evident in his earlier writings,[62] and Taberner sees an essential childishness in his works as a whole, 'a tension between the desire for authenticity — expressed in a childish predilection for fantasy — and the pressure to "grow up" and conform to external expectations that suffuses almost all of the author's oeuvre'.[63] In his 1991 novel *Die Verteidigung der Kindheit* [Defending Childhood], the protagonist Alfred Dorn suffers the trauma of witnessing the bombing of Dresden in 1945, in which he loses his maternal grandparents and the contents of the family's home, the material evidence of his blissfully happy childhood. His adult life is dominated by his attempt to retain and document the physical traces of his lost childhood. He dedicates his life to the relentless pursuit of his youth, and he becomes, in Stephen Brockmann's words, 'the one-man curator of his own personal museum'.[64] However, while Alfred Dorn collects, he never interrogates, investigates, or explores the past. He refuses to acknowledge that simply amassing the past will not help him to come to terms with it, or even engage with it in a meaningful way: 'er wird zu einem Fanatiker des Datums. Er will alles so bewahren, festhalten, wie es wirklich gewesen ist. [...] Und nicht weniger als gar alles. Und alles ganz genau. Bloß keine Fiktion' [he becomes fanatical about dates. He wants to preserve and hold on to everything as it really was. [...] And nothing less than absolutely everything. And everything just right. Only, no fictions].[65] Dorn's obsession with archiving the past and his fear of fictionalizing are the antithesis of Walser's project, in which fictionalizing and imagination are necessary to approach the past and in which experienced past takes precedence over the documented past.

In the first of three metafictional chapters that provide a commentary on the complexity of memory and historical representation, Walser constructs an analogy in which history resembles a museum. 'In der Vergangenheit, die wir alle zusammen haben, kann man herumgehen wie in einem Museum. Die eigene Vergangenheit ist nicht begehbar. Wir haben von ihr nur das, was sie von selbst preisgibt' [We can stroll around in the past we all have in common, as in a museum. One's own past is not walkable. All we have of it is what it surrenders of its own accord] (*Brunnen*, p. 9; *Fountain*, p. 3). Walser suggests a conflict between the memories of individuals, the subject of private memory, and the supposedly monolithic 'official memory culture': the narrative of history as it exists within the public sphere, in an institutional context, museums included.[66] In his view, the singular narrative of the past is reified and stories, like objects, can be selected for display. By contrast, individual memory is alive and cannot simply be called up from the archive and exhibited. Walser rejects the kinds of institutionalized narratives of official memory culture represented here by the museum, and in doing so evokes Michel Foucault's criticism that museums, as examples of heterotopias, replicate the 'social and cultural structure of the society which creates [them]'.[67] In this metaphor, the museum is the domain of 'official memory' that reinforces the narrative created by a ruling consensus. In the postscript to his autobiographical account of growing up in the Third Reich, *Ich nicht: Erinnerungen an eine Kindheit und Jugend* [Not Me: Memoirs of a German Childhood] (2008), the historian Joachim Fest also uses the metaphor of the museum to question authoritative representations of the past:

> Die Vergangenheit ist stets ein imaginäres Museum. Man zeichnet im Nachhinein nicht etwa auf, was man erlebt hat, sondern was die Zeit, die wachsende perspektivische Verschiebung sowie der eigene Formwille im Chaos halbverschütteter Erlebnisse daraus gemacht haben. Im ganzen hält man weniger fest, wie es eigentlich gewesen, sondern wie man wurde, wer man ist.[68]
>
> [The past is always an imaginary museum. One does not, in retrospect, record what one has experienced, but what time — with increasing shifts in perspective, with one's own will to create a shape out of the chaos of half-buried experiences — has made of it. By and large, one records less how it actually was than how one became who one is.][69]

Fest emphasizes the importance of the present in shaping narratives of the past, but, rather than demanding the recognition of memory alongside or even in place of history, he questions the very existence of historical representation divorced from a retrospective view. He places emphasis on the dynamic process of memory and its contribution to identity. Walser's critics might feel that his insistence on preserving the past 'as it was', and not as it is viewed from the vantage point of today, creates not a museum of collective memory but rather a 'Museum der unbewältigten Vergangenheit' [museum of the unmastered past].[70]

In *Ein springender Brunnen*, then, according to Walser's programme, the reader encounters the past primarily through the child's perspective and through his understanding of events. Johann functions as the paradigmatic innocent child who, in Nazi Germany, remains innocent because he is ignorant of the events going on around him. This point of view is largely uninterrupted throughout the novel,[71] with the exception of the three philosophical chapters on the theory of memory. As a result, there is a consistent emphasis on the domestic sphere, and on historical and political events only when they impinge upon the child's world, and then only as he perceived them at the time. The reader's first encounter with Johann is as observer: 'Johann beobachtete alles von der Küchentür aus' [Johann was watching it all from the kitchen door] (*Brunnen*, p. 10; *Fountain*, p. 4): this is a view not from below, but from a threshold, placing Johann as outsider. His observations frequently focus on objects which fascinate him, such as his father's bag (*Brunnen*, p. 52), and constitute what Coe terms the 'triviality of the childhood experience'.[72] In addition, his childlike response to external events is also a source of humour. For example, when a letter arrives announcing a real-estate auction of a local family's farm, Johann, who is playing a spelling game with his father, considers how much fun it would be to spell the word that heads the announcement: 'Anwesensversteigerung' [real estate auction] (*Brunnen*, p. 66; *Fountain*, p. 53). Of the inflation problem in the early 1930s he comments that 'immer wenn Johann von dieser Inflation etwas hörte, dachte er, das Land hat Fieber gehabt damals, 41 oder 42 Grad Fieber müssen das gewesen sein' [whenever Johann heard about the inflation, he thought the country must have been running a fever back then — 106 or 107 degrees] (*Brunnen*, p. 93; *Fountain*, p. 77).

Similarly, Johann's naive perspective creates a gap of knowledge that can be filled by the reader. Johann comments that his best friend, Adolf, 'sagte öfter Sätze über diesen Hitler, die so klangen wie alle Sätze, die Adolf bei Erwachsenen, vor allem bei seinem Vater, gehört hatte und die er dann dahersagte, auch wenn sie überhaupt nicht paßten' [often repeated sentences about this Hitler, and they all sounded like sentences he'd heard from grown-ups, especially his father. And he'd reel them off even when they weren't appropriate] (*Brunnen*, p. 80; *Fountain*, p. 66). The result of this perspective is primarily to distance the reader from the events that are described. The child's naive and innocent tone provides a fresh commentary on the historical events and conditions which will be well known to the reader. Pinfold suggests that 'those who have read countless books, watched films, and learnt about the period in history classes run the risk of [...] habitualization; they "know" about the Third Reich'.[73] The child's uncomprehending view of events is afforded to the reader as a means of defamiliarization which is designed to offer a new approach to engaging with the past. The narrative also contains frequent references to fairy tales, which form a conceptual framework for the young Johann to make sense of the world. He considers that the hairdresser resembles a 'Zauberkünstler' [magician] (*Brunnen*, p. 16; *Fountain*, p. 9), and similarly describes the way in which the itinerant photographer 'zauberte aus dem Stabartigen ein Stativ' [conjured a tripod out of his stick] (*Brunnen*, p. 21; my translation).

Johann also adopts this language from the adults around him. His father has told him that a local woman, Hermine, who cleans the villas of rich merchants, is a queen, and Johann comments in the language of the fairy tale: 'als der Vater verraten hatte, daß Helmers Hermine eine Königin sei, hatte Johann sofort gespürt, daß dieses Königinnentum in der hohen schlanken Warze links neben ihrer Nase zum Ausdruck kam' [when Father pronounced Helmer's Hermine a queen, Johann immediately sensed that her queenliness was expressed by the prominent, longish wart to the left of her nose] (*Brunnen*, p. 23; *Fountain*, p. 15). Johann similarly adopts the statement made by the family's maid, Mina, that in his photograph he looks like a 'Königssohn' [prince] whose 'Rad ist sein Roß!' [bike's his steed!] (*Brunnen*, p. 72; *Fountain*, p. 59). He describes his grandfather as 'ein Riese' [a giant] (*Brunnen*, p. 36; *Fountain*, p. 27), and when Johann receives a knitted grey jumper as a Christmas present, he believes he now resembles the knight in *Richard Löwenherz und sein Paladin* [Richard the Lionheart and his Paladin], he is 'der Silberne Ritter' [the Silver Knight] (*Brunnen*, p. 106; *Fountain*, p. 89).[74]

The innocence of childhood evoked by the fairy tale is also intertwined with Walser's evocation of the notion of Heimat. This concept was famously defined by Ernst Bloch as 'etwas, das allen in die Kindheit scheint und worin noch niemand war: *Heimat*' [something that shines into everyone's childhood, but where no one has yet been: *Heimat* (home)].[75] In his study of this discourse in Germany, Peter Blickle writes:

> the idea of Heimat is based on an imaginary space of innocence projected onto real geographical sites. Whether this innocence is religious (paradise), sexual (childhood), sociological (premodern, preindustrial), psychological (preconscious), philosophical (prerational, predialectical), or historical (pre-Holocaust) in character, in every case we find imageries of innocence laid over geographies of Heimat.[76]

The rural setting of *Ein springender Brunnen*, as well as its implicit defence of historical innocence, strongly evoke the idea of innocence associated with, and embodied by, the idea of Heimat. The term is often associated with the innocence of childhood,[77] and it is commonly designated a place of nostalgic childhood memory.[78] The yearning for a lost time and place of childhood innocence in *Ein springender Brunnen* appears to reflect Walser's desire to relieve his (and his generation's) memories of childhood of the stain of retrospective knowledge of the crimes of Nazism. Fuchs reads this as a deficiency of Walser's text, arguing that he 'deliberately taps into the *Heimat* discourse to evoke Proustian childhood memories that refuse to obey the conventions of contritional writing'.[79] As Fuchs demonstrates, Walser's evocation of this discourse is questionable because it proposes a version of the past that has been stripped of its more unsavoury elements. In doing this, Walser is asking a very fundamental question about the way the past is remembered publicly.

Amongst the criticisms directed at *Ein springender Brunnen* on *Das literarische Quartett* was the challenge that the novel failed to show the 'Schrecken des Faschismus' [horrors of fascism].[80] Walser was accused of constructing an unrealistically idyllic picture of the past.[81] In 'Über Deutschland reden', Walser asked:

ist man fähig oder gar verpflichtet, Kindheitsbilder nachträglich zu bewerten, oder darf man sich diesem allerersten Andrang einfach für immer überlassen? Ich habe das Gefühl, ich könne mit meiner Erinnerung nicht nach Belieben umgehen. Es ist mir, zum Beispiel, nicht möglich, meine Erinnerung mit Hilfe eines inzwischen erworbenen Wissens zu belehren.[82]

[Can one, or is one even obliged to, evaluate the images from one's youth ex post facto, or is one allowed simply to abandon oneself forever to this onrush of images? I have the feeling that I can't handle my memories just any way I want. For example, it's not possible for me to instruct my memory with the aid of knowledge I have obtained in the meantime.][83]

This comment encapsulates Walser's attitude and programme in *Ein springender Brunnen* and is in direct opposition to de Bruyn's approach. The images of childhood and youth here represent Walser's memories. Just as the images of childhood 'well up from the "springender Brunnen" of language and do not have to be re-created',[84] so too they cannot be, or in Walser's view should not be, informed retrospectively. Helmuth Kiesel contends that by depicting average, ordinary people during this period, Walser succeeds in showing them 'ohne Beschönigung, aber auch ohne Verteufelung' [without embellishment, but also without denigration] and ultimately makes them 'verständlich' [understandable].[85] As we shall go on to see, there are parallels with recent approaches to depicting the Nazi past, particularly in film, where a more empathetic attitude is adopted towards perpetrators and 'Mitläufer' [fellow travellers].

Walser does indeed 'make a claim' for the historical innocence of his and his generation's childhood.[86] Fuchs is critical of this approach and suggests that Walser 'represses the inevitable mediation of all our memories through the portrayal of a childhood idyll which is sealed off from the author's later historical knowledge'.[87] She argues that Walser '[pitches] the idea of an authentic recall of the past against political correctness'.[88] What Friederike Eigler calls the '"naturalness" of memory'[89] is pitted against the constructedness of official narratives of the past. Walser himself states: 'ich wollte mir die Unschuld meiner Kindheit bewahren und sie nicht durch nachträgliches Dreinreden verbessern oder schärfen oder politisch korrekter machen' [I wanted to preserve the innocence of my childhood and not improve or concentrate or make it more politically correct as a result of retrospective interference].[90] The innocence of childhood, specifically of *Walser's* childhood, is conceived as a lack of knowledge of wider events which frees the protagonist from any guilt, shame, or sense of complicity (in Nazism).

In *Ein springender Brunnen*, this takes on a Judaeo-Christian dimension as Johann's childhood comes to represent a kind of prelapsarian Eden. This is part of what Maguire considers a nostalgic stance, which, as Pinfold had argued, is part of a desire for 'hope' or 'progress' on the part of authors writing about National Socialism.[91] Yet, at the same time, a Freudian concept of childhood is at work, for which the retrospective view of childhood as a paradise is a fraud: 'das Paradies selbst ist nichts Anderes als die Massenphantasie von der Kindheit des Einzelnen' [Paradise itself is nothing but a composite phantasy from the childhood of the individual].[92] Here, childhood, like prelapsarian human existence, is conceptualized as a time free from shame, which in turn is the result of a lack of knowledge of good and evil. And yet, as Freud argues, such a state, free from guilt or shame, is a fantasy.

The three metafictional chapters to which Walser here alludes frame each of the text's three sections. They provide reflections on the process of remembering and a commentary on the difficulty of his endeavour. By exploring the constructedness of memory and historical truth, they succeed, however briefly, in undercutting the overall impression of the narrative, which gives the illusion of being an unmediated description of the past. Entitled 'Vergangenheit als Gegenwart' [The Past as Present], their function, as Schmitz argues, is to establish 'a distinction between public and private memory'.[93] Walser proposes that the past is subject to the demands of the present. It is not slumbering, waiting to be awoken and called to mind. It is always shaped by the present: 'die Vergangenheit als solche gibt es nicht. Es gibt sie nur als etwas, das in der Gegenwart enthalten ist, ausschlaggebend oder unterdrückt, dann als unterdrückte ausschlaggebend' [the past doesn't exist as such. It exists only as something contained within the present, a decisive or suppressed factor — and in the latter case, decisive, although suppressed] (*Brunnen*, p. 281; *Fountain*, p. 245). While writers like Wolf and de Bruyn express concern with the way the past continues to shape their present, Walser is preoccupied by the effect of the present on the past. This is also reflected in his placement of the 'Vorwort als Nachwort' [Foreword as Afterword] (*Brunnen*, p. 409; *Fountain*, p. 354), thereby shifting the expected structuring of the text

Ultimately, Walser himself acknowledges the complexity, and impossibility, of his desire to show the past as it was lived, without retrospective commentary, and at the same time defends his right to do so: 'ich weiß, ich schreibe von heute aus [...]. Trotzdem habe ich versucht, eine Schreibart zu entwickeln, in der die Vergangenheit mir entgegenkommt wie von selbst und keine Einmischung von heute duldet' [I know I am writing from the perspective of the present day [...]. Nevertheless, I have tried to develop a style of writing in which the past comes to meet me on its own terms, and which brooks no interference from the present].[94] Walser asserts that to write retrospectively about the crimes of Nazism, he would have to deny his and his parents' involvement in fascism, and depict himself as an anti-fascist child, forming a protective boundary of fiction around his own life story. He writes:

> ich habe nicht den Mut oder nicht die Fähigkeit, Arbeitsszenen aus Kohlenwaggons der Jahre 1940 bis 43 zu erzählen, weil sich hereindrängt, daß mit solchen Waggons auch Menschen in KZs transportiert worden sind. Ich müßte mich, um davon erzählen zu können, in ein antifaschistisches Kind verwandeln. Ich müßte also reden, wie man heute über diese Zeit redet.[95]

> [I don't have the courage, or I don't have the ability, to tell about scenes of work in freight cars filled with coal, because the knowledge that people were transported to concentration camps in the same kind of freight car intrudes. If I wanted to be able to describe these scenes, I would have to transform myself into an anti-fascist child. I would thus have to speak in the way one speaks about those times today.][96]

In doing so, he would be conforming to contemporary popular opinion, but he would not be expressing the truth. The only possibility was to write a narrative of growing up without superimposing subsequent historical awareness on that narrative. In this way, Walser's text asserts the primacy of subjectivity. Its priority is, as Christoph Parry suggests, not so much the question 'wie war es wirklich?' [what was it really like?], as the more precise question 'wie hat man es damals erlebt?' [how did one experience it back then?].[97] The authenticity for which Walser strove was not necessarily rooted in the past events but rather in the feeling of the time: in the quintessence of Welzer's 'gefühlte Geschichte'. This ultimately proves to be what Maja Zehfuss has termed an 'impossible authenticity';[98] yet it is this authenticity that Walser defends, and which for him takes on a political significance.

Amir Eshel gives a more positive account of Walser's approach within the context of his proposed move away from a 'hermeneutics of suspicion' to a 'hermeneutics of futurity' that would encompass a future-oriented and more hopeful modelling of the present through imaginative engagements with the past.[99] He argues that *Ein springender Brunnen* 'expands', rather than reduces, readers' view of the period,[100] and that its function is 'to stimulate dissensus — to provoke a serious public discussion of the nature of memory, history, and forgetting'.[101] It is then not so much the content of the text itself, but rather the effect that content has in the context of public debate, which performs a productive function. Eshel writes that 'it shocks us into considering how we relate to the past and, specifically, what forms Germany's future *Erinnerungskultur* may or should take'.[102] This reads almost like a rehabilitation of Walser's work, which, as we have seen, has been taken to task for its ahistoricity and failure to adhere to the normative framework of memory. In her critical essay on Erich Kästner, Ruth Klüger takes Kästner's *Das doppelte Lottchen* [Lottie and Lisa] to task for its ahistorical setting. Published in 1949, the text must either be set in the present, in which case there would be occupying troops everywhere, or be set in the past, in which case the war and occupation would still be to come, and in this way the 'Happy-End' of the book would be untenable.[103] Walser's text comes across for much of its length as similarly ahistorical, with its preoccupation with the child's view and pubescent development and the rites of passage of the Church. Ultimately, the fundamental question with regard to *Ein springender Brunnen* is not 'should he be permitted to write in this way?' (as though it were a question of permission), but rather 'why would Walser want to write his childhood in the way he does?'.

Grass's Onions: *Beim Häuten der Zwiebel* (2006)

In *Ein springender Brunnen*, Walser comments: 'Manche haben gelernt, ihre Vergangenheit abzulehnen. Sie entwickeln eine Vergangenheit, die jetzt als günstiger gilt. Das tun sie um der Gegenwart willen' [Some people have learned to repudiate their past. They generate a past they deem more favourable. They do it for the sake of the present] (*Brunnen*, p. 282; *Fountain*, p. 246). We can read the verb 'entwickeln' [to develop] here in two ways: first, simply as 'developing' in the sense of 'creating' or 'causing to grow', and second, as 'de-veloping' in the more literal sense of 'unwrapping'. In this latter reading, it is not simply that such individuals have rejected their past in favour of a more convenient or retrospectively auspicious version, but rather that they have sought to remove the accretions with which prevailing historical narratives have overlaid their lived experience. Whilst the stripping of this historical varnish can, on one reading, appear both morally and historiographically commendable, on another, the question of what ought to be removed is almost entirely subjective; and, to extend the metaphor, we might ask whether the layers which have been removed are in fact obscuring some other facet of the autobiography which, for whatever reason, the author does not wish to share.

Just such a charge was levelled at Günter Grass when, in an interview with the *Frankfurter Allgemeine Zeitung* in August 2006, he revealed that he had served in the *Waffen SS* 10th Tank Division 'Frundsberg' in 1944, a fact which he had not hitherto disclosed publicly. Grass had never denied his youthful involvement in Nazism, stating repeatedly in interviews and in his autobiographical literary works that he had been a Nazi.[104] Yet this new admission of having been in the SS provoked widespread criticism both for its belatedness and for Grass's apparent hypocrisy in having acted for decades as a national 'Moralprediger' [preacher of morality].[105] Grass's confession was made in advance of the publication of his autobiographical text *Beim Häuten der Zwiebel*, which provides a detailed account of his childhood and adolescence in Nazi Germany and the immediate post-war period. It culminates in the publication of his first novel, *Die Blechtrommel* [The Tin Drum] (1959), which propelled him into public life as a popular, although often rather unpopular, figure.[106]

While the *Frankfurter Allgemeine Zeitung* article broke the story of a new and previously unknown piece of information about the life of the author, in reality the book offers the reader little autobiographical information to which they had not already been privy. Grass's childhood, indeed his entire life, has consistently been public property since he first came to prominence. He draws attention to this in *Beim Häuten der Zwiebel* when he writes that everything which follows in his current narrative is 'aufgezählt und datiert, steht gedruckt und in Zeilen geordnet' [listed and dated, printed in neat lines] (*Zwiebel*, p. 471; *Onion*, p. 418). Similarly, pointing forward to his life after the publication of *Die Blechtrommel*, he comments: 'so lebte ich fortan von Seite zu Seite und zwischen Buch und Buch' [and from then on I lived from page to page and between book and book] (*Zwiebel*, p. 479; *Onion*, p. 425), referring both to his career, and to the notion that he is encased or enclosed within the very pages themselves. The case would seem to validate Reich-Ranicki's comment that autobiographical writing about childhood offers nothing original: 'leider lieben es viele Autobiographen, sich ausführlich über etwas zu verbreiten, worüber sie nur selten etwas Originelles zu sagen haben — über ihre Kindheit' [unfortunately, many autobiographers like to express themselves extensively on a subject about which they only rarely have anything original to say — about their childhood].[107] In Grass's case, the reader may indeed be forgiven for feeling that they have encountered it all before. Grass draws attention to this very point in the opening pages, asking:

> Warum überhaupt soll Kindheit und deren so unverrückbar datiertes Ende erinnert werden, wenn alles, was mir ab den ersten und seit den zweiten Zähnen widerfuhr [...] einer Person anhängt, die [...] nicht wachsen wollte, Glas in jeder Gebrauchsform zersang, zwei hölzerne Stöcke zur Hand hatte und sich dank ihrer Blechtrommel einen Namen machte [...]? (*Zwiebel*, p. 8)
>
> [Why go back to my childhood and its clear and immutable end date, when everything that happened to me between milk teeth and permanent ones [...] has since been associated with a person who [...] refused to grow and shattered all manner of glass with his song, kept two wooden sticks at the ready, and thanks to a tin drum made a name for himself [...]?] (*Onion*, p. 2)

Grass is referring here, of course, to Oskar Matzerath, the protagonist of his first and most famous novel, *Die Blechtrommel*, whose early biography was a rewriting of Grass's own childhood and youth. Grass's response to the question 'why recall childhood?' reads:

> weil dies und auch das nachgetragen werden muß. Weil vorlaut auffallend etwas fehlen könnte. Weil wer wann in den Brunnen gefallen ist: meine erst danach überdeckelten Löcher, mein nicht zu bremsendes Wachstum, mein Sprachverkehr mit verlorenen Gegenständen. Und auch dieser Grund sei genannt: weil ich das letzte Wort haben will. (*Zwiebel*, p. 8)
>
> [because this as well as that deserves to be part of the record. Because something flagrantly significant could be missing. Because certain things at certain times fell into the well before the lid went on: the holes I left uncovered until later, growth I could not halt, the linguistic give-and-take I had with lost objects. And let this, too, be said, because I wanted to have the last word.] (*Onion*, p. 8)

Grass's motivation seems to be in part a desire to reclaim his own youthful biography from the fictional use to which he put it, and to assert a full account of, and for, himself. In addition, the reference to 'Brunnen' here also recalls Walser's *Ein springender Brunnen*, and Taberner has suggested that Grass references Walser's text as part of his motivation for writing his own autobiography.[108]

The link with Oskar Matzerath at the outset of *Beim Häuten der Zwiebel* is significant, both in terms of Grass's approach to the idea of authenticity, and his idea and treatment of childhood. In *Die Blechtrommel*, the diminutive protagonist, Oskar, views the world of Nazism from below, experiencing it in the guise of a three-year-old child, albeit one who is possessed of an adult's capacity for thought and perception.[109] Oskar refuses to grow up physically, thereby insistently remaining an outsider. Pinfold terms Oskar the quintessential 'Kind-Dämon' [demon child] or 'Anti-Kind' [anti-child].[110] Oskar is a 'pseudo-child', who possesses 'many adult attributes' but also the outward appearance of a child.[111] This outward appearance enables Oskar to maintain an ironic distance from the events he describes. It also enables the adult narrator, Oskar, now thirty years old and in an asylum, to elicit sympathy from the reader. Salman Rushdie called Oskar the 'Peter Pan among the million lost boys and murderous pirates of Nazi Germany: little, stunted Oskar, the other boy in classic literature who never grew up'.[112] However, Grass, unlike Oskar, asserts a profound sense of shame at having been involved in Nazism. *Beim Häuten der Zwiebel* begins with the recollection of the end of Grass's childhood:

'auf engem Raum wurde meine Kindheit beendet, als dort, wo ich aufwuchs, an verschiedenen Stellen zeitgleich der Krieg ausbrach [...]. Mit ehernen Worten wurde [...] das Ende meiner Kinderjahre ausgerufen' [my childhood came to an end when, in the city where I grew up, the war broke out in several places at once [...]. The end of my childhood was proclaimed with words of iron] (*Zwiebel*, p. 7; *Onion*, p. 1). However, Grass continues to write about his childhood and youth for a significant proportion of the text. He draws attention to the theme of childhood, both through his depictions of his young self and through several linguistic pointers. He refers to himself using distancing techniques throughout the narrative. He is 'der Junge meines Namens' [the boy bearing my name] (*Zwiebel*, p. 27; *Onion*, p. 19), 'jener Junge, dem ich auf der Spur zu bleiben habe' [the boy whose life I feel the need to trace] (*Zwiebel*, p. 26; *Onion*, p. 18), 'jener Junge, der anscheinend ich war' [the boy I apparently was] (*Zwiebel*, p. 10; *Onion*, p. 4), and 'der Schüler meines Namens' [the art student bearing my name] (*Zwiebel*, p. 337; *Onion*, p. 299), emphasizing both his youth and the adult narrator's disassociation with this child he once was.

The contrition which is largely absent in *Zwischenbilanz* and *Ein springender Brunnen* is prominent in *Beim Häuten der Zwiebel*, which periodically reads like a confession. Grass views his childhood years as having been dominated by a silence, specifically a failure to ask questions about events and the world around him. He cites several examples: the sudden disappearance of his uncle Franz, who was executed by the National Socialists for fighting on the Polish side; his Latin teacher at school, Monsignor Stachnik, who was imprisoned in Stutthof concentration camp; a fellow recruit in the *Arbeitsdienst* — a young man dubbed 'Wirtunsowasnicht' [Wedontdothat] because of his refusal to take up arms; and a schoolfriend's father who was also sent to Stutthof concentration camp. With regard to the latter, Grass expresses regret at not having paid more attention to what was happening around him at the time. He writes: 'ich hatte mich kindlich dummgestellt, sein Verschwinden stumm hingenommen und so abermals das Wort "warum" vermieden' [I had used my status as a child to play dumb and accepted his disappearance without a murmur, and once more dodged the word *why*] (*Zwiebel*, p. 25; *Onion*, p. 18). In a sense, the phrase 'kindlich dumm' [literally 'childishly dumb'] is something of a misnomer: children are forever asking 'why?'. Here, Grass points to a childhood perverted, and in doing so evokes the idea of the 'Alibi Jugend' [alibi of youth].[113]

Grass sees this silence, this failure to ask questions, as the source of his shame. It is part of a picture he paints of uncritical conformism and the ease with which it was possible simply to comply with political and moral demands. Of the disappearance of his uncle Franz, he asks: 'Und auch ich habe, wenngleich mit Beginn des Krieges meine Kindheit beendet war, keine sich wiederholenden Fragen gestellt. Oder wagte ich nicht zu fragen, weil kein Kind mehr? Stellen, wie im Märchen, nur Kinder die richtigen Fragen?' [Nor did I, even though my childhood had ended with the onset of war, ask any insistent questions. Or was it because I was no longer a child that I dared not ask? Is it only children who, as in fairy tales, ask the right questions?] (*Zwiebel*, p. 16; *Onion*, p. 10). Grass's dilemma recalls that of Wolfram von Eschenbach's *Parzival*, in which the protagonist's entry into courtly society hinges upon his success or failure to ask a question.[114] Parzival fails to ask his host, King Anfortas, about his mysterious wound or about the magical objects that are paraded before him, recalling the advice of his tutor, Gurnemanz, not to be too curious. Had he asked Anfortas the reason for his suffering, the spell would have been broken and the king would have been restored to health. The concern to avoid curiosity stands in the way of compassion. In Wolfram's tale, Parzival's inability to ask the crucial question — 'Oeheim, waz wirret dir?' [Uncle, what troubles you?] — is the reason redemption is withheld, and the subsequent narrative is concerned with his search for righteousness. Lack of curiosity becomes tantamount to sin. The paradox is that innocence and ignorance can look rather alike. Thus, Grass describes his younger self as 'unverschämt jung' [shamelessly young] (*Zwiebel*, p. 51; *Onion*, p. 42). As in *Ein springender Brunnen*, the idea of childhood becomes synonymous with a prelapsarian state: no shame is experienced, because the child has no agency and therefore there is nothing of which to be ashamed. Parzival reaches the point where this is no longer true for him, when he learns to experience shame after his failure to question suffering. So too by analogy does Grass come to feel consumed with shame for his ongoing failure to question the fate of so many. On recalling watching a Danzig synagogue burn, he comments on his proximity to the events but unwillingness to confront them: 'Als bald nach meinem elften Geburtstag in Danzig und anderswo die Synagogen brannten [...] war ich zwar untätig, doch als neugieriger Zuschauer dabei [...]. Offenbar haben keine Zweifel meine Kinderjahre getrübt' [When shortly after my eleventh birthday synagogues in Danzig and elsewhere were set aflame [...], I took no part, yet I was very much a curious spectator] (*Zwiebel*, p. 26; *Onion*, p. 18). It is striking here that, although Grass again points out his lack of a critical approach to the events in question, he describes himself as having been curious. Thus, it is not an unchildlike lack of curiosity that plagues him in retrospect; rather, it is the inability (or failure) to have acted on that innate response.

Throughout the text, Grass brings his younger self to life, urging him, as does the figure of 'Der Alte' [the old man] in *Im Krebsgang* (2002), to help with his attempt to peel the onion and examine his past. The boy-he-once-was resists his accusations of guilt, protesting as he runs to his mother: 'Ich war doch ein Kind nur, nur ein Kind' [I was just a child, just a kid ...] (*Zwiebel*, p. 37; *Onion*, p. 29). He describes his youthful belief in Hitler as having been 'kinderleicht' [child's play] (*Zwiebel*, p. 106; *Onion*, p. 92). Even memory is imbued with the characteristics of childhood: 'die Erinnerung liebt das Versteckspiel der Kinder' [memory likes to play hide-and-seek] (*Zwiebel*, p. 8; *Onion*, p. 3). This establishes a paradigm for the rest of the text, which becomes part of a narrative formula of exculpation through exaggerated self-accusation reminiscent of the narrative pattern at work in *Die Blechtrommel*. There, Oskar recounts the death of his putative father, Jan Bronski, giving an account of the scene in which Jan is taken prisoner by the SS. He then qualifies it, however, with the words: 'soeben las ich den zuletzt geschriebenen Absatz noch einmal durch. Wenn ich auch nicht zufrieden bin, sollte es um so mehr Oskars Feder sein, denn ihr ist es gelungen [...] zu lügen. Ich möchte jedoch bei der Wahrheit bleiben' [I have just reread the last paragraph. I am not too well satisfied, but Oskar's pen ought to be, for writing tersely and succinctly, it has managed [...] to lie].[115] Oskar attempts to assert his own reliability as a narrator by claiming that his pen has lied. The narrator's claim to the reader that he will stick to the truth is a device used frequently in *Beim Häuten der Zwiebel*, in which the onion — the metaphor for the author's process of accessing the past — contradicts Grass's account of events. A similar construction in *Die Blechtrommel* involves Oskar's reaction to his receipt of a new tin drum. Oskar comments: 'und während Jan das müde Blech, ich das frische faßten, blieben Jans, Mamas, Matzeraths Augen auf Oskar gerichtet. [...] Ja dachten die denn, ich klebte am Althergebrachten, nährte Prinzipien in meiner Brust?' [as Jan gripped the tired drum and I the new one, the eyes of Jan, Mama and Matzerath were glued on Oskar; [...] did they think I clung to tradition for its own sake, that I was burdened by principles?].[116] Pinfold comments on this passage:

> We might consider Oskar's preference for a new toy over an old and broken one to be quite natural, yet the narrating Oskar apparently encourages us to see the incident as proof of a kind of unnatural amorality. However, it is also possible that this very deliberate blackening is intended to create an impression of him being too hard on his child self and so encourage reader sympathy with him or at the very least the sense that 'he can't be as bad as all that'.[117]

Oskar the narrator heaps guilt upon himself. The reader's response to his guilt and complicity in the crimes and misdemeanours he claims to have perpetrated is complicated by his status as a child, or at least his claims to be one. In the same way, in *Beim Häuten der Zwiebel*, Grass refuses any means with which his guilt might be mitigated. The anthropomorphized onion defends the young Grass: 'du [...] warst nur ein dummer Junge, hast nichts Schlimmes getan' [you were just a foolish boy, you did nothing bad] (*Zwiebel*, p. 44; *Onion*, p. 36). This assurance is later rejected by Grass, who claims: 'meine Tat läßt sich nicht zur jugendlichen Dummheit verwinzigen' [what I did cannot be put down to youthful folly] (*Zwiebel*, p. 75; *Onion*, p. 64). Yet Grass also emphasizes to the reader the 'dummer Stolz meiner jungen Jahre' [stupid pride of youth] (*Zwiebel*, p. 127; *Onion*, p. 110). As Taberner notes, 'the plea for mitigation, once rejected, is now adopted by Grass, and the reader may well feel that the author has committed only a minor sin of omission in remaining silent for so long about his foolish youthful pride'.[118]

Grass frequently draws attention to the veracity — or lack of it — of his account. He repeatedly insists that, while interred in an American prisoner of war camp in Bad Aibling, he met and befriended Joseph Ratzinger, later Pope Benedict XVI. He describes his re-telling of the story and his sister's response:

> meine Schwester glaubt meinen Erzählungen grundsätzlich nicht [...]. 'Stimmt das? Hört sich übertrieben an, ganz wie eine von deinen Geschichten!' Ich sagte: 'Also, wenn dich mein Lagerleben unter Bayerns Himmel nicht interessiert ...' Sie drauf: 'Na, erzähl schon ...'. (*Zwiebel*, p. 419)
>
> [my sister doesn't believe my stories on principle. [...] 'Are you sure? Sounds a bit far-fetched to me. Just like one of your stories.' 'Well, if my camp experiences under Bavarian skies are of no interest to you ...' I said. To which she replied, 'Oh, go ahead ...'.] (*Onion*, p. 372)

Grass has his sister anticipate the curious reader's response: we are aware that this account is another tall story, yet we simultaneously want to know more. Grass's overt fictionalizing serves merely to draw the reader in closer and to expose the reader's complicity in their own desire for 'truth', even if that truth is on the stretched side. By employing this narrative construction, Grass deliberately draws attention to the problem of authenticity in his account.

This is a common feature of Grass's writing, and one that he frequently uses to engage the reader. Kliche-Behnke compares this episode with the fantastical 'Wunder von Wasserburg' [Miracle of Wasserburg] section of *Ein springender Brunnen*, in which Johann spends two days and a night away from home pursuing the circus performer Anita, only to return home to find that he had somehow miraculously also been at home the whole time.[119] Kliche-Behnke argues that while Grass's Pope Benedict story is revealed to be part of a game, in Walser's text the overtly fictionalized sequence is viewed by Johann as real.[120] Thus, the interplay of fact and fiction has a contrasting effect: in Grass, fictionalizing is a self-conscious and self-reflexive narrative device; in Walser, it is a way of reinforcing the protagonist's innocent perspective. A further comparison bears this out. Both Grass and Walser depict the child's experience of the sacrament of confession. For Johann, this involves a protracted period of paranoia as, having made his First Confession the day before receiving the sacrament of the Eucharist for the first time at his First Holy Communion, he puts himself into a state of mortal sin by masturbating, and is too frightened of what people might think of him to go back into the confessional the following morning. In a state of heightened tension, he receives the sacrament 'unworthily', that is to say, without the requisite preparation. The intense seriousness of this episode, the psychological torture that Johann puts himself through, contrasts starkly with Grass's account of going to confession in *Beim Häuten der Zwiebel*. Grass, echoing Oskar Matzerath's flights of fancy in the confessional, insists that he managed to shock his confessor, Father Wiehnke, with stories about the outlandish and fictional exploits of his penis (*Zwiebel*, pp. 66–67). Walser uses the episode to enrich the reader's perspective on the authenticity of the Johann character; Grass, by apparently deflecting the development of character onto the unsuspecting priest, is in fact telling us all the more about his narrator.

There is a question of authenticity here, a central idea in *Beim Häuten der Zwiebel*. It is raised when Grass recounts his wartime experiences at the front. He writes:

> aber das, was hier im einzelnen geschrieben steht, habe ich ähnlich bereits woanders, bei Remarque oder Céline gelesen, wie schon Grimmelshausen bei der Schilderung der Schlacht von Wittstock, als die Schweden die Kaiserlichen in Stücke hauten, überlieferte Schreckensbilder zitierte ... (*Zwiebel*, p. 142)
>
> [but I had already read everything I write here. I had read it in Remarque or Céline, who — like Grimmelshausen before them in his description of the Battle of Wittstock, when the Swedes hacked the Kaiser's troops to pieces — were merely quoting the scenes of horror handed down to them ...] (*Onion*, p. 125)

Grass's comment that the wartime pictures he calls up from his memory are simply repetitions of pre-existing images in literary works echoes discussions about the appropriation of authenticity by means of images that correspond to existing depictions of the past. We will see this in Chapter 5 in the discussion of post-1990 filmic depictions of the Third Reich. Grass also introduces the notion that photographs are constructed, rather than being direct representations of reality, to problematize memory. He writes: 'oft gibt die Lüge, oder deren kleine Schwester, die Schummelei, den haltbarsten Teil der Erinnerung ab; niedergeschrieben klingt sie glaubhaft und prahlt mit Einzelheiten, die als fotogenau zu gelten haben' [Lie, or her younger sister, Deception, often hands over only the most acceptable part of a memory, the part that sounds plausible on paper and vaunts details to be as precise as a photograph] (*Zwiebel*, p. 9; *Onion*, p. 3). Grass emphasizes the fact that, although memories may seem to be 'fotogenau' [precise as a photograph], that is no guarantee of truth. Like de Bruyn, he ultimately concludes that the moving images merely purport to show reality. He draws attention to the constructedness of his account, hampered by memory and by his own reluctance to reveal the truth about his past.

For Grass, the title metaphor of the onion represents the elusive quality of 'Erinnerung'.[121] He writes: 'wenn ihr mit Fragen zugesetzt wird, gleicht die Erinnerung einer Zwiebel, die gehäutet sein möchte, damit freigelegt werden kann' [when pestered with questions, memory is like an onion that wishes to be peeled so we can read what is laid bare] (*Zwiebel*, p. 9; *Onion*, p. 3). The layers themselves constitute the author's memories and experiences. At the same time, they form a protective casing which makes up the onion — or rather, Grass's youth consists of layers of memory which must be peeled back, and which desire to be removed. Just as Virgil shows Dante the layers of the underworld, so the authorial persona guides us through the vagaries of his past. Like Wolf's *Kindheitsmuster*, which Elizabeth Boa terms 'a quest narrative within the mode of labyrinthine writing',[122] *Beim Häuten der Zwiebel* is presented as a search for the author's past, and for the truth of that past. At the same time, in Greek mythology King Minos's labyrinth was built to hold the Minotaur: a bull-headed creature that fed on children offered as tribute. We might follow Boa and say that for Wolf, the creature at the centre of the labyrinth is her own child-self, whose uncritical enthusiasm for Nazism frightens the adult looking back. In Grass's case, the German word for labyrinth — 'Irrgarten' — is particularly apt. While it may suggest the notion of childhood as Edenic garden, it also puts emphasis on the idea of 'sich irren' [to err]. Thus, for Grass, the labyrinthine journey towards his past as performed within the text is continually hampered by the shame he expresses for his youthful mistakes. Ultimately, however, the onion metaphor with its idea of unwrapping simultaneously symbolizes the futility of searching for the truth of the past: there *is* no seed or kernel at the centre of an onion, you peel and peel until nothing remains.

Conclusion

In *Meine Schulzeit im Dritten Reich*, Reich-Ranicki posits that our image of the Third Reich is becoming increasingly abstract: 'Aber die Wahrheit ist konkret. Und wer wäre mehr berufen, sich dem Gespenst der Abstraktion zu widersetzen, als die Schriftsteller?' [But the truth is concrete. And who could be better called to make a stand against the phantom of abstraction than writers?].[123] De Bruyn, Walser, and Grass each offer an account of their childhood and youth in the 1930s and 1940s which seems to respond, albeit indirectly, to Reich-Ranicki's rhetorical question. There is no shortage of autobiographical accounts by former members of the Hitler Youth. Yet *these* three writers speak with the authority not just of the eyewitness but of prominent writers and public intellectuals, especially well placed to give literary expression to their experiences. Their autobiographical texts promise 'privileged insights'[124] into the lives of their respective authors even if, as in Grass's case in particular, this material has already been put to use in the service of their fictional works. Their autobiographical texts are attempts both at exploring and writing private experience and at speaking on behalf of others who possess neither the skill nor the platform to articulate their experiences and memories publicly. Furthermore, given their authors' membership at the heart of Germany's 'intellektuelle Gerontokratie' [intellectual gerontocracy],[125] we inevitably read them differently from works by first-time authors who do not possess the proficiency of these literary giants.

The landscape of memory politics changed radically between the publication of *Zwischenbilanz* in 1992 and *Beim Häuten der Zwiebel* in 2006. Part of this was precipitated by these writers themselves through their public commentary and literary engagement with the development of the legacy of the GDR, the fall of the Wall, reunification, collective memory of the Third Reich and the Holocaust, collective guilt, and German wartime suffering. What, then, do these post-reunification texts offer beyond such 'privileged insights'? First, they demonstrate the breadth of experience on the part of those categorized as the Hitler Youth generation, and of life writing about childhood more generally. De Bruyn, Walser, and Grass share formative experiences, but their accounts underscore their individuality and the plurality of childhoods even within the restrictions of the Nazi state. Second, they engage in very different ways with the challenge faced by their generation: to reconcile private memories and experiences, and society's expectation that childhood be a happy, carefree period, with their retrospective knowledge of the historical facts of the Third Reich. For de Bruyn, childhood is an idyllic world that is breached as the public and political spheres encroach on the private. He demonstrates this through the juxtaposition of private memories and historical events, and by contextualizing what he remembers within his post-war knowledge of the crimes committed while he was growing up. Grass's retrospective view of his childhood is shrouded in shame for what he sees as a sin of omission in not questioning the system in which he was formed. The text seems to reveal something of his desire to atone for what he views as a failure to question the world of his youth, and to write about that in particular, whilst still performing the role of 'Günter Grass' that he establishes and develops throughout his writing. Walser defends his right to remember his childhood without that retrospective knowledge of suffering. This, for him, represents the most authentic way to write about this period. He seems to see the private world of his childhood as under threat, not just from the political sphere but also from the demands of post-war discourse that he contextualize his memories of childhood within knowledge of the Holocaust.

Each author expresses the desire to produce an account of 'how it really was': de Bruyn promises a truthful (if not complete) account of his formative years, Grass establishes the idea that *Beim Häuten der Zwiebel* will fill in the gaps left by the rest of his *oeuvre*, and Walser determines to give the reader an account of childhood free from the retrospective knowledge of Nazi crimes. The primary impetus of autobiographical writing, particularly accounts of childhood, is to give a truth about oneself and about personal experience. As Coe argues, the writer who produces autobiographical work about his childhood is 'concerned not so much with *the* truth, as with *his* truth'.[126] De Bruyn explores this idea in *Das erzählte Ich*, suggesting

> daß [...] der Begriff Dichtung nicht Erfindung bedeutet, sondern daß er als Verdichten des Geschehenen, als Konzentrieren des Vielfältigen und Zufälligen oder auch als gedankliches Durchdringen oder Deuten zu verstehen ist. Dichtung im autobiographischen Schreiben ist die Fähigkeit, das Vergangene gegenwärtig zu machen, Wesentliches in Sein und Werden zu zeigen, Teilwahrheiten zusammenzufassen zu dem Versuch der ganzen Wahrheit über das schreibende und beschriebene Ich.[127]
>
> [that [...] the term 'poetry' does not mean 'invention', but rather should be understood as condensing events, concentrating the varied and chance things, or as conceptual imbuing or pointing to. Poetry in the context of autobiographical writing means the ability to make the past present, to show the essentials 'in Sein und Werden', in Being and Becoming, to summarize half-truths in an attempt to achieve the whole truth of the I who both writes and is described.]

De Bruyn's notion of the 'Wahrheit der Kunst' [truth of art] as outlined here does not suggest that the subject of childhood in itself can guarantee authenticity; rather, the authenticity that can be achieved is always an attempt, hampered by the limits of memory and literary representation. Describing in *Zwischenbilanz* how he told stories to his friend Hannes, he comments: 'Hannes, mein Publikum, wollte ja keine exakte Geschichtsschreibung, sondern Geschichten' [Hannes, my audience, did not want a precise account of history, but rather stories] (*Zwischenbilanz*, p. 29). The reader's desire for the 'truth' of the author Günter de Bruyn's early life may well be considered in these terms. Grass's text uses precisely this idea in order to draw the reader in throughout the account: it is part of both his literary style and his persona. In an interview with Elizabeth Gaffney, he playfully contends that 'the truth is mostly very boring, and you can help it along with the lies. There is no harm in that.'[128] By drawing attention to the problematic nature of writing about one's own childhood, and in particular childhood spent under dictatorship, Grass conforms to de Bruyn's notion that the child's view and experience must always be tempered with that of the remembering adult who is, and has been since 1945, aware of the crimes perpetrated in the name of Nazism. For those who have lived through pernicious historical periods, such as the Third Reich, the imperative to comment on the events of these times is great, and both de Bruyn and Grass acknowledge this, although they execute it in different ways. In both cases, they seem to offer a kind of 'inszenierte Authentizität' [performed authenticity], a performance of truth, but it is a performance which the reader is 'in on'. Gillian Lathey attributes the popularity of autobiographical works about childhood in the Third Reich to this, writing that 'the thriving autobiography industry of recent decades has been accompanied by the promotion of life histories as a successful product. A "true story" always attracts readers — but it must still be a "story".'[129] Lathey's comments suggest not only the commodification of life stories, but also the constructedness of such accounts. For de Bruyn and Grass, the limitations of this approach are considered the unreliability of memory, the mediated quality of writing, and the confines of historical representation.

Walser also explores the constructedness of autobiographical accounts of childhood, but for him this takes on a moral dimension, as he argues that the interests of the present are what 'construct' the past. For Walser, 'Erzählen, wie es war, ist ein Traumhausbau' [telling what things were like means building a house of dreams] (*Brunnen*, p. 10; *Fountain*, p. 4); however, his concern stems not from a concern about the representability of the past, but rather about his own ability to access his memories 'authentically', by which he means without the constraints and interests of the present. Walser draws attention to this within *Ein springender Brunnen*. As Stephen Brockmann argues,

> what people may think of as the objectively true past, the narrator claims, is in fact a construction which they have created for their own purposes in the present. Every past, inasmuch as it is told in the present, is at least partly a fiction. 'Geschichte' as history is always also 'Geschichte as story'.[130]

But, rather than capitalizing on it as the other two do, Walser resists it. Instead of performed authenticity, we have a kind of 'inszenierte Naivität' [performed naivety].[131] In order to write the book of his childhood, he poeticizes memory to produce an account outside of the knowledge he acquired after 1945. Erll and Rigney suggest (drawing on Nora) that cultural memory formation, as a dynamic process of remembering and forgetting, must be seen as an 'active engagement with the past'.[132] Here, remembering is 'performative'. We can see this in each of the texts discussed above, albeit in different ways.

Ultimately, these works are concerned with the legacy of their authors' childhood experiences and the influence this formative period had on their lives, particularly their development as writers and as artists. This is a greater priority in the texts than depicting the mechanics of Nazi indoctrination and control. Walser describes *Ein springender Brunnen* as 'das Buch meiner Kindheit' [the book of my childhood],[133] while insisting that he had no interest in writing a book about the Nazi period or about childhood during the Nazi period. Nicole A. Thesz observes that Grass 'makes scant mention of his Hitler Youth membership, a topic that might have given insight into his everyday experience of Nazi Germany'.[134] De Bruyn also devotes little attention to this aspect of his youth. Their concern is not so much with the 'Wahrheit der Kunst' but rather with the 'Wahrheit des Künstlers' [truth of the artists]. Grass said that he had deliberately avoided the term 'autobiography' when writing *Beim Häuten der Zwiebel*. He comments:

> Mir kam es eher darauf an, den schwierigen Werdegang eines jungen Menschen in einer Zeit zu beschreiben, die in der Anfangsphase bestimmt war von der Zeit des Nationalsozialismus [...] der schwierige Prozess des sich Darauslösens nach dem Krieg und zugleich [...] der verstiegene Wunsch eines Zwölf-Dreizehnjährigen und die feste Vorstellung: 'ich werde Künstler'.[135]
>
> [For me, it was more about describing the difficult development of a young person in a time which was initially determined by National Socialism [...] the difficult process of breaking free from that after the war and at the same time [...] the extravagant wish of a twelve-, thirteen-year-old and the firm belief: 'I am going to be an artist'.]

Similarly, de Bruyn seeks to show the 'Reifeprozeß des jungen Menschen' [a young person's coming-of-age] within the context of a whole generation who encountered this experience and had to come to terms with it after the war.[136] Walser, in an interview conducted with his son, the journalist Jakob Augstein, in 2017, emphasized that *Ein springender Brunnen* was not intended to be another *Blechtrommel*,[137] a book standing against fascism. Rather, he sought to create a literary monument to the people with whom he grew up: 'Wenn ich ein Buch über meine Kindheit schreibe, ist das eine Grabung, und es ist das Errichten eines Denkmals, vieler Denkmäler' [If I write a book about my childhood, that is a kind of burial, and that means putting up a monument, many monuments].[138] He enshrines these people from his past in a literary monument, creating a site of memory in which they can live on, and in this way prioritizes his own life and memory above the need to warn and inform. Despite the painful legacy of a Nazi childhood, these writers enjoy a freedom when it comes to writing about it. Driven not by an imperative to 'bear witness', but by an inner compulsion both to examine their own origins and to speak authentically to their fellow Germans, they offer stories about growing up at a time when childhood was under threat. Yet, at the same time, post-war memory culture would see them as bearing a responsibility to take account of the past, to acknowledge the persecution and suffering of others, a responsibility which they decline to accept on those terms.

Notes to Chapter 2

1. Helmut Schmitz, *On their Own Terms: The Legacy of National Socialism in Post-1990 German Fiction* (Birmingham: Birmingham University Press, 2004), p. 3.
2. Christa Wolf, *Kindheitsmuster* (Munich: Luchterhand, 2002). An earlier account, published in West Germany, was Melita Maschmann's divisive autobiographical text *Fazit: Kein Rechtfertigungsversuch* (Stuttgart: Deutsche Verlags-Anstalt, 1963). See Sayner, pp. 163–209.
3. Schaumann, *Memory Matters*, p. 63.
4. Christa Wolf, 'Eine Diskussion über *Kindheitsmuster*', *German Quarterly*, 57 (1984), 91–95 (p. 92).
5. Günter Gaus coined the term in 1983. It was also used by Kohl in a speech at the Knesset in Israel in January 1984.
6. Christa Wolf, *Ansprachen* (Darmstadt: Luchterhand, 1988), p. 74.
7. Wolf, 'Eine Diskussion über *Kindheitsmuster*', p. 94.
8. Christa Wolf, *Fortgesetzter Versuch: Aufsätze, Gespräche, Essays* (Leipzig: Reclam, 1980), p. 106.
9. E.g. Renate Finckh, *Sie versprachen uns die Zukunft* (Tübingen: Silberburg, 2002 [1979]); Eva Zeller, *Solange ich denken kann: Roman einer Jugend* (Stuttgart: Ullstein, 1987 [1981]); Erich Loest, *Durch die Erde ein Riß* (Hamburg: Hoffmann und Campe, 1981); Max von der Grün, *Wie war*

das eigentlich: Kindheit und Jugend im Dritten Reich (Darmstadt: Luchterhand 1981); Margarete Hannsmann, *Der helle Tag bricht an: Ein Kind wird Nazi* (Munich: dtv, 1984 [1982]); Carola Stern, *In den Netzen der Erinnerung* (Reinbek: Rowohlt, 1986); Eva Sternheim-Peters, *Die Zeit der großen Täuschungen: Mädchenleben im Fascismus* (Bielefeld: AJZ, 1987); Gudrun Pausewang, *Fern von der Rosinkawiese* (Munich: dtv, 2004 [1989]). See also Ingrid Strobl, ed., *Das kleine Mädchen, das ich war: Schriftstellerinnen erzählen ihre Kindheit* (Munich: dtv, 1984), a collection which includes eleven accounts by women born between 1917 and 1942. Unlike Reich-Ranicki, ed., *Meine Schulzeit im Dritten Reich*, however, the volume does not focus primarily on the effects of a childhood under National Socialism.
10. Kater, p. 265.
11. Wolf, *Fortgesetzter Versuch*, p. 112. For a discussion of how this position affected Wolf's choice of narrator in *Kindheitsmuster*, see Schaumann, *Memory Matters*, pp. 92–94.
12. Christa Wolf, *The Fourth Dimension: Interviews with Christa Wolf*, trans. by Hilary Pilkington (London: Verso, 1988), pp. 44–45.
13. Gullestad, p. 8.
14. Mark Roseman, 'Introduction', in *Generations in Conflict*, ed. by Roseman, pp. 1–47 (p. 33).
15. Zeller, *Solange ich denken kann*, p. 186.
16. The most influential theory with regard to this has been Philippe Lejeune's seminal concept of 'le pacte autobiographique' [the autobiographical pact]: the author and reader enter a contract in which it is understood that the writer and narrator are one and the same. See Philippe Lejeune, *On Autobiography*, ed. by Paul John Eakin, trans. by Katherine Leary (Minneapolis: University of Minnesota Press, 1989), pp. 3–30. On the theory of autobiography and its reception in contemporary German literary studies, see Schmidt, pp. 65–71.
17. Paul John Eakin, 'Breaking Rules: The Consequences of Self-Narration', *Biography*, 24 (2001), 113–27 (p. 115).
18. Roy Pascal, *Design and Truth in Autobiography* (Cambridge: Cambridge University Press, 1960), p. 182.
19. Ibid., p. 61.
20. Ibid., p. 42.
21. Linda Anderson, *Autobiography* (London: Routledge, 2001), p. 16. Consider e.g. Augustine's *Confessions* (c. 398–400 AD), John Bunyan's *Grace Abounding to the Chief of Sinners* (1666), and William Wordsworth's *Prelude* (1888).
22. L. Anderson, p. 44.
23. Coe, p. 80.
24. Johann Wolfgang von Goethe, *Aus meinem Leben: Dichtung und Wahrheit* (Frankfurt a.M.: Deutscher Klassiker Verlag, 2007).
25. Coe, p. 41.
26. Eva Zeller, *Die Autobiographie: Selbsterkenntnis — Selbstentblößung* (Stuttgart: Akademie der Wissenschaften und der Literatur, 1995), p. 7.
27. Günter de Bruyn, *Das erzählte Ich: Über Wahrheit und Dichtung in der Autobiographie* (Frankfurt a.M.: Fischer, 1995), p. 66.
28. Günter de Bruyn, *Zwischenbilanz* (Frankfurt a.M.: Fischer, 1992). Cited henceforth as *Zwischenbilanz*.
29. Examples include Hermann Kant, *Abspann: Erinnerung an meine Gegenwart* (Berlin: Aufbau, 1991); Heiner Müller, *Krieg ohne Schlacht: Leben in zwei Diktaturen* (Cologne: Kiepenheuer & Witsch, 1992). See Julian Preece, 'Damaged Lives? (East) German Memoirs and Autobiographies, 1989–1994', in *The New Germany: Literature and Society after Unification*, ed. by Osman Durrani, Colin Good, and Kevin Hilliard (Sheffield: Sheffield Academic Press, 1995), pp. 349–64. See also James Reece, 'Remembering the GDR: Memory and Evasion in Autobiographical Writing from the Former GDR', in *Textual Responses to German Unification: Processing Historical and Social Change in Literature and Film*, ed. by Carol Anne Costabile-Heming, Rachel J. Halverson, and Kristie A. Foell (Berlin and New York: de Gruyter, 2001), pp. 59–77.
30. Dennis Tate, 'Changing Perspectives on Günter de Bruyn: An Introduction', in *Günter de Bruyn in Perspective*, ed. by Dennis Tate (Amsterdam: Rodopi, 1999), pp. 1–9 (pp. 1–2). For an excellent

analysis of *Vierzig Jahre*, see Owen Evans, '"Schlimmeres als geschah, hätte immer geschehen können": Günter de Bruyn and the GDR in *Vierzig Jahre*', in *Günter de Bruyn in Perspective*, ed. by Tate, pp. 171–89.

31. Dennis Tate, *Shifting Perspectives: East German Autobiographical Narratives before and after the End of the GDR* (Rochester, NY: Camden House, 2007), p. 180.
32. Günter de Bruyn, 'Fremd im eigenen Land', in *Über Deutschland: Schriftsteller geben Auskunft*, ed. by Thomas Reitzschel (Leipzig: Reclam, 1993), pp. 154–74 (p. 160).
33. De Bruyn, *Das erzählte Ich*, p. 51.
34. Ibid., p. 19.
35. Ibid., p. 53.
36. Uwe Wittstock, 'Interview mit Günter de Bruyn' <http://blog.uwe-wittstock.de/?p=2069> [accessed 1 July 2019].
37. De Bruyn cites autobiographical works by several authors in *Das erzählte Ich*, pp. 22–24, including Augustine, Adalbert Stifter, Theodor Fontane, Stefan Heym, Johann Wolfgang von Goethe, Erich Loest, Otto von Bismarck, Karl Phillip Moritz, Vladimir Nabokov, Jean-Jacques Rousseau, Christa Wolf, and Benjamin Franklin.
38. De Bruyn, *Das erzählte Ich*, p. 62.
39. Günter de Bruyn, *Der Hohlweg* (Halle: Mitteldeutscher Verlag, 1963). See Tate, *Shifting Perspectives*, pp. 162–63.
40. De Bruyn, *Das erzählte Ich*, p. 15.
41. Brettschneider, p. 11.
42. Chris Lewis, 'Der verkaufte Schatten? Interview mit Günter de Bruyn am 27. September 1996', in *Günter de Bruyn in Perspective*, ed. by Tate, pp. 207–29 (p. 212).
43. Jean-Jacques Rousseau, *The Confessions of Jean-Jacques Rousseau*, trans. by J. M. Cohen (London: Penguin, 1953), p. 548.
44. De Bruyn, *Das erzählte Ich*, p. 62.
45. Ibid., p. 66.
46. Ibid.
47. Tate, *Shifting Perspectives*, p. 180.
48. De Bruyn, 'Fremd im eigenen Land', p. 161.
49. On the use of the collective 'wir' in the text, see Tate, *Shifting Perspectives*, pp. 181–82.
50. Renate Rechtien, 'Gelebtes, erinnertes, erzähltes und erschriebenes Selbst: Günter de Bruyns *Zwischenbilanz* und Christa Wolfs *Kindheitsmuster*', in *Günter de Bruyn in Perspective*, ed. by Tate, pp. 151–70 (pp. 159–60).
51. Tate, *Shifting Perspectives*, p. 181.
52. *Das literarische Quartett*, 5 March 1992 <http://www.youtube.com/watch?v=LNLhVEbiIH0> [accessed 1 July 2019].
53. Owen Evans, *Ein Training im Ich-Sagen: Personal Authenticity in the Prose Work of Günter de Bruyn* (Berne: Lang, 1996), p. 297.
54. De Bruyn, *Das erzählte Ich*, p. 20.
55. See, most recently, Martin Walser and Jakob Augstein, *Das Leben wortwörtlich: Ein Gespräch* (Reinbek: Rowohlt, 2017), esp. pp. 23–95.
56. Martin Walser, *Ein springender Brunnen* (Frankfurt a.M.: Suhrkamp, 1998), henceforth cited as *Brunnen*. Unless otherwise indicated, translations are taken from Martin Walser, *A Gushing Fountain*, trans. by David Dollenmayer (New York: Skyhorse, 2015).
57. Maguire, p. 42 (see esp. pp. 39–43). On Walser's approach to the politics of memory, see esp. Stuart Taberner, 'A Manifesto for Germany's "New Right"? Martin Walser, the Past, Transcendence, Aesthetics, and *Ein springender Brunnen*', *German Life and Letters*, 53.1 (2000), 126–41; Christoph Parry, 'Die Rechtfertigung der Erinnerung vor der Last der Geschichte', in *Grenzen der Fiktionalität und der Erinnerung*, ed. by Christoph Parry and Edgar Platen (Munich: Iudicium, 2007), pp. 98–111.
58. Gillian Lathey, *The Impossible Legacy: Identity and Purpose in Autobiographical Children's Literature Set in the Third Reich and the Second World War* (Berne and New York: Lang, 1999), p. 242.
59. For a detailed textual analysis of the speech, see Bill Niven, *Facing the Nazi Past: United Germany*

and the Legacy of the Third Reich (London: Routledge, 2001), pp. 173–75; Thomas A. Kovach, 'Commentary', in Thomas A. Kovach and Martin Walser, *The Burden of the Past: Martin Walser on Modern German Identity: Texts, Contexts, Commentary* (Rochester, NY: Camden House, 2008), pp. 96–107. On its reception, see Kathrin Schödel, *Literarisches versus politisches Gedächtnis? Martin Walsers Friedenspreisrede und sein Roman 'Ein springender Brunnen'* (Würzburg: Königshausen & Neumann, 2010), esp. pp. 63–123. On the ensuing public debate between Walser and Ignatz Bubis, see Frank Schirrmacher, *Die Walser-Bubis-Debatte: Eine Dokumentation* (Frankfurt a.M.: Suhrkamp, 1999).

60. Martin Walser, *Über Deutschland reden* (Frankfurt a.M.: Suhrkamp, 1989), pp. 76–77.
61. Martin Walser, 'Speaking of Germany', in Kovach and Walser, *The Burden of the Past*, pp. 58–59 (p. 58)
62. Such works include *Ehen in Philippsburg* (1957), *Halbzeit* (1960), *Ein fliehendes Pferd* (1978), *Das Schwanenhaus* (1980), and *Jagd* (1988). See Gertrud Bauer Pickar, 'In Defense of the Past: The Life and Passion of Alfred Dorn in *Die Verteidigung der Kindheit*', in *New Critical Perspectives on Martin Walser*, ed. by Frank Pilipp (Columbia, SC: Camden House, 1994), pp. 134–56 (p. 135). My discussion here of the museum and memory previously appeared in '"Institutionalized Stories"', pp. 103-05.
63. Taberner, *Aging and Old-Age Style*, p. 141.
64. Stephen Brockmann, *Literature and German Reunification* (Cambridge: Cambridge University Press, 1999), p. 138.
65. Martin Walser, *Die Verteidigung der Kindheit* (Frankfurt a.M.: Suhrkamp, 1991), dust jacket.
66. Schmitz, *On their Own Terms*, pp. 186–87, identifies this in his analysis of *Ein springender Brunnen*.
67. Andrew Prescott, 'The Textuality of the Archive', in *What Are Archives? Cultural and Theoretical Perspectives: A Reader*, ed. by Louise Craven (Aldershot: Ashgate, 2008), pp. 31–53 (pp. 32–33).
68. Fest, *Ich nicht*, p. 366.
69. Joachim Fest, *Not Me: Memoirs of a German Childhood*, trans. by Martin Chalmers (London: Atlantic, 2012), p. 297.
70. Edgar Hilsenrath, *Berlin ... Endstation* (Berlin: Dittrich, 2006), p. 62.
71. Maguire notes that Walser challenges the Romantic association of the child with nature through the scene in which Johann remembers beating a cat to death in a sadistic act of pleasure (*Brunnen*, p. 176). At the same time, Johann's close relationship with his beloved dog, Tell, serves to counteract this to some extent.
72. Coe, p. xii.
73. Pinfold, *Child's View*, p. 26.
74. The 'Brunnen' of the novel's title is also reminiscent of the Grimms' fairy tale 'Frau Holle', in which a well conceals a door to a magical world. Fountains also appear in several fairy tales collected by the Grimms. See Axel Dickmann, *Grimms Märchen von A bis Z: Kleines Lexikon der Märchenmotive* ([n.p.]: Books on Demand, 2014), pp. 16–19.
75. Ernst Bloch, *Das Prinzip Hoffnung* (Frankfurt a.M.: Suhrkamp, 1959), p. 1628; Ernst Bloch, *The Principle of Hope*, trans. by Neville Plaice, Stephen Plaice, and Paul Knight (Cambridge: MIT Press, 1986), p. 1376.
76. Peter Blickle, *Heimat: A Critical Theory of the German Idea of Homeland* (Rochester, NY, and Woodbridge: Camden House, 2002), p. 130.
77. Blickle, p. 17.
78. Elizabeth Boa, 'Lost Heimat in Generational Novels by Reinhard Jirgl, Christoph Hein, and Angelika Overath', in *Germans as Victims*, ed. by Taberner and Berger, pp. 86–102 (p. 89).
79. Fuchs, *Phantoms of War*, p. 165.
80. See Jochen Hieber, 'Unversöhnte Lebensläufe: Zur Rhetorik der Verletzung in der Walser-Bubis-Debatte', in *Hinauf und zurück in die herzhelle Zukunft*, ed. by Michael Braun and Birgit H. Lermen (Bonn: Bouvier, 2000), pp. 543–59 (p. 544). The programme was broadcast on 14 August 1998.
81. Martin Walser, 'Die Banalität des Guten: Erfahrungen beim Verfassen einer Sonntagsrede aus Anlass der Verleihung des Friedenspreises des Deutschen Buchhandels', *Frankfurter Allgemeine Zeitung*, 12 October 1998, p. 15.

82. Walser, *Über Deutschland reden*, p. 76.
83. Walser, 'Speaking of Germany', p. 58.
84. Schmitz, *On their Own Terms*, p. 200.
85. Helmuth Kiesel, 'Zwei Modelle literarischer Erinnerung an die NS-Zeit: *Die Blechtrommel* und *Ein springender Brunnen*', *German Monitor*, 60 (2004), 343–61 (p. 360).
86. Andreas Huyssen, *Present Pasts: Urban Palimpsests and the Politics of Memory* (Stanford: Stanford University Press, 2003), p. 139.
87. Fuchs, *Phantoms of War*, p. 165.
88. Ibid.
89. Friederike Eigler, 'Engendering Cultural Memory in Selected Post-Wende Literary Texts of the 1990s', *German Quarterly*, 74 (2001), 392–406 (p. 394).
90. 'Jeder Tag bringt eine kleinere oder größere Provokation' [interview with Martin Walser], *Die Welt*, 6 October 1998 <http://www.welt.de/print-welt/article626366/Jeder-Tag-bringt-eine-kleinere-oder-groessere-Provokation.html> [accessed 1 July 2019].
91. Maguire, pp. 60–61.
92. Sigmund Freud, *Die Traumdeutung* (Frankfurt a.M.: Fischer, 2005), p. 252; Sigmund Freud, *The Interpretation of Dreams*, trans. by A. A. Brill (New York: Dover, 2015), p. 186.
93. Schmitz, *On their Own Terms*, p. 186.
94. 'Jeder Tag bringt eine kleinere oder größere Provokation'.
95. Walser, *Über Deutschland reden*, p. 77.
96. Walser, 'Speaking of Germany', pp. 58–59.
97. Parry, p. 102. See also Stuart Taberner, *German Literature of the 1990s and Beyond: Normalization and the Berlin Republic* (Rochester, NY, and Woodbridge: Camden House, 2005), p. 123.
98. Maja Zehfuss, *Wounds of Memory: The Politics of War in Germany* (Cambridge: Cambridge University Press, 2007), p. 146.
99. Eshel, pp. 93, 253.
100. Ibid., p. 69.
101. Ibid., p. 72.
102. Ibid.
103. Ruth Klüger, *Frauen lesen anders: Essays*, 2nd edn (Munich: Deutscher Taschenbuch Verlag, 1997), p. 65.
104. For an overview of this, see Julian Preece, *The Life and Work of Günter Grass: Literature, History, Politics* (Basingstoke: Palgrave Macmillan, 2004), pp. 1–9.
105. Martin Kölbel, 'Nachwort', in *Ein Buch, ein Bekenntnis: Die Debatte um Günter Grass' 'Beim Häuten der Zwiebel'*, ed. by Martin Kölbel (Göttingen: Steidl, 2007), pp. 335–57 (p. 336).
106. Günter Grass, *Beim Häuten der Zwiebel* (Göttingen: Steidl, 2006), cited henceforth as *Zwiebel*. English translations are taken from Günter Grass, *Peeling the Onion*, trans. by Michael Henry Heim (London: Harvill Secker, 2007), cited henceforth as *Onion*.
107. Marcel Reich-Ranicki, *Über Ruhestörer: Juden in der deutschen Literatur* (Munich: Piper, 1973), p. 168.
108. Stuart Taberner, 'Private Failings and Public Virtues: Günter Grass's *Beim Häuten der Zwiebel* and the Exemplary Use of Authorial Biography', *Modern Language Review*, 103 (2008), 144–54 (p. 152). A further reference is made to *Ein springender Brunnen* when Grass compares his own biography with those of 'Schriftsteller meiner Generation, die seßhaft am Bodensee [...] aufgewachsen [...] sind' [writers of my generation who grew up in one place — on Lake Constance] (*Zwiebel*, p. 64; *Onion*, p. 54). Grass also mentions Walser explicitly in the final pages in the context of the Gruppe 47 (*Zwiebel*, p. 469).
109. Günter Grass, *Die Blechtrommel* (Munich: dtv, 2003), p. 52.
110. Pinfold, *Child's View*, p. 89.
111. Ibid., p. 90.
112. Salman Rushdie, 'A Fine Pickle', *The Guardian*, 28 February 2009 <http://www.nawe.co.uk/DB/young-writers-news-3/a-fine-pickle.html> [accessed 1 July 2019].
113. Zeller, *Solange ich denken kann*, p. 186.
114. This reference provides a further link to Grass, *Die Blechtrommel*, p. 623, in which Oskar discusses the motif of three drops of blood in the snow.

115. Grass, *Die Blechtrommel*, p. 318; Günter Grass, *The Tin Drum*, trans. by Ralph Manheim (London: Vintage, 1998), p. 228.
116. Grass, *Die Blechtrommel*, p. 84; Grass, *The Tin Drum*, p. 56.
117. Pinfold, *Child's View*, p. 152.
118. Stuart Taberner, 'Günter Grass's *Peeling the Onion*', in *The Cambridge Companion to Günter Grass*, ed. by Stuart Taberner (Cambridge: Cambridge University Press, 2009), pp. 139–51 (p. 142).
119. See Kathrin Schödel, 'Martin Walser's *Ein springender Brunnen (A Gushing Fountain)*', in *The Novel in German since 1990*, ed. by Stuart Taberner (Cambridge: Cambridge University Press, 2011), pp. 108–23 (pp. 112–14).
120. Kliche-Behnke, p. 190.
121. Eva Zeller also uses onions as a metaphor for childhood memory in *Solange ich denken kann*, p. 37: 'In die Zwiebel Kindheit, in deren unterirdischen Speicher alles längst vorgebildet liegt. Es braucht nur noch zu treiben' [Into the onion of childhood, where in its subterranean storehouse everything has long lain in readiness. It only needs to sprout]. On the unreliability of memory in *Beim Häuten der Zwiebel*, see Schmidt, pp. 236–41.
122. Elizabeth Boa, 'Wolf, *Kindheitsmuster*', in *Landmarks in the German Novel (2)*, ed. by Peter Hutchinson and Michael Minden (Oxford: Lang, 2007), pp. 77–93 (p. 86).
123. Reich-Ranicki, 'Vorwort', p. 9.
124. Katharina Gerstenberger, *Truth to Tell: German Women's Autobiographies and Turn-of-the-Century Culture* (Ann Arbor: University of Michigan Press, 2000), p. 176.
125. Eva Menasse and Michael Kumpfmüller, 'Wider die intellektuelle Gerontokratie: Ein Plädoyer für weniger Grass und mehr Nahost in der Debatte', *Süddeutsche Zeitung*, 17 August 2006, p. 11, cited in Stuart Parkes, 'Günter Grass and his Contemporaries in East and West', in *The Cambridge Companion to Günter Grass*, ed. by Stuart Taberner (Cambridge: Cambridge University Press, 2009), pp. 209–23.
126. Coe, p. 80.
127. De Bruyn, *Das erzählte Ich*, p. 31.
128. Elizabeth Gaffney, 'Interview with Günter Grass', *Paris Review*, 124 (1991) <www.theparisreview.org/interviews/2191/the-art-of-fiction-no-124-gunter-grass> [accessed 1 July 2019]. Imre Kertész makes a similar comment in an interview about Wilkomirski's *Bruchstücke*: 'Lüge ist immer sehr wirkungsvoll. Lüge hört man viel lieber als die Wahrheit' [Lies are always very effective. People would always rather hear a lie than the truth] ('Wichtig ist die Öffentlichkeit: Gespräch mit Sebastian Hefti und Wolfgang Heuer', in ... *alias Wilkomirski: Die Holocaust Travestie: Enthüllung und Dokumentation eines literarischen Skandals*, ed. by Daniel Ganzfried and Sebastian Hefti (Berlin: Jüdische Verlagsanstalt, 2002), pp. 207–18 (p. 208))
129. Lathey, p. 40.
130. Stephen Brockmann, 'Martin Walser and the Presence of the German Past', *German Quarterly*, 75 (2002), 127–43 (p. 128).
131. André Fischer, *Inszenierte Naivität: Zur ästhetischen Simulation von Geschichte bei Günter Grass, Albert Drach und Walter Kempowski* (Munich: Fink, 1992). See also Barth, p. 27.
132. Erll and Rigney, p. 2.
133. Walser and Augstein, p. 60.
134. Nicole A. Thesz, *The Communicative Event in the Works of Günter Grass: Stages of Speech, 1959–2015* (Rochester, NY: Camden House, 2018), p. 184.
135. Cited in Richard E. Schade, 'Layers of Meaning, War, Art: Grass's "Beim Häuten der Zwiebel"', *German Quarterly*, 80 (2007), 279–301 (pp. 282–83).
136. Wittstock.
137. Walser and Augstein, p. 60.
138. Ibid., p. 61.

CHAPTER 3

❖

Seen, but Not Heard: Memories of Child Holocaust Survivors

Introduction: A Silent Legacy?

FIG. 3.1. Frank Meisler's sculpture *Züge in das Leben — Züge in den Tod* [Trains to Life — Trains to Death], Berlin. Photograph by the author

Outside Berlin's busy Friedrichstraße station stands a memorial to Jewish children persecuted under Nazism. Entitled *Züge in das Leben — Züge in den Tod* [Trains to Life — Trains to Death], the sculpture, by Frank Meisler, represents those children who escaped on the Kindertransports and those who were deported to concentration camps throughout Nazi-occupied Europe. These two trajectories are marked by the train tracks that surround the sculpture: suffering and death in the camps, or the possibility of escape and survival. Both trajectories confound the modern, Western understanding of childhood. Children are not supposed to encounter death or sex: for them to do so, or for someone to depict their doing so, is taboo. In Meisler's sculpture, the deported children are sent to death camps; those on the Kindertransports were forced to grow up too quickly, robbed of their childhood as they were thrust into new surroundings, experiencing loss of language, family, homeland, culture, and religion. The memorial makes visible the legacy of Jewish children's suffering during the Holocaust and draws attention to an 'unnatural' ending of childhood, through death, or the demand to grow up at an accelerated rate.[1]

While authors such as those discussed in the previous chapter were the object of National Socialism's nurture and control as children, those whom the regime deemed 'unacceptable' found themselves at risk of persecution, deportation, and death. National Socialism's racial policies disrupted many of the universal aspects of childhood and common formative experiences for these children. Susan Suleiman has termed this age cohort of Jewish children the '1.5 generation'.[2] Their experience, she suggests, was twofold: first, 'the trauma [of the Holocaust] occurred (or at least, began) before the formation of stable identity that we associate with adulthood, and in some cases before any conscious sense of self',[3] and second, children often experienced 'premature aging', as they were forced to take on adult roles. They thus become defined by their liminality and by the impossibility of their experience: they were old enough to suffer persecution and annihilation, just as adults were, but for many this was the only way of life they had ever known.

English-language accounts of Jewish children's childhood experiences under Nazism abound, but such narratives written in German are, unsurprisingly, scarce.[4] An extremely small number of Jewish children survived the war, and for those who did and who had German as their mother tongue, the impulse to bear witness was unlikely to be realized in that language. Indeed, writing in German proved both impractical, since so many survivors escaped abroad or emigrated soon after the war, and undesirable, because German was often seen to represent the language of the perpetrators. The traumatic effects of a childhood of loss, extreme suffering, and persecution also played their part. In this chapter, I discuss three autobiographical texts that foreground the Jewish experience of childhood in the Third Reich: Ruth Klüger (b. 1931), *weiter leben: Eine Jugend* [Still Alive: A Holocaust Girlhood Remembered] (1992); Georges-Arthur Goldschmidt (b. 1928), *Die Absonderung* [Seclusion] (1991); and Günter Kunert (b. 1929), *Erwachsenenspiele: Erinnerungen* [Games for Grown-Ups: Memories] (1997). Given the scarcity of German-language literary accounts of Jewish childhood, these texts, and the stories they tell, become in some way exceptional, even representative. Their authors speak when so many were forced to remain silent, and offer an invaluable insight into the child's experience, albeit from the perspective of the adult looking back.

The notion of journey encapsulated in Meisler's sculpture at Friedrichstraße pervades these texts. In *weiter leben*,[5] Klüger recounts her childhood in a ghetto and two concentration camps and her attempts at coming to terms with her past as an adult in the US. The dust jacket of the first German edition showed four pictures of the 'stations' on Klüger's journey from childhood to adulthood and freedom. As she writes within the text itself, she originally conceived of the title 'Stationen', but abandoned it as it failed to express her feelings of rootlessness. As she comments: 'ich [bin] doch eine, die nirgendwo lange war und wohnt' [I'm someone who hasn't spent and doesn't spend long anywhere] (*weiter leben*, p. 79). The painting on the cover of the Deutscher Taschenbuch Verlag's edition, by the German-Jewish artist Charlotte Salomon, depicts a woman surrounded by suitcases, reflecting the author's sense of uprootedness and the dominating presence of her own journey. Goldschmidt narrates his escape as a ten-year-old boy from Germany and his continued persecution in Nazi-occupied France. In this way, his text focuses on the effects of an actual journey, from Germany via Florence to France, and in addition thematizes adolescence as an arduous journey from childhood to adulthood. In *Erwachsenenspiele*, Kunert recalls his childhood in National Socialist Berlin and his life in the GDR before he emigrated to the Federal Republic in 1979. The title of Kunert's work already points to the anticipated destination of the journey from childhood to adulthood, and the marketing on the dust jacket promises that Kunert will recapitulate the 'Stationen seines Lebens' [stations of his life]. Like Klüger, Kunert structures his account around places, and in doing so brings out the notion of journey. In addition, he dedicates *Erwachsenenspiele* to his wife, Marianne, without whose help his 'Expedition in die Vergangenheit schon bei Beginn gescheitert wäre' [expedition into the past would have failed as soon as it began] (*Erwachsenenspiele*, p. 5). Here, he conceives of his childhood in topographical terms, as a distant land, full of potential discoveries.

By offering an account of their experience of Nazism, these authors challenge the largely symbolic representation of the Jewish child's experience of the Third Reich that we find in post-war discourse. They do this through their depiction of childhood, and their explicit or implicit engagement with earlier representations of Jewish child Holocaust victims. Klüger explores notions of childish ignorance, Goldschmidt asserts the child's burgeoning sexuality, and Kunert narrates a picaresque account of his experience of persecution. In my analysis of these texts, I address the ways in which these writers negotiate the legacy of this formative experience and examine the narrative strategies they use to portray it.

Jewish Children as Objects and Agents: Post-War Perspectives

Historians of childhood have increasingly focused on the question of historical agency in their research, and this is particularly pertinent when it comes to the history and memory of children who were victims of the Holocaust. The instrumentalization of such children in literature and visual culture, figures whom we frequently find invested with symbolic capital, can best be exemplified by the two children who have proved the most powerful and enduring representatives of the Jewish childhood experience in post-war Germany: in the West, Anne Frank, and in the former GDR, the 'Buchenwaldkind' [Buchenwald child].

The most prominent child figure depicted in East German fiction was undoubtedly the young boy in Bruno Apitz's novel *Nackt unter Wölfen* [Naked among Wolves] (1958). The novel became one of the most widely read texts in the GDR,[6] and it was made into a film by DEFA, directed by Frank Beyer and released in 1963. Apitz's novel is based on the true story of the three-year-old Stefan Jerzy Zweig, who was brought to Buchenwald with his father in 1944. Zweig's name was included on a list of two hundred children and adolescents to be transported to Auschwitz, but when the child was found to be absent (hidden in the camp's typhus ward), another youth, a sixteen-year-old Sinto boy named Willy Blum, was deported in Zweig's place.[7] The story involves the dual narrative of the 'self-liberation' of Buchenwald on 11 April 1945 by its communist prisoners, and the attempts to save the life of a young Polish-Jewish boy, renamed Stefan Cyliak by the author.[8] In the novel, Stefan is smuggled into the camp in a suitcase and, once he has been discovered by some of the prisoners, is protected by them until they manage a successful uprising against the SS guards and liberate themselves.[9]

In his study *The Buchenwald Child: Truth, Fiction, and Propaganda* (2007), Bill Niven analyses the propagandist use that was made in the GDR of the narrative of Stefan's survival. In Apitz's novel, the figure of the child is helpless and passive, and has a purely symbolic function. Given that he does not speak, the child consequently 'remains a blank surface onto which the greater glory of adult male communist achievements can be projected'.[10] This might indeed be read as a more common trope of writing about the Holocaust. As Beate Müller has argued:

> Where adult characters are faced with or confront child figures, adults have to make up their minds how to respond to the child, have to choose between right and wrong courses of action — this crucially reinstates agency (and, by implication, responsibility) in a group of people who have precious little agency left.[11]

Significantly, it is because of his youth that the boy is deemed to require protection, not because he is Jewish. Indeed, his identity as a Jew is almost entirely written out of Apitz's fictional account.[12] The novel became 'a kind of literary monument to antifascism'[13] with the child as its symbolic centrepiece.

In West Germany, Anne Frank undoubtedly provided the most public symbol of Jewish suffering in the Holocaust.[14] Her diary was first published in Germany in 1949 with a limited print run, and even when it was taken up by the publishing house Fischer in 1955, it was not initially a best-seller. It only came to prominence with *Das Tagebuch der Anne Frank*, the German translation of the American stage play *The Diary of Anne Frank*, by Frances Goodrich and Albert Hackett, which was first performed in Germany on 1 October 1956. Within months, there had been more than two thousand performances in fifty-eight cities in Germany.[15] Although Goodrich and Hackett went to great lengths to ensure the play was as authentic in representing the story as possible, it involved a good deal of artistic licence and the kinds of changes necessitated by adapting the text of a diary to the stage. It was, then, not actually Anne Frank's own voice that initially captured the imaginations and hearts of the German public, but rather the adaptation of that voice by other writers. In this way, Anne Frank became, like 'Stefan', a symbol rather than an individual. In addition, just as Anne's father, Otto Frank, had edited the diary to remove what he deemed unsuitable for publication,[16] the first German translator,

Anneliese Schütz, also made various changes, which included removing any negative references to the German language and people. As Cynthia Ozick argues: 'Almost every hand that has approached the diary with the well-meaning intention of publicizing it has contributed to the subversion of history.'[17] The result has been that Anne Frank has become representative, symbolic, iconic. A 'natural focus for mythmaking',[18] she comes to embody the Romantic ideal of childhood innocence and becomes a blank canvas onto which individual needs can be projected.

Furthermore, Anne Frank's status as child must be reinforced. It is only in this way that her total innocence, both in terms of guiltlessness and in terms of lack of knowledge, can be maintained. For example, several passages regarding her developing sexuality were omitted until the publication of the most recent critical edition.[19] Such an omission serves to infantilize her and heighten the reader's sense of her innocence. In an article on the American reception of Anne Frank, L. J. Nicoletti explores photographic representations of her in a recent Holocaust exhibition. According to Nicoletti, the curators of the exhibition observed that 'commonly, images of Anne (all of them taken before she went into hiding) are used to visualize her at a later age and in the time period when she started to write'.[20] Thus, the reception of her voice is shaped by the visual, iconic image of her as a child rather than an adolescent. The message from the case of both Anne Frank and the Buchenwald child is the same: they have been made to function as symbols to fit a wider purpose. In Apitz's novel, Stefan literally has no voice, and the symbolic use of Anne Frank's story extends far further than critical engagement with her text. In both cases, the child's experience is mapped onto the national narrative of confronting the past. As Hanno Loewy writes:

> die Rettung des [Buchenwald] Kindes wird zum Mythos der Erlösung aus der tiefsten Barbarei, der drohenden eigenen Verrohung durch den Terror des Gegners. Im Westen hingegen mußte Anne Frank, der unschuldige Opfer, tot sein, um jedes Jahr aufs Neue zum Leben erweckt werden zu können.[21]

> [the rescue of the Buchenwald child became a myth of salvation from the most profound barbarity, the threat of one's own brutalization by the enemy's terror. In the West, however, Anne Frank, the innocent victim, had to die in order to be resurrected every year anew.]

Anne Frank's enduring phrase, 'in spite of everything I still believe that people are really good at heart',[22] fits both reception narratives perfectly: the story of the prisoners' daring rescue of the child in *Nackt unter Wölfen* seeks to demonstrate nothing other than that the 'good in people' leads them to risk their lives to do what is right, and Anne Frank's words, removed from their original context, give absolution.

Furthermore, in each case a single child figure appears to offer a means with which to encounter the totality of the Holocaust. The result is a failure to represent the diversity of Jewish children's experience of the Third Reich, which might have included going into hiding, and being discovered or betrayed; escaping the continent on a Kindertransport; being interned in a ghetto; or being deported to a concentration camp, either dying there, or surviving and facing the trauma of this experience and the loss of homeland, language, and family. Primo Levi suggested that Anne Frank is so frequently identified as a single representative of the millions of people who suffered and died as she did because 'one single Anne Frank moves us more than the countless others who suffered just as she did but whose faces have remained in the shadows'.[23] He conjectures that this is a more effective means of encouraging engagement with the past: 'Perhaps it is better that way; if we were capable of taking in all the suffering of all those people, we would not be able to live.'[24] While Levi seems ultimately to accept the use of Anne Frank's role in Holocaust remembrance, he raises an important point about the representation of the victims.

Similarly, Theodor W. Adorno commented on a story he heard from a friend attending a performance of the stage play *Das Tagebuch der Anne Frank*: 'man hat mir die Geschichte einer Frau erzählt, die einer Aufführung des dramatisierten Tagebuchs der Anne Frank beiwohnte und danach erschüttert sagte: ja, aber *das Mädchen hätte man doch wenigstens leben lassen sollen*' [I once heard the story of a woman who, after attending a performance of the dramatisation of *The Diary of Anne Frank*, said in a shaken voice: 'Yes, but really, at least *that* girl ought to have been allowed to live'].[25] The literary construction of Anne Frank becomes a sentimental figure and one with whom an audience or reader can empathize without having to engage with the totality of the Holocaust, perhaps even, in Adorno's example, without having to deprecate it. For Adorno, Anne Frank becomes an 'Alibi des Ganzen' [alibi for the whole].[26]

The child's view and experience therefore provide the reader with a 'view from below' that enables a more critically engaged response to the legacy of the Holocaust. At the same time, it can function as a means of creating a purely sentimental depiction of events that allows the reader merely to identify with one child's suffering without attempting to engage with the context and the extent of the suffering.

'Für ein Kind war das anders' [For a child it was different]: *weiter leben: Eine Jugend* (1992)

Klüger's autobiographical text *weiter leben: Eine Jugend* (1992) has become the best-known German-language account of childhood in the Holocaust since reunification. Klüger's narrative recounts her childhood and youth under Nazism: in Vienna, the Theresienstadt ghetto, and the concentration camps at Auschwitz-Birkenau and Christianstadt (Groß-Rosen). The text represents both a private attempt at coming to terms with the author's own origins, and a very public commentary on literary and political topics, including the commemoration of the Holocaust in post-war and post-reunification Germany. Most significant for this study is Klüger's treatment of the child figure, including her engagement with established notions of childhood, and of Jewish child victims of the Holocaust. Throughout the text, Klüger re-imagines the common understanding of the child survivor's experience of the Holocaust, seeking to counter the view that children of the Holocaust were too young to understand what was happening to them. She asserts the fundamental difference between children's experience of the Holocaust and that of adults, but in doing so, she also underlines the need not to reduce the children's experience to that of a mute, passive group.

The narrative begins in Vienna in 1939, as the eight-year-old Klüger secretly observes the adults in her family:

> Der Tod, nicht Sex war das Geheimnis, worüber die Erwachsenen tuschelten, worüber man gern mehr gehört hätte. Ich gab vor, nicht schlafen zu können, bettelte, daß man mich auf dem Sofa im Wohnzimmer [...] einschlafen ließe, schlief dann natürlich nicht ein, [...] und hoffte, etwas von den Schreckensnachrichten aufzufangen. (*weiter leben*, p. 9)

> [Their secret was death, not sex. That's what the grown-ups were talking about, sitting up late around the table. I had pretended that I couldn't fall asleep in my bed and begged them to let me sleep on the sofa in the living room [...] Of course, I didn't intend to fall asleep, I wanted to get in on the forbidden news, the horror stories.] (*Still Alive*, p. 15)

This opening passage immediately establishes the child's view, and yet Klüger does not use it primarily as a defamiliarization technique in order to distance the reader from the events she recounts, but rather to establish her approach towards the depiction of the child's experience of Nazism. The child listens avidly to the adults as they discuss the increasing violence towards Jewish friends and relatives, including imprisonment and torture. As Carolin Duttlinger outlines in her analysis of curiosity in *weiter leben*, Klüger 'defies an image of childhood first established in Romanticism'.[27] As Duttlinger points out, the style and setting of this opening passage evoke Freud's theory of the 'Urszene' [primal scene]: 'the real or imagined event of the child witnessing the parental intercourse'.[28] By establishing a clear link in this opening scene with the Freudian notion of childhood, in which the child is aware of the sexual, Klüger emphasizes to her readers her rejection of the Romantic view of the child, which she views as the epitome of the public's view of child Holocaust victims, and sets out immediately, as Duttlinger argues, to 'debunk' the 'limitation and naivety of the child's perspective'.[29]

This proves to be a dual challenge because, as Duttlinger notes, the taboo to which Klüger bears witness in this scene is not sex, but rather the taboo of death.[30] Duttlinger examines the role of curiosity in *weiter leben* through Freud's theory of the 'Wisstrieb' [desire for knowledge]. We might also see here a Heideggerian notion of death (without commenting on his politics). For Heidegger, as much as man is always his 'Noch-nicht', so he is also always his 'Ende'.[31] Heidegger quotes from the fifteenth-century text *Der Ackermann aus Böhmen*: 'sobald ein Mensch zum Leben kommt, sogleich ist er alt genug zu sterben'.[32] This negates a notion of childhood and adulthood as separate, for both states share a common potentiality for death, which in the Holocaust context is particularly apt as the Nazis killed indiscriminately. So, by drawing indirectly on this Heideggerian notion, Klüger asserts that the child stands on an equal footing with the adults in this regard. She comments on the 'Geheimnis der Erwachsenen, die den Kindertod den Kindern verschweigen und ihnen weismachen wollen, daß es nur den Erwachsenentod gebe, daß nur sie, die Überlegenen, dem Tod gewachsen sind, und daher auch nur sie ihn erleiden. Alles Lügen' [secret of the adults who conceal from children the fact that children can die and try to fool them into thinking that only adults can die, that they, the superior ones, are equal to dying, and that consequently only they can suffer it. It's all lies] (*weiter leben*, p. 10). This comment has a particularly petulant tone, and the child's voice is clearly audible. The adults' desire to protect the child from the knowledge, both of sex and death, which they consider will end childhood (breaking a taboo, moreover, if this knowledge is attained too soon), is shown by the author to be futile. Thus, Klüger challenges not only the Romantic view of the child, but also the idea that children are inferior to adults — what Phyllis Gaffney terms the 'deficiency paradigm'.[33] In this paradigm, children are inferior by virtue of their ignorance, but superior by virtue of their innocence. In the words of the sociologist Jenny Kitzinger, 'a child is ignorant if she doesn't know what adults want her to know, but innocent if she doesn't know what adults don't want her to know'.[34]

However, Klüger does defend the idea that the child's experience is different to that of adults. Coe considers the experience of the child to constitute an 'alternative world' and that the child's view is entirely removed from that of the adult: the child 'sees differently, reasons differently, reacts differently'.[35] Similarly, Klüger stresses the unique nature of the child's experience of Nazi persecution. She asserts: 'Für ein Kind war das anders, denn mir war in den wenigen Jahren, die ich als bewußter Mensch existierte, die Lebensberechtigung Stück für Stück aberkannt worden, so daß Birkenau für mich einer gewissen Logik nicht entbehrte' [For a child it was different, for in the few years that I had lived as a conscious person, my rights had been removed piece by piece, so that Auschwitz had a kind of logic to it] (*weiter leben*, p. 113; *Still Alive*, p. 95). For the young Klüger, Auschwitz exists as a 'verkehrte Welt' [topsy-turvy world] (*weiter leben*, p. 114; *Still Alive*, p. 96), and yet it also takes on a certain normality: unlike the adults, she has little with which to compare it.

The discrepancy between the child's and adult's view is perceptible at a formal level too. There is no attempt here to create the child's voice. Rather, Klüger, looking back, asserts remembered feelings and perceptions that take the reader into her world. For example, she knows in hindsight that her great-aunt perished in the gas chambers. The child Klüger used to be nurses an intense hatred towards this woman on account of a litany of slights and complaints. The adult Klüger, faced with the prospect of visiting the son of this hated great-aunt, is at a loss: 'Was soll ich nun ihrem Sohn sagen, wenn er nach ihr fragt, er, der sie geliebt hat, mich, die sie gehaßt hat, mit schmalem, spitzem Kinderhaß?' [So what could I say to her son, who loved her as a child loves his mother, when he questioned me, who hated her with a child's needle-sharp aversion [...]?] (*weiter leben*, p. 13; *Still Alive*, p. 20). Of this episode Katja Schubert writes that, although the child's perspective dominates the narrative, Klüger does not create the illusion of being able to recreate a sustained rendering of the child's voice.[36] Instead, Klüger provides emotional authenticity in the way she remembers feeling and thinking as a child, which still shapes her at the time of writing.

The child's way of seeing things differently also provides a source of humour in the text. For example, Klüger recalls having found her father's name as it stood on the sign outside his surgery, 'Doktor Viktor Klüger', a source of amusement: 'ich fand die Verdoppelung der Silbe "tor" lustig, als ich sie zum ersten Mal richtig lesen konnte. Die Erwachsenen fanden das nicht komisch, was mich erstaunte, wie so oft, diese Diskrepanz der Wahrnehmungen' [I was amused at the double end syllable *tor*. The grown-ups didn't see the point; another surprise, this discrepancy of perception] (*weiter leben*, pp. 25–26; *Still Alive*, p. 31). Klüger also describes her first outing with her mother after attaching the now compulsory Stars of David to their clothes. A woman compliments Klüger's mother on how the star matches her blouse, which Klüger finds 'mutig und witzig' [plucky and witty] (*weiter leben*, p. 50; *Still Alive*, p. 49); however, this is not echoed by her mother. Such moments of humour are not, though, intended to elicit a sentimental response from the reader, but rather help to establish a stark generational opposition throughout the text, which contributes to part of Klüger's project: to address what she regards as the problems of German remembrance culture.

Klüger considers that when the adults are not trying to keep knowledge from the child, they wilfully fail to acknowledge its cognisance, writing of adults' need to call into question children's ability to experience what is going on around them (*weiter leben*, p. 74). She cites the example of a recent television programme she has watched, in which footage of a group of hostages was shown. One of them, a child, was subsequently described in a newspaper as having been bored because it was apparently unable to understand what was happening. Klüger counters this, saying: 'das Kind war jedoch alt genug, um zu wissen, was mit ihm geschah, und war weder blind noch taub. Verdrängungsbedarf der Erwachsenen. Ich kenn das gut' [the child was old enough to know what was happening to it, and was neither blind nor deaf. Adults' need for repression. I know it well] (*weiter leben*, p. 73). In an essay on the child's voice in Holocaust literature, Naomi Sokoloff undertakes a comparison of the retrospective writing of childhood by adults with poetry written by children at the time, such as is included in *I Never Saw Another Butterfly*,[37] a collection of children's poetry written in the Theresienstadt ghetto in the early 1940s. Sokoloff observes:

> while the children in adult texts are often uncomprehending, the children's own poetry frequently features attempts at explanation — by way of philosophical observations or generalizations that take on the quality of aphorism, and that demonstrate an unmistakable desire to comprehend.[38]

Sokoloff attributes far greater cognitive powers to the children than do some of the adult writers she discusses, such as Louis Begley and Uri Orlev. Similarly, Klüger describes how, as an adult, she encounters incredulity at her having survived the Holocaust as a child, though more particularly at her having been conscious of her surroundings and experiences at the time. She recounts how she is asked, or rather told by people, both Germans and Americans: 'aber Sie waren doch viel zu jung, um sich an diese schreckliche Zeit erinnern zu können' [but surely you were far too young to be able to remember that terrible time!] (*weiter leben*, p. 73). Klüger responds: 'Ich denke dann, die wollen mir mein Leben nehmen, denn das Leben ist doch nur die verbrachte Zeit, das einzige, was wir haben, das machen sie mir streitig, wenn sie mir das Recht des Erinnerns in Frage stellen' [Then I think they want to take my life away from me, for isn't life only time that has passed, the only thing we have, and they challenge me for it, when they call into question my right to remember] (*weiter leben*, p. 73). At the same time, Suleiman writes of the trauma incurred by child victims who were forced to grow up too quickly, particularly before 'the formation of stable identity that we associate with adulthood'.[39] This echoes Klüger's comment on Levi's testimony *If This Is a Man* (1947), in which he explores the effects of Auschwitz on the individual's concept of identity. Klüger points out that, in contrast to her, he came to Auschwitz 'mit dem Selbstgefühl eines erwachsenen, fertigen Europäers dahin, [...] beheimatet und gefestigt' [with the self-esteem of a grown European, a rationalist, at home in Italy, secure in his identity] (*weiter leben*, p. 113; *Still Alive*, p. 95).

While Klüger seeks to deprecate what she sees as the adult's underestimation of the child by undermining it, she also uses this model to reflect more generally on German remembrance of the Holocaust and its victims. Klüger rejects what she considers the role of innocent victim that has been assigned to her. She describes a recent meeting with two young German students who have just completed their 'Zivildienst' [alternative national service] whitewashing the fences in Auschwitz (*weiter leben*, p. 69). Klüger writes that, while they were willing to believe anything about their own grandfathers, they would not believe a single bad word about the victims (*weiter leben*, p. 78). She considers that the national narrative has come to encourage such young people to be attuned to the stark differentiation between victims and perpetrators, the result of which is that they hold up the victims on pedestals (*weiter leben*, p. 85) and, in doing so, fail to engage meaningfully with their experience. Furthermore, Klüger considers there to be a lack of differentiation amongst victim groups that denies individual suffering and experience. She is critical of the fence-painters' failure to distinguish between Polish and Jewish concentration camp inmates (*weiter leben*, p. 71). In Klüger's view, such public remembrance of the victims as does take place is reductionist and blocks a more constructive engagement with the past: 'so werden alle Opfer, alle Lager in der Zusammenfassung nivelliert' [in this way all the victims and all the camps are generalized and placed on the same level] (*weiter leben*, p. 83).

Moreover, Klüger seeks to break down the stark binary between victim and perpetrator, emphasizing her point by recounting how, even as a child, she rejected the label of 'innocent victim'. She cites two examples of this. First, she recalls a tram journey in Vienna, during which a stranger (a non-Jew) handed her an orange as the tram passed through a tunnel. Her reaction, she recalls, was not one of gratitude, but rather of outrage: 'ich gefiel mir nicht in dieser Rolle. Ich wollte mich als oppositionell statt als Opfer sehen' [I didn't like the role of the passive victim [...]. I wanted an assertive, oppositional role] (*weiter leben*, p. 51; *Still Alive*, p. 49). The act, which involved some risk for the giver, did little to help in her view, and was in essence no more than a 'sentimentale Geste' [sentimental gesture] (*weiter leben*, p. 51; *Still Alive*, p. 49).

Second, she recalls how, after the end of the war, she submitted two poems she had composed about her experience of Auschwitz to the local Bavarian newspaper. One of her poems was published, but only half of it was printed, and it was included in the context of a story about children in the Holocaust intended for a 'kinderliebendes Publikum' [child-loving public] (*weiter leben*, p. 200). In addition, the text was accompanied by 'eine Zeichnung, ein verlumptes, verschrecktes Kind darstellend' [a drawing of a ragged, terrorized child] (*weiter leben*, p. 200; *Still Alive*, p. 154), which, much to the young author's annoyance, bears a faint resemblance to her. The graphic allusion to the child victim in the article is exactly contrary to Klüger's desired depiction. Klüger recalls her strong reaction against this labelling: 'ich wollte ja als eine junge Lyrikerin gelten, die im Lager gewesen war, nicht als das Umgekehrte, das KZ-Kind, das Verse geschrieben hatte' [I wanted to be a young poet who had been in the camps, not a former child prisoner who had written some heart-wrenching verses] (*weiter leben*, p. 200; *Still Alive*, p. 155). As Caroline Schaumann argues, 'characteristic of a German nadir of confronting the past at the time, the editors deprived Klüger of her voice, reduced her to a passive, helpless victim pleading for compassion, and stifled her identity as a survivor with sentimental preconceptions'.[40] This episode proves representative for a broader argument that Klüger constructs throughout her text with regard to German memory culture and the commemoration of the Holocaust. By the reduction of her experience to a sentimental tale of misfortune, Klüger considers her story and, consequently, her experience, to have been both disregarded and de-individualized. This, she argues, leads to an avoidance of critical engagement with the victims on a broader scale. It also resonates with criticism of Anne Frank's reception, and Adorno's comments cited above, to the effect that Anne Frank provides a single, innocent identification-figure, which prevents any real engagement with the totality and variety of the horror of Nazi persecution.[41] Klüger revisits this idea later in the text, recounting a speech she delivered on memoirs by camp survivors. The problem with such accounts is, in her view, the fact that the author is alive at the end (*weiter leben*, p. 140). In the tale of survival, which represents an exception, lies the risk that the dead will be forgotten.

Having asserted her dissatisfaction with the traditional view of the innocent, passive, and unknowing child in the context of the Holocaust, Klüger expands on this throughout her text with a critical evaluation of works which have used this approach. She cites in particular the example of the Buchenwald child. The success of the film version of Apitz's *Nackt unter Wölfen*, which was internationally well received, was due, in Apitz's opinion, to the fact that the rescue of the Jewish child represented a 'sentimentaler Brennpunkt' [sentimental focal point].[42] It is precisely this, however, which Klüger condemns. She considers that the story of the innocent child being rescued has a reductive effect on the suffering of those in the concentration camps to a point where critical engagement and memory work is no longer possible. She claims that those who propagated this tale 'infantilisierten, verkleinerten und verkitschten damit den großen Völkermord [...] im 20. Jahrhundert' [thus infantilized, shrank, and sentimentalized the great genocide [...] of the twentieth century] (*weiter leben*, p. 75). Although Apitz's novel has been translated into over thirty languages and was hailed, certainly in the GDR, as a seminal Holocaust text, it might also be charged with a sentimentalizing tendency. In an article to mark the centenary of Apitz's birth, Volker Müller comments:

> Es steht nicht im Roman, dass für Stefan, der im letzten Moment von der Todestransportliste genommen wurde, der Sinto-Junge Willy Blum ins Gas musste. Das zu sagen ist des Historikers Pflicht. Auch wenn es eine willkommene Legende stört.[43]
>
> [Nowhere in the novel does it state that in order for Stefan to be taken off the transport list at the last moment, the Sinto-boy Willy Blum had to go to the gas chamber. It is the historian's duty to say that. Even if it destroys a comforting legend.]

Klüger, for whom such sentimentalizing is anathema, concludes: 'und der Roman über dieses Kind ist trotz der Achtung, die er genießt, ein Kitschroman' [and the novel about this child is, in spite of the attention that it enjoys, a pulp novel] (*weiter leben*, p. 75). Her objection to kitsch runs deep and can, as Jerry Schuchalter has argued, be interpreted as 'a form of denial, a means of averting complexity and contradiction. In art it leads to sentimentality and autocratic rule over the interpretation of reality.'[44] And the trouble with kitsch, too, as Klüger herself states, is that it is 'immer plausibel, bis man ihn durchschaut und die Wahrheit ihn in seiner Lächerlichkeit entlarvt' [always credible until you see through it and the truth exposes it in all its ridiculousness].[45]

In a further rejection of the role of innocent victim, Klüger recounts a visit to the cinema, to see Walt Disney's *Snow White* (1938). In doing so, she violated race laws which forbade Jews from attending. During the film, Klüger realizes that she is sitting near the baker's daughter, whose family were hard-line Nazis. At the end of the film, the girl stops Klüger and declares that, if she sees her in the cinema again, she will report her to the authorities. Klüger uses the story of *Snow White*, which the children had just viewed, as a frame for recounting her experience of persecution. Jennifer Taylor reads this episode as a reflection of Klüger's relationship with her mother, suggesting that Klüger 'likens her mother to the fairy tale Witch and herself to Snow White, the innocent victim',[46] since her mother had insisted that she attend the performance. However, it is also possible to see the baker's daughter cast in the role of the wicked queen. She stands 'im eigenen Hause, den Spiegel ihrer rassischen Reinheit vor Augen' [in her own house, the magic mirror of her racial purity before her eyes] (*weiter leben*, p. 48; *Still Alive*, p. 47). Yet Klüger also deliberately complicates even this constellation of roles, for the baker's daughter, seen here in the role of the wicked stepmother, is herself a child and consequently, as Schaumann puts it, the victim of the 'poisonous pedagogy'[47] with which she was being socialized at the time.

Klüger's inclusion of this episode is not used as an opportunity to evoke pity or sentimentality, though her outrage is infectious. She is scathing of the desire for a fairy-tale happy ending: 'Nur darf der wahrheitsliebende Leser das Happy-End meiner Kindheitsirrfahrten (wenn man das einfache Weiterleben überhaupt als Happy-End bezeichnen will) nicht auf ein Hoffnungskonto [...] setzen' [All I can do is warn the reader not to invest in optimism vouchers and not to give credit [...] for the happy end of my childhood's odyssey — if indeed simple survival can be called a happy end] (*weiter leben*, p. 108; *Still Alive*, p. 91). In an essay on the function of fairy tales in Holocaust fiction, Lawrence Langer writes: '"Once upon a time," the traditional refuge for children always ended "and they lived happily ever after," assuring an uninterrupted adventure from past to future.'[48] For Klüger, her survival is not reason enough to take away a positive message from her text. This would only result in the kind of response that, she argues, is unhelpful in coming to terms with the legacy of Nazism. We find this reflected in the title of her text: 'weiter leben' represents a complex and difficult endeavour to live on with the memory of the trajectory her life has taken. It is not to be taken as a signal of relief or recuperation.

By offering a text in which the child's experience is so entirely removed from the sentimental, Klüger insists that her readers engage with her narrative and reflect more critically on the commemoration of the victims of the Holocaust in post-reunification Germany. Amongst German contemporaries, Klüger feels that her own memories are still marginalized. She describes a scene in which she and some German friends in Göttingen are discussing situations in which they have felt trapped. Klüger automatically thinks of her journey to Auschwitz, yet she feels unable to recall this story as it is not 'salonfähig' [socially acceptable] (*weiter leben*, p. 110). She addresses the German reader directly: 'über eure Kriegserlebnisse dürft und könnt ihr sprechen, liebe Freunde, ich über meine nicht. Meine Kindheit fällt in das schwarze Loch dieser Diskrepanz' [you are permitted to and can speak about your war experiences, dear friends, but I am not and cannot. My childhood falls into the black hole that is this discrepancy] (*weiter leben*, p. 111). Klüger demands to know why tales of the bombing war, expulsions, and death are deemed topics for possible discussion, and yet the relevant portion of her own experience, the journey on the transport to Auschwitz, is not. This scene demonstrates what she sees as the fundamental issue with memorial culture in post-reunification Germany: that the version of the past considered 'appropriate' marginalizes the full spectrum of memories of this period of German history. Her aim throughout the text is to provoke her readers to engage critically and constructively with this issue, rather than passively acknowledging Jewish suffering en masse. She exhorts her readers: 'laßt euch doch mindestens reizen, verschanzt euch nicht, sagt nicht von vornherein, das gehe euch nichts an [...]. Werdet streitsüchtig, sucht die Auseinandersetzung' [allow yourselves at least to be provoked, don't dig yourselves in, don't say from the outset that it doesn't affect you [...]. Be argumentative, seek debate] (*weiter leben*, p. 142). This is precisely what the German text especially, dedicated specifically to 'den Göttinger Freunden — ein deutsches Buch' [Göttingen friends — a German book] (*weiter leben*, p. 284), sets out to achieve. Her autobiography was intended, as she stated in an interview in 1995, not 'als Selbsttherapie, sondern als Kommunikation' [as catharsis but as communication].[49] As Schaumann suggests, Klüger's text becomes 'an invitation to a dialogue' that is 'particularly courageous and daring'.[50] Klüger rejects clear-cut paradigms of victims and perpetrators that she considers both unhelpful and even dangerous. The figures in her text are, as Stephan Braese comments, not forced into a straightforward victim–perpetrator binary: 'ihre Opfer sind keine Engel, ihre Täter keine Bestien' [her victims are not angels, her perpetrators are not beasts].[51] Her call is for a more pluralistic approach: a version of the past in the public sphere that accommodates the range of experiences and memories of Nazism and that, Klüger argues, would result in a more critical and productive commemoration of the past.

'Ich bin ein Lebensschmuggler' [I am a smuggler of life]: *Die Absonderung* (1991)

Like Klüger, Georges-Arthur Goldschmidt left the country of his birth during childhood and has lived in France for most of his adult life. Born just outside Hamburg in 1928 into a Jewish family that had converted to Protestantism in the nineteenth century, Goldschmidt spent his early childhood unaware of his Jewish heritage. However, in 1938, his parents sent him and his brother out of Germany, to live with an acquaintance in Florence. This separation from his parents, whom he never saw again, marked the 'Grundzäsur' [fundamental caesura] of his formative years.[52] After the introduction of the Race Laws in Italy in 1939, the two boys were forced to seek refuge with an aristocratic relative in France, where they were housed in a Catholic boarding school in the Savoy Alps. The German occupation of the region in 1942 constituted a further threat to the boy's safety and he was hidden by farmers. After the war, he ended up in a Jewish orphanage in Paris, and after completing his schooling and studying at the Sorbonne he became a secondary-school teacher of German, and a writer, essayist, and prolific translator of German works into French.[53]

A further similarity between Goldschmidt and Klüger is that, despite having lived in France for the greater part of his adult life, Goldschmidt chose to write an autobiographical account of childhood in German. *Die Absonderung* is one of a number of broadly autobiographical texts by Goldschmidt that he has written over a thirty-year period.[54] He first wrote three autobiographical works in French: *Le Miroir quotidien* [The Daily Mirror] (1981), *Un jardin en Allemagne* [A Garden in Germany] (1986), and *La Forêt interrompue* [The Interrupted Forest] (1991). In the afterword to the German edition of *Un jardin en Allemagne*, *Ein Garten in Deutschland* [A Garden in Germany], Goldschmidt asserts that he could not have written an account of his childhood in Germany *in German*: 'eine Erzählung wie "Ein Garten in Deutschland" hätte in der Muttersprache (das Deutsche) wegen der erlebten Vergangenheit und der Erfahrung der Trennung nicht so entstehen können, wie sie eben im Französischen entstanden ist' [a story like *A Garden in Germany* could not have emerged in my mother tongue (German) as it did in French because of the past I underwent and the experience of separation].[55] It was, he writes, not possible to write about his Heimat in his mother tongue.

Goldschmidt's initial inability to write autobiographically in German (despite teaching it to others and working as a translator) is characterized by his sense of dislocation from his homeland and the trauma of separation from his parents, whom he never saw again after his flight from Germany. He differentiates elsewhere between his 'Muttersprache' (German) and his 'Lebenssprache' (French).[56]

Goldschmidt managed, however, to overcome this linguistic crisis to write the third of his autobiographical texts, *Die Absonderung*, which was published in spring 1991 and was the first book Goldschmidt had written in German. His decision to use German to write about his experience of persecution was made consciously: 'Meine autobiografischen Bücher habe ich [...] auf Deutsch geschrieben, auch als Provokation, um den Deutschen zu zeigen, dass sie mich nicht totgekriegt hatten' [I [...] wrote my autobiographical books in German, also as a provocation, to show the Germans that they hadn't managed to kill me].[57]

Die Absonderung was awarded the Geschwister-Scholl-Preis in 1991 and was received overwhelmingly positively in the German press.[58] The narrative begins in 1938 as Goldschmidt and his elder brother are travelling to Florence. The text has a third-person narrator, referred to only as 'er' throughout the text, and it is striking that, of the authors discussed in this chapter, Goldschmidt is the only one who does not use a first-person narrator. The protagonist remains unnamed throughout the account. Goldschmidt's entire *oeuvre* treats the long-term effects of his exile as a child in some way, but, as Stefan Willer points out in his essay on language in Goldschmidt's texts, it is only in *Über die Flüsse* [Crossing the Rivers] that 'a memorizing and authenticating "I" is introduced'.[59] Thus, in *Die Absonderung* there is a marked distance within the text between author and subject, as well as the distance between the remembering adult and the child he used to be.

Unlike the retrospective narrative perspective in *weiter leben*, in *Die Absonderung* the child's perspective dominates and is almost entirely uninterrupted by interjections which might show the reader that the events are being recalled from over fifty years later. The narrative spans the period from 1938 to 1944. The child spends almost the entire war in the boarding school in Savoy where, though he is not consciously aware of it, he is being hidden from the authorities. The immediate threat to the boy's safety comes, however, not from the Nazis but from his fellow pupils and his teachers, at whose hands he suffers abuse. He endures this life at the school until the Nazi occupation of the region makes it too dangerous for him to stay there, and the narrative ends as he departs the school, aided by the headmistress, in the hope of hiding more effectively from the Nazis in the mountains.

Like Klüger's text, *Die Absonderung* begins with an aura of secrecy and taboo which can be framed in Freudian terms.[60] Goldschmidt recalls the way in which his parents kept his Jewish ancestry from him, and that this led him to associate Judaism with shame and guilt: 'zu Hause, es war 1938 gewesen, hatte er nicht bleiben dürfen: er war schuldig, von ihm hatte man etwas gewußt, was er selber noch nicht wußte' [in 1938 he had no longer been allowed to remain at home: he was guilty; people had known something about him which he did not even know himself] (*Absonderung*, p. 14). For the child, there is 'etwas Unheimliches' [something uncanny] (*Absonderung*, p. 15) about being Jewish which he does not understand. He recalls:

> Die Eltern schwiegen, wenn er eintrat, saßen steif da, als wollten sie zeigen, daß sie gar nicht von ihm redeten. [...] Sie flüsterten sich ununterbrochen zu [...]. Das Wort 'Jude' kam immer wieder vor, ein Wort aus der Bibel, er hatte nicht verstanden, warum sie so unruhig waren, wo sie doch von der Bibel sprachen. Aber dann war ihm plötzlich eingefallen, daß in der Sonntagsschule, wenn das

Wort Jude fiel, der Pastor ihn immer angeschaut hatte, und das Wort hatte ihm Angst gemacht. (*Absonderung*, pp. 14–15)

[His parents were silent when he entered, sitting there stiffly as though they wanted to show that they had not just been talking about him. [...] They whispered to one another constantly [...]. The word 'Jew' kept coming up, a word from the Bible, he had not understood why they should be so troubled when they were talking about the Bible, of all things. But then it suddenly came to him that, during Sunday School, when the word 'Jew' came up, the pastor had always looked at him, and the word frightened him.]

His parents' reluctance to talk about the subject, coupled with the stern looks of the pastor, lead him to believe that being Jewish is something shameful. He immediately associates this with the shame he feels at having masturbated for the first time, and consequently his Jewish identity becomes inextricably linked with his emerging sexuality.[61] From this point onwards, the narrative is dominated by the child's obsession with his body, which holds a terrible fascination for him, being both the source of exploration and pleasure, but simultaneously the source of his separation from his home and his parents. His mother, a devoted follower of the teaching of the Lutheran theologian Johann Hinrich Wichern, maintained a view of sex and sexuality which was 'geprägt von strenger autoritärer Triebunterdrückung und Körperfeindlichkeit' [characterized by strict, authoritarian repression and hostility towards the body].[62] This is shown to have had a profound influence on the young Goldschmidt.

Thus, the onset of puberty, which ought to mark the beginning of the physical development into adulthood, is negatively connoted, and the natural trajectory of childhood is stifled by overwhelming feelings of guilt and shame. In this way, for Goldschmidt the body becomes the site of his childhood trauma, both literally and as a symbol of violence and loss. Eva Lezzi considers the body to be the 'Austauschorgan zwischen Außenwelt und inneren Vorstellungen, zwischen Vergangenheit und Gegenwart, Landschaftswahrnehmung und Erinnerung' [organ of exchange between the external and inner worlds, between past and present, perception of landscape and memory].[63] For example, the boy's sense of physical, social, and linguistic dislocation on arriving at the school is reflected in his frequent sensation that he has no control over his body. As a punishment for having become lost and returned late from a walk, he is caned. He recalls: 'Da hielt er sich die Finger vors Gesicht, zusammengedrückt [...], eine Geste, die er an sich selber noch nicht gekannt hatte' [He held up his fingers, pressed together [...], a gesture he had not noticed himself making before] (*Absonderung*, p. 83). Similarly, when he visits his guardian, he feels he cannot control his body out of fear: 'Erst auf dem Weg zurück ins Kinderheim kam er zu sich selbst und konnte wieder ganz Körper werden' [Only when he was on his way back to the children's home again could he relax and be completely at one with his body] (*Absonderung*, p. 54). Baker persuasively reads the boy's masochistic and increasingly sado-masochistic fantasies as 'the literary re-enactment of his traumatization as a child'.[64]

Indeed, masturbation and sexual fantasies constitute the child's means of dealing with loss, pain, and exile. He endures violent abuse throughout his childhood and adolescence at the school, including physical beatings and sodomy. It is ironic that, after the war breaks out, this persecution is due to his nationality, and he recalls being ashamed to be German and associated with the enemy (*Absonderung*, p. 56). As a victim, he develops means with which to deal with his experience: 'Er tat, wenn er geohrfeigt wurde, als wäre er das Opfer. Schon lange war der Schmerz vorbei, als er noch den Verzweifelten spielte' [When he was beaten, he acted as though he were the victim. Even long after the pain had gone, he still played the part of the desperate one] (*Absonderung*, p. 102). While the child fears such beatings, he also expresses a sense of pride at having been the recipient of such attacks:

> wenn man wüßte, wie weh das tut, würde man ihn nicht prügeln. Seltsam, aber zugleich dieser Stolz in ihm, daß er es war, den man da züchtigte, daß er es war, der sich wand und der heulte, daß ihn alle anderen dabei sehen konnten. (*Absonderung*, p. 69)
>
> [if they knew how much it hurt, they wouldn't beat him. Strange, though, that at the same time he felt a sense of pride that he was the one being punished, that he was the one who was writhing and howling, that they could all see him doing it.]

For Goldschmidt, trauma is mapped onto the site of the body: flight, exile, and persecution are visible scars. The boy's journey into puberty is also the journey through persecution. The explicit nature of the boy's sexuality makes this text unusual among those that narrate the child's experience of the Holocaust. In *Die Absonderung*, the child's innocence is removed; and indeed, his sexuality is a central aspect of the text. In addition, the perverse pride he takes in the beatings received complicates the reader's view of him as an innocent victim, though it is possible to recognize this as a way of coping which enables him to endure the persecution. Not only the narrative but also childhood itself is pervaded by images of the sexual. As Barbara Breysach suggests: 'das Bild dieser Kindheit ist [...] von Anfang an stark sexualisiert und niemals "unschuldig"' [this view of childhood is [...] from the very start strongly sexualized and never 'innocent'].[65]

And yet the boy is also still a child. When he encounters three *Wehrmacht* officers (having just left the school in order to evade discovery and deportation), they remind him of his toys at home in Germany: 'zwei behelmte Soldaten — genau wie damals noch seine Bleisoldaten' [two soldiers wearing helmets — just like his old tin soldiers] (*Absonderung*, p. 171). The child observes them, and the reader, through the child's perspective, sees the soldiers as the toys:

> ein Kommandowagen der Wehrmacht mit auf die Kühlerhaube herabgeklappter Windschutzscheibe, breit mit genau den gelb-grünen Tarnflecken, die es auch auf seinen Spielfahrzeugen gegeben hatte, als er den Feldmarschall Mackensen auf der Lafette eines Geschützes durch das Zimmer fahren ließ. (*Absonderung*, p. 172)
>
> [a *Wehrmacht* command vehicle, the windscreen folded down over the bonnet, broad and with the very same yellow-green camouflage that had been on his toy vehicles when he had driven Field Marshal Mackensen through the room on the gun carriage of a heavy artillery piece.]

Similarly, Goldschmidt depicts the boy with a gentle irony at times. For example, when it becomes clear that the Germans are rounding up Jewish children, the headmistress helps to conceal him. As she hands him his coat, sending him off to hide, he performs a gesture which seems intended to put her at ease:

> Im Vorzimmer wurde ihm der dicke Wintermantel weit offen von der Anstaltsleiterin entgegengehalten [...]. Wie um zu zeigen, daß er es gewohnt war, bedient zu werden, drehte er sich um und streckte die Arme hinter sich aus, wie er es seinen Vater hatte tun sehen. (*Absonderung*, p. 169)
>
> [In the hall, the headmistress held up the thick winter coat wide open for him [...]. As though to show that he was used to being served, he turned around and stuck out his arms behind him as he had seen his father do.]

The text also includes voids in which the reader understands more than the child can know or express. For example, as his passport is checked, the boy considers it odd that certain passports bear the letter 'J', since they belong to elderly people and he knows that the 'J' stands for 'Jugendlicher' [youth]. However, it then suddenly occurs to him, immediately after it will have occurred to the reader, 'es konnte auch "Jude" heißen' [it could also mean 'Jew'] (*Absonderung*, pp. 22–23). In addition, the reader's outrage at the abuse he suffers at the hands not only of the other schoolboys, but also the teachers and the headmistress, is exacerbated by the boy's own acceptance of the situation as normal. In another episode, after the boy has been hiding from the Germans, he is warmed and given fresh clothes: 'er stand da, nackt, weiß, kindhaft und schuldlos, ein zu hoch geschossener, noch unreifer kleiner Junge' [he stood there, naked, white, childlike and innocent, a boy who had shot up too much, but who was still immature and little] (*Absonderung*, p. 176). In this moment, the dual shame he feels of masturbation and Jewishness disappears, and his burgeoning sexuality is allowed to be what it is: the beginning of growing up. As he comments at the end of this passage: 'Er fühlte sein Gesicht vor Röte glühen, vielleicht wußte man, daß er an sich das große Wunder entdeckt hatte' [He felt his face glow red, perhaps someone knew that he discovered the great marvel by himself] (*Absonderung*, p. 176). In contrast to earlier accounts, his self-exploration is described in positive terms: the taboo, having been broken, is now bypassed. The positive connotations of 'glühen' [to glow] and 'Wunder' [marvel] reinforce this shift.

In *Die Absonderung*, childhood becomes inextricably linked with place rather than with knowledge, or the lack of it, and an important underlying concern of the text is the search for Heimat. Goldschmidt describes this in the opening pages:

> damals 1944, in Hoch-Savoyen, als man wieder tief und unruhig atmen konnte. Immer richtete sich dann, in der Deutlichkeit des Abends, der Blick in die Richtung der Heimat. Denn es wurde eine ganze Kindheit damit verbracht, sich die Heimat zu vergegenwärtigen. (*Absonderung*, p. 14)
>
> [back in 1944, in Upper Savoy, when you could breathe deep and loudly again. Then the gaze always returned, in the clarity of evening, in the direction of home. For a whole childhood was spent trying to visualize home.]

His entire childhood becomes an effort at conjuring up his lost homeland. Goldschmidt's flight from Germany as a child leads to a rupture from the site of his childhood, in a real and a metaphorical sense. Breysach describes Goldschmidt's situation as an exile from his mother tongue and, consequently, from childhood: 'ausgeschlossen aus dem Deutschen, der Ausdrucksweise der Empfindung, wurde Kindheit zu einem Anderswo, zu etwas Unerschließbaren' [barred from German, the expression of feelings, childhood became an otherwhere, something inaccessible].[66] The fact that he is always longing for his Heimat is also reflected in his journeying on. Nowhere is safe, and the end of the narrative sees him about to move on again to another farm where he may or may not be safe for long, as the Germans are still out looking for Jews. Again, his trajectory is the result of other influences.

German is the language responsible for the trauma of Goldschmidt's early childhood: the separation from his parents and from his homeland. As an adult, he retains the association between loss and childhood, as German remains the 'Sprache der Kindheit' [language of childhood].[67] In his introduction to the first edition of the text, Peter Handke writes:

> Goldschmidt hat so etwas wie ein Traumbuch geschrieben: in dem Sinn, daß er für Situationen und Ereignisse, für die es bis dahin keine Sprache gab, wie somnambul, planlos, vorsatzlos, dafür um so klarer und unmittelbarer eine solche — nicht findet, sondern einfach hinsetzt.[68]
>
> [Goldschmidt has written something approaching a dream book: in the sense that he sets down (not finds) situations and events for which previously there had been no language, as though sleepwalking, without plan or purpose, and because of this does it more clearly and directly.]

Thus, in Handke's view, Goldschmidt has not only overcome his own *Sprachkrise* by writing in his native tongue but has also overcome the more common problem of finding a language with which to express the trauma of his youth. This has, in a sense, been the impetus behind all his literary works. Indeed, Goldschmidt has claimed that he is not an author and that he could not write a convincingly fictionalized account: 'er könne nur über sein Leben erzählen und nicht mehr' [he can tell the story of his life and nothing more].[69] This is precisely what he achieves in *Die Absonderung*, and what offers a fresh approach to the subject of growing up and the effects of racial persecution in the Third Reich. Goldschmidt's text, part of a broader autobiographical project, gives the reader an account of feelings, of the effects of loss, fear, separation, and trauma. In Barth's view, the child's lack of understanding — he does not know why he has been sent away — causes the reader to experience his persecution more directly, 'da er [Goldschmidt] einer an Fakten mageren, aber an emotionalen Reaktionen umso reicheren Narrative folgt' [since he [Goldschmidt] pursues a narrative which is short on facts but rich in emotional reactions].[70] At the same time, Goldschmidt eschews sentimentality, and never presents himself as a victim. In her comparison of *Die Absonderung* and *Bruchstücke* [Fragments], Baker argues that, unlike Wilkomirski, whom I discuss in the following chapter, Goldschmidt 'appears first and foremost as a writer and translator', and never as a victim 'asking for the reader's empathy, pity, or understanding'.[71] In this way, he fights against the misuse of his childhood, pressing the reader to *think* as well as feel.

Childhood's Games: *Erwachsenenspiele* (1997)

Günter Kunert's *Erwachsenenspiele* was one of several autobiographical texts published in the 1990s in which the author sought to deal with a double legacy: of having grown up under Nazism and having lived as an adult in the GDR.[72] Kunert's text stands out among them in that his experience of the Third Reich was one of persecution at the hands of the Nazis. As the son of a Jewish mother and non-Jewish father, he was classed as a 'Mischling ersten Grades' ['Mischling' of the first degree] by the state.[73] This categorization put Kunert, and those like him, in a precarious position: on the one hand he was protected from deportation by virtue of his 'Aryan' heritage, yet on the other he was unable to complete his secondary education and lived in constant fear that his protected status would be revoked (*Erwachsenenspiele*, p. 52). His mother and father survived, but many other members of his family were deported and killed.

In *Erwachsenenspiele*, Kunert narrates his life from his birth in 1929 to his emigration from the GDR in 1979 following the expulsion of Wolf Biermann. The sections recounting Kunert's life in the GDR have received the greatest portion of critical attention, and responses have been mixed.[74] Here, I want to focus on his account of childhood, which constitutes the first of nine books that make up the text and which ends with the arrival of the Soviets in Berlin and the end of the Second World War. In spite of the grave nature of the events in *Erwachsenenspiele* and its ultimately pessimistic outlook, Kunert's account is characterized by a playfulness that is alluded to in the title. In contrast to the opening of Klüger's and Goldschmidt's texts, which are rooted in an aura of secrecy and taboo, Kunert's autobiography begins with the child at play: 'oben auf dem Schrank hockt ein Indianer, das Gewehr im Anschlag. Gespannter Blick über Kimme und Korn in Erwartung der Feinde. [...] Das Visier ist auf hundert Meter Entfernung eingestellt. Der Indianer lauert reglos. Der Indianer bin ich' [up on the cupboard an Indian is crouching, weapon at the ready. Gaze focused through the sights in expectation of the enemy. [...] The aim is set at 100 metres' distance. The Indian lies in wait. The Indian is me] (*Erwachsenenspiele*, p. 9). This initial scene is striking in that, while it establishes the child as the focus of the narrative, the young Kunert is shown in a position of height, looking down on the scene. In contrast to the more conventional child's perspective, the view from below, here the young Kunert is looking down on the world and, what is more, he is armed. The fact that it is only at the end of the first paragraph that Kunert reveals that he is the Indian reinforces this, and reminds the reader of many of Kunert's contemporaries, who would indeed be armed with guns only a few years later. It also signals Kunert's very particular position in the Third Reich as the son of 'mixed' parentage. On the one hand, he can be viewed retrospectively as having been a victim of National Socialism, and indeed most of his family on his mother's side was deported; on the other hand, he is protected by his 'German blood'. In the course of the text, the 'Indianer' [Indian] also becomes a symbol of the process of growing up. Kunert explains that 'es ist keineswegs leicht und einfach, Indianer zu werden' [it is not at all easy or straightforward to become an Indian] (*Erwachsenenspiele*, p. 12): rites of passage must be undertaken before the child can consider himself, and be considered, a true Indian. Here Kunert couples the self-assured tone of the child's voice with the notion of coming of age, which will be a focus of the text.

For Kunert, the state of being a child is one of creative freedom, and when the individual grows up, this quality can be lost or retained. In an interview with *Die Welt*, Kunert cited his love of biographies, including one of Albert Einstein. He commented: 'auch Einstein hat ein starkes Maß an Kindlichkeit besessen, sonst hätte er nie so unbelastet seine Entdeckungen machen können. Wenn die Psyche eingeklammert und verfestigt ist, kommt nichts mehr' [Einstein, too, had a good deal of childishness about him, otherwise he would not have been able to make his discoveries in so unencumbered a way. When the psyche is closed off and rigid, nothing new can happen].[75] While the first part of *Erwachsenenspiele* is concerned with the child's experience of the Third Reich, the child's perspective as a narrative device is used sparingly. Kunert employs it primarily to comic effect and to demonstrate the uniqueness of the child's view of Nazism. In order to demonstrate his experience of the Allied bombing of Berlin, for example, Kunert uses the language of the fairy tale, in a manner similar to Martin Walser in *Ein springender Brunnen*. He writes: 'sodann kündigt sich von weit her den verängstigten Liliputanern das Heranschreiten eines blinden, übermächtigen Gulliver an. [...] Hysterie erfaßt die Kellerinsassen. Gulliver stapft davon, das Licht flammt auf, die Gesichter haben die Farbe der Wände angenommen' [then, from far away, the approach of a blind, overwhelming Gulliver announces itself to the frightened Lilliputians. [...] The occupants of the cellar became hysterical. Gulliver stomps away, light flares up, faces became the same colour as the walls] (*Erwachsenenspiele*, p. 45). In his description of bombing as the trudging of Gulliver, and in drawing an affinity between the terrified German civilians and the fictional Lilliputians, Kunert encourages the reader to view this experience from below, conveying a more emotionally charged sense of terror and confusion, not least because, as Kunert reminds his reader, he was secretly on the side of the bombers.

This is not an attempt at creating the child's perspective, but rather a self-reflexive performance of a view from below. Elsewhere in the text, the child's voice is framed by the ironic tone of the adult narrator, thus removing any hint of childish naivety. In a scene which echoes Goldschmidt's account of mistaking the 'J' on a passport for 'Jugendlicher' [youth] (rather than 'Jude' [Jew]), Kunert recalls examining his mother's identity papers. He comments: 'Zwar muss sie keinen Stern tragen, doch ihre Kennkarte und ihre Lebensmittelkarten weisen unübersehbar das "J" auf, von dem keiner annehmen würde, dass es die Abkürzung für Japaner wäre' [Although she does not have to wear the star, her identity card and ration cards are marked unmistakably with a 'J': no-one would suppose it was an abbreviation for 'Japanese'] (*Erwachsenenspiele*, pp. 52–53). Rather than supplying a void for the reader to fill with their knowledge of the period, Kunert colludes with the reader, and in doing so exposes the absurdity of Nazi race laws, at the hands of which he suffered throughout his youth.

Like both Klüger and Goldschmidt, Kunert recounts how, during his childhood, his parents withheld knowledge and information from him. He writes that there were tensions within families which were never explained and silence reigned: 'Nähere ich mich einer Streiterei, verstummen die Streitenden' [If I get near a dispute, the disputing parties are silent] (*Erwachsenenspiele*, p. 26). His parents seek to protect him by shielding him from problems which he is deemed too young to understand. In response, the young Kunert becomes increasingly curious, eager to discover more. He recalls: 'auf die Sprache, auf das Sprechen, auf die Sprechenden sind meine Ohren fledermausartig ausgerichtet. Da wird vom "Affidavit" geredet, was für mich komisch und zoologisch klingt' [my ears, like a bat's, are oriented towards language, speaking, and speakers. Someone talks about 'affidavit', which to my ears sounds strange and zoological] (*Erwachsenenspiele*, p. 29). This comment echoes Klüger's recollection of her childish delight in words and sounds, as well as her curiosity. In his depiction of this scene, Kunert draws attention to the autonomy of the child, its capacity for knowledge, and the curiosity which would seem to characterize it.

Kunert views his life as having been repeatedly disrupted by historical events, even during his childhood. He considers that his generation has been marked by the Third Reich and by the *Wende*. He criticizes the demand for his life story to be divided according to historical events: 'heute sind wir gezwungen, zwei Perioden zu unterscheiden und sie, ohne Spur von Blasphemie, analog und kurz zu benennen: vor Hitler und nach Hitler' [nowadays we are forced to distinguish between two periods and to name them, analogously and succinctly, without a trace of blasphemy: before Hitler and after Hitler].[76] Similarly, he considers the Berlin Wall to have been a 'Daseinzäsur für die Betroffenen' [existential caesura for those affected] (*Erwachsenenspiele*, p. 221): people distinguish between the time before the Wall and after it. While the latter is a self-imposed caesura, for those who, like Kunert, experienced both Nazism and the GDR, these thresholds come to mark their life retrospectively. Like de Bruyn in *Zwischenbilanz*, Kunert situates the account of his childhood in Berlin in the 1920s and 1930s firmly within the political and social developments of the day. He alludes to events in passing, and demonstrates their interrelatedness, both within the arch-narrative of history and within his own experience. For example, of the events of Kristallnacht he writes: 'ich nehme nur eine tobende Meute wahr, höre Geschrei, Glas splittert [...]. Man zieht mich vom Fenster zurück. Da ist der Teufel los, der deutsche Teufel. Der Kalender nennt das Datum: 9. November 1938' [I'm only aware of a riotous mob, I hear screams, glass shattering [...]. Someone pulls me back from the window. All hell has broken loose, a German hell. The calendar reads 9 November 1938] (*Erwachsenenspiele*, p. 36). Here his own recollections are placed alongside the retrospective knowledge that the event was a highly significant one. Similarly, he comments: 'inzwischen tagt die "Wannseekonferenz zur Endlösung der Judenfrage", mit deren Beschlüssen die fröhliche Skatrunde insgesamt zu Verlierern wird' [meanwhile the 'Wannsee Conference on the Final Solution to the Jewish Question' is taking place, at which decisions will be taken that turn the whole happy company of skat players into losers] (*Erwachsenenspiele*, p. 42). In the opening pages, he describes listening to the radio. He recounts:

Hinter zwei Klappen verbergen sich zwei ungleich große Schalltrichter, aus denen mir die Stimme Kurt Gerrons quäkend entgegenschallt: 'Und der Haifisch, der hat Zähne ...' Mein Lieblingslied. Noch weiß man nicht, daß es überhaupt einen Ort namens Theresienstadt gibt. Dort dreht Kurt Gerron einen Film, betitelt: 'Der Führer schenkt den Juden eine Stadt', und wird nach Ende der Dreharbeiten zu einem anderen Platz transportiert, der Auschwitz heißt. Von dem weiß man auch noch nichts. (*Erwachsenenspiele*, p. 10)

[Behind two flaps are concealed two unequally large horns out of which rings the voice of Kurt Gerron croaking: 'And the shark has teeth ...'. My favourite song. No one knows yet that there is a place called Theresienstadt. There, Kurt Gerron will make a film called *The Führer Gives a City to the Jews*, and when the filming is complete, he will be transported to a place called Auschwitz. No one knows anything about that yet either.]

This passage points the reader backwards towards the narrated timeframe, to the events situated in the past, and also forwards, to the Holocaust. For a reader looking back on the events, there is a strong sense of foreboding, as well as an evocation of a time before Auschwitz, which, in this depiction at least, has a quality of innocence about it. The phrase 'noch weiß man nicht' [no one knows yet] suggests the innocent ignorance of the child's perspective, and through this evokes the notion of a time of historical innocence, before the Holocaust had been perpetrated.

Like Grass in *Beim Häuten der Zwiebel*, Kunert aligns himself with the protagonist of Grimmelshausen's *Der Abenteuerliche Simplicissimus Teutsch* [The Adventures of Simplicius Simplicissimus] (1668), who embodies the 'quintessential German example for describing the horrors of war through the picaresque lens'.[77] The source of Kunert's sense of affinity with Simplicissimus can be identified in a comment made in Chapter 4 of Grimmelshausen's text. Addressing the reader, the narrator, Simplicissimus, declares that, although he would prefer not to show the reader the atrocities of war, 'so erfordert jedoch die Folge meiner Histori, daß ich der lieben Posterität hinterlasse, was vors Grausamkeiten in diesem unserm Teutschen Krieg hin und wieder verübet worden, zumalen mit meinem eigenen Exempel zu bezeugen' [my story demands that I set down for posterity the cruel atrocities that were committed from time to time in our German wars [...], as my own example demonstrates].[78] By writing about his own experience of the Third Reich, Kunert uses his life story as an example, and in doing so provides an account of the horrors of oppression and war for posterity. Kunert asserts: 'ich bin ein Nachfahre des Simplicius Simplicissimus. Einer, der dank seiner überwältigenden Naivität fast unangefochten durch die Schrecken und Scheußlichkeiten praktizierter Historie schlendert' [I am a descendant of Simplicius Simplicissimus; of one who, thanks to his overwhelming naivety, ambles almost entirely unchallenged through the terrors and abominations of history as practised] (*Erwachsenenspiele*, p. 57). 'Naivety' has a double meaning here: it describes not only the ignorance of the child figure unable to see the larger historical picture, but also his inability to comprehend the systematic deportation and murder of the Jewish people precisely because it was so utterly incredible. It also points to a continuity in his life since he again makes this link when writing about the GDR, referring to East Berlin as 'das sozialistische

Narrenparadies' [the socialist fools' paradise] (*Erwachsenenspiele*, p. 356). As has been said, Kunert uses the child's perspective primarily as a means with which to emphasize the uniqueness of the child's experience, and for comic effect. He does *not* argue that the child has a lack of understanding. The naivety he points to in this comment represents far more the confines of knowledge which are established by his parents, and the historical accident which seems to place him again and again at the centre of world events.

In all the works addressed so far in this study, we have seen the unsettling effects of the juxtaposition of the private and public realms. Kunert views his own youth as a 'staatlich verpfuschte Kindheit' [childhood botched by the state].[79] In the same way as Grass, de Bruyn, and Walser in the previous chapter, Kunert highlights the way in which the political has impinged upon the private: external events have destroyed his childhood. As Carsten Gansel observes: 'die erinnerte frühe Kindheit Kunerts erscheint dem Dichter als eine noch heile Welt — eine "Noch-nicht-Lebensphase", in der die späteren Ortsnamen des Schreckens "noch" keine Assoziationen bilden lassen' [the early childhood Kunert remembers appears to the poet as a still idyllic world — a 'Not-Yet stage of life' in which the place names later inextricably linked with terror as yet evoke no such associations].[80] Gansel's use of the phrase 'heile Welt' is reminiscent of de Bruyn's usage in *Zwischenbilanz*, and, just as de Bruyn laments the end of his childhood, which has been shattered by war and conflict,[81] so Kunert refers to his own youth as a 'verstörte Kindheit' [shell-shocked childhood].[82] Vees-Gulani argues that Kunert's childhood is curtailed by the war and by Nazism.[83] The abrupt end of Kunert's childhood through political events disrupts ideas about what it means to be a child.

However, Kunert counters this unnatural ending of childhood with several vivid accounts of his sexual development in puberty, emphasizing a more natural transition from childhood to adulthood. Indeed, this is even alluded to in the 'adult games' of the title, which Kunert plays as part of his first sexual encounters. He describes his sexual awakening in the following way: 'Nahrung für meine haltlose Fantasie stöbere ich überall auf. Was Pubertät sei, ist mir bekannt. Denn ich studiere mit zunehmender Ungeduld "Frühlings Erwachen" von Wedekind und vermisse enttäuscht die erhofften Stellen' [I find sustenance for my unstoppable imagination everywhere. I know what puberty is. For I have impatiently studied Wedekind's *Spring Awakening*, missing with disappointment the landmarks for which I have been led to hope] (*Erwachsenenspiele*, p. 17). When he receives his pocket-money, he uses it to buy

> ein Pariser Nudistenblatt mit zahllosen hübschen, nackten Mädchen auf Schiern im Schnee [...]. Von den nebenstehenden Texten erwarte ich eine zusätzliche Steigerungsmöglichkeit, aber ich verstehe kein einziges Wort. Mit Hilfe eines französischen Wörterbuches klaube ich mir einiges fragmentarisch zusammen, ohne davon berührt zu sein. Ich halte mich fernerhin an die Fotos. Das scheint mir solider. (*Erwachsenenspiele*, pp. 17–18)

> [a Parisian nudist publication with innumerable pretty naked girls on skis in the snow [...]. I anticipate that the texts alongside the pictures will provide an additional source of arousal, but I can't understand a single word. With the help

of a French dictionary, I piece together a few fragments, but without any effect. In future, I stick with the photographs. That seems sounder.]

While the young Kunert experiences shame when his mother eventually finds and confiscates the 'Nudistenblatt' [nudist publication], the episode contrasts starkly with Goldschmidt's account of puberty. In another episode, Kunert returns to the family's former home, which has been bombed, in order to view the destruction. He describes the return to the house as a return to the site of childhood: 'ans Geländer gedrückt, schleiche ich die Treppen hinauf, löse den Drahtverschluß und betrete meine kürzlich abrupt abgebrochene Kindheit' [squeezed against the railings, I creep up the steps, unfasten the wire, and enter my childhood which had recently been abruptly cut short] (*Erwachsenenspiele*, p. 64). On his arrival, he encounters a girl he knew when he was younger and who, as he notices, has reached puberty. He describes her ironically as a 'Mädchenfrau' [girl-woman] (*Erwachsenenspiele*, p. 65) and threatens to drop an unexploded bomb unless she agrees to undress. However, this initially disturbing scene of sexual power games is quickly revealed to be a game of equals. Kunert comments: 'doch meine Gefangene spielt mit, entkleidet sich mit verdächtiger Geschwindigkeit und begibt sich umstandslos aufs Bett, damit ich meine geringen anatomischen Kenntnisse vervollständigen kann' [but my prisoner plays along, undresses suspiciously quickly, and without further ado gets into the bed, so that I can expand my meagre knowledge of anatomy] (*Erwachsenenspiele*, p. 65).

This part of Kunert's adolescence is a prominent aspect of the text and draws attention to the notion of journey in that it narrates the protagonist's development from pre-pubescence to adulthood. It also draws attention to the development of identity, which was complicated for Kunert by his ambiguous position in the Third Reich as the son of a Jewish mother and non-Jewish father. He was protected by virtue of his 'Aryan' father from deportation but was also ostracized for his Jewish identity. Kunert is unable to fit into one category or the other, and growing up becomes a complex search for identity. As I have outlined elsewhere in this study, identity is at the core of coming of age, and so the ambivalent position in which the young Kunert finds himself upsets this process. In this context, role-playing becomes important, and indeed, the dust jacket for the hardback edition of the text depicts Kunert as a child, standing next to a toy theatre. This aspect of Kunert's youth, as well as the playful style of his account, is reminiscent of the picaresque style of Agnieszka Holland's film *Hitlerjunge Salomon*, which I discuss in Chapter 5. When Kunert undergoes an inspection by the military to assess his fitness to be drafted into the *Wehrmacht*, the officer in charge of the process, impressed by Kunert's physical prowess, declares that the regime needs such young men (*Erwachsenenspiele*, p. 69). However, on discovering that Kunert is a 'Mischling', the officer must declare him unfit to serve. In the same way as we will see in Holland's film, this exposes the senselessness of the Nazis' race laws and the Third Reich.

Finally, like Klüger, Kunert provides a searing critique of both politics and memory politics in twentieth-century Germany. The title, *Erwachsenenspiele*, also alludes to Kunert's contempt for those who cause suffering, war, and oppression.

Within his autobiography, it refers both to his experiences in the Third Reich and those in the GDR, where he opposed the strict censorship and oppressive methods of state control. Kunert mocks the endeavours of adults throughout the century who have engaged in games of power, control, war, and persecution. Of his peers being drafted into the army he comments: 'offenkundig sind sie von der Schulbank ausgerissen, um wie die Erwachsenen Krieg zu spielen' [evidently they were torn from their school desks to play at war like the grown-ups] (*Erwachsenenspiele*, p. 86). Similarly, he describes a weapon as 'ein Spielzeug, wie es auch Erwachsene verwenden' [a toy that grown-ups also use] (*Erwachsenenspiele*, p. 14). Like Klüger, Kunert is extremely critical of what he views as a general complacency in German memory culture, both immediately after the war and following reunification. He recalls how, after Hitler's death had been announced, people began to burn their now incriminating papers:

> ab ins Fegefeuer mit dem belastenden Material, auf daß man selber gereinigt und geläutert aus dem Keller in eine neue Zeit hervorgehe. Ich ahne nicht, daß es kaum einen Tag dauert, bis jeder der verzweifelt Agierenden einen jüdischen Bekannten gehabt haben würde [...]. Morgen früh werde ich mich unter lauter Opfer des Faschismus befinden. (*Erwachsenenspiele*, p. 85)

> [throw the incriminating material into the purgatorial fire, so that you can come out from the cellar purified and reformed ready for a new age. I didn't foresee that it would barely take a day before each of the disappointed activists turns out to have had a Jewish acquaintance [...]. Tomorrow morning I'll find myself surrounded by victims of fascism.][84]

The use of the term 'Fegefeuer' [purgatory] suggests the purging of sin and adds a religious dimension to Kunert's criticism. It draws out his condemnation of a memory culture in which the past can simply be erased, and with it, guilt and responsibility.

Conclusion

Klüger, Goldschmidt, and Kunert all make legible experiences of growing up in order to place them alongside better-known, but more symbolic, versions of Jewish childhood and, by doing so, question the received symbolic portrayal of the Jewish child victim of the Holocaust. To write autobiographically about their childhood experiences of persecution and suffering, each of these authors confronts a painful past. Unlike the authors in the previous chapter, Klüger, Kunert, and Goldschmidt cannot hope to act as representatives of their generation. They are the exception: they survived. Their texts thus fill a void of narrated experience: not only of the experience of the children caught up in the Holocaust, but also of the legacy of that experience in their adult lives. Their texts also contribute to a small body of autobiographical material originally written *in German*, a language with complex meanings and associations for those who were persecuted.

Klüger, Goldschmidt, and Kunert each write their own childhood, though with different approaches and different degrees of poeticizing. Klüger is very clear about what autobiography is (and is not). In *Dichter und Historiker: Fakten und Fiktionen*

[Poets and Historians: Facts and Fictions], she writes that 'Autobiographie ist Geschichte in der Ichform. Weil sie dank ihrer Subjektivität Dinge enthält, die nicht nachprüfbar sind — Gefühle und Gedanken —, wird sie öfters und leicht mit dem Roman verwechselt' [Autobiography is history in the first person. Because, due to its subjectivity, it contains things that are not verifiable — thoughts and feelings — it is often and easily mistaken for the novel].[85] As 'Geschichte in der Ichform', *weiter leben* gives an account of the author's childhood and the process of growing up under persecution, as well as speaking to wider issues of gender politics, cultural memory, and memorialization. For Kunert, writing childhood has been a complex endeavour, first because of his precarious and ambiguous position as the son of a Jewish mother and non-Jewish father, afraid of deportation, of losing relatives and friends, and in Berlin during the bombing, and second because of his later experiences in the GDR. Goldschmidt's *Die Absonderung* represents part of a larger whole, an attempt at writing childhood at a distance, and a first attempt at doing so in German, the language of his early years.

Klüger, Goldschmidt, and Kunert frame their conceptions of childhood within different physical, psychological, moral, and social spaces. For Klüger, childhood is a struggle against oppressive forces that, in her adult life, comes to embody in particular a resistance to patriarchy. For Goldschmidt, childhood is the site of physical abuse, pain, and loss. His narrative recounts a journey towards self-understanding and independence. For Kunert, childhood is a state of innocence in which the creative faculties are uninhibited, but also the site of fear for one's life. Klüger, Goldschmidt, and Kunert resist the narrative of child Holocaust victims as it has been co-opted by the paradigmatic examples of the Buchenwald child and Anne Frank. Indeed, their accounts challenge this kind of instrumentalization of the child, offering the reader a picture of childhood that takes into account the range of the child's part in the Holocaust between the two poles of experience which these figures have come to represent. Each of the authors attempts to highlight and to overcome forces which propel them from outside to follow certain trajectories, and which deny them their voice and their agency.

These works also demonstrate the plurality of experience, which is especially important given the symbolic portrayal of Jewish child Holocaust victims that we saw exemplified by Anne Frank and the Buchenwald child. Klüger, a Viennese Jew, is deported to Theresienstadt and Auschwitz; Goldschmidt, brought up in a Protestant household, was sent into hiding totally unaware of his Jewish heritage. He recalls reading Heinrich Heine's untitled poem 'Ich weiß nicht, was soll es bedeuten' (1822) in his school textbook, under which appeared the words 'Dichter unbekannt' [poet unknown], the poet's Jewish heritage having been officially effaced. He innocently asked his parents whether the poet's surname was 'Unbekannt'.[86] In contrast, Kunert was all too aware of his own 'unacceptable' identity. In a parallel scene to Goldschmidt's, he comments in *Erwachsenenspiele* that Heine's poem is printed in his school reading book and he, unlike his classmates, knows that it is by Heine. He and Heine are, he thinks, part of the same club: 'Der Unbekannte ist einer von uns' [The 'unknown' is one of us] (*Erwachsenenspiele*, p. 21).

Rather than asking for pity, these three writers call for a productive critical engagement with the experience of racial persecution in Nazi Germany: one which acknowledges the pluralistic nature of memory and of experience, and which provokes a productive engagement with the past in the present. It is striking that these authors reject the title and role of 'victim'. Klüger repeatedly expresses her frustration at being treated as a 'victim' in the sense that her own story is reduced to simplistic models of this experience. Similarly, Goldschmidt resists the role of victim, calling himself a 'Lebensschmuggler' [smuggler of life] and a 'Schwarzfahrer des Lebens' [fare-dodger of life].[87] Not only does Goldschmidt deny his status as a victim of the Holocaust; the concept of the 'Lebensschmuggler' suggests an image of the child as having cunningly outwitted his foes. Kunert, by depicting his burgeoning sexuality during adolescence, also resists any status he might have as simply an innocent, passive victim. Yet, as Vees-Gulani has argued, it is also possible to read his almost relentless playfulness as a mask for traumatic experiences that occasionally become perceptible in the text.[88]

Their resistance to becoming symbolic or objectified as child survivors is also evident in the way each writer narrates their process of growing up as a journey. As a child deported to Auschwitz, Klüger represents an apparently uncomplicated view of the child Holocaust victim; however, as her autobiography demonstrates, she has since incorporated that experience into a meaningful engagement with Holocaust remembrance. In Klüger's view, there is still a trajectory which is imposed on the Holocaust child and which, even if it cannot be overturned, might be recuperated. Goldschmidt's exile becomes defined by the loss of his native language and his subsequent estrangement from it as a means of expressing his own life in literature. When he is estranged from his homeland and his mother tongue, he enters a self-imposed isolation that he develops as a coping mechanism in reaction to the trauma of sexual and physical abuse. In writing the account of his childhood and by using his native German to do so, Goldschmidt passes through the boundary of self-imposed linguistic exile and manages to reclaim the journey he has in fact made. As a 'Mischling', Kunert finds himself on the side of the victims and of the perpetrators. And, as *Erwachsenenspiele* shows, his life after the war is once more overshadowed by the political: 'ich bin ja durch eine Bezeichnung stigmatisiert, welche mir vierzig Jahre später, obschon aus anderen Gründen, noch einmal als Markenzeichen verliehen werden wird: Dissident' [I have been stigmatized with a label which, forty years later, for different reasons, has again branded me: dissident] (*Erwachsenenspiele*, p. 21). While he does not compare the two regimes, he sees his role as outsider and dissident as having been a continuation from the Third Reich to the GDR. By leaving the GDR, and by writing about his experiences, he managed to overcome the trajectory. Thus, these texts resist an overly emotional response by refusing to provide a depiction of the objectified suffering Holocaust child: the authors call for critical engagement, dispute, ethical and intellectual judgement.

Notes to Chapter 3

1. On this subject, see Robert Krell, 'Elderly Children as Grown Ups: Child Survivors of the Holocaust', *Psychoanalytic Perspectives*, 5 (2007), 13–21.
2. Susan R. Suleiman, 'The 1.5 Generation: Thinking about Child Survivors and the Holocaust', *American Imago*, 59 (2002), 277–95 (p. 277). See also Steven Jaron, who terms them the 'liminal generation' ('Autobiography and the Holocaust: An Examination of the Liminal Generation in France', *French Studies*, 56 (2002), 207–19).
3. Suleiman, 'The 1.5 Generation', p. 277.
4. See Dwork, p. xi. In addition to the texts discussed in this chapter, see Robert Schopflocher (b. 1923), *Eine Kindheit* (Göttingen: Wallstein, 1998), in which the author recounts his flight from Germany to Argentina aged fourteen; Ralph Giordano (b. 1923), *Erinnerungen eines Davongekommenen* (Cologne: Kiepenheuer & Witsch, 2007), who grew up in Hamburg, endured persecution, and spent the last months of the war in hiding; and George Heller (b. 1929), *Das Kind, das er war: Die Geschichte des Johann Avellis* (Berlin: Rowohlt, 2006), an autobiographical novel about the author's childhood in Germany as the son of a Jewish father and Protestant mother, including a period in a forced labour camp.
5. Ruth Klüger, *weiter leben: Eine Jugend* (Munich: dtv, 2008), henceforth cited in the main text as *weiter leben*. The English-language publication of the text, *Still Alive: A Holocaust Girlhood Remembered* (New York: The Feminist Press, 2012), is not a direct translation but a new version written by Klüger. Where possible, translations provided here are taken from this version, cited in the main text as *Still Alive*; all other translations are my own. On the reception of *Still Alive* in the US, see Linda Schulte-Sasse, ' "Living On" in the American Press: Ruth Klüger's "Still Alive" and its Challenge to a Cherished Holocaust Paradigm', *German Studies Review*, 27 (2004), 469–75. My discussion of *weiter leben* has previously been published as 'Writing Childhood in Ruth Klüger's *weiter leben: Eine Jugend*', *Forum for Modern Language Studies*, 49 (2013), 175-183.
6. Hanno Loewy, 'Das gerettete Kind: Die "Universalisierung" der Anne Frank', in *Deutsche Nachkriegsliteratur und der Holocaust*, ed. by Stephan Braese and others (Frankfurt: Campus, 1998), pp. 19–43 (p. 35). In contrast, the boy's own father published an account, Zacharias Zweig, *'Mein Vater, was machst du hier ...?' Zwischen Buchenwald und Auschwitz: Der Bericht des Zacharias Zweig* (Frankfurt a.M.: dipa, 1987), which Reiter, 'Memory and Authenticity', p. 136, posits few people have read.
7. This fact is mentioned neither in the novel nor in the film adaptation. See Susanne zur Nieden, ' "... stärker als der Tod" — Bruno Apitz' Roman *Nackt unter Wölfen* und die Holocaust-Rezeption in der DDR', in *Bilder des Holocaust: Literatur — Film — Bildende Kunst*, ed. by Manuel Köppen and Klaus R. Scherpe (Cologne: Böhlau, 1997), pp. 97–109 (p. 106).
8. Bill Niven, *The Buchenwald Child: Truth, Fiction, and Propaganda* (Rochester, NY: Camden House, 2007), p. 103.
9. Bruno Apitz, *Nackt unter Wölfen* (Halle: Mitteldeutscher Verlag, 1958).
10. B. Niven, *The Buchenwald Child*, p. 115.
11. Beate Müller, 'Agency, Ethics and Responsibility in Holocaust Fiction: Child Figures as Catalysts in Bruno Apitz's *Nackt unter Wölfen* (1958) and Edgar Hilsenrath's *Nacht* (1964)', *Internationales Archiv für Sozialgeschichte der deutschen Literatur*, 36 (2011), 85–114.
12. See also B. Niven, *The Buchenwald Child*, pp. 112–13.
13. Ibid., p. 123.
14. Sylke Kirschnick demonstrates, in *Anne Frank und die DDR: Politische Deutungen und persönliche Lesarten des berühmten Tagebuchs* (Berlin: Links, 2009), that Anne Frank did indeed have more influence in the GDR than has previously been acknowledged. However, it is still in the West that her resonance proved greatest.
15. Gene A. Plunka, *Holocaust Drama: The Theater of Atrocity* (Cambridge: Cambridge University Press, 2009), p. 104. A film adaptation of the play, directed by George Stevens, was shown in the FRG in 1959.
16. Cynthia Ozick, 'Who Owns Anne Frank?', *New Yorker*, 28 September 1997 <http://www.newyorker.com/magazine/1997/10/06/who-owns-anne-frank> [accessed 1 July 2019]. See also

André Lefevere, *Translation, Rewriting, and the Manipulation of Literary Fame* (London and New York: Routledge, 1992), pp. 45–55; Alvin H. Rosenfeld, 'Popularization and Memory: The Case of Anne Frank', in *Lessons and Legacies: The Meaning of the Holocaust in a Changing World*, ed. by Peter Hayes (Evanston: Northwestern University Press, 1991), pp. 243–79.
17. Ozick.
18. Pinfold, *Child's View*, p. 94.
19. *The Diary of Anne Frank: The Critical Edition*, ed. by David Barnouw and Gerrold van der Stroom (London: Viking, 1989). There have been several cases in the US of uncensored versions of the diary being banned from schools because of its sexual content. See Francine Prose, *Anne Frank: The Book, the Life, the Afterlife* (London: Atlantic, 2010), pp. 253–71.
20. Klaus Müller, e-mail communication, 6 January 2004, cited in L. J. Nicoletti, 'No Child Left Behind: Anne Frank Exhibits, American Abduction Narratives, and Nazi Bogeymen', in *Visualizing the Holocaust: Documents, Aesthetics, Memory*, ed. by David Bathrick, Brad Prager, and Michael D. Richardson (Rochester, NY: Camden House, 2008), pp. 86–114 (p. 107).
21. Loewy, p. 35.
22. *The Diary of Anne Frank*, p. 694.
23. Primo Levi, cited in Anne Frank Stichting, Janrense Boonstra, and Marie-José Rijnders, *Anne Frank House: A Museum with a Story*, trans. by Nancy Forest-Flier (Amsterdam: Anne Frank Stichting, 2000), p. 237.
24. Ibid.
25. Theodor W. Adorno, 'Was bedeutet: Aufarbeitung der Vergangenheit', in Theodor W. Adorno, *Gesammelte Schriften*, ed. by Rolf Tiedemann with Gretel Adorno and others, 2 vols (Frankfurt a.M.: Suhrkamp, 1970–1986), x.2: *Kulturkritik und Gesellschaft II* (1977), 555–73 (p. 570); Theodor Adorno, 'What Does Coming to Terms with the Past Mean?', in *Bitburg in Moral and Political Perspective*, ed. by Geoffrey H. Hartman (Bloomington: Indiana University Press, 1986), pp. 114–29 (p. 127).
26. Ibid.
27. Carolin Duttlinger, 'The Ethics of Curiosity: Ruth Klüger, *weiter leben*', in *Curiosity in German Literature and Culture from 1700 to the Present*, ed. by Carolin Duttlinger and Johannes Birgfeld (= special issue of *Oxford German Studies*, 38 (2009)), pp. 218–32 (p. 221).
28. Ibid., p. 219.
29. Ibid., p. 221.
30. Ibid., p. 219.
31. Martin Heidegger, *Sein und Zeit* (Tübingen: Niemeyer, 1979), p. 245.
32. Johannes von Tepl, *Der Ackermann aus Böhmen: Im Auftrage der Königl. preussischen Akademie der Wissenschaften*, ed. by Alois Bernt and Konrad Burdach (Berlin: Weidmannnsche Buchhandlung, 1917), p. 46. Cited in Heidegger, p. 245.
33. Phyllis Gaffney, *Constructions of Childhood and Youth in Old French Narrative* (Farnham and Burlington, VT: Ashgate, 2011), p. 10.
34. Jenny Kitzinger, 'Who Are You Kidding? Children, Power, and the Struggle against Sexual Abuse', in *Constructing and Reconstructing Childhood: Contemporary Issues in the Sociological Study of Childhood*, ed. by Allison James and Alan Prout (London: Falmer, 1997), pp. 165–90 (p. 169).
35. Coe, p. 1.
36. Katja Schubert, *Notwendige Umwege: Gedächtnis und Zeugenschaft in Texten jüdischer Autorinnen in Deutschland und Frankreich nach Auschwitz = Voies de traverse oblige* (Hildesheim: Olms, 2001), p. 317.
37. *I Never Saw Another Butterfly: Children's Drawings and Poems from Terezin Concentration Camp 1942–1944*, ed. by Hana Volavková (New York: McGraw-Hill, 1964).
38. Naomi Sokoloff, 'Childhood Lost: Children's Voices in Holocaust Literature', in *Infant Tongues: The Voice of the Child in Literature*, ed. by Elizabeth Goodenough, Mark A. Heberle, and Naomi Sokoloff (Michigan: Wayne State University Press, 1994), pp. 259–75 (p. 264).
39. Suleiman, 'The 1.5 Generation', p. 277.
40. Schaumann, *Memory Matters*, p. 100.
41. Lawrence Langer, *Using and Abusing the Holocaust* (Bloomington: Indiana University Press, 2006), p. 27.

42. Josef-Hermann Sauter, 'Interview mit Bruno Apitz', *Weimarer Beiträge*, 19 (1973), 26–37 (p. 34).
43. Volker Müller, 'Das willkommene Heldenlied', *Berliner Zeitung*, 28 April 2000 <http://www.berliner-zeitung.de/archiv/er-schrieb-das-buch--nackt-unter-woelfen---heute-vor-100-jahren-wurde-bruno-apitz-geboren-das-willkommene-heldenlied,10810590,9794632.html> [accessed 1 July 2019].
44. Jerry Schuchalter, *Poetry and Truth: Variations on Holocaust Testimony* (Oxford: Lang, 2009), p. 97.
45. Ruth Klüger, *Dichter und Historiker: Fakten und Fiktionen* (Vienna: Picus, 2000), p. 48.
46. Jennifer Taylor, 'Ruth Klüger's *weiter leben: Eine Jugend*: A Jewish Woman's Letter to her Mother', in *Out from the Shadows: Essays on Contemporary Austrian Women Writers and Filmmakers*, ed. by Margarete Lamb-Faffelberger (Riverside, CA: Ariadne Press, 1997), pp. 77–88 (p. 81).
47. This term was coined by Alice Miller, *Am Anfang war Erziehung* (Frankfurt a.M.: Suhrkamp, 1980), cited in Schaumann, *Memory Matters*, p. 30.
48. Lawrence Langer, *The Holocaust and the Literary Imagination* (New Haven and London: Yale University Press, 1975), p. 158.
49. Marita Pletter, 'Der Pazifik hat die richtige Farbe', *Die Zeit*, 3 March 1995, p. 67.
50. Caroline Schaumann, 'From *weiter leben* (1992) to *Still Alive* (2001): Ruth Klüger's Cultural Translation of her "German Book" for an American Audience', *German Quarterly*, 77 (2004), 324–39 (p. 325).
51. Irene Heidelberger-Leonard, 'Ruth Klüger *weiter leben* — ein Grundstein zu einem neuen Auschwitz-"Kanon"', in *Deutsche Nachkriegsliteratur und der Holocaust*, ed. by Braese and others, pp. 157–73 (p. 159).
52. Günter Rüther, 'Ein Schriftsteller, der keiner sein will: Einführung in Leben und Werk von Georges-Arthur Goldschmidt' <http://www.kas.de/wf/doc/kas_7553-544-1-30.pdf?051118133259> [accessed 1 July 2019], p. 6. His mother died of natural causes in 1942, and his father was deported to Theresienstadt. He died in 1947.
53. Among others, Goldschmidt has translated works by Franz Kafka, Friedrich Nietzsche, Peter Handke, and Walter Benjamin.
54. See esp. Julia Baker, '*Fragments* and Beyond: Childhood Trauma in Binjamin Wilkomirski's and Georges-Arthur Goldschmidt's Holocaust Testimonies and Life-Writing', in *Trajectories of Memory*, ed. by Guenther and Griech-Polelle, pp. 279–313. *Die Absonderung* was followed by *Die Aussetzung: Eine Erzählung* (Zurich: Ammann, 1996); *La Traversée des fleuves: Autobiographie* (Paris: Seuil, 1999), which Goldschmidt translated into German himself as *Über die Flüsse: Autobiografie* (Zurich: Ammann, 2001); *Le Recours* (Paris: Verdiers, 2005), translated by Goldschmidt and published in German as *Der Ausweg: Eine Erzählung* (Frankfurt a.M.: Fischer, 2014); *Die Befreiung* (Zurich: Ammann, 2007); and *Ein Wiederkommen: Erzählung* (Frankfurt a.M.: Fischer, 2012).
55. Georges-Arthur Goldschmidt, *Ein Garten in Deutschland*, trans. by Eugen Helmlé (Zurich: Ammann, 1988), p. 184.
56. 'Joseph-Breitbach-Preis an Georges-Arthur Goldschmidt', *Frankfurter Allgemeine Zeitung*, 28 July 2005 <http://www.faz.net/aktuell/rhein-main/kultur/auszeichnung-joseph-breitbach-preis-an-georges-arthur-goldschmidt-1255911.html> [accessed 1 July 2019].
57. Georges-Arthur Goldschmidt, 'Ich hoffe, dass Deutschland nicht vergaulandet', *Die Zeit*, 18 December 2018 [accessed 1 July 2019].
58. Georges-Arthur Goldschmidt, *Die Absonderung* (Zurich: Ammann, 1991), henceforth cited in the main text as *Absonderung*. For an account of its reception, see Martin Rector, 'Frühe Absonderung, später Abschied: Adoleszenz und Faschismus in den autobiographischen Erzählungen von Georges-Arthur Goldschmidt und Peter Weiss', *Peter Weiss Jahrbuch*, 4 (1995), 122–39 (pp. 122–23).
59. Stefan Willer, 'Being Translated: Exile, Childhood, and Multilingualism in G.-A. Goldschmidt and W. G. Sebald', in *German Memory Contests*, ed. by Fuchs, Cosgrove, and Grote, pp. 87–107 (p. 90).
60. In addition to translating Freud into French, Goldschmidt has published two books on Freud and the German language: *Quand Freud voit la mer* (Paris: Buchet-Chastel, 1988) and *Quand Freud attend le verbe* (Paris: Buchet-Chastel, 1996). See Willer, pp. 94–95.
61. Rector, p. 129.

62. Ibid., p. 124.
63. Lezzi, p. 321. For a discussion of trauma in *Die Absonderung*, see Baker, pp. 279–313.
64. Baker, p. 303.
65. Barbara Breysach, 'Verfolgte Kindheit: Überlegungen zu Ilse Aichingers frühem Roman und Georges-Arthur Goldschmidts autobiographischer Prosa', in *Bilder des Holocaust*, ed. by Köppen and Scherpe, pp. 47–63 (p. 55).
66. Breysach, p. 58.
67. Joachim Fritz-Vannahme, 'Der Anwalt, der Komplize: Doppelporträt der Übersetzer Goldschmidt und Lortholary', *Die Zeit*, 13 October 1989, p. 6.
68. Peter Handke, 'Vorwort', in Goldschmidt, *Die Absonderung*, pp. 7–9 (p. 9).
69. Rüther, p. 2.
70. Barth, p. 91.
71. Baker, p. 283.
72. Günter Kunert, *Erwachsenenspiele: Erinnerung* (Munich: Hanser 1997), henceforth cited in the main text as *Erwachsenenspiele*.
73. The 'Gesetz zum Schutze des deutschen Blutes und der deutschen Ehre' [Act for the Protection of German Blood and German Honour] passed in September 1935 marked a watershed in the 'legal' persecution of the Jews. It excluded Jews from citizenship rights, and prohibited marriage and sexual contact between Jews and Aryans. It also addressed the question as to how to define a 'Jew'. Party officials favoured a wide-ranging definition which would incorporate anyone with any Jewish blood. Many state and justice officials, on the other hand, considered it necessary to distinguish between 'Volljuden' and 'Mischlinge'; see Eric Johnson, *The Nazi Terror: The Gestapo, Jews, and Ordinary Germans* (London: Murray, 2000), p. 105. As Raul Hilberg writes, 'the party "combatted" the part-Jew as a carrier of the "Jewish influence"; the civil service wanted to protect in the "part-Jew" that part which is German' (*The Destruction of the European Jews* (London: Allen, 1961), p. 47, cited in Johnson, p. 105). In the end, the definition of 'Mischling' was written into the law.
74. Tate, *Shifting Perspectives*, p. 53, describes these sections as 'disappointing'. On criticisms of *Erwachsenenspiele*, see Evans, *Contours of Oppression*, pp. 183–87.
75. Christoph Klimke, 'Es gibt keinen vernünftigen Grund, ein Gedicht zu schreiben!', *Die Welt*, 28 February 2009 <http://www.welt.de/welt_print/article3290188/Es-gibt-keinen-vernuenftigen-Grund-ein-Gedicht-zu-schreiben.html> [accessed 1 July 2019].
76. Günter Kunert, *Die letzten Indianer Europas: Kommentare zum Traum, der Leben heißt* (Munich: Hanser, 1991), p. 241.
77. Susanne Vees-Gulani, *Trauma and Guilt: Literature of Wartime Bombing in Germany* (Berlin: de Gruyter, 2003), p. 155. Vees-Gulani, pp. 154–55, reads Kunert's intertextual link to Grimmelshausen, and his playful and satirical tone, as part of a coping mechanism for the trauma Kunert suffered during the Nazi era and particularly during the Allied bombing of Berlin.
78. Hans Jakob Christoph von Grimmelshausen, *Der abenteuerliche Simplicissimus* (Stuttgart: Reclam, 2001), p. 25; Johann Jakob Christoffel von Grimmelshausen, *The Adventures of Simplicius Simplicissimus*, trans. by Mike Mitchell (Cambridge: Dedalus, 1999), p. 25.
79. Günter Kunert, *Notizen in Kreide: Gedichte* (Leipzig: Reclam, 1970), p. 12. See Evans, *Ein Training im Ich-Sagen*, p. 181.
80. Carsten Gansel, *Rhetorik der Erinnerung: Literatur und Gedächtnis in den 'geschlossenen Gesellschaften' des Real-Sozialismus* (Göttingen: V&R unipress, 2009), p. 120.
81. De Bruyn, *Zwischenbilanz*, p. 14, writes: 'die heile Kindheitswelt brach mir entzwei' [my idyllic childhood world was shattered].
82. Günter Kunert, *Warum schreiben? Notizen zur Literatur* (Berlin: Aufbau, 1978), p. 191.
83. Vees-Gulani, p. 155.
84. He takes a similarly cynical view in his 1950 poem 'Über einige Davongekommene' [About Some Who Got Away], in which a man who has been bombed out says: 'Nie wieder | Jedenfalls nicht gleich' [Never Again | At least not yet]. Cited and translated in Vees-Gulani, p. 151.
85. Klüger, *Dichter und Historiker*, p. 4.
86. Georges-Arthur Goldschmidt in conversation with Susanne Wittek, 6 November 2014 <http://www.youtube.com/watch?v=cQLn90VF2YM> [accessed 1 July 2019].

87. Georges-Arthur Goldschmidt and Hans-Jürgen Heinrichs, *Schwarzfahrer des Lebens* (Frankfurt a.M.: Fischer, 2013), p. 8. There is a striking link here to Salomon Perel's view of his story of survival, as I discuss in Chapter 5.
88. Vees-Gulani, p. 154.

CHAPTER 4

Imagined Childhoods: Writing Fictional Lives

Introduction

With the awareness that the last eyewitnesses to Nazism will soon be gone, and, with them, new accounts of the period, there comes a shift from communicative memory to cultural memory. Eyewitness accounts increasingly give way to purely imaginative responses by those who have no biographical involvement with the Third Reich, or who have no direct experience of the events they are narrating. In this chapter, I examine three fictional works about childhood in the Third Reich whose authors' own trajectories do not correspond to those of the children in their literary works. The authors embody three levels of distance from the imagined children in their texts. W. G. Sebald was born in Bavaria in 1944, and his father fought in the *Wehrmacht*. In his novel *Austerlitz* (2001), Sebald tells the story of a child, Jacques Austerlitz, who was sent by his Jewish mother from Prague to England on one of the last Kindertransports to depart the continent in 1939. *Austerlitz* is a complex narrative in which Sebald interweaves several themes and ideas to approach the fundamental issues of historical consciousness, the relationship between the past and the present, and the representability of history. The depiction of the protagonist, his search for his childhood self, and indeed the psychological and visual traces of the child which remain, are central to Sebald's overall project.

Binjamin Wilkomirski's *Bruchstücke: Aus einer Kindheit 1939–1948* [Fragments: Memories of a Childhood, 1939–1948] (1995) raises the question of fictionalization to an ethical level. Susan R. Suleiman has called it 'not a novel but a false — or better, a deluded — memoir'.[1] In this text, the close association of the child and authenticity is exploited to validate the authenticity of the narrative. However, the complex reception of Wilkomirski's text has raised questions about the extent to which his account might in fact be considered 'emotionally authentic' despite its exposure as a fraud and the consequent general acknowledgement that it should be discredited as a document of witness. Finally, in her young-adult fiction novel *Reise im August* [The Final Journey] (1992), Gudrun Pausewang offers an imagined account of the Jewish childhood experience. Her text is narrated from the perspective of the eleven-year-old Alice Dubsky, who is travelling on a transport to Auschwitz. At the same age as her fictional protagonist, Pausewang was a member of the *Bund deutscher Mädel* [League of German Girls] (BDM), and her text thus questions both the aesthetic creation of the child's voice and the ethical legitimacy of writing the narrative of a Holocaust victim from the standpoint of one who, at the same time, was on the side of the perpetrators.

Here, I address the different ways in which these three writers portray the child's experience of, and perspective on, the Third Reich. I ask in what ways they seek to reinforce or undermine the challenge of authenticity in Holocaust writing. Because of the very different nature of these texts, I do not wish to provide a direct comparison; rather, I seek to examine the ways in which each text evokes or challenges authenticity through an imagined depiction of childhood under Nazism. Finally, I consider the discussion these texts provoke about the way in which the experience of childhood in the Third Reich will be made legible after the last eyewitnesses have disappeared.

Negative Revelations: *Austerlitz* (2001)

W. G. Sebald's final novel, *Austerlitz*, documents the protagonist Jacques Austerlitz's reconstruction of identity from the remnants of his lost childhood.[2] Born in 1934 in Prague to Jewish parents, Austerlitz travels to England on a Kindertransport in 1939. Like the young unnamed protagonist in *Die Absonderung*, the character Austerlitz is displaced by the events of the Holocaust: sent into exile by his parents as a means of protecting him from deportation to the concentration camps. The exile from home and family, however, results in a different kind of trauma, as the young protagonist's origins and identity are swiftly hidden by his foster-parents and he is furnished with a new name (Dafydd Elias), language, family, and way of life. The narrative, told from the perspective of a nameless narrator who encounters Austerlitz several times over a period of some years, charts Austerlitz's difficult adulthood, mental breakdown, and subsequent uncovering of his true identity. When the narrator meets Austerlitz again by chance in the mid-1990s, Austerlitz tells him the story of his long-repressed childhood that he himself has discovered shortly before, and which he now feels compelled to communicate to someone.

The narrative focuses primarily on Austerlitz's search for his origins and identity, which is motivated by his admission that 'seit meiner Kindheit und Jugend [...] habe ich nicht gewußt, wer ich in Wahrheit bin' [since my childhood and youth [...] I have never known who I really was] (*Austerlitz*, p. 68; trans. by Bell, p. 61). The initial trauma of separation from family and home has a lasting effect upon Austerlitz. As he comments later in the text: 'irgendwann in der Vergangenheit, dachte ich, habe ich einen Fehler gemacht und bin jetzt in einem falschen Leben' [at some time in the past, I thought, I must have made a mistake, and now I am living the wrong life] (*Austerlitz*, p. 306; trans. by Bell, p. 298). In addition to this, the manner in which this trauma is negotiated, both by Austerlitz and by others, contributes further to his inability to establish a stable identity. The erasure of his origins as a five-year-old child is shown to have had a profound effect on his adult life, causing 'emotional impotence'[3] and a refusal to engage with recent historical events: he will not read newspapers and fixates on pre-twentieth-century history. As an adult, Austerlitz recalls and describes the claustrophobic atmosphere of the Welsh manse in which he grew up, where the closed doors and windows represent the stifling environment, as well as the secrecy and concealment, which pervade his childhood. The lack of paragraphing in the text also emphasizes this notion. The manse is the first of many locations which Austerlitz experiences as uncanny. He is unable to feel any sense of belonging and comments: 'noch heute träumt es mir manchmal, daß eine der verschlossenen Türen sich auftut und ich über die Schwelle trete in eine freundlichere, weniger fremde Welt' [even today I still sometimes dream that one of those locked doors opens and I step through it, into a friendlier, more familiar world] (*Austerlitz*, p. 69; trans. by Bell, p. 61).

At the age of fifteen, Austerlitz learns his real name from his boarding-school headmaster, though he receives no further information about his origins. It is the exoticism of the name which, the adult recalls, most unsettled the adolescent. He comments: 'wäre mein neuer Name Morgan oder Jones, dann hätte ich das beziehen können auf die Wirklichkeit' [if my new name had been Morgan or Jones, I could have related it to reality] (*Austerlitz*, p. 102; trans. by Bell, p. 94). Anne Fuchs addresses the way in which Sebald uses the protagonist's reflections on his birth-name to explore the formation of his emerging identity. While one's proper name is, under normal circumstances, a positive guarantor of individuality inasmuch as it shows one's origins, this very particularity was 'das sichere Todesurteil' [a certain death sentence] for the protagonist's family and all Jewish victims of the Holocaust.[4] However, neither of these forms of self-identification is initially available to Austerlitz, whose inability to imagine himself as the bearer of this strange name is also a reflection of his inability to root his identity in a specific tradition or genealogy. As Fuchs writes, 'die Namensproblematik veranschaulicht beispielhaft, dass in Austerlitzens Leben die Verbindung zu seiner Familie und jüdischen Vorgeschichte gekappt wurde' [the difficulties surrounding his name exemplify the fact that, in Austerlitz's life, his connection to his family and his Jewish background has been severed].[5] It is only when a schoolmaster indicates that Austerlitz is also the name of a battle that the protagonist is able to invest the name with some concrete reality, and to begin to view it as a source of identity, rather than of unease and shame.[6]

It is, of course, also ironic that Austerlitz's adoptive name, Dafydd Elias, has greater Old Testament connotations than his real name, Jacques Austerlitz. I have discussed in previous chapters the significance of adolescence for identity formation; significantly, Austerlitz learns of his alternate identity precisely during the period when his emerging sense of self is most vulnerable to disruption. Arguably, it is after this point that Austerlitz is truly unable to develop further. The notion of journey is central to *Austerlitz*, including the literal journeys he makes, both as a child to England, and as an adult across Europe, as well as his figurative journey into the past. It is at this moment, as he discovers his alternate identity, that, to follow the metaphor, the journey abruptly stops. It only resumes after he experiences a mental breakdown and resolves to discover his origins in more detail.

Austerlitz becomes a static figure, not physically or intellectually, but in terms of his inner life. This is exemplified throughout the text in his social interactions, most particularly in his relationship with women. Helen Finch writes that Austerlitz 'functions like an uncanny doll, possessing no autonomous sexual identity'.[7] This stasis is also alluded to by the narrator. In the text's opening pages, the narrator recounts a visit to the Antwerp zoo, where a racoon reminds him of Austerlitz. He comments on his observations:

> Wirklich gegenwärtig geblieben ist mir eigentlich nur der Waschbär, den ich lange beobachtete, wie er mit ernstem Gesicht bei einem Bächlein saß und immer wieder denselben Apfelschnitz wusch, als hoffe er, durch dieses, weit über jede vernünftige Gründlichkeit hinausgehende Waschen entkommen zu können aus der falschen Welt, in die er gewissermaßen ohne sein eigenes Zutun geraten war. (*Austerlitz*, pp. 10–11)
>
> [The only animal which has remained lingering in my memory is the racoon. I watched it for a long time as it sat beside a little stream with a serious expression on its face, washing the same piece of apple over and over again, as if it hoped that all this washing, which went far beyond any reasonable thoroughness, would help it to escape the unreal world in which it had arrived, so to speak, through no fault of its own.] (*Austerlitz*, trans. by Bell, pp. 2–3)

The 'falsche Welt' [unreal world] recalls Austerlitz's own statements regarding his feeling of alienation from reality. It also draws attention to his lack of development and stasis in that the racoon repeatedly washes the same piece of fruit. The best example of this idea of Austerlitz's stasis is in a photograph. Within the narrative, the discovery of this photograph proves to be the culmination of Austerlitz's search for his origins. Having travelled to Prague, Austerlitz encounters Věra, a friend of his deceased mother, who cared for him as a child. During his stay, Věra finds the photograph by chance and shows it to Austerlitz, providing its context for him: it was taken in February 1939 at a masked ball which Austerlitz was permitted to attend with his mother, six months before he left Prague. At this point, the photograph is reproduced within the text itself. It is an integral part of the narrative and plays an important role in the reader's reception of the text, and the image of the 'young Austerlitz', aged five, is also shown on multiple versions of the dust jacket and cover of the book.

Considerable critical attention has been paid to Sebald's use of photographs in his works, examining the interplay of text and image, the lack of captioning, the documentary qualities associated with photography, the mnemonic role of photographs, photography as a model for negotiating traumatic memory, and the role of photographs in developing the texts' ambiguity between fact and fiction.[8] In an essay on the interaction of narrative and photography, and their contribution to the conceptions of history and memory in Sebald's 1992 text *Die Ausgewanderten* [The Emigrants], J. J. Long suggests that such photographs function both in combination with the text and in juxtaposition with other photographs. They are situated within 'a nexus of interrelations that mirrors metaphorically the overall thematics of the verbal narrative'.[9] He writes:

within the narrative economy of Sebald's text, photographs acquire their meaning through acts of captioning and commentary that are circumscribed by the familial and affiliative gaze. Reading the family album emerges as one way in which something permanent can be salvaged from the passing of time and the ravages of history.[10]

This is, he argues, part of 'an attempt, at the level of form, to counteract the dispersal, dissipation, and rupture inherent in the historical process'.[11] However, within *Austerlitz*, although the photograph has endured and appears to offer a direct link to the past (because it is an image of the protagonist as a child), it does not offer any more than a basic record of the fact of that past. Indeed, rather than aiding Austerlitz in his quest for his childhood, the photograph actually works against him. As Maya Barzilai has discussed, it becomes what Roland Barthes calls a 'counter-memory': it 'blocks' memory instead of stimulating it.[12] Austerlitz refers to the child in the picture as 'der Knabe' [the boy], the 'Kinderkavalier' [child cavalier], and 'der Page' [the page boy] (*Austerlitz*, pp. 267, 268, 264; trans. by Bell, pp. 258, 260). The use of synecdoche here in referring to his younger self echoes other authors in this study who, writing autobiographically, use this technique to express the divide they feel from their younger self. For Austerlitz, though, this divide is not the result of shame or retrospective knowledge about Nazi crimes, but rather a psychological inability to recognize himself as a result of trauma. In the photograph, the effect of the child's 'otherness' is heightened by the strange costume with its old-fashioned style and his presence in what looks to be a field, the reason for which remains unknown. That the photograph is so highly stylized further complicates Austerlitz's relationship with the child it depicts. The boy remains remote and mysterious, both to the reader and to Austerlitz himself. In addition, it possesses a haunting quality, as the child, with his shock of blonde hair, creates an ethereal image, heightened by the old-fashioned theatrical costume. Maguire has linked the photograph to the Gainsborough school, and indeed it is strikingly reminiscent in its composition of Thomas Gainsborough's *The Blue Boy* (1779), a painting which was world-famous in the nineteenth century and which contributed significantly to a sentimental view of the child in the period.[13]

Austerlitz can observe his child-self by looking at the photograph, but finds it impossible to identify with the figure he sees. Not only is he unable to engage with the child in the photograph; he is further distanced from his origins because he cannot even engage with the memory of the child he used to be. Austerlitz confesses:

> an mich selber in dieser Rolle aber erinnerte ich mich nicht, so sehr ich mich an jenem Abend und später auch mühte. Wohl erkannte ich den ungewöhnlichen, schräg über die Stirne verlaufenden Haaransatz, doch sonst war alles in mir ausgelöscht von einem überwältigenden Gefühl der Vergangenheit. (*Austerlitz*, p. 267)
>
> [yet hard as I tried both that evening and later, I could not recollect myself in the part. I did recognize the unusual hairline running at a slant over the forehead, but otherwise all memory was extinguished in me by an overwhelming sense of the long years that had passed.] (*Austerlitz*, trans. by Bell, p. 259)

The 'Rolle' refers here both to the part of page boy which Austerlitz played at the masked ball, but also to the 'part' of the child which he used to play. He did not in fact *play* this role — he *was* the boy in the photograph — but he can find no affinity with him. In her study of photography and memory in contemporary German texts, *Nachbilder: Fotografie und Gedächtnis in der deutschen Gegenwartsliteratur* [Afterimages: Photography and Memory in Contemporary German Literature] (2009), Silke Horstkotte suggests that, while Austerlitz's 'früheres, kindliches Ich' [earlier, childhood self] finally materializes in this photograph,[14] the image ultimately raises more questions than it answers: 'Während die Fotografie ihrem Betrachter keinen Zugang zur Vergangenheit eröffnet, sondern eher Rätsel aufgibt [...], fordert der kleine Page selbst als Wiedergänger sein Recht vom Betrachter' [While the photograph fails to provide the viewer with access to the past, instead posing riddles [...], the little page boy, as a revenant, demands his rights from the viewer].[15] In Horstkotte's reading, the child in the photograph is figured as one who returns, a 'Wiedergänger', a figure in German myth who, though deceased, returns to the world of the living. He is a haunting figure, entirely separated from the adult Austerlitz gazing at the photograph, who cannot access the past through the act of seeing. The child nonetheless makes a claim on him. In addition, Horstkotte draws attention to the 'Zukunftsversprechen der Fotografie' [future promised by the photograph], which is undermined by the fact that this future can no longer be realized: the adult Austerlitz is looking back at his own, albeit unfamiliar, past.[16] This makes sense particularly in the context of the previous photograph, which (possibly) portrays Austerlitz's parents. Věra finds it 'durch einen Zufall' [by chance], and without quite knowing how or why, in a volume of works by Balzac (*Austerlitz*, p. 266; trans. by Bell, p. 256). As Hirsch points out, the eponymous protagonist of *Le Colonel Chabert* [Colonel Chabert], the volume in question, is himself a revenant, returning from the dead to regain what he has lost.[17] Yet, unlike Chabert, Austerlitz as revenant cannot hope to recover what he has lost: first, because he has no actual memories of it, and second, because it has been destroyed. Ultimately, the photograph fails to provide an image of the past for Austerlitz, who possesses almost no memories of childhood from this period. This causes him to have a postmemorial response to the photograph.[18] For Austerlitz, there is a generational distance between himself and the photograph. He is in his sixties as he views it. Although it is of him, he reacts as though it is of somebody else, somebody who is familiar (he recognizes the figure's distinctive hair as similar to his own), but who is ultimately a different person from a different time. He attempts to reach the boy through imagination and reflection, but ultimately fails.[19]

In her study of photographs of children used on book covers and dust jackets, Douglas emphasizes the importance of the book cover as 'the first meeting place between reader and book',[20] and suggests that this image will shape the reader's expectations and interpretations of the text. She suggests that, while fictional books tend to use artistic images for the covers, autobiographies of childhood frequently depict a photographic image of the author/protagonist as a child. The association of the photograph, autobiography, and childhood with authenticity proves a 'powerful mix'.²¹ The picture on the front of Sebald's *Austerlitz* may, therefore, point to a specific genre designation as autobiography for the uninformed reader. Indeed, the photograph of the child in *Austerlitz* appears in some way on the cover of all editions of the book and functions within the text like a genuine photograph or film still of the central figure of a conventional autobiography. However, Austerlitz is of course a fictional character and the real subject of the photograph does not share his story.²² Thus, this seeming touchstone of realism and authenticity is in fact illusory and represents a comment on the idea of authenticity which the conventional deployment of such images is intended to invoke.

Douglas also suggests that images of children used on book covers often fall into certain prevalent categories: the 'playful child', smiling straight into the camera or looking 'serenely' away; the close-up of 'angelic child faces' used to emotive effect; and a small image engulfed by the page which is used to 'emphasize the vulnerability of the figure'.²³ The photograph on the cover of *Austerlitz* eludes these categorizations: the image is otherworldly, and the child's enigmatic gaze has an unsettling effect. For Anne Higonnet, Gainsborough's Blue Boy evokes nostalgia — this eighteenth-century boy is wearing a costume from a century earlier.²⁴ Something similar is happening with the image of the child Austerlitz. This effect is heightened by the fairy-tale costume of the page from the *Rosenkönigin* [Rose Queen], a traditional tale in which the queen dies, leaving her only son abandoned. Thus, this seemingly benign image also proves strangely prophetic, hinting at the loss which Austerlitz will later experience.²⁵

Furthermore, although the photograph was apparently taken outside, perhaps in a garden or field, the child's pose lends it something of the photographer's studio. This further complicates the kind of nostalgia to which it alludes. Of the nostalgic use of images of children in advertising, Nancy Martha West writes: 'unlike the actual child, photographs are represented as pure objects not taken up in the changing sphere of lived reality. Like the *idea* of childhood, as opposed to its reality, photographs remain complete, whole, timeless.'²⁶ The child becomes associated with an atemporal world, outside time. Indeed, as Stefanie Boese notes, the photograph is devoid of 'authentic history' in its evocation of a fairy-tale world.²⁷ This photograph could not be further removed in effect from the other photograph of 'Austerlitz' in the text, which depicts him at school with his rugby team (*Austerlitz*, p. 114) and which provides a conventional image from within the context of an English school. The strangeness of the Prague photograph is exacerbated by what Barzilai views as the 'uncanniness of photography' in Sebald's works: the fact that they are all black and white, often grainy, from earlier times, and, from their ambivalent position, 'not fully integrated into the body of the text, yet dependent on the narrative for their significance'.²⁸

Despite the prominence of the image of Austerlitz as a child, this figure remains elusive throughout the text. He has, we learn, always been a silent figure. On a visit to the spa at Marienbad with a friend, he experiences a sense of the uncanny. His companion, Marie, asks: 'warum sehe ich, wie deine Lippen sich öffnen, wie du etwas sagen, vielleicht sogar ausrufen willst, und dann höre ich nichts?' [why do I see your lips opening as if you were about to say something, maybe even cry out loud, and then I hear not the slightest sound?] (*Austerlitz*, p. 311; trans. by Bell, p. 303). Austerlitz's self-imposed silence, rooted in his childhood trauma, is echoed by the silence of the child he used to be. It is only when he travels to Prague and the Czech language of his childhood is awoken, that he is shown to be able to truly communicate. This is reminiscent of Emine Sevgi Özdamar's notion of the relationship between an individual's mother tongue and their childhood, and her suggestion that 'in der Fremdsprache haben Wörter keine Kindheit' [in a foreign tongue, words have no childhood].[29] In his mother tongue, Austerlitz can begin to find the words to express what he needs to and to attempt to recover his lost origins. This recalls the overcoming of distance from the German language which Klüger and Goldschmidt express in their autobiographical works. However, it is less contested as Austerlitz reclaims Czech, rather than the German associated with the language of the perpetrators.

Through his inclusion of the photographs in the narrative, Sebald both evokes and challenges the authenticity of depictions and accounts of the past. However, the use of an anonymous image of a real child as the basis of these considerations must raise questions about authenticity and our response to the text: to borrow another's image or account for literary purposes is potentially problematic when this is uncredited within the book. This is not the only such area of difficulty in this text: in an interview about *Austerlitz*, Sebald commented on the problem of whether someone who has not suffered under the Nazis can legitimately speak for, or at least about, a Jewish victim of National Socialist persecution.[30] Sebald comments:

> meine Überlegung dazu war, dass das, was von deutschen Autoren nichtjüdischer Herkunft über dieses Thema der Verfolgung und der versuchten Ausrottung des jüdischen Volks geschrieben worden ist, im Allgemeinen unzulänglich ist und über weite Strecken aus Peinlichkeiten besteht, auch aus Usurpationen.[31]
>
> [my thoughts on that were, that what German writers with no Jewish heritage have written on the theme of the persecution and attempted extermination of the Jewish people is inadequate and consists to a great extent of embarrassments, and usurpations.]

Yet it was just such a usurpation of which *Austerlitz* was accused by Susi Bechhöfer, whose ghostwritten account of her experience as a Kindertransport child had provided a model for Sebald's character Jacques Austerlitz.[32] Bechhöfer explained in an article in the *Sunday Times* that she had contacted Sebald, that they had been in correspondence, and that he had confirmed that *Austerlitz* was indeed based in part on her story. Bechhöfer expressed her outrage at having had her story appropriated in this way without being formally acknowledged, asserting that 'I felt once more that my identity had been usurped'.[33] Sebald explained in an interview that 'the details of Susie Bechhofer's [sic] life [...] are far more horrific than anything in *Austerlitz*. But I didn't want to make use of it because I haven't the right. I try to keep at a distance and never invade'.[34] In an article on *Austerlitz*, Elizabeth Baer rightly argues that Sebald's appropriation of Bechhöfer's story must be seen within the context of his wider literary project and the critical approach he takes.[35]

Ultimately, though, it makes us consider the limits, and ethics, of representation in both literature and visual culture.

Imagined Authenticity: *Bruchstücke* (1995)

As I have examined in previous chapters, the notion of a counterfactual autobiography was appealing to many of those who grew up in the Third Reich. This is precisely what the writer Binjamin Wilkomirski constructed in his apparently autobiographical text *Bruchstücke: Aus einer Kindheit 1939–1948*,[36] first published by Suhrkamp's Jüdischer Verlag [Jewish Publishing House] in 1995.[37] It contained what Wilkomirski claimed to be his own experiences of persecution as a Jewish child in Eastern Europe: born in 1938 or 1939 in Latvia, he escaped from the persecution of the Jews in Riga, was imprisoned in concentration camps in Poland, and survived, ending up in a children's home in Switzerland after the war.

Bruchstücke received several awards,[38] and reviewers spoke of Wilkomirski in the same breath as Elie Wiesel, Anne Frank, and Primo Levi.[39] Daniel Jonah Goldhagen, author of the controversial *Hitler's Willing Executioners* (1996), said of *Bruchstücke*: 'Dieses fesselnde Buch ist auch für jene lehrreich, die mit der Literatur über den Holocaust vertraut sind. Es wird jeden tief bewegen' [Even those conversant with the literature of the Holocaust will be educated by this arresting book. All will be deeply moved].[40] Critics praised Wilkomirski's use of the child's perspective, an uncommon technique in a retrospective, autobiographical account of the Holocaust (perhaps because of its ubiquity in works of fiction on this subject). Only some years later did it transpire that, prior to publication, Hanno Helbling, former head of the *Feuilleton* of the *Neue Zürcher Zeitung* had raised concerns about the veracity of Wilkomirski's story. Helbling had heard rumours from acquaintances of Wilkomirski that the account was not authentic. He therefore advocated its publication provided it was framed as a work of fiction. His concern was not that the work was without literary merit. Rather, it hinged on whether the publisher intended to present the text as an '"Auschwitz-Roman", dem der Verfasser die literarische Form der Ich-Erzählung gegeben hat [...]; oder als "echtes" Erinnerungsbuch, das aber wohl früher oder später als fiktiv erkannt werden dürfte' ['Auschwitz novel', to which the author has given the literary form of a first-person narrative [...]; or as 'genuine' memoirs that sooner or later may be identified as fiction].[41] Suhrkamp halted printing while Eva Koralnik, Wilkomirski's literary agent, questioned him as to the truth of his account. Satisfied that Wilkomirski was indeed who he claimed to be, publication went ahead and the book was presented as an autobiographical account.

Then, in August 1998, an article appeared in the Swiss magazine *Weltwoche* in which the author and journalist Daniel Ganzfried disputed the truth of Wilkomirski's account.[42] Ganzfried suggested in the strongest terms that Wilkomirski was not in fact a Holocaust survivor at all, but rather the Swiss-born Bruno Dösekker, who, after his mother was unable to care for him, was fostered by various families before finally being adopted by a Swiss doctor and his wife in 1945. Ganzfried's article created a public uproar, and finally the historian and writer Stefan Mächler was engaged to investigate the case. Mächler's findings were published in the volume *Der Fall Wilkomirski: Über die Wahrheit einer Biographie* [The Wilkomirski Affair: A Study in Biographical Truth] (2000), in which he persuasively demonstrates the likelihood of Ganzfried's conclusion that Wilkomirski was 'nie als Insasse in einem Konzentrationslager' [never imprisoned in a concentration camp].[43] Mächler suggests rather that Wilkomirski, whose early childhood had been extremely problematic to say the least, engaged in a course of memory recovery techniques, as a result of which he was able to situate his memories of childhood in a Holocaust context. This was also the view of Elena Lappin, who after detailed research and interviews with Wilkomirski, concluded that the most plausible scenario seemed to be that Wilkomirski had mapped his own experience onto his knowledge of Holocaust experience.[44]

Critical approaches have tended to focus on issues of authenticity[45] and the construction of a child's perspective.[46] I want to argue here that these two aspects of the work are intertwined. First, Wilkomirski insists upon the child's perspective because the adult's perspective would only distort the truth of his account: 'Will ich darüber schreiben, muß ich auf die ordnende Logik, die Perspektive des Erwachsenen verzichten. Sie würde das Geschehene nur verfälschen' [If I'm going to write about it, I have to give up on the ordering logic of grown-ups; it would only distort what happened] (*Bruchstücke*, p. 8; *Fragments*, p. 4). Without wishing to draw a direct comparison between the two, there are certainly echoes here of Walser's insistence on his right to remember without the corrective of the adult's retrospective view. Wilkomirski appears to suffer from the essential tension between what, to all intents and purposes, he believes his individual, personal memories to be, and the claims made by history, by the publicly documented facts of his life. Thus, he can write in the afterword: 'Die juristisch beglaubigte Wahrheit ist eine Sache, die eines Lebens eine andere' [Legally accredited truth is one thing — the truth of a life another] (*Bruchstücke*, p. 143; *Fragments*, p. 154).

Second, Wilkomirski begins his text by seeking to establish the 'truth-value' of his account. He writes: 'ich bin kein Dichter, kein Schriftsteller. Ich kann nur versuchen, mit Worten das Erlebte, das Gesehene so exakt wie möglich abzuzeichnen — so genau, wie es eben mein Kindergedächtnis aufbewahrt hat: noch ohne Kenntnis von Perspektive und Fluchtpunkt' [I'm not a poet or a writer. I can only try to use words to draw as exactly as possible what happened, what I saw; exactly the way my child's memory has held on to it; with no benefit of perspective or vanishing point] (*Bruchstücke*, p. 8; *Fragments*, pp. 4–5). Here, Wilkomirski suggests that the historical discrepancies and contradictions do not undermine the authenticity of his account but rather serve to underline it.[47] However, this argument proves problematic. Whilst authors of autobiography commonly draw attention to the problems of memory, here Wilkomirski fails even to entertain the concept of the unreliability of memory. A central aspect of the theory of childhood autobiography is the extent of the writer's reliance on memory to write their account. In a study of the Austrian author Julian Schutting, Gerhard Zeillinger argues that childhood memories are necessarily 'bruchstückhaft' [fragmentary]: 'Grundsätzlich gilt darüber hinaus, daß das Erinnern eine Phantasietätigkeit im nachhinein ist, die eine Echtheit von Kindheitserinnerungen automatisch in Zweifel zieht' [It is fundamentally the case that memory is a retrospective act of imagination which automatically calls into question the authenticity of memories of childhood].[48] Zeillinger's comment appears to indirectly endorse the approach which Wilkomirski pursues; however, it also raises the point that memory involves an act of imagination ('Phantasietätigkeit') which calls the remembrance of past events into question. As I discussed in the previous chapter, a challenge of autobiographical writing about childhood in the Holocaust is to reconcile the demand for veracity with the awareness of the vicissitudes of memory.

Ironically, though, it is precisely the presence of imagination that Wilkomirski seeks to refute in the opening to his text. Apparently uncritically, he writes: 'meine frühen Kindheitserinnerungen gründen in erster Linie auf den exakten Bildern meines fotografischen Gedächtnisses und den dazu bewahrten Gefühlen' [my early childhood memories are planted, first and foremost, in exact snapshots of my photographic memory and in the feelings imprinted in them] (*Bruchstücke*, p. 7; *Fragments*, p. 4). Wilkomirski uses the analogy of memory with the photograph to prove the veracity of his account.[49] He urges his reader to trust him and his recollections because the story he is telling is true and can be proved by such evidence as his 'photographic memory'. Lappin commented that this was likely true, but not in the way Wilkomirski meant it. Rather, his 'memories' were the result of the many films and documentaries he had watched about the camps, all part of his extensive personal archive of Holocaust material. They were, it seems, more reel than real.

In the light of the analysis of *Austerlitz* above, this uncritical deployment of photography as offering referential truth proves extremely problematic. Mächler draws attention to this issue in his study of Wilkomirski's text, framing it as a pact between writer and reader:

> der Pakt, den Wilkomirski einem Leser implizit abverlangt, heißt: Du mußt meinen Text als fotografisch genaue Wiedergabe meiner erinnerten Erfahrungen lesen; ich bin kein Geschichten erfindender Dichter. In den Genuß der Wahrheit kommst du nur, wenn du verstehst, zwischen den Zeilen zu lesen und das Nichtgesagte zu erahnen, denn die Sprache ist nicht mein eigentliches Ausdrucksmittel, und für das Wesentliche fehlen mir die Worte. [...] ich komme aus einer Welt, die sich zweiteilt in Opfer und Täter, und ich gehöre selbst zu den unschuldigsten aller Opfer, die sich statt an Mutter und Vater nur an ihre Ursprünge in KZ-Baracken erinnern. Willst du meine Erzählung verstehen, mußt du auf die ordnende Logik des Erwachsenen verzichten und meine Kinderperspektive einnehmen. Wählst du die Seite der Ordnung, wählst du die Seite der Täter, die mich und meinesgleichen zu ermorden planten.[50]
>
> [The pact Wilkomirski implicitly demands of his readers is as follows: You must read my text as a photographically exact copy of my remembered experience. I am no poet inventing stories. You will come to know the truth if you learn to read between the lines and surmise what is not said, for language is not my real mode of expression and I lack words for what is most essential. [...] I come from

a world divided into victims and villains, and I am among the most innocent of all victims, whose remembered origins are not mother and father but a barrack in a death camp. If you want to understand my story, you must give up your adult's logic and assume my child's perspective. If you choose order, you are on the side of the villains who planned to murder me and those like me.][50]

Furthermore, and as Mächler observes here, Wilkomirski establishes a binary opposition between the perpetrators and the victims which, in the context of his narrative, requires the reader to take the side of the innocent child rather than the 'guilty' adult. This perpetrator–victim binary was, as I have shown, precisely what Ruth Klüger had argued against in *weiter leben*. Indeed, Klüger commented on *Bruchstücke* in an article originally published in the *Süddeutsche Zeitung* in 1998 that 'es war ermüdend, dieses Einerlei der Sprache, die Klischees, die Perspektiven eines Kindes' [it was exhausting to read: this monotony of language, the clichés, the perspectives of a child].[52] According to Klüger's interpretation, texts such as Wilkomirski's reduce the child victim to a cliché, devoid of agency and unable to have engaged cognitively and actively in the world around them. The charge of being 'kitsch' which she levels at *Bruchstücke* stems primarily from the use of the child's perspective unqualified by that of the remembering adult, from the naivety, and from the gaps between what is observed and what is understood.[53]

Klüger's criticism is not unfounded. The child protagonist in *Bruchstücke* does not develop throughout the text, so that, as Suleiman observes, 'the narrative moves forward and back, producing new experiences and new memories but no new understanding — until the final chapter',[54] when the boy watches a documentary in his history class about the liberation of Mauthausen and realizes the war is over. This ensures that the child's perspective does not change throughout the text. His seemingly innocent responses to what will prove to be difficult and traumatic events elicit pity. Having become separated from his mother and brothers, he encounters a female SS officer: 'Aber Stiefel hatte sie — noch nie hatte ich so schöne gesehen! Die graue Uniform war aus einem Stoff, wie ich ihn nicht kannte — glatt und sauber, ohne Risse, ohne Löcher, ohne einen Flecken. Sie mußte etwas Besonderes sein!' [And she had boots — I'd never seen any as grand as hers. The gray uniform was made of some kind of material I didn't know — smooth and clean, no tears, no holes, no stains. She must be someone special] (*Bruchstücke*, p. 35; *Fragments*, p. 35). When she tells him he is going to Majdanek, he responds positively, 'der Name klang so schön!' [the name was so pretty] (*Bruchstücke*, p. 36; *Fragments*, p. 36), and exclaims: 'ich konnte es kaum erwarten' [I couldn't wait] (*Bruchstücke*, p. 37; *Fragments*, p. 36). Elsewhere, the child reacts positively to a new situation, only to discover its true violent and horrific nature. The second response is often inappropriate, at least in the reader's estimation. We can read it as either childhood curiosity uncensored by the morality of adult understanding, or simply as badly written prose.

A further example of this can be found in the description of one night at Majdanek, during which two babies are brought into the children's freezing-cold barracks. During the night, the protagonist notices that the babies' fingertips are black; this, he is told, is frostbite. In the morning, the babies are found frozen, and their fingertips are now white. Desperately hungry, they have chewed their numbed fingers down to the bone. The child protagonist's response after being told what has happened is not the instinctive shock and disgust experienced by the reader, but rather fascination: 'ich konnte mir zum ersten Mal vorstellen, wie meine Knochen aussehen. Ich hatte das erhabene Gefühl, eine große Entdeckung gemacht zu haben' [for the first time I could picture what my bones looked like. I felt a sense of superiority, as if I'd just made a great discovery] (*Bruchstücke*, p. 67; *Fragments*, p. 71). This kind of curiosity about the human and natural world is a recognizable attribute of childhood; thus, Wilkomirski appears to create an authentically childish viewpoint. However, in the context of the Holocaust, where the events themselves are so thoroughly shocking, such responses as this take on a taboo quality. This is compounded by his description of his friend, Jankl's, response to the scene: he weeps bitterly (*Bruchstücke*, p. 68). This astonishes the narrator, who seems unable to understand why dead babies would be something to cry about.

The protagonist's naive perspective continues throughout the book: furthermore, because, when he is in the post-war children's home, he is unaware that the war is over, the world of the camps lives on, albeit it in a different place and time. These seemingly disjointed reactions could be viewed as a presentation of a kind of coping mechanism. Lappin found, in her analysis of the Wilkomirski affair, that the child's voice was being used as 'both a shield and a weapon: the author can effectively hide behind its imprecision and its vulnerability, and, at the same time, disarm a potentially sceptical reader with its emotional power'.[55] Ross Chambers argues along similar lines: the implausibility of the narrative, which had been picked up on by some historians, 'was sometimes cited as paradoxical evidence of the text's authenticity, or at least as evidence that did not disprove its authenticity'.[56] The child's voice in itself performed an authenticating function, guaranteeing the text's truth-value. As Julia Baker has also argued, *Bruchstücke* confirmed what critics expected to find in a literary depiction of trauma.[57]

A common trope in literature and art that seeks to engage with the Holocaust has been silence, as both a symbol of absence and loss, and as a means with which to say the unsayable, pointing to the indescribability of the scale and horror of the persecution. We find this explored in physical form, for example, in Daniel Libeskind's design for the Berlin Jewish Museum's extension. The zigzag construction, spanning 161,000 square feet, resembles an unravelled Star of David. Using silence, light, and empty spaces, it evokes the loss of those who died in the Holocaust and the memory of their suffering. Emptiness dominates the space, precluding 'any voyeuristic desire to see traces of the extermination'.[58] This approach, which we frequently find in literary accounts of the Holocaust, is eschewed by Wilkomirski, who instead fills such voids with scenes of explicit and graphic violence. These not only shock the reader but are presented in so uncritical a fashion that they do indeed border on the voyeuristic.

At the same time, silence is a recurring trope in the text, a feature that makes it all the more plausible, because it speaks to the inarticulation of trauma and a trope associated with writing about the Holocaust. Robert Krell, an academic and child

Holocaust survivor, comments that 'silence is the language of the child survivors'.⁵⁹ The need for, and expectation of, silence apparently continues into the post-war period for Wilkomirski, who writes in the afterword: 'Wie einfach ist es doch, ein Kindergedächtnis zu verunsichern, ein Kind zum Schweigen zu bringen. [...] ich wollte nicht mehr schweigen' [It is so easy to make a child mistrust his own reflections, to take away his voice. [...] I wanted my voice back] (*Bruchstücke*, p. 142; *Fragments*, p. 154). By writing about silence in this way, Wilkomirski invokes a trope not only of writing about the Holocaust, but also of the reception of the Holocaust in post-war culture: the silencing of the victims. He describes the silence imposed on him by his foster-parents, who apparently insisted that he not mention his experience in the camps; the silence of the Jewish experience in post-war Switzerland and Germany; and the silence of the child during his ordeal as he discovers that the safest course is to remain silent. Wilkomirski deliberately sets out to fill any such voids as a response to what he considers the void of the child's experience as a topic in post-war memory culture.

Yet, to break the silence, he puts words into the child's mouth and attempts to 'reconstruct' the child's voice. In the afterword to *Bruchstücke*, Wilkomirski cites silence as the primary motivating factor for his text, that he grew up in a time and a place where 'his experiences' were marginalized: '"Kinder haben kein Gedächtnis, Kinder vergessen schnell, du mußt alles vergessen, alles war nur ein böser Traum" — so die stets wiederholten Worte, mit denen man mir meine Erinnerungen löschen, mich seit meiner Schulzeit zum Schweigen bringen wollte' ['Children have no memories, children forget quickly, you must forget it all, it was just a bad dream.' These were the words, endlessly repeated, that were used on me from my schooldays to erase my past and make me keep quiet] (*Bruchstücke*, p. 142; *Fragments*, p. 153). His stated hope was also that his text would encourage others to find the strength to voice their memories and that their accounts and feelings, their trauma, would be taken seriously:

> Ich schrieb in der Hoffnung, daß vielleicht Menschen in vergleichbarer Situation auch die nötige Unterstützung und Kraft finden, ihre traumatischen Kindheitserinnerungen endlich in Worte zu fassen und auszusprechen, um dann zu erfahren, daß es heute noch Menschen gibt, die sie ernst nehmen. (*Bruchstücke*, p. 143)

> [I wrote [...] with the hope that perhaps other people in the same situation would find the necessary support and strength to cry out their own traumatic childhood memories, so that they too could learn that there really are people today who will take them seriously.] (*Fragments*, p. 155)

This comment is strikingly like Klüger's attitude towards German memory politics, and her demand for a considered and critical engagement with the Jewish victims of Nazism. It is striking, then, that Wilkomirski manages in the text to simulate not only the experiences of childhood in the camps, but also the post-war representation of that experience. He appropriates not only the original experience but also its legacy. Also, like Klüger in Germany, Wilkomirski argues for a wider recognition of the experiences of children during the Holocaust in Switzerland. It is ironic, then, that his account might be deemed to have in fact damaged their cause.

On one level, the question of the boundary between truth and fiction is clear-cut in Wilkomirski's case: his claim to have been in Majdanek and Birkenau is not true. He was never there. In this sense, the case of Wilkomirski is a paradigm of the phenomenon of 'autobiographical disenchantment',[60] exacerbated of course by the ethical dimension which caused widespread outrage and profound concern: that he claimed to be a Holocaust survivor when he was not one. Yet critics have questioned whether there might also be a truth in Wilkomirski's text which is beyond the truth of referentiality.[61] Misia Leibel, a former employee of one of the children's homes in which Wilkomirski claims to have been during the war, told Mächler in an interview that, although she could not remember Wilkomirski as one of the children in the home, she considered the book itself to be 'grausam wahr' [cruelly true] and found the description of fear 'sehr ehrlich' [very honest].[62] Berel Lang observes that defenders of the book have 'claimed that since his account is authentic *emotionally* that basis also certifies something akin or even identical to historical authenticity'.[63]

This raises an important question: while Wilkomirski's text does not necessarily convey the truth of his own autobiography, in the sense that he was not ever in a concentration camp, can it be said to reveal a more universal truth about history, what Linda Anderson has termed 'the pathology of history whose traumatic effects spread uncontrollably and implicate us in ways we do not as yet understand'?[64] I want to return briefly to Brettschneider's claim that the 'truth' unequivocally comes out through the poetic depiction of one's own childhood. If taken too literally, Brettschneider's comments are problematic.[65] However, they seem peculiarly apt in Wilkomirski's case. His claims to have suffered as a persecuted Jewish child have been discredited (he is not Jewish and was never in a concentration camp), and yet it is still possible to discuss (as I am doing) the ethical and stylistic aspects of his text. Schmidt argues that *Bruchstücke* can be called authentic not in terms of 'traditionelle Referenzauthentizität' [traditional referential authenticity] but because: 'Wenn die autobiographische Fälschung auch keine auf dokumentarische Fakten bzw. "verifizierbare" Daten beruhende Authentizität repräsentiert, so doch letztlich eine kollektiv anerkannte und in diskursiv-normativen Mustern verankerte Authentizität' [Even if the autobiographical fraud does not represent an authenticity based on documentary facts or 'verifiable' data, ultimately it is an authenticity which is grounded in collectively recognized and in discursive-normative patterns].[66] Andrea Reiter argues that, despite its status as a fraudulent text, it can still be considered aesthetically and psychologically authentic.[67] Scholars have called for a reappraisal of the work as fiction and, despite its tendency towards the sentimental in its uncomplicated use of the child's perspective, it has nevertheless provoked discussion and debate about the representability of the Holocaust in the post-reunification era.

While in Walser's case, the issue was the *way* in which he sets out to write his childhood, with Wilkomirski it is a question of *whether* he should be able to write a childhood which he then claims, falsely, to be his own. The critical discussion of his work has become increasingly recuperative: is there something which his account of childhood can be said to represent which in some way compensates for the fraud? Daniel Ganzfried argued that not only was Wilkomirski a fraud, he had fundamentally and dangerously affected the way in which people respond to the Holocaust:

> hier ist Mitleid ein erhebendes Gefühl. [...] Er nimmt uns die Aufgabe des Nachdenkens und die erschütternde Erfahrung des Versagens unseres Menschenverstandes vor dem Faktum Auschwitz ab. Wir benützen das Erleben des andern, um nicht denkend wettmachen zu müssen, was sich der Vorstellungskraft entzieht. Gedankenlos mitleidend, finden wir im Opfer den Helden, mit dem wir uns auf der Seite der Moral verbrüdern können: Binjamin Wilkomirski.[68]
>
> [here pity is an uplifting feeling. [...] He relieves us of the task of reflection, and of the shocking experience of the failure of our conception of what it is to be human in the face of the fact of Auschwitz. We use the experience of another, because we have uncritically to make up for what eludes our power of imagination. Minds blank, pitying, we find in the victim the hero with whom we can stand shoulder-to-shoulder on the right side of morality: Binjamin Wilkomirski.]

That the protagonist is so consciously and deliberately presented as an innocent and baffled child only serves to make this 'Mitleidsucht' [pathological need for pity] more affecting. It recalls the kind of empathy that the child's experience is seen to evoke. It also further underlines Adorno's comment on what he perceived as the overly empathetic and uncritical reception of Anne Frank's story. It signals one of the potential problems with the notion of 'gefühlte Geschichte': that emotional responses will come to outweigh critical engagement. This was exacerbated by the claims that the text was an account of trauma experienced by a writer, offering *this* suffering childhood as his own: claims proven to be false.

Through the Looking Glass: *Reise im August* (1992)

In her novel *Reise im August* (1992), Gudrun Pausewang writes from the perspective of an eleven-year-old Jewish protagonist, Alice Dubsky, who with her grandfather is travelling on a transport to Auschwitz.[69] The narrative begins as Alice, her grandfather, and forty-seven other prisoners are loaded onto a wagon. During the journey, Alice, from whom the truth of Jewish persecution has been kept secret, talks with other children and adults, and gradually discovers the reality of the situation. The narrative ends as Alice, now alone, stands in a gas chamber awaiting the 'Wasser des Lebens' [water of life] (*Reise*, p. 175; *Journey*, p. 154) of the shower which, as the reader knows, will in fact result in her death. Unlike the fictional constructs of Austerlitz and Wilkomirski, Alice does not experience long-term adulthood. Her trajectory from the beginning of the text results not in the usual taboo (for this kind of writing) of premature adulthood, but rather in premature death at the hands of the Nazis.

Reise im August engages directly with the question of whether someone who has not suffered under the Nazis can legitimately speak for, or at least about, a Jewish victim of National Socialist persecution. Pausewang was born in 1928 in the Sudetenland, whence she and her family fled during the Soviet advance at the end of the war.[70] At the same age as her protagonist in *Reise im August*, she was a member of the *Bund deutscher Mädel*. The book is intended primarily for a teenage market, as part of a genre identified by Susan Tebbutt as 'socially critical "Jugendliteratur" [young-adult literature]'.[71] In this way, it is intended to inform contemporary youth about the reality of the Holocaust. The text foregrounds the felt experience of the journey. Alice is a child who is easily disgusted, who hates dirt, and who has been kept shielded from the unsavoury elements of life. Throughout the journey, she encounters vomit, menstrual blood, diarrhoea, and childbirth. Tebbutt suggests that such elements are 'unconventional in the context of children's novels'.[72] However, striking here is that not only these, but also the themes and events of adult Holocaust literature, are dealt with realistically and uncompromisingly. Unlike Wilkomirski's text, though, these elements are 'not just prurient voyeurism or exploitation of the horror-genre, but part of Pausewang's use of dystopian images to transmit a utopian vision'.[73]

The journey of the title is both physical and metaphorical: it marks the journey to Auschwitz and simultaneously Alice's journey from childhood to adulthood. In *Reise im August*, childhood is synonymous with a lack of knowledge. Like the young Klüger and Goldschmidt, discussed in the previous chapter, the fictional Alice has been protected from a dark secret by her family. Yet, while Klüger's curiosity leads her to uncover the secret, and Goldschmidt comes quickly to a realization of the truth, Alice only gradually learns the reality of her situation. The systematic process of Jewish persecution has been kept from Alice by her parents and grandparents who, two years previously, went into hiding in the cellar of their old apartment building. This period in the basement flat is evoked in flashbacks and memories throughout the novel; it was, as Alice comes gradually to realize, not what it seemed. For example, when Alice asks why they cannot go out into the streets anymore, her grandmother explains: 'es ist jetzt so schmutzig in den Straßen [...]. In diesem Schmutz kann man sich den Tod holen' [it's so dirty out in the streets now [...] You could catch your death in that dirt] (*Reise*, p. 53; *Journey*, pp. 40–41). There is an irony here, for going out onto the street will indeed mean death, but of a different kind. It is sustained through Alice's naive perspective. Later, when Alice does go out for the first time in two years after soldiers come to the flat and round up her and her grandparents, she notices that the streets are not dirty after all. She first wonders whether her grandmother has told her a lie, and then asks herself: 'Und warum hatten ihr Mami und Papi nicht die Wahrheit gesagt?' [And why had Mummy and Daddy not told her the truth?] (*Reise*, p. 55; *Journey*, p. 43).

Alice's innocence, which in this case is considered the equivalent of not knowing, is symbolized by the cellar in which the family hides before deportation. The cellar protects her from the many truths about which her family feels she need not know. Alice recalls staring longingly up into the outside world: 'an diesen Fenstern hatte

Alice stundenlang gesessen und geträumt. Sie hatte sich danach gesehnt, jenseits der Mauer zu sein, im Garten herumzutoben und auf der Schaukel zu sitzen' [Alice had sat for hours beside the windows, dreaming. She had yearned to be on the other side of the wall, to tear around the garden, or sit on the swing] (*Reise*, p. 43; *Journey*, p. 32). As soon as they leave the cellar, the grandparents continue to try to protect her from all kinds of truths. For example, Alice entreats another girl her age, Rebekka, to tell her 'alles, was ich wissen muss' [what I ought to know] (*Reise*, p. 41; *Journey*, p. 31), but the grandfather calls her away. The other children also initially try to shield Alice from the truth when they realize that she knows nothing of the racial persecution taking place throughout the Third Reich. The narrative echoes Klüger's criticism of adults' false estimation of what children can comprehend. When Alice finally comes to understand the reality of the situation — that they are prisoners, being sent to a camp because they are Jewish — she accuses her grandfather of having kept it from her. He is unable to give much of a reply, protesting: 'Du bist doch noch so jung!' [You are still so young] (*Reise*, p. 85; *Journey*, p. 71). He then points out that, since the adults barely comprehend what is happening, they could not have expected a child to begin to. The narrative focalizer is Alice, however, who expresses outrage at having been lied to and infantilized, insisting that she *would* have been able to understand.

While the cellar provides protection, it has also stunted her personal development. Many accounts of children in the Holocaust tell of encountering the standard taboo of having to grow up too quickly, to take the place of absent parents, looking after themselves and younger siblings.[74] Alice, however, has had the opposite experience: her youthful innocence has been preserved and her childhood unnaturally prolonged to shield her from the horrors of reality. In this constellation, then, the wagon represents both another prison, but also a means of release from a state which, while not a taboo, is nonetheless an uncomfortable one for the reader to imagine. For it is here that Alice can catch up on all she has missed. When her grandfather dies during the course of the journey, Alice comments: 'Großvater war tot. Es gab niemand mehr, der über sie bestimmen konnte. [...] Jetzt war Schluss mit dem Keller. Jetzt begann das richtige Leben' [Grandfather was dead. Now there was no one to make decisions for her. [...] The basement was in the past; real life was about to begin] (*Reise*, p. 120; *Journey*, p. 103). This is another irony for the adult reader, for whom it must be clear, especially given that Alice has been said to be small for her age, that she will perish.

Having had no contact with her peer group, and having been protected from any kind of sexual knowledge by her parents and grandparents, Alice has no awareness of her burgeoning sexuality. The physical and emotional development which comes with puberty is one of the ways in which Alice is shown to move from childhood to adulthood. The final step on this journey is marked by the onset of menstruation as she and the others stand in the gas chamber: the physical mark of her movement into adulthood is the last event before her death. Alice's final thoughts include a moment's reflection on the attractiveness of one of the boys: the only man she had ever previously seen naked was her grandfather. This final scene is, on one hand, extremely crass; yet, on the other hand, Pausewang succeeds in demonstrating the futility of Alice's death, just as her adult life is shown to begin, and provides a more complex image of the child on the threshold of becoming sexually aware.

Indeed, Alice is no innocent victim figure whom the author depicts uncritically so as to elicit a purely sentimental response from the reader. Alice is depicted as petulant. She verbally attacks her grandfather for having kept the truth of Nazi persecution from her. His death occurs during her tirade. The text seems in this way to respond indirectly to Klüger's call for a more critical view of the victims, in that Alice is not presented as nothing more than a passive victim. Alice's response to her grandfather's collapse is similarly shocking: 'auf einem fremden Rucksack sah Alice eine große, zusammengeklappte Brotschnitte liegen. Instinktiv griff sie nach ihr und stopfte die mit Griebenschmalz bestrichene Schnitte in sich hinein' [on someone else's rucksack Alice saw a large, folded slice of bread. Instinctively she grabbed it and stuffed the dripping-spread slice into her mouth] (*Reise*, p. 87; *Journey*, p. 73). The action is uncharacteristic and shocking, preventing a purely sentimental response.

Like so many narratives of childhood, *Reise im August* contains allusions to fairy tales which have both a comforting, but also sinister quality. In response to Alice's admission that she has no idea about what is happening to the Jews, one of the boys exclaims: 'deine Leute haben dich aber ganz schön ahnungslos gehalten. Haben die dich in einen Rapunzelturm gesteckt?' [your people have left you absolutely clueless. Did they keep you in Rapunzel's tower?] (*Reise*, p. 83; *Journey*, p. 69). Here the cellar is transformed, in the language of the children, into Rapunzel's tower, which keeps the princess hidden from the outside world. Isolde, a name rich with fictional allusions, is the name of the child who says they should tell her the truth because Alice is 'zu alt für diese Kindermärchen' [too old for those fairy-stories] (*Reise*, p. 83; *Journey*, p. 68).

Most prominent of these intertextual allusions, however, is the link between Alice and the protagonist of Lewis Carroll's classic, *Alice's Adventures in Wonderland* (1865), and *Through the Looking-Glass* (1871). Like Carroll's Alice, Alice Dubsky recites advice and commands given by her parents and grandmother during the initial stage of the journey. In addition, Alice's development causes her to question her own identity, as does Alice in 'Wonderland'. At one point she muses:

> I wonder if I've been changed in the night? Let me think: *was* I the same when I got up this morning? I almost think I can remember feeling a little different. But if I'm not the same, the next question is 'Who in the world am I?' Ah, *that's* the great puzzle![75]

The passive construction employed here raises questions of agency: by what forces are the children's lives being guided, and what will be their destination? And yet, a juxtaposition of 'Wonderland' and Auschwitz initially seems incongruous and is loaded with bitter irony,[76] for Carroll's text has been regarded in popular culture as a tale of the fantastical. And yet, the 'Wonderland' of the title also suggests a world turned upside-down; indeed, more than one critic has noted the sinister nature of Carroll's fictional world. It is reminiscent of Klüger's definition of Auschwitz as a 'verkehrte Welt' [world turned upside-down] where all logic is gone. Like the world of Carroll's text, time appears suspended and scenes appear to merge into one another in a dream-like sequence. 'Wonderland' has reversed the true and proper meanings of things. Virginia Woolf wrote of *Alice in Wonderland* that

> to become a child is to be very literal; to find everything so strange that nothing is surprising; to be heartless, to be ruthless, yet to be so passionate that a snub or a shadow drapes the world in gloom. It is so to be in *Alice in Wonderland*.[77]

It may be this quality of literalness, of finding everything so new that nothing shocks, which we find disturbing about *Reise im August* and perhaps about children's views of the Holocaust.

Alice's child's perspective is initially a conventional narrative means of encouraging the reader to fill in the gaps left by her lack of knowledge. The reader is given clues and is left to piece together the truth from the ironies. For example, Alice recalls that, after her parents had departed from the cellar never to return, she received two letters from them. She observes: 'merkwürdig war nur, daß Mami und Papi dort, wo sie jetzt waren, eine Schreibmaschine hatten, bei der das große P ganz ähnlich klemmte wie bei Großvaters alter Schreibmaschine' [the only extraordinary thing was that where they were now, Mummy and Daddy had a typewriter in which the capital D stuck just like the one on Grandfather's old typewriter] (*Reise*, p. 56; *Journey*, p. 44). When Alice draws his attention to this, the grandfather is silent and then is reported to have said 'was für eine scharfe Beobachtungsgabe sie doch habe!' [and how observant she was!] (*Reise*, p. 56; *Final Journey*, p. 44). Alice recalls many such instances of the adult protecting the child from knowledge. The terrible irony of this, however, is that even those who are adults do not know what awaits them at Auschwitz. Thus, while Alice has become an adult through her acquisition of knowledge throughout the journey, she remains, like her companions, a victim of ignorance of the true capacity for evil which awaits them in the gas chambers.

By writing this account, Pausewang seeks to make legible the Jewish child's experience, to warn and inform young readers about the dangers of extremism and the human capacity to inflict suffering. However, *Reise im August* raises ethical questions about the legitimacy of a former BDM member writing a first-person account of a Jewish child's experience of the Holocaust. Indeed, the novel has the potential to be inflammatory: it is a fictional text about a child victim of the Holocaust which depicts not only this experience from the protagonist's perspective, but also shows the moment of her death in the gas chambers. Tebbutt has argued that Pausewang has that right;[78] and, seen within the context of her life-long literary project, Pausewang's text should be viewed as an attempt to assert an experience which she considers neglected in memory culture and which, she believes, will prove educational to subsequent generations of Germans.

Conclusion: The Ethics of Memory and Problems of Authenticity

In all three texts discussed in this chapter, childhood is fashioned as a period of confinement. This is an ambiguous concept: on the one hand, it provides security and protection from the dangers of the world. On the other, it can act as a means of stifling the child, denying it the knowledge and tools it requires to engage with these complexities. In *Austerlitz*, the protagonist recalls the claustrophobic atmosphere of the manse, and Sebald depicts the self-imposed psychological confinement that separates the adult Austerlitz from the memories of his early childhood in Prague. For the child in *Bruchstücke*, childhood is spent in the physical confinement of the ghettos and camps. He is unable to understand that the war is over, and so experiences what he believes to be a continued state of conflict: the atmosphere of confinement thus remains for Wilkomirski. For Alice Dubsky, the cellar is a prison that keeps her in a perpetual state of childhood, protected from persecution, but also shielded from development into adolescence and beyond. It is ironic that the wagon to Auschwitz simultaneously facilitates the beginnings of her adult life, but also its end. Like the texts in the previous chapter, those discussed here describe a range of experience: deportation, survival in the camps, exile. In addition, they explore the notion of journey; however, while Austerlitz, the protagonist of Wilkomirski's text, and Alice all undertake a journey in the physical sense, they do not experience a psychological journey into adolescence. Where Klüger, Goldschmidt, and Kunert used this idea of journey to challenge the static, symbolic representation of the Jewish child victim of the Holocaust, the authors in this chapter seem rather to reinforce it.

Yet, above all, these texts raise questions of the legitimacy of writing about the Holocaust from the perspective of those who experience it themselves. At one extreme, we find Elie Wiesel's statement that 'literature of the Holocaust does not exist, cannot exist. It is a contradiction in terms [...]. A novel about Treblinka is either not a novel, or not about Treblinka.'[79] At the other, we find Timothy Dow Adams's question, posed in his study of American autobiographical texts, about whether 'it [is] more important to be true or to ring true'.[80] In the particular case of Holocaust writing, and especially as shown by the reactions to *Bruchstücke*, these questions are invested with an urgent ethical dimension. In this context, Rousseau's notion of the 'truth of feelings', as cultivated in his *Confessions*, proves inadequate, as it fails to respond to the weight of the Holocaust's documentary burden.

Sebald writes as a member of the second generation, born in 1944, with no first-hand memory of the war or Nazism, but with a close familial connection to it. In an interview with Christian Scholz, Sebald revealed his own response to leafing through family photograph albums:

> as a rule, you look through these albums as a child, completely naively, without any sense for history or of history or any knowledge of the Third Reich. You didn't know what role your parents played during this period of history, what position they adopted. [...] And then you left them lying in a drawer. When you get them in your hands again, say as a forty-year-old, after a gap of twenty or twenty-five years, the whole thing is something of a negative revelation. Because in the interim you've learned what history is.[81]

The historical knowledge gleaned in the intervening time between childhood and adulthood casts the photographs and family memory in a new light.

Sebald engages with the issue of legitimacy within *Austerlitz*, most particularly by examining questions of authenticity through his combination of fictional narrative and documentary sources, both in the composition of the text and in the use of photographs. *Austerlitz* was one of a number of texts, published from the late 1990s onwards, which 'explore the tension between photographic evidence, the imaginative reconstruction of the past and the pursuit of historical truth'.[82] Despite its status as a fictional work, Nicholas Lezard, writing in the *Guardian*, described *Austerlitz* as possessing 'an unimpugnable tang of veracity'.[83] Yet Sebald challenges the authenticity-value attributed to photographs, and his approach takes on an integrity precisely through this questioning which he sets up within the narrative. At every turn, he reminds the reader of the inherent unreliability and subjectivity of the photograph. Patricia Holland argues, in *Picturing Childhood: The Myth of the Child in Popular Imagery* (2004), that children appear to be perfect photographical subjects because they are 'innocent' and 'make no attempt to shape their own image'.[84] This results, as Holland contends, in an adult gaze which takes pleasure in the innocence of childhood, and which exerts power over that subject. But, she argues, 'the innocence of the child and that of the photographic image have proved equally deceptive'.[85] Thus, when the image of the 'child Austerlitz' appears, a dual deception commences. By being manipulated, Sebald's photographs take on a 'tang of veracity'; in being used for fictional ends, the deployment of the innocent child victim of the Holocaust is used to achieve the same result.

In contrast, Wilkomirski presses the analogy between memory and the photograph into service to prove the veracity of his account. The photograph becomes a guarantor of authenticity. As Hirsch observes, 'photography's promise to offer an access to the event itself, and its easy assumption of iconic and symbolic power, makes it a uniquely powerful medium for the transmission of events that remain unimaginable'.[86] In addition, the construction of the child's voice in *Bruchstücke* has invited criticism, yet it was also what was considered the text's most compelling aspect. It bears out Douglas's claim in *Contesting Childhood* that 'when the naïve child voice enters the text, this commonly functions as a gesture of authenticity'.[87] The child's voice in *Bruchstücke* acts as a guarantor of truth.

We can look at this another way, by placing our fictional, or imagined, texts alongside the life writing examined in the previous chapter. *Bruchstücke* is, on the face of it, strikingly like Goldschmidt's *Die Absonderung*, both in its style and in some of its primary concerns.[88] The two respective protagonists are separated from their parents at an early age; both endure hardship and terror in a school environment; and both are the victims of violence, persecution, and fear. In addition, the style of both works is not dissimilar: both are structured in a series of short chapters which are only loosely linked, and which depict moments in the protagonists' childhood. Just as in *Die Absonderung* the body is conceptualized as a site in which trauma can be found, so in *Bruchstücke* the physical effects of the camps are the most prominent aspect. However, while Goldschmidt offers a complex literary account into which he incorporates the qualifying view of the remembering adult, and which is written in a neutral and measured style, Wilkomirski's naive perspective of the child offers the reader what ends up reading like a 'Greuelmärchen' [atrocity story].

The questioning approach associated with the naive child is extended to the adult characters in Pausewang's text. When Alice angrily demands of her grandfather his reasons for not telling her the truth about the persecution of the Jews, one of the other passengers comments on the problematic notion of truth in general: '"wenn man nur immer wüsste, was Lüge und was Wahrheit ist", sagte Herr Blum. "Wer weiß, ob gerade das die Wahrheit ist, was wir jetzt für Wahrheit halten"' ['if only one knew what was lies and what was the truth,' said Mr Blum. 'Who knows if what we now think is true really *is* the truth?'] (*Reise*, p. 86; *Journey*, p. 72). Here, Pausewang transfers the idea of the dream-like world of 'Wonderland' to the world of the Holocaust, in which reality has become so absurd that it seems to be incomprehensible to those experiencing it. Herr Blum's uncertainty about the nature of reality also draws attention to the fictional nature of Pausewang's text. As Zohar Shavit writes:

> unlike the prevalent German discourse, which seeks to lend a sense of authenticity to narratives by resorting to a perspective that provides an account of the events 'as they were', Pausewang undermines the truth-value of the story provided by the structure of the perspective.[89]

But, if the adults' questioning serves to undermine the story's truth-value in this way, by allowing them to be presented as, to a degree, infantilized, then Alice's almost completely unquestioning approach does so even more, since this lack of curiosity is not what we expect from a child.

In her introduction to *Children with a Star: Jewish Youth in Nazi Europe* (1993), Dwork defends the title of her text against those who point out that the many children who suffered as a result of the Holocaust never wore a Star of David. Those in hiding for example, or children under the age of six, ten, or twelve years of age (depending on the location), were in fact not required to wear it. Dwork views the star as an 'icon': 'It is a symbolic image which embodies more than mere description; it transcends historical accuracy for the sake of historical truth.'[90] The image on the dust jacket of the most recent paperback edition of *Reise im August* also serves to contradict the narrative in this way. The cover illustration shows Alice and her grandfather carrying their suitcases. The figures are painted entirely in a dark, murky green and depicted on a red background. The title appears in yellow, and both figures are wearing a bright yellow Star of David. This image does not correspond to the narrative contained within, however. Early on in the novel, Alice asks her grandfather why *they* are not wearing stars like the other prisoners. He explains that because they have not been out in the street, they have not had to wear them (*Reise*, p. 30). Naturally, the book cover needs to signal its contents, especially since the title does not.[91] Here, the cover illustration performs a symbolic function, rather like Dwork's use of the 'Star of David' in the title of her historical account. It announces that this is a novel about the Holocaust, whether or not the characters in fact wear the stars. The semiotics of the Holocaust novel include such devices;

the question is whether 'authentic' accounts of childhood in the Third Reich can be said to be employing the conventions of the child narrator in the same way as they employ the photograph or other received images of the victims. The child as subject becomes the guarantor of authenticity, and there is a conventional mode of expression given to the child which, when used, signifies a desire to project 'authenticity'.

The manner of their reception suggests that these texts are indeed considered to offer 'authenticity', and that this is achieved precisely through their depiction of childhood. Thus, the focus on children in these texts is significant. Hirsch examines the power of the Jewish child Holocaust victim as an image, particularly within photographs, and posits that these have a singular effect. She writes that 'every child whose image we see is, at least metaphorically, one who perished' and that 'images of children readily lend themselves to such universalization'.[92] Because of the ideas associated with childhood by Western culture, which Hirsch identifies here as innocence and vulnerability, the photographic image of the child 'elicits an affiliative and identificatory as well as a protective spectatorial look marked by these investments'.[93] Images of child victims of the Holocaust are so ubiquitous because of their identificatory potential, and because they 'bring home the utter senselessness of Holocaust destruction'.[94]

However, the danger of this, which I have identified as a concern throughout this study, is that it can preclude a critical engagement with the past. Hirsch considers Wilkomirski's text to be problematic precisely because it asks the reader to identify with the child figure. This image of the child victim

> facilitates an identification in which the viewer can too easily become a surrogate victim. Most important, the easy identification with children, their virtually universal availability for projection, risks the blurring of important areas of difference and alterity: context, specificity, responsibility, history.[95]

An alternative, as Hirsch suggests, might be found in the concept of 'working through', which, in Dominick LaCapra's analysis, involves a response which 'implies the possibility of judgement [...], self-questioning, and [is] related in mediated ways to action'.[96] It encourages learning from the past.

This has significant implications for the way in which the Jewish experience of childhood in the Third Reich will be made legible after the last eyewitnesses have disappeared. These texts offer a representation of the child's experience, and, through their close association with authenticity, through the conditions of the texts' composition and the deployment of the child figure, there is a suggestion that they will contain an account of lived experience. The kind of response that this might elicit has, as I have outlined, its own problems. These three texts contribute to contemporary discussions about identity and origins by provoking a debate about the extent to which the appearance of authenticity can be a legitimate goal of those tackling historical subjects, particularly one as ethically charged as the Holocaust. They encourage us to ask whether the texts might, even as imagined accounts, tell us something 'emotionally authentic' about the past, which makes it more 'accessible' to those coming after. At the same time, our scrutiny of these texts contributes further to that debate.

Notes to Chapter 4

1. Susan R. Suleiman, 'Problems of Memory and Factuality in Recent Holocaust Memoirs: Wilkomirski/Wiesel', *Poetics Today*, 21 (2000), 543–59 (p. 552).
2. W. G. Sebald, *Austerlitz* (Frankfurt a.M.: Fischer Taschenbuch, 2001). Translations are taken from *Austerlitz*, trans. by Anthea Bell (London: Hamilton, 2001), cited in the main text as 'trans. by Bell'. On Sebald's own childhood, see Mark M. Anderson, 'A Childhood in the Allgäu: Wertach, 1944–52', in *Saturn's Moons: W. G. Sebald: A Handbook*, ed. by Jo Catling and Richard Hibbitt (London: Legenda, 2011), pp. 16–42.
3. Mark Richard McCulloh, *Understanding Sebald* (Columbia: University of South Carolina Press, 2003), p. 136.
4. Anne Fuchs, *Die Schmerzensspuren der Geschichte: Zur Poetik der Erinnerung in W. G. Sebalds Prosa* (Cologne: Böhlau, 2004), p. 56.
5. Fuchs, *Schmerzensspuren*, p. 57.
6. See ibid., pp. 56–57.
7. Helen Finch, ' "Die irdische Erfüllung": Peter Handke's Poetic Landscapes and W. G. Sebald's Metaphysics of History', in *W. G. Sebald and the Writing of History*, ed. by Anne Fuchs and J. J. Long (Würzburg: Königshausen & Neumann, 2007), pp. 179–97 (p. 196).
8. Carolin Duttlinger draws on Freud and Benjamin to examine the interrelation between photography and traumatic memory, suggesting that photography can also be linked to forgetting (Carolin Duttlinger, 'Traumatic Photographs: Remembrance and the Technical Media in W. G. Sebald's *Austerlitz*', in *W. G. Sebald: A Critical Companion*, ed. by J. J. Long and Anne Whitehead (Edinburgh: Edinburgh University Press, 2006), pp. 155–75 (p. 158)). Stefanie Harris argues that the combination of text and image in *Die Ausgewanderten* serves to 'address questions of representation and representability' (Stefanie Harris, 'The Return of the Dead: Memory and Photography in W. G. Sebald's *Die Ausgewanderten*', *German Quarterly*, 74 (2001), 379–91 (p. 381), while Maya Barzilai considers the photographs to function at an 'affective-aesthetic level', providing an experiential sense of the way deep memory functions which, I would argue, can be extended to Austerlitz (Maya Barzilai, 'On Exposures: Photography and Uncanny Memory in W. G. Sebald's *Die Ausgewanderten* and *Austerlitz*', in *W. G. Sebald: History — Memory — Trauma*, ed. by Scott Denham and Mark McCulloh (Berlin: de Gruyter, 2006), pp. 205–19 (p. 207). Nina Pelikan Straus reads the juxtaposition of text and image as part of a Wittgensteinian framework, suggesting that 'a form of pictorial healing is symbolically achieved by connecting what has been disconnected through the juxtapositions of language and photographs' (Nina Pelikan Straus, 'Sebald, Wittgenstein, and the Ethics of Memory', *Comparative Literature*, 61 (2009), 43–53 (p. 46)).
9. J. J. Long, 'History, Narrative, and Photography in W. G. Sebald's "Die Ausgewanderten"', *Modern Language Review*, 98 (2003), 117–37 (p. 137).
10. Long, pp. 131–32.
11. Long, p. 137.
12. Roland Barthes, *Camera Lucida: Reflections on Photography*, trans. by Richard Howard (New York: Hill and Wang, 1993), p. 91. See Barzilai.
13. Maguire, p. 153.
14. Silke Horstkotte, *Nachbilder: Fotografie und Gedächtnis in der deutschen Gegenwartsliteratur* (Cologne: Böhlau, 2009), p. 240. Horstkotte, pp. 215–16, reads Sebald's inclusion of photographic material in the text, and his thematizing of photography within the narrative, as part of a discourse centred on intergenerational transfer of memory.
15. Ibid., p. 239.
16. Ibid., p. 240.
17. On the photographs of 'Austerlitz' in the text, see the excellent analysis by Kevin Brazil, *Art, History, and Postwar Fiction* (Oxford: Oxford University Press, 2018), pp. 159–63.
18. See Hirsch, *Generation of Postmemory*, pp. 49–52.
19. On the role of postmemory in Sebald's works, see Long, pp. 122–37.
20. Douglas, p. 44.
21. Ibid., p. 45.

22. The photograph depicts an architectural historian and friend of Sebald as a child; see Maya Jaggi, 'Recovered Memories', *The Guardian*, 22 September 2001 <http://www.guardian.co.uk/books/2001/sep/22/artsandhumanities.highereducation> [accessed 1 July 2019].
23. Douglas, p. 60.
24. Sina Najafi, 'Picturing Innocence: An Interview with Anne Higonnet' <http://www.cabinetmagazine.org/issues/9/picturing_innocence.php> [accessed 1 July 2019].
25. Ludwig Bechstein, *Deutsches Märchenbuch* (Leipzig: Wigand, 1847), p. 35. Margaret Olin reads this differently, arguing that the child in the photograph is reminiscent of Oktavian, the title character in Hugo von Hofmannsthal's *Der Rosenkavalier*, evoking the complexity of identity; see Margaret Olin, *Touching Photographs* (Chicago: University of Chicago Press, 2012), p. 93.
26. Nancy Martha West, *Kodak and the Lens of Nostalgia* (London: University Press of Virginia, 2000), p. 84.
27. Stefanie Boese, '"Forever Just Occurring": Postwar Belatedness in W. G. Sebald's Austerlitz', *Journal of Modern Literature*, 39.4 (2016), 104–21 (p. 114).
28. Barzilai, p. 214.
29. Emine Sevgi Özdamar, *Mutterzunge: Erzählungen* (Cologne: Kiepenheuer & Witsch, 1998), p. 44; Emine Sevgi Özdamar, *Mother Tongue*, trans. by Craig Thomas (Toronto: Coach House Press, 1994), p. 52.
30. Katja Garloff, 'The Task of the Narrator: Moments of Symbolic Investiture in W. G. Sebald's *Austerlitz*', in *W. G. Sebald*, ed. by Denham and McCulloh, pp. 157–71 (p. 168).
31. Martin Doerry and Volker Hage, 'Ich fürchte das Melodramatische' [interview with W. G. Sebald], *Der Spiegel*, 12 March 2001, pp. 228–34 (p. 232).
32. Jeremy Josephs with Susi Bechhöfer, *Rosa's Child: The True Story of One Woman's Quest for a Lost Mother and a Vanished Past* (London: I. B. Tauris, 1996). See Martin Modlinger, '"You can't change names and feel the same": The Kindertransport Experience of Susi Bechhöfer in W. G. Sebald's *Austerlitz*', in *The Kindertransport to Britain*, ed. by Hammel and Lewkowicz, pp. 219–32.
33. Susi Bechhöfer, 'Stripped of my Past by a Bestselling Author', *Sunday Times*, 30 June 2002.
34. Jaggi.
35. Elizabeth Baer, 'W. G. Sebald's *Austerlitz*: Adaptation as Restitution', in *Adaptations in Film, the Arts, and Popular Culture: Reworking the German Past*, ed. by Susan G. Figge and Jenifer K. Ward (Rochester, NY: Camden House, 2010), pp. 181–203.
36. Quotations are taken from Binjamin Wilkomirski, *Bruchstücke: Aus einer Kindheit 1939–1948* (Frankfurt a.M.: Suhrkamp, 1998), henceforth cited in the main text as *Bruchstücke*. Translations are taken from *Fragments: Memories of a Childhood, 1939–1948*, trans. by Carol Brown Janeway (London: Picador, 1996), cited in the main text as *Fragments*.
37. It is interesting to note that Suhrkamp had deemed *weiter leben* insufficiently 'literary'. See Ursula März, 'Nur Unversöhnlichkeit hilft weiter' <http://www.zeit.de/2008/42/L-Klueger-Besuch> [accessed 1 July 2019].
38. See Anne Whitehead, 'Telling Tales: Trauma and Testimony in Binjamin Wilkomirski's *Fragments*', *Discourse*, 25 (2003), 119–37 (p. 120).
39. Stefan Mächler, *Der Fall Wilkomirski: Über die Wahrheit einer Biographie* (Zurich: Pendo, 2000), pp. 127–29.
40. Cited in Mächler, *Der Fall Wilkomirski*, pp. 130–31; Stefan Maechler, *The Wilkomirski Affair: A Study in Biographical Truth*, trans. by John E. Woods (London: Picador, 2001), p. 116.
41. Hanno Helbling, letter to Siegfried Unseld, 9 February 1995, cited in Mächler, *Der Fall Wilkomirski*, p. 109; Maechler, *The Wilkomirski Affair*, p. 94.
42. Daniel Ganzfried, 'Die geliehene Holocaust-Biographie', *Die Weltwoche*, 27 August 1998, p. 45. This was one of a number of articles Ganzfried wrote on the subject between August 1998 and November 1999.
43. Ganzfried.
44. Elena Lappin, 'The Man with Two Heads' <https://granta.com/the-man-with-two-heads> [accessed 1 July 2019].
45. See esp. Reiter, 'Memory and Authenticity'; Suleiman, 'Problems of Memory and Factuality'; Schmidt, pp. 201–18.

46. See e.g. Vice, pp. 155–59.
47. Mächler, *Der Fall Wilkomirski*, p. 298.
48. Gerhard Zeillinger, *Kindheit und Schreiben: Zur Biographie und Poetik des Schriftstellers Julian Schutting* (Stuttgart: Heinz, 1995), p. 47.
49. Lappin.
50. Mächler, *Der Fall Wilkomirski*, p. 295.
51. Maechler, *The Wilkomirski Affair*, p. 276.
52. Ruth Klüger, 'Kitsch ist immer plausibel: Was man aus den erfundenen Erinnerungen des Binjamin Wilkomirski lernen kann', in *... alias Wilkomirski*, ed. by Ganzfried and Hefti, pp. 225–29 (p. 226).
53. Reiter, 'Memory and Authenticity', p. 141, contests Klüger's conclusions here.
54. Susan R. Suleiman, 'Do Facts Matter in Holocaust Memoirs? Wilkomirski/Wiesel', in *Obliged by Memory: Literature, Religion, Ethics*, ed. by Steven T. Katz and Alan Rosen (Syracuse: Syracuse University Press, 2006), pp. 21–43 (p. 28).
55. Lappin.
56. Ross Chambers, 'Orphaned Memories, Foster-Writing, Phantom Pain: The *Fragments* Affair', in *Extremities: Trauma, Testimony and Community*, ed. by Nancy K. Miller and Jason Tougaw (Urbana: University of Illinois Press, 2002), pp. 92–112 (pp. 98–99). Reiter, 'Memory and Authenticity', p. 134, explains that she herself found the 'apparent lack of logic' to be evidence of the text's authenticity.
57. Baker, p. 308.
58. Eric Kligerman, *Sites of the Uncanny: Paul Celan, Specularity and the Visual Arts* (Berlin: de Gruyter, 2007), p. 250.
59. Krell, 'Elderly Children as Grown Ups', p. 16.
60. Michael Jopling, *Re-Placing the Self: Fictional and Autobiographical Interplay in Modern German Narrative (Elias Canetti, Thomas Bernhard, Peter Weiss, Christa Wolf)* (Stuttgart: Heinz, 2001), p. 272.
61. See e.g. Suleiman, 'Problems of Memory and Factuality'.
62. Mächler, *Der Fall Wilkomirski*, p. 194; Maechler, *The Wilkomirski Affair*, p. 178.
63. Berel Lang, *Post-Holocaust: Interpretation, Misinterpretation, and the Claims of History* (Bloomington: Indiana University Press, 2005), p. 83.
64. L. Anderson, p. 133.
65. Brettschneider, p. 5.
66. Schmidt, p. 270.
67. Reiter, 'Memory and Authenticity', p. 140.
68. Ganzfried.
69. Gudrun Pausewang, *Reise im August* (Ravensburg: Ravensburger Buchverlag, 1997), cited in the main text as *Reise*. Translations are taken from *The Final Journey*, trans. by Patricia Crampton (London: Puffin, 1998), cited in the main text as *Journey*.
70. Pausewang recounts her experiences growing up in her autobiographical trilogy *Rosinkawiese*, published between 1980 and 1990. For a discussion of these texts, see Kati Tonkin, 'From "Sudetendeutsche" to "Adlergebirgler": Gudrun Pausewang's *Rosinkawiese* Trilogy', in *Coming Home to Germany? The Integration of Ethnic Germans from Central and Eastern Europe in the Federal Republic*, ed. by David Rock and Stefan Wolff (New York: Berghahn, 2002), pp. 119–213.
71. See Susan Tebbutt, *Gudrun Pausewang in Context: Socially Critical 'Jugendliteratur'* (Frankfurt a.M.: Lang, 1994).
72. Susan Tebbutt, 'Journey to an Unknown Destination: Gudrun Pausewang's Transgressive Teenage Novel *Reise im August*', in *German Culture and the Uncomfortable Past*, ed. by Schmitz, pp. 165–83 (p. 176). English-language novels for children and teenagers of eleven and upwards have been dealing with these themes for over forty years (e.g. Judy Blume, *Are You There, God? It's Me, Margaret* (London: Pan Piper, 1970)).
73. Tebbutt, *Gudrun Pausewang in Context*, p. 165.
74. Sokoloff, p. 259.
75. Lewis Carroll, *Alice's Adventures in Wonderland* (London: Penguin, 2006), p. 17. The text is available to German readers in over thirty translated versions.

76. Rüdiger Steinlein, '*Sternkinder* und *Tote Engel* — Bilder des Holocaust in der Kinder- und Jugendliteratur zwischen pädagogisch-moralischer Wiedergutmachung und dokumentarisch-katastrophischer Wirkungsästhethik', in *Bilder des Holocaust*, ed. by Köppen and Scherpe, pp. 63–97 (p. 89).
77. Virginia Woolf, 'Lewis Carroll', in *Aspects of Alice: Lewis Carroll's Dreamchild as Seen through the Critics' Looking-Glasses, 1865–1971*, ed. by Robert Philips (London: Gollancz, 1972), pp. 47–50 (p. 48).
78. Tebbutt, 'Journey to an Unknown Destination', p. 174.
79. Elie Wiesel, 'Art and Culture after the Holocaust', in *Auschwitz: Beginning of a New Era? Reflections on the Holocaust*, ed. by Eva Fleischner (New York: KTAV, 1977), pp. 403–15 (p. 405).
80. Timothy Dow Adams, *Telling Lies in Modern American Autobiography* (Chapel Hill and London: University of North Carolina Press, 1990), p. 9.
81. Christian Scholz, 'Aber das Geschriebene ist ja kein wahres Dokument: Ein Gespräch mit dem Schriftsteller W. G. Sebald über Literatur und Photographie', *Neue Zürcher Zeitung*, 26 February 2000, p. 77.
82. Taberner, *German Literature of the 1990s and Beyond*, p. 111.
83. Nicholas Lezard, '*Austerlitz* by W. G. Sebald', *The Guardian*, 13 July 2002, p. 31.
84. P. Holland, p. 10.
85. Ibid.
86. Marianne Hirsch, 'The Generation of Postmemory', *Poetics Today*, 29 (2008), 103–28 (pp. 107–08).
87. Douglas, p. 89.
88. For a detailed comparison of the two, see Baker.
89. Zohar Shavit, *A Past without a Shadow: Constructing the Past in German Books for Children* (London: Routledge, 2005), p. 239.
90. Dwork, p. xvii.
91. Other editions depict an illustration of the gatehouse building at the entrance to Auschwitz-Birkenau.
92. Hirsch, 'Projected Memory', p. 12.
93. Ibid., p. 13.
94. Ibid., p. 12.
95. Ibid., p. 17.
96. Dominick LaCapra, *Representing the Holocaust: History, Theory, Trauma* (Ithaca and London: Cornell University Press, 1998), p. 196.

CHAPTER 5

The Fascination of Fascism in Contemporary Film

Introduction

With the gradual transition from communicative to cultural memory, film has increasingly been recognized as a significant medium with which to transmit narratives and images of the past, and to engage in memory work. Christian Schneider has argued that 'im Übergang vom kommunikativen zum kulturellen Gedächtnis, das heißt mit dem Aussterben der Zeitzeugen wird der Film — gleichgültig ob als Dokumentation, Doku-Drama oder Spielfilm mit historischen Zitaten — das mächtigste Mittel der Geschichtsdarstellung werden' [in the transition from communicative to cultural memory, that is to say with the disappearance of the eyewitnesses, film — whether documentary, docu-drama, or fiction film with historical references — will become the most powerful means of depicting history].[1] Thus, as the 'organic' memory of the Third Reich increasingly disappears, German cinema becomes the 'primary site of transmitting memory between generations who have never lived through the actual events'.[2]

Since reunification, and particularly since the early 2000s, German film has been dominated by stories about Nazism and its legacy in the present, with an emphasis in mass-market cinema on the truth-value of narratives about the past.[3] The referentiality of figures, places, and events is foregrounded in promotional material, the *mise en scène* is painstakingly researched, actors perfect the vocal timbre and mannerisms of their subjects, and the reception follows suit, assessing the extent to which such films reproduce historical reality. This in itself is not novel: as Marcia Landy writes, 'from earliest embodiments in the cinema, the penchant for documenting the past has been evident', and this has always entailed a 'demand for "veracity" and "facticity" [...] especially around staged events on film purported to be "authentic"'.[4] Indeed, a sociological study published in 2002 as *Opa war kein Nazi* [Grandfather Wasn't a Nazi] concluded that film was frequently seen as evidence of the way historical events had 'really' played out, and that eyewitness accounts were being assessed against the supposed veracity of filmic depictions.[5]

In this chapter, I discuss three films which explore the fascination of National Socialism for the young and which make for a productive discussion of the place of childhood and authenticity within contemporary cinema. First, I compare

Agnieszka Holland's *Hitlerjunge Salomon* [Europa Europa] (1990) and Dennis Gansel's *NaPolA: Elite für den Führer* [Before the Fall] (2005), both of which depict a young male protagonist's coming-of-age journey and explore the techniques used by the National Socialists to indoctrinate the young. The films share some formal and thematic elements; however, through their contrasting treatment of the experience of growing up in the Third Reich, they raise questions about the ways in which childhood and adolescence are constructed and represented in cinema. The analysis of the films' reception suggests that the authenticity associated with them is frequently attributed not to their historical accuracy, but rather to their perceived ability to reveal a 'deeper truth' about the experience of the past. Like the imagined accounts discussed in the previous chapter, this authenticity is bound up with the works' focus on juvenile protagonists, though it is also a symptom of the filmic medium. Thus, my discussion of these two films builds on ideas about historical representation, while opening out the debate to consider how genre might also affect this. I then turn to a more recent cinematic depiction of childhood and Nazism, Cate Shortland's 2012 film *Lore*, which follows a female protagonist at the end of the war. It traces the eponymous heroine's journey with her siblings from their home in southern Germany to the apparent safety of their grandmother's house in Hamburg.[6] The film offers another perspective on the portrayal of the young under Nazism, one that combines elements of Holland's and Gansel's respective approaches.

'Das glaubt dir kein Mensch' [Nobody will believe you]: *Hitlerjunge Salomon* (1990)

The Polish director Agnieszka Holland's provocative film *Hitlerjunge Salomon* had its premiere in Paris in November 1990 and was first released in Germany in October 1991.[7] It explores the Third Reich from a Jewish perspective; it is based on the true story of Solomon 'Solly' Perel, born in Peine (Lower Saxony) in 1925, and traces his journey from childhood to adulthood. The incredible and picaresque account as shown in the film begins on the eve of Solly's bar mitzvah, which coincides with Kristallnacht, during which the family's shop is attacked and his sister is killed. Consequently, the family relocates to Łódź. When the Germans invade Poland, he and his brother Isaak (René Hofschneider) escape with the intention of heading east, but become separated. Solly is placed in a Soviet orphanage in Grodno, in Soviet-occupied Poland, where he enrols as a member of the youth wing of the Communist Party of the Soviet Union, the *Komsomol*. After a *Wehrmacht* attack on the school, he is separated from his teachers and schoolmates and taken prisoner by the Nazis. When asked whether he is a Jew, he denies it, claiming instead to be a 'Volksdeutscher' [ethnic German], a term purportedly coined by Hitler to describe those, mainly in the East, who were of German origins but who did not hold German citizenship.[8] With a new identity as Josef 'Jupp' Peters, Solly becomes an interpreter for a *Wehrmacht* unit.[9] Here he forms a friendship with a former actor, Robert Kellermann (André Wilms), who discovers Solly's secret Jewish identity, but swears to keep silent. After Robert is killed, Solly attempts to defect to the Soviets and, in doing so, unwittingly leads the German troops to their position. As a result, he is declared a German war hero by the assembled unit. He is adopted by a German officer and sent to an elite National Socialist school in Germany, where he spends the rest of the war until he is dispatched, along with the other pupils, to defend Berlin against the final Soviet advance. After his capture, Solly attempts to reassert his Jewish identity, but this proves problematic. On the point of being shot by the Russians, he is saved by a final coincidence: his brother Isaak, who has just been liberated from a concentration camp, vouches for Solly, and the penultimate sequence depicts the two brothers walking arm-in-arm into the distance, having resolved to resettle in Palestine. The final scene shows the real-life Perel, thus at once apparently confirming the authenticity of the film's diegesis and reminding the audience of the continuity between the events of the film and the present day.

The film is based on Perel's account of his childhood and youth as published in his memoir *Europa Europa: A Memoir of World War Two*.[10] As he explores in the text, the difficulty in confronting his own youthful experiences in the Third Reich was that he had been on both sides of the war. He lived in fear of the Nazis, hidden in plain sight, but, as he writes, '[I] had worn their uniform [...] and had yelled "Heil Hitler" as though I really identified with their criminal ideology and their barbaric goals'.[11] The title of Perel's memoir and of the English-language release of Holland's film echoes Elia Kazan's 1963 film *America, America*, based on his book of the same name, published in 1962, and inspired by Voltaire's *Candide*.[12] Given his picaresque story of survival, it is not surprising that Holland saw Perel as a kind of 'Candide of the twentieth century'.[13] The film's German title is an ironic reference to the Nazi propaganda film *Hitlerjunge Quex: Ein Film vom Opfergeist der deutschen Jugend* [Hitler Youth Quex: A Film about the Spirit of Self-Sacrifice of Germany's Youth] (Ufa, 1933), directed by Hans Steinhoff and based on a novel by Karl Aloys Schenzinger.[14] In this story, the protagonist, Heini Völker, defies his fiercely anti-fascist father and joins the Hitler Youth, where he earns the nickname 'Quex', an abbreviation of 'Quecksilber' [quicksilver/mercury]. Steinhoff's film was extraordinarily popular and has been dubbed 'an integral part of Nazi ideology'.[15] The romanticized martyrdom of the film's young protagonist for the National Socialist cause was designed to promote the values of comradeship, courage, and idealism, and was intended to serve as a model for imitation and emulation.[16] This glorification of youth was part of the Nazis' highly developed 'generational profile', which they utilized in their policies and propaganda.[17] The reference to *Hitlerjunge Quex* in the title of Holland's film is of course ironic, for it is Solly's quick-wittedness which enables him to evade discovery, deportation, and death at the hands of the Nazis. It serves to signal the picaresque and provocative qualities of the film itself. Critics have proposed that this humorous and playful approach was one of the reasons why *Hitlerjunge Salomon* did not do well in Germany, despite the fact that Holland had previously enjoyed success there.[18] This reached its apex when a panel overseen by the German Export Film Union refused to nominate the film as a candidate for the German entry in the 1992 Academy Awards.[19] In response, thirty German directors, including Volker Schlöndorff, Wolfgang Peterson, Michael Verhoeven, Margarethe von Trotta, and Werner Herzog, signed an open letter to Holland congratulating her on the film and expressing disappointment that it had not been nominated in the category of Best Foreign Film.[20] In Holland's view, this was the result of German 'arrogance and xenophobia' which had surfaced since reunification.[21]

The strained reception of the film also finds expression in German fiction. In his novel *Ohne einander* [Without Each Other] (1993), Martin Walser draws attention to what he views as a restrictive political correctness, using Holland's film as an example.[22] The novel's protagonist, Ellen, is a journalist who is required to write a positive review of *Hitlerjunge Salomon* to counter the effects of a previous article that might be interpreted as anti-Semitic. According to Taberner, the character 'endures the characteristic Walserian clash between her desire for personal authenticity and the requirement to be socially and politically "correct"'.[23] What, then, were the objections? After all, Holland's film did well in the US, while conversely, as Janet Lungstrum points out, *Schindler's List* (1995), went on to do very well in German cinemas.[24] The answer may on the one hand be simply the timing: in the early 1990s, Germany was preoccupied with quite different concerns. Another explanation, offered by William Collins Donahue, is that 'by placing Solly side-by-side with Germans almost throughout the war (and throughout the film)', German viewers 'are denied any substantive opportunity to identify themselves as victims of any kind'.[25] It also seems plausible that Holland's unlikely and challenging depiction of the Jewish protagonist may have been unwelcome. This explanation is put forward by Claudius Seidl, who suggested it was not Germans' anti-Semitism but rather their philo-Semitism that made them unwilling to tolerate this complex version of a young Jewish protagonist on screen.[26] Central to this is Solly's age, and the film's depiction of youth. Solly's 'non victim-like opportunism', as Lungstrum terms it,[27] challenges received images of the Jewish child victim of the Holocaust. Solly shifts chameleon-like from one identity to another as he attempts to survive within war-torn Europe. He is delighted when war breaks out because it means he will no longer be in trouble for having broken a shopkeeper's pane of glass (*Hitlerjunge Salomon*, 00:10:04). Captivated by his attractive young *Komsomol* teacher, he proudly asserts that 'we call religion the opium of the masses' (*Hitlerjunge Salomon*, 00:21:06–00:21:09). He dons the uniform of the *Komsomol*, of the *Wehrmacht*, of the Hitler Youth, and finally trades his German army uniform for the striped uniform of the concentration camp prisoners after being reunited with his brother.

Thus, there is an essential tension in the film: Solly is shown to be a victim of the political conditions of his time as he and his family are persecuted and uprooted, and his actions are almost always informed by his need to survive. At the same time, he is portrayed as a kind of shapeshifter, adapting as necessary to stay alive, and in this way, he is afforded a crucial degree of agency. This, as we have seen, is unusual in the portrayal of Holocaust victims, who are commonly seen to lose agency when they become inhabitants of ghettos or prisoners of concentration camps, or when they are forced into hiding.[28] Solly is not simply portrayed as a symbol of victimhood, which, for Omer Bartov, Jewish child victims of the Holocaust in cinema embody.²⁹ His decision to deny his Jewish identity to the *Wehrmacht* is unquestionably brought about by outside forces, yet Solly is shown to make this choice consciously. In a series of medium shots, we see the German soldiers inspecting the prisoners' papers and sorting them into groups. Machine-gun fire is heard in the background. The camera pans across the group, including Solly, then cuts back to a close-up of him. He is clearly frightened, but also observing events keenly. Having stuffed his identification papers down the front of his trousers (which in the framework of the film now conceal two dangerous former identities), he tells the soldier that his papers were stolen. As another jokes 'Vielleicht ist er Jude' [Maybe he's a Jew], Solly raises his head to the sky, and, as though divinely encouraged, he embarks further on his lie. This unsettles the clear-cut presentation of the character: he no longer symbolizes the passive victimhood associated with the child, but rather, by acting with agency (however limited), he takes on a more complex role. At the school, we see Solly participating in an exercise in which students are required to bayonet a doll which represents a caricature of a Jewish man. Solly is clearly troubled, as the atonal and percussive musical score underlines, but participates, albeit under duress. It is only in the final days of the war, when Solly is required to fight the advancing Soviet Army, that he refuses to fire his weapon and surrenders, finally breaking out of the ambiguous role he has been playing throughout the film.

Hitlerjunge Salomon sets up its narrative clearly as the coming-of-age journey of its protagonist. The opening sequence of the film proper depicts Solly's circumcision:³⁰ a rite of passage which places him within a clear religious and social context. The rite of passage which ought to follow it, his bar mitzvah, is shown to be disrupted by Kristallnacht and, significantly, it is from this moment that Solly's identity becomes fragmented. Certainly, identity was a theme which attracted Holland to the project,³¹ and Holland did not shy away from showing the sexual development of her protagonist. At each stage on his journey, Solly engages in some form of romantic encounter. Having hidden naked in a barrel during Kristallnacht, Solly asks a young neighbour, Kati (Kama Kowalewska), to fetch him some clothes, and is clearly ashamed of his nakedness.³² He forms the beginning of a relationship with the proprietor of the local cinema in Łódź, and with his *Komsomol* teacher in Grodno. Solly also unexpectedly succeeds in a sexual encounter with the female NSDAP envoy sent to escort him to his new National Socialist school. This scene is both comic and grotesque: the envoy learns that Solly shares the same birthday as Hitler, and his complexion and dark hair lead him to be likened physically, and favourably, to him.³³ Thus, Solly's identity as a victim of Nazism is complicated not only by his engagement in the Nazi structures of the *Wehrmacht*, and its educational institutions, but also by his apparent essential connection to the Führer. The woman makes sexual advances, and the scene's initial function seems to be to demonstrate the corrupting power of Nazism on the young Jewish boy.³⁴ However, this scene cuts immediately to a shot of Solly triumphantly shouting in an exhilarated manner from the train window, suggestive of the fact that he has had his first successful sexual experience and that, rather than experiencing shame or degradation, he is in

FIG. 5.1. Solly and Isaak set off into their future (*Hitlerjunge Salomon*, 01:44:53)

fact proud of it. That the rite of passage Solly engages in is a sexual one is significant, as it disrupts his own, and the audience's, notion of him as a child. At the school, he begins a romantic relationship with one of the BDM girls who works there, Leni (Julie Delpy). Her fanatical anti-Semitism prevents him revealing the physical mark of his Jewish identity, and so he is forced to abstain from sexual intercourse and becomes obsessed by his absent foreskin. Frustrated by Solly's lack of interest, Leni becomes pregnant by his friend, Gerd (Ashley Wanninger), in order to give up her child as part of the SS-run *Lebensborn* project. Among a cast of German characters who appear 'ludic and two-dimensional',[35] Leni is an exception: she is a product of the system's indoctrination and control, fanatical, to the extent that she has alienated her own mother, who sadly comments: 'Die Kinder sind ... heutzutage so anders' [Children today are so different ...] (*Hitlerjunge Salomon*, 01:34:31–01:34:35).

Neil Sinyard has observed that 'children are the war film's handiest symbol of innocent victims, and their fate is designed to register on adult sensibilities'.[36] However, as Sinyard also observes, the problem with this is that it risks prompting a purely sentimental response from the viewer, rather than one which is able to engage critically with the topic.[37] *Hitlerjunge Salomon* encourages critical engagement at every turn, never permitting the audience to indulge in Solly's suffering. In keeping with the comic style of *Hitlerjunge Salomon*, Holland makes visual references to National Socialist aesthetics, and Margaret Olin identifies 'intertextual, parodistic allusions to the likes of Leni Riefenstahl's Nazi propaganda film *Triumph of the Will*'.[38] These include scenes showing young men and women engaging in sporting activities, night scenes in which flaming torches light up the screen, and a scene in which the over-enthusiastic teacher who, in a pre-dinner pronouncement in the place of grace, reminds the students to use their cutlery correctly, to respect their 'deutsches Brot' [German bread], before wishing them 'Guten Appetit!' [Enjoy the meal] in a tone of hilariously exaggerated quasi-religious fervour (*Hitlerjunge Salomon*, 01:04:10–01:04:12).

After being reunited with his brother, Solly changes clothes once again, into the striped uniform of the concentration camp prisoner, and he and Isaak are shown walking away from the lens, surrounded by trees and bathed in sunlight. Pinfold notes that Jewish child Holocaust victims often function as a means of suggesting the 'moral triumph of an innocent child over Nazism'.[39] Such figures embody notions of victimhood and a redemptive hope for the future. Yet, as I have shown, Solly does not embody the image of the 'innocent child'. Nor is the final image an unambiguously hopeful one. As Solly and his brother walk into the distance, the path snaking through the middle of the frame suggests hope for the future, but the path that lies behind them in the foreground of the frame also signals the troubled journey they have already made: a journey through Nazi Europe, through survival, and a journey from childhood to adulthood.

Hitler's Elite: *NaPolA: Elite für den Führer* (2005)

Dennis Gansel's *NaPolA: Elite für den Führer* premiered in Munich in January 2005, appearing as one in a number of memory-boom films, including most famously Oliver Hirschbiegel's *Der Untergang* [Downfall], which had premiered in September 2004.[40] Although nowhere near as commercially successful as *Der Untergang*, *NaPolA* won several awards and did moderately well at the box office.[41] The narrative is a straightforward coming-of-age tale which charts the moral development of its protagonist from a state of ignorance to a fuller understanding of the flawed ideological values inherent in the National Socialist system. In late summer 1942, seventeen-year-old Friedrich Weimar (Max Riemelt), a talented boxer, is spotted by a teacher from the NaPolA in Allenstein, East Prussia (now Olsztyn, Poland). He is lifted out of his monotonous life in the suburb of Berlin-Wedding and offered the chance to enrol at the school. Here, he becomes friends with the son of the local Gauleiter, Albrecht Stein (Tom Schilling), an artistic and sensitive youth who is sceptical of National Socialism's values and the dazzling opportunities it appears to offer. Friedrich, on the other hand, is enthralled by the school's exceptional facilities, the comradeship of the other pupils, and the promise of his future role as a member of the National Socialist elite. However, he also witnesses the cruelty and lack of pity shown towards those who fail to meet the school's expectations, in particular his classmate Siegfried Gladen (Martin Goeres), who is routinely persecuted for bedwetting. The film's turning point comes when pupils from Friedrich's class are required by Gauleiter Stein (Justus von Dohnànyi), Albrecht's overbearing father, to participate in a nocturnal military operation in the woods surrounding the school. Because of their knowledge of these woods, the young men are to assist in the capture of some escaped prisoners-of-war. However, it swiftly becomes clear that the escapees they shoot and kill are in fact Russian children. In response to the episode, Albrecht writes an anti-fascist essay in which he criticizes both the school and the Nazi regime. Facing punishment by his father (the Gauleiter), enforced enrolment in the *Waffen SS*, and immediate transfer to active combat on the Eastern Front, he commits suicide during a sporting exercise on the school lake. Through Albrecht's moral stand, Friedrich gains the strength and understanding to make his own act of resistance by deliberately losing an important school boxing match against the NaPolA at Potsdam. As a result, he is expelled from the school, and the film's final sequence shows him walking away from the building into an uncertain future, presumably attempting to return to his family in Berlin to rebuild the bridges he burned at the start of the film.

While *Hitlerjunge Salomon* primarily plays on the title alone of *Hitlerjunge Quex*, *NaPolA* is informed both by the plot and the style of the Nazi propaganda film. Like Heini Völker in *Hitlerjunge Quex*, Friedrich functions as a kind of everyman figure, and the name 'Friedrich Weimar' suggests both a universality which is also to be found in the name 'Heini Völker' and the pre-National Socialist political system, the Weimar Republic and the *Kampfzeit*. In addition, physically Friedrich embodies the Nazis' ideal young German male: blonde, blue-eyed, muscular, and willing to denounce his own family in favour of Nazism (even if this is motivated more by his desire to attend an elite school than by his ideological commitment). Like Quex, both in Schenzinger's novel and in Steinhoff's film, we see the way the Hitler Youth offers possibilities which are not to be found elsewhere.[42] In *NaPolA*, Friedrich's father is obviously opposed to Nazism, and forbids his son from entering the elite school on the grounds that 'mit diesen Leuten [den Nationalsozialisten] haben wir nichts zu schaffen' [we have nothing to do with these people [National Socialists]].[43] Like Heini, Friedrich is captivated by what the Nazis seem to be offering and by what he sees embodied in its young people. In a scene in Schenzinger's novel, Heini's first meeting with a company of the Hitler Youth is described in the following way:

> 'Deutschland, Deutschland über alles', fiel es mit tausend Stimmen wie eine heiße Welle über ihn her. [...] Er wollte mitsingen, aber seine Stimme versagte. Dies war deutscher Boden, deutscher Wald, dies waren deutsche Jungens, und er sah, daß er abseits stand, allein, ohne Hilfe, daß er nicht wusste, wohin mit diesem jähen großen Gefühl.[44]
>
> ['Germany, Germany above everything', it came over him from a thousand voices like a hot wave. [...] He wanted to sing with them, but his voice failed. This was German soil, German forest, these were Germans youths, and he saw that he was standing apart, alone, helpless, and that he didn't know what he should do with this sudden great feeling.]

Precisely this mood is created through music and camerawork in *NaPolA*. Friedrich begins the film as an outsider, innocent and discovering the possibilities of Nazism for the first time. In one of the first scenes in the school in *NaPolA*, all the pupils are assembled in the main hall and the camera pans across ranks of pupils in their uniforms, singing the Hitler Youth marching song 'Uns're Fahne flattert uns voran' [Our Flag Waves before Us]. It is, notably, this song which begins and ends

Hitlerjunge Quex, and the first line of which is uttered by the dying Heini Völker with his final breath, followed swiftly by the sound of marching and the lusty singing of the song by an off-screen chorus of young people. In *NaPolA*, as in *Quex*, we are presented with an 'idealized community of young people'.[45] A montage of Friedrich's activities in the school towards the middle of the film emphasizes the pupils' comradeship, and the uplifting orchestral soundtrack reinforces this positive image. Gansel emphasizes the attractive elements of the school and Friedrich's initial enjoyment of it.

The sense of community is central to *NaPolA*'s depiction of the hold of Nazism over the young. Several scenes depict Friedrich boxing and evoke earlier National Socialist images which place emphasis on robust, healthy young bodies. Randall Halle has criticized the film, arguing that the audience is expected to 'abjure' National Socialism, but only by ignoring all the positive aspects of Nazism shown in the film's first act.[46] However, I would argue that precisely the opposite is true: that the film shows how *difficult* it would be to say no to the attractions and enticements on offer. We can read this as part of Gansel's aim to depict 'wie Verführung funktioniert' [how temptation works],[47] and to portray the young protagonists in a way that the audience could sympathize with and understand. He comments:

> ich glaube, wer verführen will, muss Verführerisches zeigen. Nur so hat dieses System funktioniert, und das muss man auch einmal zeigen und emotional nach erfahrbar machen auch für eine junge Generation. Weil ansonsten steht man vor einem Bücherhaufen der Geschichte und fragt sich: Wie ist es möglich?[48]

> [in my view, anyone who wants to ensnare people has to show something tempting. It is only in this way that the system functioned, and you have to show that and make it possible for the young generation to experience that emotionally. Because otherwise, you stand in front of a pile of history books and ask yourself: how was it possible?]

Gansel prioritizes making the young men more 'human' and aims to show how easily they were corrupted to serve ideological ends. His determination to avoid judging youth reflects the broader empathetic attitude in post-reunification Germany towards those who experienced Nazism. It also corresponds to the way 'gefühlte Geschichte' works: once again it is the history of feelings which is being foregrounded here.

Unlike *Hitlerjunge Salomon*, which seeks to blur the boundaries between young people's status as victims and as perpetrators, *NaPolA* establishes a paradigm of the innocence of youth. In the first instance, the film focuses on Friedrich's moral journey, and as such it sidelines his adolescent development and depicts him as sexually innocent throughout. In a strikingly similar sequence to one in *Hitlerjunge Salomon*, Friedrich and Albrecht attempt to watch a girl undressing.[49] While the scene does suggest the boys' burgeoning sexuality, the air of innocence, and its isolation within the rest of the film and from the rest of the plot, led Daniel Kulle to comment: 'man hat fast den Eindruck, als diene [die Szene] eher dazu, den möglichen Verdacht einer homosexuellen Beziehung zwischen den beiden

Freunden auszuräumen' [one almost has the impression that the scene is there to rule out any suspicions of a homosexual relationship between the two friends].[50] The desexualization of the boys contributes to a process of infantilization which runs throughout the film, and which contrasts starkly with Solly's coming-of-age tale in *Hitlerjunge Salomon*.

This paradigm of innocence is also constructed through the generational conflicts presented between children and adults in the film. For example, Gauleiter Stein is portrayed as the embodiment of Nazi dominance and cruelty, as demonstrated in several scenes, most notably when at his birthday party he forces Albrecht and Friedrich to box, knowing full well that his son is no match for Friedrich's strength and skill. Albrecht's slight frame contrasts starkly with the Gauleiter's thick-set and muscular build, and they are presented as polar opposites in their sensibilities and morality. Stein's comment on hearing of Albrecht's death in the icy waters of the school lake is that his son was 'einfach zu schwach' [simply too weak] (*NaPolA*, 01:34:40), referring both to Albrecht's physical condition and, ironically, his refusal to conform. Indeed, Albrecht demonstrates to the viewer his strength in resisting his father's duress, though the only way to do this is through suicide.

The adult teaching staff at the NaPolA are also presented as predominantly negative figures, depicted largely one-dimensionally. This is certainly true of the nameless sport teacher (Michael Schenk) who is a caricature of a Nazi, and who evokes the kind of turn-of-the-century school stories in which boys are persecuted by their schoolmasters (we might think of Rilke's 'Die Turnstunde' [The Gym Class] (1902) or Frank Wedekind's *Frühlings Erwachen* [Spring Awakening] (1891)). The more ambivalent Heinrich Vogler, the boxing teacher who 'discovers' Friedrich, appears more sympathetic, but is exposed as exploitative later in the film when Friedrich fails to fulfil the school's demand for him to win the boxing match. Even Friedrich's father (Alexander Held) is portrayed in a negative light, despite his opposition to Nazism. When he is forbidden from enrolling in the school, Friedrich defies his father, departing secretly from the family home and leaving behind a letter in which he swears he will report his father's anti-fascist comments should he attempt to remove Friedrich from the school.[51] Although Herr Weimar represents anti-fascism and is, in this sense, himself a victim (we learn subsequently that he has been investigated by the Gestapo), he nonetheless *appears* oppressive and authoritarian because the film has established the primacy of Friedrich's perspective. This view is only reinforced by Herr Weimar's violent response to Friedrich's departure: he proceeds immediately to the basement and angrily smashes Friedrich's bicycle. In this constellation, the audience comes implicitly to identify itself with the young Nazis through its empathy with Friedrich.

As Daniel Kulle comments:

> die empathisch zugänglichen und sympathischen Figuren sind allesamt unschuldig und stehen einem übergeordneten, nationalsozialistischen System gegenüber, zu welchem sie Stellung beziehen müssen. Die Jugendlichkeit der Protagonisten befreit sie gleichzeitig von einer Mitschuld.[52]

[the empathetically accessible, sympathetic characters are all innocent and face a superior National Socialist system, which they must oppose. The protagonists' youth frees them at once from any complicity.]

Here we find an echo of the idea of the 'alibi of youth'. The pupils' lack of agency in *NaPolA* provides a largely uncomplicated picture of German youth in the Third Reich, seeking as it does to present them as victims of the system, and to try to show how it was possible *not* to stand up to Nazism. Thus, when the pupils are sent out to kill the escaped prisoners-of-war, they have no idea that the latter are in fact children and adolescent civilians. The film casts no judgement on the youths who shoot, nor on their response, which contrasts starkly with that of Albrecht, who is a model of compassion. At the same time, the NaPolA pupils are shown to shoot out of fear, and not because they are consumed with hatred for the enemy.

NaPolA employs established cinematic images of childhood, most notably the motif of the fairy tale, which had been utilized by the Nazis in their propaganda.[53] The fairy tale thus represents the innocence associated with childhood as well as the potential for exploitation and corruption.[54] In *NaPolA*, the building which houses the school is a Gothic castle, surrounded by woodland, and the frequent wide shots of the school which punctuate the film initially set up a stark contrast between the claustrophobic, dingy world of Friedrich's life in Berlin and the open, fairy-tale landscape of the school and its surroundings in what resembles a Romantic painting.[55] Daniel Kulle rightly identifies the boarding-school aspects of the film, and the wide shots of the castle resemble strikingly the images of Hogwarts in the film posters for the 2001 adaptation *Harry Potter and the Philosopher's Stone*, which was undoubtedly the most popular and best-known 'school story' when *NaPolA* was made and released.

Initially the school and the forest that surrounds it represent freedom and opportunity. Friedrich first sees the school in a photograph at the try-outs. Yet the forest also comes to signify the liminality of adolescence through its evocation of the fairy tale. The forest has a long history in literary allusion. In Middle High German literature, heroes commonly embark on quests which lead them into the forest where they earn their status in society. In Wolfram von Eschenbach's *Parzival*, the protagonist journeys through the forest to fulfil his destiny. He takes many paths through the forest, often false ones, before he reaches the required moral and societal maturity. Parzival is an archetype of the literary outsider figure commonly associated with the mad and with children.

In the early nineteenth century, the Brothers Grimm became fascinated by the forest in German folklore. As Jack David Zipes writes:

> the heroes of the Grimms' tales customarily march or drift into the forest and they are rarely the same people when they leave it. The forest provides them with all they need, if they know how to interpret the signs.[56]

The forest is a site in which moral betterment is possible, and as such often plays a particular role in the fairy tale, which is about those who stray from the path and, in doing so, become more self-aware and stronger. Bruno Bettelheim writes: 'only by going out into the world can the fairy-tale hero (child) find himself there [...].

Fig. 5.2. The NaPolA school at Allenstein (*NaPolA*, 41:48)

The fairy tale is future-oriented and guides the child [...] to relinquish his infantile dependency wishes and achieve a more satisfying independent existence.'⁵⁷ For Friedrich, the path through the forest leads him to kill the Russian children, but also to witness Albrecht's compassionate response to the 'enemy', as he defies his father and attempts to dress one of the Russian boys' wounds. For Friedrich, the forest provides the site of the liminal stage of adolescence: as he witnesses Albrecht's empathy, he is shown finally to have left his childhood behind, and yet he is still 'betwixt and between': the forest has provided him with all he needs, but he has not yet learnt how to interpret the signs. Albrecht's own awareness of the evil of Nazism is crystallized in this sequence, and is confirmed the following day, when he writes a critique of Nazism in an essay. He writes his essay using the language and tropes of the fairy tale:

> So kindlich es auch sein mag, so erfüllt uns Menschen die Winterzeit und der Anblick von frischgefallenem Schnee, immer mit einem unerklärlichen Gefühl von Glückseligkeit. [...] Ich jedenfalls war in meinen Vorstellungen ein Held, der Drachen besiegt und Jungfrauen rettet. Jemand der die Welt von dem Bösen befreit. Und als wir gestern loszogen, um die Gefangenen zu finden, da kam ich mir wieder vor wie dieser kleine Junge, der die Welt vor dem Bösen retten will. [...] Und als wir zurückkamen, da war mir klar geworden, dass ich selbst Teil des Bösen bin, vor dem ich die Welt immer bewahren wollte. (*NaPolA*, 01:21:26–01:22:08)

> [As childish as it may seem, winter and the sight of freshly fallen snow always fills us with an unaccountable feeling of happiness. [...] I, at least, was in my imagination a hero who conquers dragons and saves maidens. Someone who frees the world from evil. And when we set off yesterday to find the prisoners, I saw myself once again as that little boy who wants to save the world from evil. [...] And when we returned, it was clear to me that I had become part of the evil from which I had always wanted to protect the world.]

Albrecht's experience is constructed as a fairy tale, but he has come to realize that it is one in which he is the figure of evil, rather than the hero-protagonist as he had been trained to believe. Albrecht's insight is expressed in the language of the child,

Fig. 5.3. Friedrich (Max Riemelt) leaves the NaPolA (*NaPolA*, 01:44:16)

who views the world as a struggle between the hero and evil. His use of the fairy tale does not serve to infantilize him; on the contrary, the maturity of Albrecht's realization is presented in language simple enough for a child to understand, thus underlining the moral bankruptcy of the regime. Furthermore, by using intellectual means to resist — the written word — he evokes the resistance mounted by the *Weiße Rose* [White Rose], whose leaflets called on Germans to resist Nazism and contribute to an end to the war.[58] The leaflets were being printed and distributed during roughly the same time period in which *NaPolA* is set.

In *NaPolA*, Gansel aims to depict National Socialism's effect on German youth, both by demonstrating how attractive it appeared to them and by showing young people in a more sympathetic light. Ultimately, Friedrich is portrayed as a victim of Nazism: a young man who is dazzled by the attractive opportunities for advancement and power, a juvenile victim of adult manipulation and corruption. The infantilization of his character reinforces this view. Friedrich leaves the school, stripped of his uniform and back in his now ill-fitting short trousers. The final shot depicts him walking away from the school, which has transformed from a fairy-tale castle into a site of terror and oppression (reflected in the shift from extreme long shots to medium, long-angle shots of the castle). The natural setting of the final frame is also significant: the affinity of childhood and the natural world is a well-established trope,[59] both in literature and film, and also in the fairy tale, as discussed above. By aligning Friedrich with nature here, *NaPolA* reinforces the childlike status of its protagonist, thereby emphasizing notions of innocence and passivity. In addition, the seasons have reflected Friedrich's journey, and the spring of his youth has become a wintry landscape. It echoes Margaret Meek's comment that maturation 'leads the individual from a lost magical state of innocence and perception into the prosaic state of regretful adulthood'.[60] The innocence of the first half of the film has been gradually worn away, and Friedrich has been shown to have come of age morally, albeit through a painful process. The similarity between this frame composition and that at the end of *Hitlerjunge Salomon* is striking and

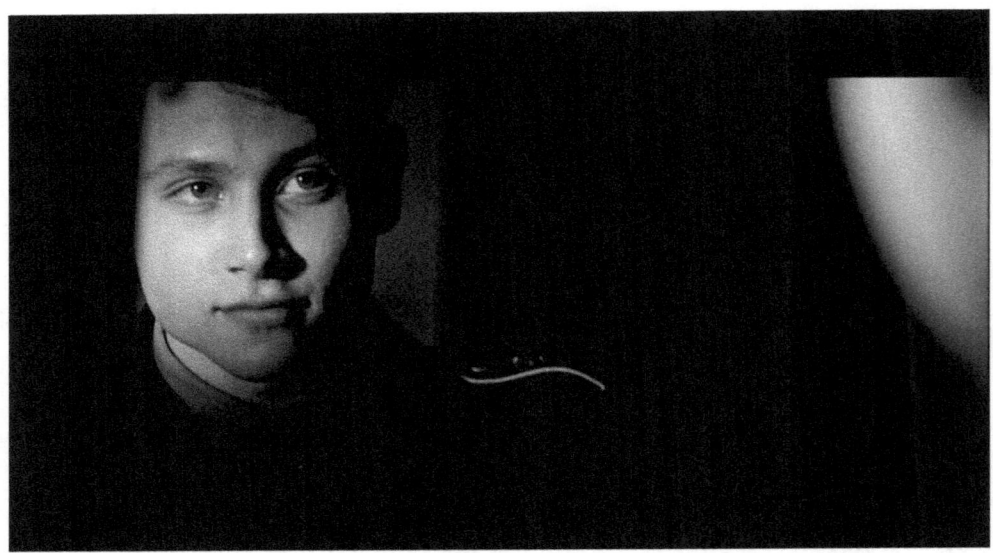

Fig. 5.4. Friedrich (Max Riemelt) surveys his new uniform (*NaPolA*, 00:16:28)

Fig. 5.5. Solly (Marco Hofschneider) practises the Nazi salute
(*Hitlerjunge Salomon*, 01:02:48)

can be found elsewhere in post-unification cinema.[61] It signals the journey which still has to be made through the intervening post-war period in order to reach the audience in the present.

Authenticating Discourses in Contemporary Film

In addition to the shot of the protagonist walking away from the camera at the films' end, there are several scenes in the two films which are strikingly similar. One in particular demonstrates well the contrast between their respective approaches. In both films, the newly arrived pupil surveys himself in his uniform with a level of satisfaction. Friedrich, no longer in his short trousers and tattered shirt, is shown in a uniform which for him represents the beginning of a new life away from war-torn east Berlin, in the ranks of the elite. This moment signals hope, optimism, and joy. In contrast, Solly stands in front of the mirror, pleased with his appearance as a good-looking young man, though conscious of the dangers before him as he tries to uphold the secret of his identity. In its inimitable comic style, Solly's practising of the Nazi salute transforms into a whimsical tap dance before we cut to the next scene. While Holland satirizes, mocks, and casts a critical light on the events of the past, Gansel takes an empathetic approach drawing on the model of 'gefühlte Geschichte', attempting through melodrama and emotionalization to elicit an emotional and empathetic response from his audience. This fundamental difference in approach may also go some way to explaining the different reception stories of these films, and for this we need to consider the way each film operates in relation to the depiction of childhood and the way it functions as an authenticating discourse.

In his cynical review of *Hitlerjunge Salomon*, Hans Günther Pflaum commented on the film's final scene, in which Solomon Perel himself steps in front of the camera: 'Ein Epilog zeigt den authentischen, nach Palästina ausgewanderten Salomon Perel. Agnieszka Holland stellt ihn aus, um den Wahrheitsgehalt ihres Films zu belegen. Wer der Inszenierung mißtraut, zweifelt am Bericht eines Opfers' [An epilogue shows the authentic Salomon Perel who emigrated to Palestine. Agnieszka Holland puts him on display to verify her film's truth content. Anyone who doubts the production is doubting a victim's testimony].[62] More recently, Schneider has argued that historical films about Nazism use their claims to authenticity and their access to footage of authentic eyewitnesses in order to legitimize their own depictions of the past.[63] Filmmakers emphasize the 'authenticity' of their production through historical figures like Traudl Junge in *Der Untergang*.[64] Schneider suggests: 'die Bekundung der Zeitzeugin macht das Geschehen, das der *Untergang* zeigt, zu einer historischen Urszene' [the evidence of the eyewitness makes the events shown in *Downfall* into a primal scene of history].[65] The result of this is that viewers leave the cinema regarding themselves not as audience members who have seen a film, but rather as witnesses to an event. Schneider's comment not only suggests that the presence of the eyewitness performs a kind of authenticating function; his use of Freud's notion of the 'Urszene' also strikingly positions the viewer in the place of a child looking up at the monolith of history.

Yet, ironically, as Lungstrum has argued, it was the 'apparent lack of "truth referentiality"' expected in portrayals of the Holocaust which turned German critics against the film.[66] *Hitlerjunge Salomon* was marketed as a 'true story' with an emphasis on its basis in fact and Perel's memoir as its source.[67] In the film

Fig. 5.6. Solomon Perel (as himself) in the final sequence of the *Hitlerjunge Salomon* (01:45:27)

adaptation, the central action is frequently commented upon, and framed, by a voice-over narration, spoken by Marco Hofschneider as Solly. Here, the question of authenticity is raised at the outset, as he states in the first lines of the voice-over: 'niemand wollte mir je glauben, dass ich mich an den Tag meiner Beschneidung erinnere' [you won't believe it, but I remember my circumcision] (*Hitlerjunge Salomon*, 00:02:45–00:02:48). While referring directly to his circumcision, the comment also has a broader relevance by raising the theme of credibility and believability at the outset. There is a certain audacity here: an unreliable narrator might utter this kind of phrase in order for the author to signal to the reader (or viewer) that they are not to be trusted. Yet Solly as a Holocaust survivor with an extraordinary tale of survival — and indeed, aren't all such stories remarkable? — is expected to be believed and to give an objective and uncomplicated account of his experiences. Yet, in contrast to the events depicted in the rest of the film, Solly's barefaced lie that he could remember his circumcision puts the viewer on their guard and stops them, right from the beginning, simply over-identifying with this Holocaust victim.

This unbelievability is acknowledged elsewhere within the diegesis: in a scene shortly after Solly and Isaak's reunion, Isaak commands his brother never to tell his story because 'das glaubt dir niemand. Das glaubt dir kein Mensch' [nobody will believe you] (*Hitlerjunge Salomon*, 01:43:50). Here authenticity is linked to plausibility. His story of survival is so unlikely that it would be better to remain silent. This comment also jars with the post-war imperative for Holocaust survivors to relate their experiences in order to warn and inform subsequent generations. That Solly will not be believed echoes his experience with the Soviet camp liberators whom he encounters shortly before the reunion with Isaak. First, dressed in the uniform of the Hitler Youth and looking relatively healthy, Solly does not 'look like' a Jew. In the same way, the story of his survival does not conform to the popular idea of the Holocaust victim. Perhaps authenticity is only that when it conforms to a pre-existing image or code. The implication is that images which are deemed 'authentic' may merely consist of reconstructions of previously 'authentic' images. Just as in a museum, where toys are usually considered to best represent children's experience because they correspond to a fixed image of 'childhood', so, in the case of the depiction of Perel, it may be that his story and image challenge the common conception of the Holocaust child victim. Although much like the authors discussed in Chapter 3, Perel would certainly reject that label. Bartholeyns suggests that the visual signs used in cinema to situate a film in a particular historical period may well work because they 'correspond to models of representation that precede the film'.[68] Thus a film will be deemed 'historical' if the audience recognizes the signifiers used. It may well be that *Hitlerjunge Salomon* failed to resonate precisely because it offered such an unconventional depiction of this subject matter.

When Solly is taken prisoner by the Soviet liberators at the end of the war, he protests that he is Jewish. In response, they confront him with photographs of Jewish concentration camp victims. Pointing at the pictures, one of the Soviet soldiers tells Solly: 'wenn du Jude wärst, würdest du so aussehen. Sieh her! Tote, Schädel, Kinder ... Siehst du sie?' [if you were a Jew, you'd look like this. Look. Look! Corpses, heads ... These children, see them?] (*Hitlerjunge Salomon*, 01:40:19–01:40:29). Solly, shocked and uncomprehending, simply repeats what his *Wehrmacht* captain had told him: that the Jews had been sent to live in Madagascar. This is an important moment. Earlier in the film it was necessary for Solly to travel twice through the ghetto in Łódź. From the tram window, he sees a woman whom he believes to be his mother, though (rather like Sebald's fictional Austerlitz) he remains unsure. He sees her twice, once on each journey. On the second occasion, he sees her in an alleyway being beaten to the ground. That Solly should have seen such things, and still utters a phrase so condemned in post-war discourse, that he simply 'didn't know', makes a powerful comment on the indoctrination of youth in the Third Reich and by extension the process of *Vergangenheitsbewältigung* in the post-war period. In an interview, Perel addresses this event in particular as an example of the tension between what he needed to do to remain safe and his authentic emotions: 'Äußerlich musste ich gleichgültig erscheinen. Die Tränen flossen nach innen' [On the outside, I had to look indifferent. On the inside, the tears were flowing].[69] At the same time, the indoctrination of the system had its effect. Perel writes in his autobiography that 'the system I was entangled in sharpened my senses, but it also anesthetized them'.[70] He never questioned why he had only seen adults in the ghetto and no children. It had not occurred to him to ask why. The film naturally condemns this stance, but it also shows how it might have been possible to cling to it. Thus, the Nazi Germans in the film may all be stereotypes, but the way indoctrination could seize the young in particular plays out in a most plausible fashion.

Lungstrum observes that German reviewers noted, and disapproved of, perceived liberties taken with Perel's own account of his life.[71] Holland acknowledges making artistic choices and changing details of Perel's account to make them work better on screen. She recalls Perel's response to the film thus:

> I'm happy to tell you that [Perel] loved the film, totally loved it. And when a scene would come on that I had invented, he would say 'Oh yeah! It was like that.' What I had added became a part of his memories.[72]

Perel here appears to confirm the authenticity of the film, even though the events he views are not what he experienced. It seems that, for Perel, what he considered the film revealed about his experience, and the experience of living through this historical period, transcended the factual discrepancies between the film's narrative, his own autobiography, and his memory. He commented in an interview that Holland may have exaggerated somewhat here and there, but 'eigentlich hat sie die Stimmung getroffen' [essentially she captured the mood].[73] This echoes Imre Kertész's comments on *La vita é bella*, discussed in Chapter 1, that authenticity is more than adherence to historical facts, that through poeticizing a deeper truth can be revealed.

NaPolA does not tell one individual's story but drew on multiple memories. Indeed, the final frame offers a historical coda, informing the audience that there were around forty such elite schools in the Third Reich with over 15,000 pupils. Gansel stressed that the screenplay had taken around three years to put together, and that he interviewed thirty-five eyewitnesses.[74] Gansel's approach stems in part from his own family history, as his grandfather was a pupil at a National Socialist elite school.[75] The production enlisted the assistance of a former elite-school pupil, Hans Müncheberg, who was to act as a historical advisor for the production, having spent five years as a 'Jungmann' at the NaPolA in Potsdam.[76] However, Müncheberg subsequently distanced himself from the project after he was troubled by the great liberties being taken with the subject matter and setting, despite the filmmakers' apparent preoccupation with historical accuracy.[77] Among several points of criticism, Müncheberg cites the implausibility of Friedrich's apparent total avoidance of National Socialism and his relative ignorance of it until he enrols in the NaPolA.[78] The Nazis' control of the web of youth organizations, as well as their total control of educational policy and staffing, made children and adolescents 'the targets of political propaganda to an unprecedented degree'.[79] That Friedrich is portrayed as apparently completely ignorant of Nazism appears to be an extremely constructed situation. It reveals, perhaps, something of contemporary ideas about childhood: we more readily engage with the ideal than the reality. This is indeed problematic, since Friedrich is the film's principal focalizer, and while his limited insight encourages the viewer to fill in the gaps, it also risks reinforcing a false view of the ignorance of those who were involved in Nazism.

In the sociological study *Opa war kein Nazi*, Welzer, Moller, and Tschuggnall assert that

> filmische Medien besitzen, obwohl sie nur momentane und mikroskopische Ausschnitte von Geschehenszusammenhängen oder gestellten Ereignissen sind, eine Art Überzeitlichkeit: Sie manifestieren scheinbar authentische, in Wirklichkeit aber höchst artifizielle Perspektiven auf Geschehensverläufe, und damit werden sie zu Deutungsvorgaben, zu Interpretamenten dafür, wie etwas gewesen ist.[80]

[although they are momentary and microscopic excerpts of historical context or staged events, filmic media possess a kind of timelessness: they manifest apparently authentic, but in reality highly artificial perspectives on crises, and in this way they become models, interpreters for how something happened.]

The phrase 'scheinbar authentisch' [apparently authentic] resonates here. To what extent can the *appearance* of authenticity be a legitimate goal of filmmakers tackling historical subjects, particularly one as ethically charged as the Holocaust? How significant is the 'truth-value' of a historical film? Films which are 'about history' are expected to 'tell the truth' about the past. James Schofield Saeger argues that the public perception of historical events is more likely to be affected by films set in the past than by historians' accounts.[81] By visually recreating 'historical reality',[82] films appear to offer a picture of the past which is 'authentic', and the question of authenticity in cinema has often been reduced to 'the normative question of the historical accuracy of movies set in the past'.[83]

Similarly, Bartholeyns writes:

> the historicity of a film can legitimately be measured by external criteria: costumes, set and language. However, it should not be confused with the rarer impression of authenticity, which is not dependent on what does or does not conform to the original. 'Authenticity' has no relationship with historical accuracy. It is neither its cause nor its consequence, and should instead be understood as the character of that which expresses a profound truth about man.[84]

In Batholeyns's view, the authenticity of the historical film lies not in its referentiality, but rather in its ability to reveal a deeper truth about the experience of the past. Oskar Roehler's feature film *Jud Süß: Film ohne Gewissen* [Jew Suss: Rise and Fall] (2010) is a case in point. The film, which depicts the production of Veit Harlan's notorious anti-Semitic propaganda film *Jud Süß* (1940) from the perspective of its star, Ferdinand Marian, was poorly received in Germany, not least because of the numerous liberties taken with the account of Marian's personal life. The screenwriter, Klaus Richter, responded to these criticisms directly, and, when asked whether he thought it was legitimate to fictionalize the life of a real person to such a great extent, commented that

> es gibt auch eine innere, eine psychologische Wahrheit, die manchmal mit der Historie nicht übereinstimmt. Der Fall Marian steht auch für die vielen anderen Schauspieler im Dritten Reich, die wegen ihren jüdischen Partnern Probleme bekamen. [...] Außerdem glaubten wir den Vorteil zu haben, dass das tatsächliche Leben Marians gar nicht bekannt ist.[85]

> [there is an inner, a psychological truth which does not always match up with history. The case of Marian stands for that of many other actors in the Third Reich who had problems because of their Jewish partners. [...] Besides, we felt we had an advantage in that Marian's life is not very well known.]

Richter's desire to access the 'inner truth' suggests not only that cinema can legitimately alter the past in order to access a deeper, or more universal truth, but that the cinema as an artistic medium will make this possible. Yet this has significant implications for the legitimacy of such an approach to historical representation, particularly when the historical subject is the fate of European Jews in the Holocaust.

Isabella Reicher, reviewing *NaPolA* in the Austrian newspaper *Der Standard*, noted that the 'Farbtönung der Bilder, ihre künstlich hergestellte Patina, entspricht den Konventionen der Historienmalerei des zeitgenössischen populären Kinos' [the hue of the images, the artificially constructed patina, conforms to the conventions of history painting in contemporary popular cinema].[86] In precisely this way, *NaPolA* is visually characteristic of post-reunification films about Nazism. It reproduces historic film from the Third Reich, and histor*ical* film from the post-*Wende* period. In doing so, it corresponds not only to a historical image but also to a contemporary recreation of that image: its aesthetics are thus doubly recognizable to a post-*Wende* audience, and perhaps, therefore, doubly acceptable.

Coming to Terms with the Past: *Lore* (2012)

Finally, I want to look briefly at a more recent treatment of youth and Nazism in German-language film. *Lore* (2012) was Cate Shortland's second full-length film, and the first she had made in German, a language she herself does not speak. This, Roger Hillman argues, gave her a kind of 'Narrenfreiheit' [fool's freedom] in being able to approach the story, and the history, from a different perspective.[87] The film is based on the second of three novellas which make up Rachel Seiffert's 2001 award-winning text *The Dark Room*, which in turn was based on Seiffert's mother's experience as a child at the end of the war.[88] In this way, the film draws on both a historical and a literary source. Shortland wrote the screenplay with Robin Mukherjee, and it was translated into German for filming. She worked with the cast of German actors through an interpreter, filming on location in Germany. Despite her apparent distance from the legacy of German fascism, she revealed in interviews that her husband's family is Jewish, and that his grandmother had left Germany in 1937, aged nineteen. Props used at the end of the film, a series of photographs, are of her husband's family. These props have an authenticating function, but also a deeply personal one for Shortland.

Unlike the events of *Hilterjunge Salomon* and *NaPolA*, which take place during the Third Reich, *Lore* begins as the war is close to its end, in April 1945. After her parents are arrested for their involvement in National Socialist crimes, the fourteen-year-old heroine Lore Dressler must lead her four younger siblings, for the most part on foot, from the Black Forest in southern Germany to their grandmother in Hamburg, a journey of about five hundred miles. En route, the children encounter an enigmatic young man, Thomas, who appears to be a concentration camp survivor, and he accompanies them. At the beginning of the film, Lore is shown to be fiercely anti-Semitic, but gradually, through her awkward adolescent encounter with Thomas, she comes to reject the National Socialist ideology with which she was indoctrinated. The film is simultaneously a coming-of-age narrative, focusing on Lore's burgeoning adolescence, the desperate situation for civilians in Germany at the end of the war, and the question of German engagement with the legacy of

Fig. 5.7. Lore and her siblings journey into the forest (*Lore*, 00:25:08)

Nazism for individuals. In contrast to Holland's and Gansel's films, therefore, we do not see the indoctrination of the children, only a gradual process of disillusionment and denazification. Shortland is not trying to show how it was possible for Lore to become as she is; rather, she shows the painful process of coming to terms with the moral bankruptcy of the system. This differs from *NaPolA* since Friedrich is never presented as fanatical; indeed, as we have seen, he is implausibly almost totally ignorant of Nazism by 1942, when the film begins.

Roger Hillman suggests that the subtitle of Michael Haneke's film about a (possibly) sinister band of children in Wilhelmine Germany, *Das weiße Band — Eine deutsche Kindergeschichte* [The White Ribbon: A German Children's Story], would do well as a tagline for *Lore*.[89] Abandoned by their parents, Lore and her siblings must traverse the length of Germany, passing through the forest to reach their grandmother's house, thus passing through the quintessentially German setting of the fairy-tale forest. Indeed, this aspect of the film was noted by several reviewers, with Jörg Schöning commenting 'von den Grimmschen Fantasien ist vor allem das Grauen geblieben' [what remains of the Grimms' fantasies is, above all, the horror].[90] For English-speakers, it is even there in the title: 'Lore'. When the children finally reach their grandmother and she asks where they have come from, there is a double meaning in Lore's reply: 'Aus dem Schwarzwald, Omi' [From the Black Forest, Omi] (*Lore*, 01:44:30). During their trek, the children at one point come across a house in the woods, inhabited by a witch-like figure, depicted from the children's perspective as physically grotesque, while the Nazi ideals to which she clings make her doubly troubling to the audience. The black sheets which hang outside her house and the black staining of her hands from the dye cause her to resemble the figure from a German children's rhyme, 'Ist die schwarze Köchin da?' [Is the Black Cook There?].[91] This effect is heightened when she suggests keeping Lore's baby brother for food. The audience is, of course, aware that she means she

Fig. 5.8. Lore smashes her grandmother's porcelain figurines (*Lore*, 01:39:27)

will get extra food rations because of the infant, yet there is a Hansel-and-Gretel hint of something more sinister which the focalization encourages. Like Friedrich, Lore does not find that her journey through the forest results ultimately in the kind of *Bildungsroman* conclusion we might anticipate. Rather than learning a moral lesson and being able to fit into society, Lore sees society exposed. As John Patterson, writing in the *Guardian* observed of *Lore*, 'the things that are learned in adolescent extremis do not equip one to join society on equal terms; they prompt one to reject it utterly'.[92] Friedrich is shown leaving Nazism behind and going back, presumably, to his anti-fascist parents. Lore, by contrast, realizes she has reached grandma's house too late — the wolf is already there, but there is no *deus-ex-machina* woodcutter to save her. This is encapsulated in the film's final scene: her grandmother has a collection of porcelain figurines, one of which, a deer, Lore faithfully and carefully carried with her on the trek from the Black Forest. Lore angrily takes each one of the figurines and smashes them under her boot. She saves the one she brought with her until last, but finally she smashes that too. There is no walking into the middle distance for this protagonist.

Elizabeth Ward reads this as an act that 'brings the past, present, and future into collision'.[93] The figurine Lore had brought with her from home, which represented security and a renewed sense of 'belonging' at the safety of grandmother's house, is destroyed, and with it 'the physical connection to her past'.[94] The broken pieces of the figurine direct the audience to consider how this broken nation can ever be put back together again. As Ward asks: 'The pieces can be glued back together, but will the form ultimately remain the same?'.[95] The answer must surely be a resounding 'no', but it is not only an impossibility — it is an imperative. For Lore's rebellion in smashing the figurines is provoked not simply by teenage rebellion against the dictates of her elders, nor even the outrage and frustration that comes from being repositioned in the submissive role of child after having led her siblings on a perilous trek across the country. Rather, it is the profound recognition of deception. The scene is immediately preceded by one of the family at dinner. The grandmother admonishes Jürgen harshly when he takes a slice of bread without asking: 'Ein braver Junge wartet bis er serviert wird' [A good boy waits until he is served] (*Lore*, 01:44:30). This authoritarian pedagogy is now so bankrupt that Lore's only response can be to stuff a slice of bread into her mouth, knock over her milk and scoop it up from the table, and to destroy what she can of the old order. Buffinga aptly describes her as 'unlearning the past'.[96]

The film also consciously engages with the aesthetics of Nazism and its historical period, rather than the aesthetics of post-Wall cinema. *Lore* was shot on 16mm in washed-out and over-saturated colours, reminiscent of films of Hitler and the Nazis made in the 1930s and 1940s. Shortland was interested in using Nazi aesthetics and specifically 'the connection to nature within that ideology'.[97] As a result, there are frequent close-ups of flowers, leaves, and trees, and of the vulnerable children juxtaposed with the sublime enormity of nature. Yet this is not the Romantic innocence of the child's affinity with nature: here, the forest is overwhelming, dangerous, and has been politicized. There is a tension between the forest as fairy-tale space, as a site of possibility as well as otherness, and, in the film's realist setting, as a space which has become reterritorialized as a consequence of war. Lore comes to understand that Germany has been divided into sectors as a result of its defeat, and that the journey to Hamburg will now prove even more perilous as they move into and out of the Soviet zone of occupation. It is while attempting to cross this zone by night that one of Lore's siblings, Günter, is shot and killed. Strikingly, when Lore later reports this death to her grandmother, she states that it happened 'in Russland' [in Russia] (*Lore*, 01:031:05).

Buffinga argues that, as well as evoking a National Socialist aesthetic, the film evokes Heimat cinema of the 1940s and 1950s.[98] This may well be true, but the film also offers scenes of the aftermath of violence. We see early on the remains of a bombed-out town, where children are drawing in chalk on a spent artillery shell and walking through the rubble, a close-up of their boots crunching on the debris (*Lore*, 00:32:10–00:33:55). Earlier, on entering an empty farmhouse to look for food, Lore unwittingly comes upon the corpse of a woman, her upper thighs exposed and bloodied. An extreme close-up shows ants crawling over crimson flesh. In the town through which the children pass, Lore joins a crowd looking at photographs of concentration camp victims displayed to educate the population. In this scene, as Pinfold has shown, we find an aesthetics of touch employed throughout the film, with frequent close-ups of hands, feet, and the natural world, which evoke more the idea of empathy and a history of feelings, rather than something that demands our identification and empathy. This also contributes to a central thematic strand of the film, one which we find throughout post-reunification representations of the Hitler Youth generation. Lore is shown here and throughout the film to experience a tension between her childhood memories of her parents, particularly her father, and the public knowledge that men like her father, and indeed her father himself, had perpetrated the violence which is shown through the photographs she sees of concentration camp victims.

Like *Hitlerjunge Salomon* and *NaPolA*, the production of *Lore* had credentials of historical authenticity. The sets and costumes were meticulously researched and reproduced, though not always to great effect, with one critic suggesting that the girls' floral dresses sometimes looked a little too 'Laura Ashley'.[99] To achieve the almost documentary aesthetic of much of the film, Shortland wanted the children to 'act' as little as possible. She explains: 'We tried to build it up gradually from the skin instead of starting with the text, so that they already had an organic idea of the world before we introduced it and said, "Okay, now you've got to say this".'[100] In preparation for filming, the child actors learned propaganda songs and dances, they learned about food, schooling, and the BDM during the period, and they watched documentaries. It seems that, even if the audience did not, the children had a kind of immersive experience of the past in the manner of emotionally experienced history.

Nevertheless, this film takes a critical approach to its subject, and as a character Lore is presented in a morally ambiguous way. Stephen Holden, writing in the *New York Times*, rightly noted 'there is no Nazi stereotype on whom to pin your loathing'.[101] This contrasts starkly with *NaPolA*, in which the young characters are presented as innocent in opposition to the 'guilty' adults, or with *Hitlerjunge Salomon*, where fanatical National Socialists are cast as one-dimensional villains. Lore is shown to have been indoctrinated, and we see the beginnings of the painful process of coming to terms with what that means. The film's final moments stress the aftermath of having grown up in the Third Reich and the Second World War. Hillman argues that *Lore* can be seen as a 'challenge to German cultural memory' from the perspective of an outsider, and from 'the direction of a more transcultural memory of Germany'.[102] Lore as a character, and *Lore* as a film, are pervaded with complexity. In this sense, the film realizes Aleida Assmann's claim for the 'compatibility of guilt and suffering'. As I discussed in Chapter 1, Assmann suggests that 'recognition of the family memory of suffering must not lead to ignoring the national memory of guilt, but the national memory of guilt cannot be a barrier closing off the stories of experienced suffering'.[103] *Lore* presents the suffering of German children, the aftermath of violence and the bombing, the turmoil of the war's end, alongside the reality of the concentration camps and the immeasurable loss of those who were persecuted.

Conclusion

Aleida Assmann writes that, after periods first of silence and then of accusation in the post-war period, German memory culture has now entered 'eine dritte Phase des Imaginierens, das heißt des Verstehenwollens und vor allem Nacherlebenwollens' [a third phase of imagination, of wanting to understand and, above all, to relive].[104] We see this clearly within post-reunification film, where the filmic medium appears to provide a particularly potent means of presenting history to the public. The production and reception of *Hitlerjunge Salomon* and *NaPolA* show that the authenticity which is associated with these films is attributed not to their historical accuracy, but rather to the perceived ability of film to reveal a 'deeper truth' about the experience of the past. This, it would seem, is again linked specifically to the depiction of the young. Importantly, *Hitlerjunge Salomon* and *NaPolA* demonstrate the appeal of Nazism. Friedrich, as an emblematic German youth, is seduced by National Socialism's promise of advancement and community. Similarly, even Solly, a Jewish boy in hiding, who has witnessed his sister's murder by the Nazis, and who has seen his family interned in the Łódź ghetto, is briefly seduced by National Socialism; the film's aesthetics, emphasizing at times the grandeur of Nazism, drive the point home. Rather than showing the process of indoctrination, *Lore* explores the protagonist's encounter with the 'other', and her gradual realization that the system in which she grew up was morally bankrupt. As is the case with many immediate post-war films, in *Hitlerjunge Salomon*, *NaPolA*, and *Lore*, the young are deployed in order to 'navigate and negotiate the most difficult questions about Germany's [...] history'.[105]

More even than the literary texts I have examined in this study, post-1990 cinema uses childhood as an authenticating discourse. Both *Hitlerjunge Salomon* and *NaPolA* depict the experience of coming of age under Nazism, and in doing so, portray on screen the appearance of this historical era, and explore personal experiences and their emotional effects. Both films seek to impress upon the viewer the positive aspects which Nazism was frequently seen to offer for the young. This is done by depicting what Lutz Koepnick has termed the 'visual attractions and aural pleasures' of heritage cinema.[106] In *Hitlerjunge Salomon*, even Solly, a Jewish boy in hiding who has witnessed his sister's murder by the Nazis, and who has seen his family interned in the Łódź ghetto, is temporarily seduced by National Socialism, and this is directly linked to his adolescence. Perel has expressed publicly how even he was not immune to what he describes as the 'poison' of National Socialist education,[107] to the extent that he recalls: 'ich war sogar etwas traurig, dass Deutschland den Krieg verloren hat' [I was even somewhat sad that Germany had lost the war].[108] *NaPolA* demonstrates the way in which an 'ordinary' German boy could have been indoctrinated (albeit implausibly late in the day), both through the film's coming-of-age narrative and through the reproduction of National Socialist aesthetics. By demonstrating the extent of the appeal of Nazism to the young, both films succeed in communicating how the process of Nazi indoctrination was possible. In this way, they come closer to the authenticity they signal: not necessarily an authentic picture of the past (and what is?), but an authentic picture, in so much as it ever can be, of the effect of education and indoctrination on the young.

Lore offers a picture of the effects of Nazism on those children and young people deemed 'acceptable' by the regime, and the strange beauty and horror of the German landscape in the aftermath of war. It combines aspects of both Holland's and Gansel's approaches, focusing on emotional engagement and the history of feelings, but simultaneously eschewing sentimentality. Aesthetically there is a desire to immerse the viewer in the world of the past, but this is done without trying to elicit an identificatory or emotionalizing response. What Pinfold calls Shortland's 'visceral aesthetic' indeed functions to appeal to 'a generation saturated with information about the Third Reich without being able to feel any personal connection to it'.[109] Echoing Reich-Ranicki's concern that the public is 'überinformiert und trotzdem unwissend' [overinformed and yet, at the same time, ignorant],[110] this suggests that *Lore* has potential to engage those who feel they 'know' the Third Reich. The film does not offer easy answers, and indeed its complicated protagonist prevents it from becoming purely a cathartic or uncritical treatment of the war. In an interview, Shortland expressed the essential drive of the film's take on this history:

> What I really felt with this film was there had to be a shadow narrative that the audience can inhabit, and there's room for the audience to think and to make up their own minds. Otherwise, we're smacking [sic] the same kind of redemptive films that have been made before and that does not further any dialogue or any discussion about totalitarianism or even what 1945 was.[111]

It is this desire for dialogue for which all three filmmakers strive (with varying degrees of success) and which connects the cinema audiences of the present with the historical actors whose stories, whose lives, are depicted on screen.

Shortland's use of the word 'redemptive' is interesting here. Perel saw his autobiography as reconciliatory. He was, after all, in the highly unusual position of being able to see the war from both sides and from both extremes. Jack Zipes writes that, without becoming sentimental or resorting to melodrama, 'Perel takes great pains to forgive Germans who caused him great pain'.[112] This is less perceptible in the film, where it is only Nazis such as Robert Kellermann or Solly's schoolfriend Gerd (Ashley Wanninger) for whom pity is elicited through the violence and poignancy of their deaths. Still, there is no suggestion of retribution or revenge. Indeed, the song Perel sings in the final shot, 'Heenay Ma Tov', based on Psalm 133, suggests a more hopeful stance: 'How good it is for brethren to dwell together in unity.' Shortland was concerned that *Lore* would be seen as 'apologist',[113] and explains that German victimhood was not at the heart of the film. Instead, it was concerned with the effects of indoctrination and control, with 'what it means when your parents have lied to you and your government is completely corrupt. How do you become a good person, and how do you find empathy again?'.[114] In this way, *Lore* puts on screen what has so often been articulated by members of the Hitler Youth generation: the sense of confusion and betrayal when, in 1945, it became clear that things were not as they had seemed. *NaPolA* engages with Nazi persecution only inasmuch as it affects Friedrich; with the Russian prisoners-of-war, who turn out to be children; and with his friend Albrecht, who resists Nazism by removing himself from the system through suicide. In its use of conventional cinematic tropes, and its uncomplicated portrayal of Friedrich, the film does not offer a challenging depiction of the Third Reich. It does, however, attempt to offer a depiction of *how it was possible* for a young person to be swept up by Nazism. In this way, it provides an important contribution to the cultural memory of the Third Reich. Despite Gansel's reflective comments on his aims as a director, the film ultimately does not attempt anything like the literary craft of Grass, Walser, and de Bruyn. However, it is here and in *Lore*, directed by an Australian, a non-German and 'outsider', that we seem to find the most readily accepted responses to the desire, expressed by the

Hitler Youth generation and those who have come after, for representations of 'what it was really like'. Surely this has as much to do with the medium as the content.

Notes to Chapter 5

1. Christian Schneider, 'Sehen, Hören, Glauben: Zur Konstruktion von Authentizität', in *Das Böse im Blick: Die Gegenwart des Nationalsozialismus im Film*, ed. by Margrit Fröhlich, Christian Schneider, and Karsten Visarius (Munich: Text + Kritik, 2007), pp. 15–30 (p. 18). See also Erll, p. 394.
2. Lutz Koepnick, 'Reframing the Past: Heritage Cinema and Holocaust in the 1990s', *New German Critique*, 87 (2002), 47–82 (p. 57).
3. E.g. Max Färberböck, dir. *Aimée & Jaguar* (Senator, 1998); Caroline Link, dir., *Nirgendwo in Afrika* (Ascot Elite Home Entertainment, 2001); Oliver Hirschbiegel, dir., *Der Untergang* (Constantin, 2004); Volker Schlöndorff, dir., *Der neunte Tag* (Progress Film-Verleih, 2004); Marc Rothemund, dir., *Sophie Scholl: Die letzten Tage* (Warner Bros. Pictures, 2005); Dennis Gansel, dir., *Die Welle* (Constantin, 2008); Wolfgang Panzer, dir., *Die Brücke* (Warner Bros. Pictures, 2008); Oskar Roehler, *Jud Süß — Film ohne Gewissen* (Concorde Filmverleih, 2010).
4. Marcia Landy, 'Introduction', in *The Historical Film: History and Memory in Media*, ed. by Marcia Landy (London: Athlone, 2001), pp. 1–25 (p. 7).
5. Harald Welzer, Sabine Moller, and Karoline Tschuggnall, *Opa war kein Nazi: Nationalsozialismus und Holocaust im Familiengedächtnis* (Frankfurt a.M.: Fischer, 2010), p. 106.
6. Cate Shortland, dir., *Lore* (Artificial Eye, 2013).
7. Agnieszka Holland, dir., *Hitlerjunge Salomon* (Central Cinema Company Film, 1992); translations are taken from the English-language release of the DVD (Optimum Releasing, 1992). The film is a French–German–Polish co-production; the director is Polish and much of the film was shot in Poland. It was co-produced by Artur Brauner, a Polish-born Holocaust survivor who became one of Germany's most prominent film producers. The film's primary language is German, and it was funded by the German Filmförderungsanstalt [Federal Film Board].
8. See Doris L. Bergen, 'The Nazi Concept of "Volksdeutsche" and the Exacerbation of Anti-Semitism in Eastern Europe, 1939–45', *Journal of Contemporary History*, 29 (1994), 569–82.
9. The name recalls the protagonist of the anti-British Nazi propaganda film *Carl Peters*, dir. by Herbert Selpin (Ufa, 1941).
10. Solomon Perel, *Europa Europa: A Memoir of World War II* (New York: John Wiley & Sons, 1997). Perel wrote it in the 1980s in Hebrew, and it was first published in French in 1990. The German edition, *Ich war Hitlerjunge Salomon* (Munich: Heyne, 1993), was published in 1993.
11. Perel, *Europa Europa*, p. xi.
12. See George Wilkes, 'Changing Attitudes to the "European-ness" of the Holocaust and of its Victims', in *Remembering for the Future: The Holocaust in an Age of Genocide*, ed. by John K. Roth and Elisabeth Maxwell, 3 vols (New York: Palgrave, 2001), I: *History*, pp. 130–55 (p. 143).
13. Cited in Perel, *Europa Europa*, p. xii.
14. Karl Aloys Schenzinger, *Der Hitlerjunge Quex: Roman* (Berlin: Zeitgeschichte, 1932). The plot is based on the true story of Herbert Norkus, a Hitler Youth member who was killed by communists in a street battle in June 1932.
15. Jay W. Baird, 'From Berlin to Neubabelsberg: Nazi Film Propaganda and *Hitlerjunge Quex*', *Journal of Contemporary History*, 18 (1983), 495–515 (p. 495).
16. Karl-Heinz Schoeps, *Literature and Film in the Third Reich* (Rochester, NY: Camden House, 2003), p. 81.
17. Fisher, p. 2. This is also reflected in the hundreds of images of Hitler with children and adolescents which were designed to reinforce this conceptual link. Hitler's final appearance in public before his suicide was with a group of Hitler Youth boys, a scene painstakingly reproduced in Hirschbiegel's *Der Untergang*.
18. See Janet Lungstrum, 'Foreskin Fetishism: Jewish Male Difference in *Europa, Europa*', *Screen*, 39 (1998), 53–66 (p. 54).

19. Hamid Naficy, *An Accented Cinema: Exilic and Diasporic Filmmaking* (Princeton and Oxford: Princeton University Press, 2001), p. 54.
20. Bernard Weinraub, 'German Filmmakers Express Support for "Europa"', *New York Times*, 18 January 1992, p. 11.
21. Bernard Weinraub, 'The Talk of Hollywood; "Europa" Surfaces in Oscar Angling', *New York Times*, 14 January 1992, p. 11. See also Andreas Kilb, 'Ohne Oscar', *Die Zeit*, 31 January 1992 <http://www.zeit.de/1992/06/ohne-oscar> [accessed 1 July 2019].
22. Martin Walser, *Ohne einander* (Frankfurt a.M.: Suhrkamp, 1993).
23. Stuart Taberner, ' "Deutsche Geschichte darf auch einmal gutgehen": Martin Walser, Auschwitz, and the "German Question" from *Ehen in Philippsburg* to *Ein springender Brunnen*', in *German Culture and the Uncomfortable Past*, ed. by Schmitz, pp. 45–65 (p. 59).
24. Lungstrum, p. 54. See also William J. Niven, 'The Reception of Steven Spielberg's *Schindler's List* in the German Media', *Journal of European Studies*, 25 (1995), 165–89.
25. William Collins Donahue, 'Pretty Boys and Nasty Girls: The Holocaust Figured in Two German Films of the 1990s', *New England Review*, 21 (2000), 108–24 (pp. 117–18).
26. Claudius Seidl, 'Blamage mit Folgen', *Der Spiegel*, 27 January 1992 <http://www.spiegel.de/spiegel/print/d-13680018.html> [accessed 1 July 2019].
27. Lungstrum, p. 55.
28. B. Müller, p. 87.
29. Omer Bartov, *The 'Jew' in Cinema: From* The Golem *to* Don't Touch my Holocaust (Bloomington: Indiana University Press, 2005), p. 114.
30. The first sequence in the film, which precedes the introductory credits, depicts Solly (Hofschneider) underwater, wearing his Hitler Youth uniform, fighting to reach the surface.
31. Allan Tong, ' "The only place to execute some kind of power was the film set": Agnieszka Holland on her Career' <http://www.filmmakermagazine.com/85231-the-only-place-to-execute-some-kind-of-power-was-the-film-set-agnieszka-holland-on-her-career/> [accessed 1 July 2019].
32. Donahue suggests that, while the frequency with which Hofschneider is shown in a state of undress on screen serves to underscore his vulnerability, it also makes 'the experience of much of the film unequivocally erotic' (p. 112). The Solly of Holland's film, he argues, is shown to be irresistible to the Nazi characters, and in this way the film applies the male gaze and 'feminizes' him. As a result, the film is 'suspiciously sensuous' (p. 115).
33. This is an example of one of the places where Holland took artistic license (Perel's birthday is in fact 21 April rather than 20 April).
34. This scene is composed of several close-up shots of National Socialist properties, including a swastika-decorated cigarette case and a cigarette lighter in the shape of a bullet, visually reinforcing the woman's commitment to Nazism.
35. Donahue, p. 114.
36. Neil Sinyard, *Children in the Movies* (London: Batsford, 1992), p. 35.
37. Ibid., p. 12.
38. Margaret Olin, 'Lanzmann's *Shoah* and the Topography of the Holocaust Film', *Representations*, 57 (1997), 1–23 (p. 8).
39. Pinfold, *Child's View*, p. 104.
40. Dennis Gansel, dir., *NaPolA: Elite für den Führer* (Olga Film, 2004), henceforth cited as *NaPolA*.
41. For admissions figures, see the *Lumiere* database <http://lumiere.obs.coe.int/web/search/> [accessed 1 July 2019]. It was awarded the Deutscher Filmpreis [German Film Prize] for best non-adapted screenplay (2004), the Bayrischer Filmpreis [Bavarian Film Prize] for best director (2004), and the award for best film at the Viareggio European Film Festival. The financial backing came from the German Federal Film Board and FilmFernsehFonds, Bayern. It was produced by Olga Film, Munich, in co-production with Constantin Film Production, Munich, and Seven Pictures Film. On its reception in the press, see Bangert, pp. 79–81.
42. John Daniel Stahl, 'Moral Despair and the Child as Symbol of Hope in Pre-World War II Berlin', *Children's Literature*, 14 (1986), 83–104 (p. 92).
43. *NaPolA*, 00:08:03.

44. Schenzinger, p. 47.
45. Hilmar Hoffmann, *The Triumph of Propaganda*, trans. by John Broadwin and Volker R. Berghahn (Providence: Berghahn, 1996), p. 51.
46. Randall Halle, *German Film after Germany* (Urbana: University of Illinois Press, 2008), p. 126.
47. *NaPolA*, DVD commentary.
48. Jörg Taszman, ' "NaPolA — Elite für den Führer": Gespräch mit dem Regisseur Dennis Gansel' <http://www.deutschlandradio.de/archiv/dlr/sendungen/fazit/338801/index.html> [accessed 1 July 2019].
49. In *Hitlerjunge Salomon*, the girl is the young *Komsomol* teacher; in *NaPolA*, she is a BDM member. There is also a very similar scene in Walser's *Ein springender Brunnen*, in which Johann and Adolf try to catch a glimpse of the circus performer Anita undressing in her trailer.
50. Daniel Kulle, ' "Tut so was ein deutscher Junge?": Verantwortung und Mitleid in *Napola — Elite für den Führer*', in *Das Böse im Blick*, ed. by Fröhlich, Schneider, and Visarius, pp. 219–31 (p. 222). There is in fact a deleted scene included as an extra on the DVD in which Albrecht secretly meets and shares a kiss with one of the BDM girls who serves at the school.
51. Kulle, p. 221, rightly identifies a parallel scene to this one in *Hitlerjunge Quex*, where the protagonist, Heini Völker, tries to convince his communist father to allow him to enrol in the Hitler Youth.
52. Kulle, p. 229.
53. After the Second World War, the Allied occupation forces banned the reproduction of traditional fairy tales. See Jack David Zipes, 'Introduction', in *Fairy Tales and Fables from Weimar Days*, ed. and trans. by Jack David Zipes (Hanover and London: University Press of New England, 1989), pp. 3–31 (p. 25). In contrast, *Alice in Wonderland* appeared in eleven new translations into German between 1945 and 1955; see Emer O'Sullivan, 'Englishness in German Translations of *Alice in Wonderland*', in *Interconnecting Translation Studies and Imagology*, ed. by Luc van Doorslaer, Peter Flynn, and Joep Leerssen (Amsterdam: Benjamins, 2016), pp. 87–109.
54. See Pinfold, *Child's View*, p. 86.
55. The actual location is the fourteenth-century Buozov Castle in the Czech Republic.
56. Jack David Zipes, *The Brothers Grimm: From Enchanted Forests to the Modern World* (Basingstoke: Palgrave Macmillan, 2002), p. 89.
57. Bruno Bettelheim, *The Uses of Enchantment: The Meaning and Importance of Fairy Tales* (London: Peregrine, 1978), p. 8.
58. Marc Rothemund's film *Sophie Scholl: Die letzten Tage* would premiere in competition at the Berlin Film Festival in February 2005.
59. Sinyard, *Children in the Movies*, p. 7.
60. Margaret Meek and Victor Watson, *Coming of Age in Children's Literature* (London: Continuum, 2003), p. 8.
61. In Hirschbiegel's *Der Untergang*, the final shot of the main part of the film shows the figures of Traudl Junge and the Hitler Youth member, Peter Kranz, cycling through the forest together into the future.
62. H. G. Pflaum, 'Keine Zeit für Trauer: Agnieszka Hollands zum Politikum gewordener Film "Hitlerjunge Salomon"', *Süddeutsche Zeitung*, 8 February 1992.
63. Schneider, p. 21.
64. Excerpts from the interview with Traudl Junge, released as *Im toten Winkel — Hitlers Sekretärin*, dir. by André Heller and Othmar Schmiderer (Der österreichische Film — Edition der Standard, 2002), appear at the beginning and end of *Der Untergang*.
65. Schneider, p. 21.
66. Lungstrum, p. 56.
67. The German translation was published in 1993, two years after the film's release, and drew on the title of the film, rather than on the book's original title or the English-language film title, *Europa Europa*. Thus, in a curious way, the 'factual' source text seems to seek to confirm its truth-value through its association with the creative project: the film adaptation of Perel's life story.
68. Gil Bartholeyns, 'Representation of the Past in Films: Between Historicity and Authenticity', *Diogenes*, 48 (2000), 31–47 (p. 40).

69. Bettina Musall und Nikolaus von Festenberg, 'Die Tränen flossen nach innen' [interview with Solomon Perel], *Der Spiegel*, 16 March 1992 <http://www.spiegel.de/spiegel/print/d-9275452.html> [accessed 1 July 2019].
70. Perel, *Europa Europa*, p. 192.
71. Lungstrum, p. 55.
72. John C. Tibbetts, 'An Interview with Agnieszka Holland: The Politics of Ambiguity', *Quarterly Review of Film and Video*, 25 (2008), 132–43 (p. 138).
73. Musall und von Festenberg.
74. Taszman.
75. Ibid.
76. He wrote an autobiographical account of his experiences: Hans Müncheberg, *Gelobt sei, was hart macht: Aus dem Leben eines Zöglings der Nationalpolitischen Erziehungsanstalt Potsdam* (Salenstein: Morgenbuch, 1991).
77. Hans Müncheberg, 'Die Geschichte der Geschichte', *Freitag*, 14 January 2005 <http://www.freitag.de/autoren/der-freitag/die-geschichte-der-geschichte> [accessed 1 July 2019].
78. Halle, p. 114, also makes this point.
79. Lathey, p. 61.
80. Welzer, Moller, and Tschuggnall, p. 105.
81. James Schofield Saeger, 'The Mission and Historical Missions: Film and the Writing of History', *The Americas*, 31 (1995), 393–415 (p. 393).
82. Bartholeyns, p. 43.
83. Bruno de Wever, 'Prologue: Historical Film as Palimpsest', in *Perspectives on European Film and History*, ed. by Leen Engelen and Roel Vande Winkel (Ghent: Academia, 2007), pp. 5–12 (p. 5).
84. Bartholeyns, p. 34.
85. Hanns-Georg Rodek, '"Jud Süß" sollte Spiel-, kein Dokumentarfilm sein' [conversation with Klaus Richter], *Die Welt*, 21 September 2010 <http://www.welt.de/kultur/article9775361/Jud-Suess-sollte-Spiel-kein-Dokumentarfilm-sein.html> [accessed 1 July 2019].
86. Isabella Reicher, 'Schule für den Heldentod', *Der Standard*, 22 April 2005 <http://www.derstandard.at/2023249/Schule-fuer-den-Heldentod> [accessed 1 July 2019].
87. Roger Hillman, 'Europe's Children across the Borders of Memory', in *The Young Victims of the Nazi Regime*, ed. by Gigliotti and Tempian, pp. 321–36 (p. 323).
88. Alex Kecskes, 'Director Cate Shortland on her Post-WW II film, "Lore"' <http://www.acedmagazine.com/director-cate-shortland-on-her-post-ww-ii-film-lore> [accessed 1 July 2019].
89. Hillman, p. 326. On the depiction of childhood in Haneke's *oeuvre*, see Alexandra Lloyd, 'Songs of Innocence and Experience: Michael Haneke's Cinematic Visions of Childhood', *Modern Language Review*, 111 (2016), 183–207. John O. Buffinga provides a comparison of practices of transnational memory in 'Transnational Memory in Michael Haneke's *The White Ribbon* and Cate Shortland's *Lore*', in *The Changing Place of Europe in Global Memory Cultures: Usable Pasts and Futures*, ed. by Christina Kraenzle and Maria Mayr (Cham: Palgrave Macmillan), pp. 103–19.
90. Jörg Schöning, 'Kinodrama *Lore*: Deutsches Mädel, deutsches Monster', *Der Spiegel*, 30 October 2012 <http://www.spiegel.de/kultur/kino/lore-cate-shortlands-starkes-nachkriegsdrama-kommt-in-die-kinos-a-862880.html> [accessed 1 July 2019].
91. This children's game plays an important role in Grass's *Die Blechtrommel*.
92. John Patterson, '*Lore*: Cate Shortland's Latest Isn't your Standard Second World War Movie', 16 February 2013 <http://www.theguardian.com/film/2013/feb/18/lore-cate-shortland> [accessed 1 July 2019].
93. Elizabeth M. Ward, 'Dismantling the Third Reich in Cate Shortland's *Lore* (2012)', *Film & History: An Interdisciplinary Journal*, 47.1 (2017), 18–27 (p. 24).
94. Ibid.
95. Ibid., pp. 24–25.
96. Buffinga, p. 118.
97. Victoria Ahearn, '*Lore* Film Shows Second World War through Eyes of Children of Nazi SS Parents' <http://www.infotel.ca/newsitem/film-lore/cp23588447> [accessed 1 July 2019].

98. Buffinga, p. 111. Shortland cites Elem Klimov's *Come and See* as an inspiration for *Lore*. See Steven Erickson, 'Director Cate Shortland on *Lore*', 5 February 2013 <https://filmmakermagazine.com/64599-director-cate-shortland-on-lore/> [accessed 1 July 2019].
99. Schöning.
100. Sheila Roberts, 'Cate Shortland Talks *Lore*' <http://www.collider.com/cate-shortland-lore-interview> [accessed 30 June 2018].
101. Stephen Holden, 'No ordinary Trip to Grandma's House', *New York Times*, 7 February 2013 <http://www.nytimes.com/2013/02/08/movies/lore-by-cate-shortland-views-children-in-postwar-germany.html> [accessed 1 January 2020].
102. Hillman, p. 323.
103. Aleida Assmann, 'On the (In)Compatibility of Guilt and Suffering in German Memory', *German Life and Letters*, 59 (2006), 187–200 (p. 199).
104. Aleida Assmann, 'Lichtstrahlen in die Black Box: Bernd Eichingers *Der Untergang*', in *Das Böse im Blick*, ed. by Fröhlich, Schneider, and Visarius, pp. 45–56 (p. 47).
105. Fisher, p. 2.
106. Koepnick, p. 50.
107. Geneviève Wood, 'Er war "Hitlerjunge Salomon" und führte ein Doppelleben', *Hamburger Abendblatt*, 27 January 2011 <http://www.abendblatt.de/hamburg/article1769348/Er-war-Hitlerjunge-Salomon-und-fuehrte-ein-Doppelleben.html> [accessed 1 July 2019].
108. Philipp Gessler, 'Tödliches Misstrauen', *Die Tageszeitung*, 6 October 2009 <http://www.taz.de/!41787> [accessed 1 July 2019].
109. Debbie Pinfold, 'The Sins of the Fathers: Mark Herman's *The Boy in the Striped Pyjamas* (2008) and Cate Shortland's *Lore* (2012)', in *Childhood in German Film after 1989*, ed. by Alexandra Lloyd and Ute Wölfel (= special issue of *Oxford German Studies*, 44 (2015)), pp. 254–71 (p. 269).
110. Reich-Ranicki, 'Vorwort', p. 9.
111. Roberts.
112. Jack Zipes, 'The Contemporary German Fascination for Things Jewish: Toward a Minor Jewish Culture', in *Reemerging Jewish Culture in Germany: Life and Literature since 1989*, ed. by Sander L. Gilman and Karen Remmler (New York and London: New York University Press, 1994), pp. 15–46 (p. 38).
113. Erickson.
114. Ibid.

CONCLUSION

The works discussed in this study all tell stories about what it was like to grow up in the Third Reich. These stories are framed within different genres, modes, and media. By looking at a diverse range of representational practices, a broad picture has been drawn of the way discourses of childhood under Nazism operate within the cultural memory of the Berlin Republic. This, too, contributes to our understanding of the processes of making sense of the Nazi past since reunification: the increasing historical distance, the imminent disappearance of the last eyewitnesses, and the shifting perceptions and reception of the period as the years pass. The means of 'accessing' or 'encountering' the past have come increasingly to rely on forms which seek to compensate for a dearth of direct experience. While the purposes and modes of expression of the narratives discussed in this book are by no means uniform, underlying each of them is a concern to articulate the *experience* of formative years spent in the Third Reich and, in many cases, what that has meant for their authors' adult lives. They thereby engage with Reich-Ranicki's concern that people are 'überinformiert und trotzdem unwissend' [overinformed and yet, at the same time, ignorant] by demonstrating something of what it was like not 'auf der Ebene, auf der Geschichte entschieden wird' [on the level on which history is written], but rather 'auf der niederen Ebene' [on the lower level] of history.[1] In doing so, they not only offer theories with regard to what it was like to grow up under Nazism, but simultaneously examine and discuss *how* this experience is understood and transmitted in the present.

In choosing to represent the experience of growing up in the Third Reich, whether as a historical narrative, an autobiographical appraisal, a fiction, or a fictionalized interpretation of a witness's account, these works necessarily entertain the notion that the child's experience can provide a means with which to engage readers and viewers with the subject of the Third Reich. Because everyone has been a child — even if the specific nature and context of that childhood was different — common aspects emerge which speak to the visitor, reader, or viewer. In addition, the special place of childhood within public discourse and thought, which sees childhood as 'familiar to us and yet strange',[2] offers a renewed perspective on events which are both known and yet unknown. This potential relies not only on the defamiliarizing effect of literary and filmic narratives about, and from the perspective of, children, as critics have shown,[3] but also on the fascination with childhood and children, their privileged status within contemporary culture, and protectionist attitudes towards them.

Given that the narratives under discussion here all depict the experience of growing up during the same period, we find a number of common tropes and memories. At times, this crosses the boundaries drawn by the Nazis, for whom there were both 'acceptable' and 'unacceptable' children: Jewish and non-Jewish children had some shared experiences. In autobiographical accounts, reading is often foregrounded, as is the cinema that is often cited as a formative experience. Fairy tales appear as points of reference, as inter-texts, and as a way of framing young protagonists' own expressions. An important recurring theme is curiosity. In Klüger's *weiter leben*, the child's curiosity is part of a wish to know the truth about existence, which, for the young Klüger, lies not in the origins of life, but in its end: she finds that what she really desires to know about is death. As Klüger becomes an adult, this desire becomes part of a need to confront the truth about the past. Similarly, Kunert recalls his curiosity and his desire to discover the secrets that his parents were keeping from him. Their silence only increased that curiosity. Part of Grass's shame as an adult lies in his failure to respond to his childish curiosity. Faced with the unexplained disappearance of friends and family members, whom he realizes, retrospectively, had been imprisoned or deported, the child Grass failed to question these events; even without this later knowledge, he might have been expected to be curious about where they were. Grass sees his own silence not as a lack of curiosity, but, like Parzival, as a failure to articulate his questions. In Pausewang's *Reise im August*, the child Alice, like her namesake in Carroll's 'Wonderland', is curious about the strange world around her. But where, like Kunert, her curiosity has been discouraged by her family, Pausewang's character necessarily lacks the subsequent knowledge attained in adulthood, even if the reader does have that knowledge.

Curiosity about sex is also a recurring trope, one that is often more readily associated with adolescence. In autobiographical writing, and in *Hitlerjunge Salomon*, pubescent boys' exploits (alone and with members of the same and opposite sex) are recounted, often with pride and relish, though also, especially in Goldschmidt's case, with a profound sense of fear and shame. The sexual encounters alluded to in the *Erwachsenenspiele* of Kunert's title, and in *Hitlerjunge Salomon*, did not conform to previous images of the passive Jewish child victim of the Holocaust, thus challenging them. Fictional girls are also shown to develop sexually in the course of the narratives. For Lore in Shortland's film, who is three years older than the literary character on whom she is based, puberty becomes confused with political and moral re-education. As Shortland commented, 'she's awakening to the world at the same time that her sexuality is awakening'.[4] The same is true of Alice in *Reise im August*. Her pre-adolescent crush on Paul, one of the prisoners who is killed during the journey, is part of her gradual coming to understand that being Jewish means being persecuted. In these cases, and in the opening of *weiter leben*, sex and death are close neighbours, both taboos associated with the premature end of childhood. It is striking that of all the works discussed here, *Austerlitz*, *Bruchstücke*, and *NaPolA* are the only ones that do not thematize sex or sexual development. Friedrich's friendship with Albrecht has been read as homoerotic, but the film does not particularly pursue this, sticking to a more conventional 'buddy movie' framework. Austerlitz's failed relationship with Marie is indicative of his arrested development; and the protagonist of Wilkomirski's *Bruchstücke* is a very (indeed implausibly) young child whose absence of sexuality serves to reinforce the view of him as innocent, and, in a Romantic view, uncorrupted.

In *Childness and the Writing of the German Past*, Maguire concludes that, in the texts on which she focuses, 'attempts to "queer" or deconstruct' the myth of innocence in recent representations of childhood in the Third Reich 'ultimately tend to feed back into it'.[5] Many of the works discussed here suggest otherwise. That is not to say there are not exculpatory manoeuvres: Gansel's Friedrich is made implausibly ignorant and thus innocent of Nazism; Johann in *Ein springender Brunnen* is allowed to retain his innocence despite what his author knows after 1945; and Grass casts the first stone at his younger self, only to encourage a more sympathetic view by doing so. Yet there are challenges to this myth. Wilkomirski's performance of the innocent child Holocaust victim in *Bruchstücke* is resisted and challenged by Kunert, Klüger, and Goldschmidt — all of whom were persecuted because of their Jewish identity. Holland's adaptation of Perel's story in *Hitlerjunge Salomon* challenges the myth too, as does Shortland's *Lore*. Perhaps, to expand on Maguire's conclusion, more successful deconstructions of the innocence myth are found in narratives from those who, then as now, are 'beyond the establishment'.

Another important question raised by the material discussed here concerns legitimacy and the right to remember, and the ethics of writing about this past. Who is permitted to write about what, and in what way? And, as importantly, who is it that grants the permission? Of all the works discussed here, only *weiter leben* and *Erwachsenenspiele* present themselves unequivocally as 'autobiography' and sustain a 'truth-telling' attitude throughout the narrative. De Bruyn and Grass knowingly perform authenticity, and Walser and Goldschmidt use a fictional framework to write about their own past. Through his combination of text and documentary traces such as photographs, Sebald writes fiction imbued with the aura of authenticity (which he systematically undermines). *Reise im August* offers a kind of autobiography in the subjunctive: Pausewang writes the story of a girl who, at the age when she herself was in the Hitler Youth, is deported to Auschwitz. I do not think it would go too far to argue that Alice's obsession with knowledge, and her profound uneasiness at being kept in the dark about social and political realities, echoes Pausewang's own discomfort after the war at not having known what was really happening around her. The extent to which Pausewang is in any way culpable for this ignorance, however much it discomforts her, is a question which all the authors face, regardless of whether they go on to decide they are or are not. *Bruchstücke* is a fictional text about the Holocaust, but based on an amassing of documentary evidence and, if we are to believe that it is an *unconscious* fraud, on the internalizing of that information to create a new identity. The films all draw on literary sources: autobiographical in the case of Holland, historical for Gansel, and from the realm of familial memory in Shortland's case. Films, with their potential to reach mass audiences, to engage and influence, today have the greatest influence in how the past is portrayed.[6] Randall Halle has argued that films of the 'Hitler Boom' such as *Der Untergang* and *NaPolA* address international audiences, and also particularly target twenty-somethings, offering 'strong points of identification to a youthful audience'.[7] If cinema is indeed about to become 'the most powerful means of depicting history', then cinema-goers themselves should engage critically with what is being depicted on screen, an attitude which hardly accords with the passive reception suggested in Landsberg's prosthetic memory.

The post-1990 debate about the commemoration of German wartime suffering has unsettled traditional post-war notions of victims and perpetrators in public discourse. Similarly, post-reunification events, including the rededication of the Neue Wache in Berlin to all victims of the war, the building of the *Denkmal für die ermordeten Juden Europas*, debates such as that between Martin Walser and Ignatz Bubis following Walser's 'Friedenspreisrede' in 1998, and Grass's SS revelations, have demonstrated that 'attempts to diffuse or suspend traditional categories of victim and perpetrator elicit an intensity of emotion'.[8] In its depiction of a Jewish boy seduced by Nazism, *Hitlerjunge Salomon* does not seek to fit its protagonist simply into a victim–perpetrator binary. Similarly, Klüger discusses the right to remember, positioning her own memories of deportation alongside the war memories of her contemporaries. In the early 1990s, even though the normative framework for remembrance is that of the Holocaust (Assmann), Klüger finds that this operates only on the 'official' level. Privately, amongst German friends and colleagues of the same generation, she feels her memories of Auschwitz are not 'salonfähig' [socially acceptable] (*weiter leben*, p. 110).

Throughout this study, I have explored how childhood and the figure of the child can perform an authenticating function. This is either because of the particular expectations of the medium, or results from claims made by the authors or filmmakers. It also emerges from the collective endeavour to show something of what it was *really* like to grow up in the Third Reich. The 'authentic' appears to be confirmed only when representations conform to a pre-existing image or code. Images which are deemed 'authentic' may merely consist of reconstructions of previously 'authentic' images: either images from the period in question, or later representations which are collectively received as 'authentic'. Furthermore, images of the past may be deemed 'authentic' if they reveal a truth about the past which, though it may not necessarily be historically accurate, is nevertheless deemed to offer a picture of 'what it was really like'.

This is what we find in the fictional treatments of the Holocaust by Sebald, Wilkomirski, and Pausewang, which have been received as 'authentic', emotionally and artistically. Even though their own backgrounds are distant from the experiences that they relate, and even though that distance is highly controversial in relation to their subject matter, this is overcome by their use of child protagonists in their stories. The texts are written from three distinct perspectives, each of which carries its own unique questions of legitimacy: Sebald, as a non-Jewish member of the post-war generation, writes the story of a Jewish child; yet the aesthetic means with which he depicts this experience seem to justify his approach. In contrast, Wilkomirski has been exposed as a fraud: although his account of childhood was purported to be a representation of his own experiences, he was never in a concentration camp. Yet his text has encouraged discussion about the nature of 'authenticity', suggesting that although his account is not historically referential, it *may* nevertheless reflect a 'poetic truth' about children's suffering. As a former member of the BDM, Pausewang occupies a more subtly complex position. The child's voice which she constructs in *Reise im August* is often implausible in its exaggerated naivety, and her depiction of the gas chambers is aesthetically questionable; yet the text brings into focus the issue of how this experience will be depicted when those of her generation, Jewish and non-Jewish, are no longer able to relate it. Indeed, the reception of these texts suggests that, while the narratives they contain are acknowledged to be imagined, they nevertheless are considered to offer something 'authentic' about the past. It is precisely the focus on childhood and children that acts as a guarantor of authenticity, where authenticity signifies a kind of 'innere Wahrheit' [inner truth].[9] It reveals a truth about the past which is rooted in experience and which appeals to the emotions. Ironically, we see this exemplified best in Wilkomirski's *Bruchstücke*, which, even after it was revealed to be a fake memoir, was nevertheless declared to be 'grausam wahr' [cruelly true]. This was not because it recounted true events, but because of what critics felt it revealed about the experience of a child facing loss and persecution, which the Holocaust survivor could recognize from their own experience.

However, such an approach is not without potential problems. Concern is frequently expressed that, while representations of children have a universal appeal and thus a positive potential, they may simultaneously engender an overly emotional response which precludes the kind of critical engagement with the past which remembrance and commemoration demand. In the case of depictions of Jewish child victims of the Holocaust, this concern has been repeatedly raised. As we saw in the case of Anne Frank and the Buchenwald child, individual children can be burdened with representation, standing in for countless others. It is precisely this against which Klüger so vehemently argues in *weiter leben*, and which Kunert, Goldschmidt, and Perel (through Holland's film), challenge in their constructions of childhood. *Bruchstücke* satisfied 'a desire for the authentic emotion and experience',[10] but also offered an account in which not only the child, but the adult author, was commended to the reader as an innocent victim in need of pity. Even *Austerlitz*, generally praised as engaging with childhood and the Holocaust in a responsible and above all critical mode, has been criticized by Klüger, who writes: 'alle Melancholie einer untergehenden Kultur [wird] in das eine Schicksal des jüdischen Kindes gelegt' [all the melancholy of a declining culture [is] laid on the fate of a Jewish child].[11]

The depiction of children as the 'victims of history' emerges from the idea of children as passive and devoid of agency. When this image of childhood is employed in exhibitions, literary texts, or films it can have a dual effect: it can both preclude a critical engagement with the topic at hand, and, at the same time, the child's passivity can deny important aspects of the way in which Nazism sought to indoctrinate and control. In a similar way, the employment of the image of the Jewish child Holocaust victim as a symbol of hope, or of the inhumanity of the Final Solution, is seen to encourage an emotionally charged response that becomes problematic when it prevents any further engagement or action.

The Search for a Usable Childhood?

Finally, I want to consider how these works contribute to the cultural memory of the Third Reich in the Berlin Republic. As I have explored throughout this study, childhood is often conceptually linked to origins. As Sinyard writes, 'the artist looking back to his own childhood as a clue to his modern existence is all part of an endless attempt, on all our behalfs, to rewrite and analyse our own history'.[12] Contemporary Germany continues to negotiate its post-reunification identity around the thirtieth anniversary of the fall of the Berlin Wall. This identity is inextricably linked to family history, for 'the entanglement of virtually every German family story in the Third Reich history means that this quest necessarily involves a confrontation both with the past of a private family and with that of a wider nation'.[13] Post-reunification representations of childhood and youth in the Third Reich can be viewed as a kind of search for a usable childhood. Based on Robert G. Moeller's notion of 'the search for a usable past', the 'search for a usable childhood' is not a normative term confirming versions of the past which are 'usable', in the sense of acceptable. Rather, it is a descriptive term which incorporates a range of narratives that seek to engage with personal, family, and national stories of the past, rooted in the experience of growing up. It points to the usefulness of certain constructions of that experience to the national narrative of post-reunification Germany, which have been both reinforced and challenged, and which contribute to national and collective identity in the Berlin Republic.

The 'search for a usable past', as described by Moeller, first took place during the 1950s in order to find a way for Germans to negotiate recent history. Moeller suggests that this process has continued following reunification:

> the search for a usable past is not at an end. It must include the continued study of National Socialism, European Jewry before the Holocaust, the 'final solution,' the Second World War, the collective experience of German loss and suffering that embraced millions of unique stories, the emergence of the Cold War, and attempts to write a complex history of the war's end, one in which all these strands appear.[14]

Similarly, Cohen-Pfister and Weinroeder-Skinner see this search for a usable past being taken up again in the Berlin Republic, writing that 'with the caesura of 1989–1990 — marking the end to Germany's division at the end of WWII — the search for a usable past has emerged in the Berlin Republic as part of the process of "normalization"'.[15] This process seeks to make sense not only of the Third Reich but also the resulting division of Germany during the post-war era.

We can understand normalization within the social, political, and cultural changes that Germany has undergone since reunification in two ways: first, as a term associated with conservatives desiring to draw a line under Germany's Nazi past and reinstate German national identity.[16] Critics, especially on the Left, perceived this kind of normalization as part of an attempt to relativize the Nazi past by questioning the singularity of the National Socialist regime and, by association, the Holocaust. Here, it is perceived as part of an endeavour to construct a national identity that emphasizes German victimhood and produces 'an imagined community defined by the experience of loss and displacement during the Second World War'.[17] Second, and since the mid-1990s, normalization has become less controversial, and part of the political landscape in Germany, as well as of its social and cultural discourse. It emerged as a concerted search for an integration of multiple memories, the 'totale Erinnerung' which accepts Germans' role both as victims and perpetrators, and which might facilitate a dialogue between different victim groups.[18] As Niven has argued:

> there is now a broader awareness of the true extent of National Socialist criminality and of the range of victims and that this inclusiveness can be understood as an 'ongoing process of broadening understanding' of the project of 'coming to terms with the past' in Germany.[19]

Niven, like Aleida Assmann and others, argues that a context has developed in which multiple narratives of the past can and do exist contemporaneously, without the one denigrating the significance of the other.

It is within this context that the search for a 'usable childhood' can be read. The term describes the contribution that the narratives in this study make to the wider debate about the ongoing legacy of Nazism, and its meaning and implications for the present. It does not suggest or denote a version of childhood, or rather of Germany's past, which is deemed acceptable, or 'salonfähig' [socially acceptable], to use Klüger's term (*weiter leben*, p. 110); rather, it is intended to suggest a construction of the past which incorporates the wide spectrum of experience that can be engaged with critically. In the same way as the concept of 'memory contests', which 'reflect a pluralistic memory culture which does not enshrine a particular normative understanding of the past',[20] these accounts of childhood under Nazism are part of a broad discourse of identity, origins, and memory.

The search for a usable childhood takes a number of forms: it involves an engagement with personal, family, and national narratives of the past in order to articulate this experience, or to challenge existing narratives. For Klüger, a usable childhood is one which instigates critical engagement with the past. Her work is intended not 'als Selbsttherapie, sondern als Kommunikation' [as self-help, but as communication].[21] Like de Bruyn, Kunert faces a personal history that has been delegitimized not once, but twice, through his dealings with the GDR authorities. His account, like those of both Goldschmidt and Klüger, seeks to deal publicly with the effects of persecution and with the complex relationship with the German language and nation which is the result of that experience. *Die Absonderung* is part of a thirty-year attempt at coming to terms with a disrupted childhood characterized by suffering and loss. And, while critics have interpreted this autobiographical project as therapeutic, like Klüger, Goldschmidt also sees it as a provocation to those who tried, and failed, to kill him.

For de Bruyn, Grass, and Walser, the search for a usable childhood is both a means to negotiate something of what Fuchs terms their 'delegitimized past',[22] and also the result of their commitment to shaping German public discourse. It is also, in Walser's case, part of a drive to defend private memory from what he considers the 'political correctness' of public discourse. Ultimately, though, these writers are more interested in *their* childhoods, in writing the 'Wahrheit des Künstlers', than with writing about the Third Reich. Indeed, Shortland's *Lore* comes closer to depicting the turmoil of the Hitler Youth generation, documented by so many in the 1970s and 1980s, than the autobiographical works discussed here.

The literary accounts of growing up in the Third Reich by Sebald, Pausewang, and Wilkomirski demonstrate how imagined accounts contribute to the search for a usable childhood. The fact that, in their reception, these works have been praised for their authenticity, that is to say, the 'inner truth' which they portray, suggests that a usable childhood in the future might be one which relies on communicating the feeling of the experience, even if this experience itself is not historically accurate. This contributes to a wider discussion of the legitimacy of writing fiction about the Holocaust, and one that is likely to intensify after the disappearance of the last eyewitnesses and survivors. We see already, in the discussion of Holland's, Gansel's, and Shortland's films, that films about growing up in the Third Reich provide a means with which to understand complex histories, and to explore, from a period of historical distance, how the events of the past could take place.

The ongoing fascination with childhood and the Third Reich continues, shaped by the changing context, particularly the recent refugee crisis and resurgence across Europe of the extreme Right. We might view this cynically as the narrator of Wolf's *Kindheitsmuster* did in the 1970s, commenting that 'der Tourismus in halbversunkene Kinderwelten blüht' [the tourist trade to half-buried childhoods is also booming].[23] In the Berlin Republic, this 'tourism' has continued, perhaps in part aided by the fact that, as Kate Douglas contends, autobiographical accounts of childhood 'pledge to offer experiences and stories of childhood for adult consumption, allowing adults to fantasise about their collective pasts and futures. Childhood lives are presented as available, desirable, and consumable'.[24] This interest has been intergenerational: on the part of those who lived through the events and are speaking only now, many for the first time, about their experiences; and on the part of those who, coming after, attempt to make sense of their parents' and grandparents' formative years. In our present world, images and accounts of suffering, of indoctrination, of political control, and of the painful process of engaging with the past — individually or as a collective — now more than ever provide a powerful means with which to shape and change the present and the future.

Notes to the Conclusion

1. Reich-Ranicki, 'Vorwort', p. 9.
2. Chris Jenks, *Childhood* (London: Routledge, 2005), pp. 2–3.
3. See e.g. Pinfold, *Child's View*; Barth.
4. Bijan Tehrani, 'Cate Shortland Talks about LORE', 13 February 2013 <https://cinemawithoutborders.com/3311-cate-shortland-lore/> [accessed 1 July 2019].
5. Maguire, p. 167.
6. It would be fruitful to consider, too, how this discourse has developed in television, particularly given the popularity and significance not only of historical documentaries (like those produced by Guido Knopp), but also TV movies and fictional series, such as *Unsere Mütter, unsere Väter* (2013).

7. Halle, p. 113.
8. Laurel Cohen-Pfister and Dagmar Weinroeder-Skinner, 'Introduction: History and the Memory of Suffering: Rethinking 1933–1945', in *Victims and Perpetrators*, ed. by Cohen-Pfister and Weinroeder-Skinner, pp. 3–29 (p. 8).
9. Rodek.
10. Reiter, 'Memory and Authenticity', p. 139.
11. Ruth Klüger, 'Wanderer zwischen falschen Leben: Über W. G. Sebald', in *W. G. Sebald*, ed. by Heinz Ludwig Arnold (Munich: Text + Kritik, 2003), pp. 95–102 (p. 100), cited in Maguire, p. 145.
12. Sinyard, p. 8.
13. Marie Louise Wasmeier, 'The Past in the Making: Invented Images and Fabricated Family History in Marcel Beyer's *Spione*', in *New German Literature: Life-Writing and Dialogue with the Arts*, ed. by Julian Preece, Frank Finlay, and Ruth J. Owen (Berne and Oxford: Lang, 2007), pp. 343–58 (p. 343).
14. Robert G. Moeller, *War Stories: The Search for a Usable Past in the Federal Republic of Germany* (Berkeley: University of California Press, 2001), p. 20.
15. Cohen-Pfister and Weinroeder-Skinner, p. 7.
16. For a discussion of this, see Taberner and Cooke.
17. Moeller, p. 6.
18. Gerrit Bartels, 'Die totale Erinnerung', *Tageszeitung*, 29 March 2003 <http://www.taz.de/1/archiv/archiv/?dig=2003/03/29/a0120> [accessed 1 July 2019].
19. B. Niven, *Facing the Nazi Past*, p. 4.
20. Fuchs and Cosgrove, p. 2.
21. Pletter.
22. Fuchs, *Phantoms of War*, p. 164.
23. Wolf, *Kindheitsmuster*, p. 19; Christa Wolf, *Patterns of Childhood*, trans. by Ursule Molinaro and Hedwig Rappolt (New York: Farrar, Straus and Giroux, 1980), p. 7.
24. Douglas, p. 44.

REFERENCES

Main Primary Texts and Films

DE BRUYN, GÜNTER, *Zwischenbilanz* (Frankfurt a.M.: Fischer, 1992)
GANSEL, DENNIS, dir., *NaPolA: Elite für den Führer* (Olga Film GmbH, 2004)
GOLDSCHMIDT, GEORGES-ARTHUR, *Die Absonderung* (Zurich: Ammann, 1991)
GRASS, GÜNTER, *Beim Häuten der Zwiebel* (Göttingen: Steidl, 2006)
—— *Peeling the Onion*, trans. by Michael Henry Heim (London: Harvill Secker, 2007)
HOLLAND, AGNIESZKA, dir., *Hitlerjunge Salomon* (Central Cinema Company Film, 1992)
KLÜGER, RUTH, *weiter leben: Eine Jugend* (Munich: dtv, 2008)
—— *Still Alive: A Holocaust Girlhood Remembered* (New York: The Feminist Press, 2012)
KUNERT, GÜNTER, *Erwachsenenspiele: Erinnerung* (Munich: Hanser, 1997)
PAUSEWANG, GUDRUN, *Reise im August* (Ravensburg: Ravensburger Buchverlag, 1997)
—— *The Final Journey*, trans. by Patricia Crampton (London: Puffin, 1998)
SEBALD, W. G., *Austerlitz* (Frankfurt a.M.: Fischer Taschenbuch, 2001)
—— *Austerlitz*, trans. by Anthea Bell (London: Hamilton, 2001)
SHORTLAND, CATE, dir., *Lore* (Artificial Eye, 2013)
WALSER, MARTIN, *Ein springender Brunnen* (Frankfurt a.M.: Suhrkamp, 1998)
—— *A Gushing Fountain*, trans. by David Dollenmayer (New York: Skyhorse, 2015)
WILKOMIRSKI, BINJAMIN, *Fragments: Memories of a Childhood, 1939–1948*, trans. by Carol Brown Janeway (London: Picador, 1996)
—— *Bruchstücke: Aus einer Kindheit 1939–1948* (Frankfurt a.M.: Suhrkamp, 1998)

Other Primary Texts

APITZ, BRUNO, *Nackt unter Wölfen* (Halle: Mitteldeutscher Verlag, 1958)
BECHSTEIN, LUDWIG, *Deutsches Märchenbuch* (Leipzig: Wigand, 1847)
BERKÉWICZ, ULLA, *Engel sind schwarz und weiß* (Frankfurt a.M.: Suhrkamp, 1994 [1992])
BEYER, MARCEL, *Flughunde* (Frankfurt a.M.: Suhrkamp, 1996)
BLUME, JUDY, *Are You There, God? It's Me, Margaret* (London: Pan Piper, 1970)
CARROLL, LEWIS, *Alice's Adventures in Wonderland* (London: Penguin, 2006)
DE BRUYN, GÜNTER, *Der Hohlweg* (Halle: Mitteldeutscher Verlag, 1963)
—— 'Fremd im eigenen Land', in *Über Deutschland: Schriftsteller geben Auskunft*, ed. by Thomas Reitzschel (Leipzig: Reclam, 1993), pp. 154–74
—— *Das erzählte Ich: Über Wahrheit und Dichtung in der Autobiographie* (Frankfurt a.M.: Fischer, 1995)
DÜCKERS, TANJA, *Himmelskörper* (Berlin: Aufbau Taschenbuch Verlag, 2004)
FEST, JOACHIM, *Ich nicht: Erinnerungen an eine Kindheit und Jugend* (Reinbek: Rowohlt, 2008)
—— *Not Me: Memoirs of a German Childhood*, trans. by Martin Chalmers (London: Atlantic, 2012)
FINCKH, RENATE, *Sie versprachen uns die Zukunft: Eine Jugend im Nationalsozialismus* (Tübingen: Silberburg, 2002 [1979])

FORTE, DIETER, *Der Junge mit den blutigen Schuhen* (Frankfurt a.M.: Fischer, 1995)
FRANK, ANNE, *The Diary of Anne Frank: The Critical Edition*, ed. by David Barnouw and Gerrold van der Stroom (London: Viking, 1989)
FREUD, SIGMUND, *Die Traumdeutung* (Frankfurt a.M.: Fischer, 2005)
—— *The Interpretation of Dreams*, trans. by A. A. Brill (New York: Dover, 2015)
GIORDANO, RALPH, *Erinnerungen eines Davongekommenen* (Cologne: Kiepenheuer & Witsch, 2007)
GOETHE, JOHANN WOLFGANG VON, *Aus meinem Leben: Dichtung und Wahrheit* (Frankfurt a.M.: Deutscher Klassiker Verlag, 2007)
GOLDSCHMIDT, GEORGES-ARTHUR, *Le Miroir quotidien* (Paris: Seuil, 1981)
—— *Un jardin en Allemagne* (Paris: Seuil, 1986)
—— *Ein Garten in Deutschland*, trans. by Eugen Helmlé (Zurich: Ammann, 1988)
—— *Quand Freud voit la mer* (Paris: Buchet-Chastel, 1988)
—— *La Forêt interrompue* (Paris: Seuil, 1991)
—— *Die Aussetzung: Eine Erzählung* (Zurich: Ammann, 1996)
—— *Quand Freud attend le verbe* (Paris: Buchet-Chastel, 1996)
—— *La Traversée des fleuves: Autobiographie* (Paris: Seuil, 1999)
—— *Über die Flüsse: Autobiografie* (Zurich: Ammann, 2001)
—— *Le Recours* (Paris: Verdiers, 2005)
—— *Die Befreiung* (Zurich: Ammann, 2007)
—— *Ein Wiederkommen: Erzählung* (Frankfurt a.M.: Fischer, 2012)
—— *Der Ausweg: Eine Erzählung* (Frankfurt a.M.: Fischer, 2014)
GOLDSCHMIDT, GEORGES-ARTHUR, and HANS-JÜRGEN HEINRICHS, *Schwarzfahrer des Lebens* (Frankfurt a.M.: Fischer, 2013)
GRASS, GÜNTER, *The Tin Drum*, trans. by Ralph Manheim (London: Vintage, 1998)
—— *Im Krebsgang* (Munich: dtv, 2002)
—— *Die Blechtrommel* (Munich: dtv, 2003)
GRIMMELSHAUSEN, HANS JAKOB CHRISTOPH VON, *The Adventures of Simplicius Simplicissimus*, trans. by Mike Mitchell (Cambridge: Dedalus, 1999)
—— *Der abenteuerliche Simplicissimus* (Stuttgart: Reclam, 2001)
HANNSMANN, MARGARETE, *Der helle Tag bricht an: Ein Kind wird Nazi* (Munich: dtv, 1984 [1982])
HARIG, LUDWIG, *Weh dem, der aus der Reihe tanzt* (Munich: Hanser, 1990)
HEIDEGGER, MARTIN, *Sein und Zeit* (Tübingen: Niemeyer, 1979)
HELLER, GEORGE, *Das Kind, das er war: Die Geschichte des Johann Avellis* (Berlin: Rowohlt, 2006)
HILSENRATH, EDGAR, *Berlin ... Endstation* (Berlin: Dittrich, 2006)
JOSEPHS, JEREMY, WITH SUSI BECHHÖFER, *Rosa's Child: The True Story of One Woman's Quest for a Lost Mother and a Vanished Past* (London: I. B. Tauris, 1996)
KANT, HERMANN, *Abspann: Erinnerung an meine Gegenwart* (Berlin: Aufbau, 1991)
KERTÉSZ, IMRE, *Fateless*, trans. by Tom Wilkinson (London: Vintage, 2006)
KLÜGER, RUTH, *Frauen lesen anders: Essays*, 2nd edn (Munich: Deutscher Taschenbuch Verlag, 1997)
—— *Dichter und Historiker: Fakten und Fiktionen* (Vienna: Picus, 2000)
KUNERT, GÜNTER, *Notizen in Kreide: Gedichte* (Leipzig: Reclam, 1970)
—— *Warum schreiben? Notizen zur Literatur* (Berlin: Aufbau, 1978)
—— *Die letzten Indianer Europas: Kommentare zum Traum, der Leben heißt* (Munich: Hanser, 1991)
LOEST, ERICH, *Durch die Erde ein Riß* (Hamburg: Hoffmann und Campe, 1981)
MASCHMANN, MELITA, *Fazit: Kein Rechtfertigungsversuch* (Stuttgart: Deutsche Verlags-Anstalt, 1963)

MÜLLER, HEINER, *Krieg ohne Schlacht: Leben in zwei Diktaturen* (Cologne: Kiepenheuer & Witsch, 1992)
MÜNCHEBERG, HANS, *Gelobt sei, was hart macht: Aus dem Leben eines Zöglings der Nationalpolitischen Erziehungsanstalt Potsdam* (Salenstein: Morgenbuch, 1991)
PAUSEWANG, GUDRUN, *Rosinkawiese — Damals und heute* (Munich: dtv, 2004)
—— *Fern von der Rosinkawiese* (Munich: dtv, 2004 [1989])
—— *Ich war dabei: Geschichten gegen das Vergessen* (Frankfurt a.M.: Fischer, 2015)
PEREL, SOLOMON [SALLY PEREL], *Ich war Hitlerjunge Salomon* (Munich: Heyne, 1993)
—— *Europa Europa: A Memoir of World War II* (New York: John Wiley & Sons, 1997)
RATZINGER, JOSEPH, *Aus meinem Leben: Erinnerungen, 1927–1977* (Stuttgart: DVA, 1998)
ROUSSEAU, JEAN-JACQUES, *The Confessions of Jean-Jacques Rousseau*, trans. by J. M. Cohen (London: Penguin, 1953)
—— *Émile; or, On Education*, trans. by Allan Bloom (New York: Basic Books, 1979)
SCHENZINGER, KARL ALOYS, *Der Hitlerjunge Quex: Roman* (Berlin: Zeitgeschichte, 1932)
SCHOPFLOCHER, ROBERT, *Eine Kindheit* (Göttingen: Wallstein, 1998)
STERN, CAROLA, *In den Netzen der Erinnerung* (Reinbek: Rowohlt, 1986)
STERNHEIM-PETERS, EVA, *Die Zeit der großen Täuschungen: Mädchenleben im Faschismus* (Bielefeld: AJZ, 1987)
VON DER GRÜN, MAX, *Wie war das eigentlich: Kindheit und Jugend im Dritten Reich* (Darmstadt: Luchterhand, 1981)
VON TEPL, JOHANNES, *Der Ackermann aus Böhmen: Im Auftrage der Königl. preussischen Akademie der Wissenschaften*, ed. by Alois Bernt and Konrad Burdach (Berlin: Weidmannnsche Buchhandlung, 1917)
WALSER, MARTIN, *Über Deutschland reden* (Frankfurt a.M.: Suhrkamp, 1989)
—— *Die Verteidigung der Kindheit* (Frankfurt a.M.: Suhrkamp, 1991)
—— *Ohne einander* (Frankfurt a.M.: Suhrkamp, 1993)
—— 'Speaking of Germany', in Thomas A. Kovach and Martin Walser, *The Burden of the Past: Martin Walser on Modern German Identity: Texts, Contexts, Commentary* (Rochester, NY: Camden House, 2008)
WALSER, MARTIN, and JAKOB AUGSTEIN, *Das Leben wortwörtlich: Ein Gespräch* (Reinbek: Rowohlt, 2017)
WOLF, CHRISTA, *Fortgesetzter Versuch: Aufsätze, Gespräche, Essays* (Leipzig: Reclam, 1980)
—— *Patterns of Childhood*, trans. by Ursule Molinaro and Hedwig Rappolt (New York: Farrar, Straus and Giroux, 1980)
—— *Ansprachen* (Darmstadt: Luchterhand, 1988)
—— *Kindheitsmuster* (Munich: Luchterhand, 2002)
ZELLER, EVA, *Solange ich denken kann: Roman einer Jugend* (Stuttgart: Ullstein, 1987 [1981])
—— *Die Autobiographie: Selbsterkenntnis — Selbstentblößung* (Stuttgart: Akademie der Wissenschaften und der Literatur, 1995)
ZWEIG, ZACHARIAS, *'Mein Vater, was machst du hier ...?' Zwischen Buchenwald und Auschwitz: Der Bericht des Zacharias Zweig* (Frankfurt a.M.: dipa, 1987)

Other Films

FÄBERBÖCK, MAX, DIR. *Aimée & Jaguar* (Senator, 1998)
GANSEL, DENNIS, DIR., *Die Welle* (Constantin, 2008)
HELLER, ANDRÉ, and OTHMAR SCHMIDERER, DIRS, *Im toten Winkel — Hitlers Sekretärin* (Der österreichische Film — Edition der Standard, 2002)
HIRSCHBIEGEL, OLIVER, DIR., *Der Untergang* (Constantin, 2004)
LINK, CAROLINE, DIR., *Nirgendwo in Afrika* (Ascot Elite Home Entertainment, 2001)

Panzer, Wolfgang, dir., *Die Brücke* (Warner Bros. Pictures, 2008)
Richter, Roland Suso, dir., *Dresden* (ZDF, 2006)
Roehler, Oskar, dir., *Jud Süß — Film ohne Gewissen* (Concorde Filmverleih, 2010)
Rothemund, Marc, dir., *Sophie Scholl: Die letzten Tage* (Warner Bros. Pictures, 2005)
Schlöndorff, Volker, dir., *Der neunte Tag* (Progress Film-Verleih, 2004)
Selpin, Herbert, dir., *Carl Peters* (Ufa, 1941)
Steinhoff, Hans, dir., *Hitlerjunge Quex: Ein Film vom Opfergeist der deutschen Jugend* (Ufa, 1933)

Newspaper Reviews and Articles

Ahearn, Victoria, '*Lore* Film Shows Second World War through Eyes of Children of Nazi SS Parents' <http://www.infotel.ca/newsitem/film-lore/cp23588447> [accessed 1 July 2019]

Bartels, Gerrit, 'Die totale Erinnerung', *Tageszeitung*, 29 March 2003 <http://www.taz.de/1/archiv/archiv/?dig=2003/03/29/a0120> [accessed 1 July 2019]

Bechhöfer, Susi, 'Stripped of my Past by a Bestselling Author', *Sunday Times*, 30 June 2002

Ensor, Josie, 'Photo of my Dead Son has Changed Nothing', *The Telegraph*, 3 September 2016 <http://www.telegraph.co.uk/news/2016/09/01/photo-of-my-dead-son-has-changed-nothing-says-father-of-drowned> [accessed 1 July 2019]

Erickson, Steven, 'Director Cate Shortland on *Lore*', 5 February 2013 <https://filmmakermagazine.com/64599-director-cate-shortland-on-lore/> [accessed 1 July 2019]

Frei, Norbert, 'Gefühlte Geschichte', *Die Zeit*, 21 October 2004 <http://www.zeit.de/2004/44/kriegsende> [accessed 1 July 2019]

Fritz-Vannahme, Joachim, 'Der Anwalt, der Komplize: Doppelporträt der Übersetzer Goldschmidt und Lortholary', *Die Zeit*, 13 October 1989, p. 6

Ganzfried, Daniel, 'Die geliehene Holocaust-Biographie', *Die Weltwoche*, 27 August 1998, p. 45

Gessler, Philipp, 'Tödliches Misstrauen', *Die Tageszeitung*, 6 October 2009 <http://www.taz.de/!41787> [accessed 1 July 2019]

Holden, Stephen, 'No ordinary Trip to Grandma's House', *New York Times*, 7 February 2013 <http://www.nytimes.com/2013/02/08/movies/lore-by-cate-shortland-views-children-in-postwar-germany.html> [accessed 1 January 2020]

Jaggi, Maya, 'Recovered Memories', *The Guardian*, 22 September 2001 <http://www.guardian.co.uk/books/2001/sep/22/artsandhumanities.highereducation> [accessed 1 July 2019]

Kecskes, Alex, 'Director Cate Shortland on her Post-WW II film, "Lore"' <http://www.acedmagazine.com/director-cate-shortland-on-her-post-ww-ii-film-lore> [accessed 1 July 2019]

Kertész, Imre, 'Wem gehört Auschwitz?', *Die Zeit*, 19 November 1998 <http://www.zeit.de/1998/48/Wem_gehoert_Auschwitz_> [accessed 1 July 2019]

Kilb, Andreas, 'Ohne Oscar', *Die Zeit*, 31 January 1992 <http://www.zeit.de/1992/06/ohne-oscar> [accessed 1 July 2019]

Klimke, Christoph, 'Es gibt keinen vernünftigen Grund, ein Gedicht zu schreiben!', *Die Welt*, 28 February 2009 <http://www.welt.de/welt_print/article3290188/Es-gibt-keinen-vernuenftigen-Grund-ein-Gedicht-zu-schreiben.html> [accessed 1 July 2019]

Lappin, Elena, 'The Man with Two Heads' <https://granta.com/the-man-with-two-heads> [accessed 1 July 2019]

Lezard, Nicholas, '*Austerlitz* by W. G. Sebald', *The Guardian*, 13 July 2002, p. 31

MÄRZ, URSULA, 'Nur Unversöhnlichkeit hilft weiter' <http://www.zeit.de/2008/42/L-Klueger-Besuch> [accessed 1 July 2019]

MENASSE, EVA, and MICHAEL KUMPFMÜLLER, 'Wider die intellektuelle Gerontokratie: Ein Plädoyer für weniger Grass und mehr Nahost in der Debatte', *Süddeutsche Zeitung*, 17 August 2006, p. 11

MÜLLER, VOLKER, 'Das willkommene Heldenlied', *Berliner Zeitung*, 28 April 2000 <http://www.berliner-zeitung.de/archiv/er-schrieb-das-buch--nackt-unter-woelfen---heute-vor-100-jahren-wurde-bruno-apitz-geboren-das-willkommene-heldenlied,10810590,9794632.html> [accessed 1 July 2019]

MÜNCHEBERG, HANS, 'Die Geschichte der Geschichte', *Freitag*, 14 January 2005 <http://www.freitag.de/autoren/der-freitag/die-geschichte-der-geschichte> [accessed 1 July 2019]

OZICK, CYNTHIA, 'Who Owns Anne Frank?', *New Yorker*, 28 September 1997 <http://www.newyorker.com/magazine/1997/10/06/who-owns-anne-frank> [accessed 1 July 2019]

PATTERSON, JOHN, 'Lore: Cate Shortland's Latest Isn't your Standard Second World War Movie', *The Guardian*, 16 February 2013 <http://www.theguardian.com/film/2013/feb/18/lore-cate-shortland> [accessed 1 July 2019]

PFLAUM, H. G., 'Keine Zeit für Trauer: Agnieszka Hollands zum Politikum gewordener Film "Hitlerjunge Salomon"', *Süddeutsche Zeitung*, 8 February 1992

PLETTER, MARITA, 'Der Pazifik hat die richtige Farbe', *Die Zeit*, 3 March 1995, p. 67

REICHER, ISABELLA, 'Schule für den Heldentod', *Der Standard*, 22 April 2005 <http://www.derstandard.at/2023249/Schule-fuer-den-Heldentod> [accessed 1 July 2019]

RODEK, HANNS-GEORG, ' "Jud Süß" sollte Spiel-, kein Dokumentarfilm sein' [conversation with Klaus Richter], *Die Welt*, 21 September 2010 <http://www.welt.de/kultur/article9775361/Jud-Suess-sollte-Spiel-kein-Dokumentarfilm-sein.html> [accessed 1 July 2019]

RUSHDIE, SALMAN, 'A Fine Pickle', *The Guardian*, 28 February 2009 <http://www.nawe.co.uk/DB/young-writers-news-3/a-fine-pickle.html> [accessed 1 July 2019]

SCHÖNING, JÖRG, 'Kinodrama *Lore*: Deutsches Mädel, deutsches Monster', *Der Spiegel*, 30 October 2012 <http://www.spiegel.de/kultur/kino/lore-cate-shortlands-starkes-nachkriegsdrama-kommt-in-die-kinos-a-862880.html> [accessed 1 July 2019]

SEIDL, CLAUDIUS, 'Blamage mit Folgen', *Der Spiegel*, 27 January 1992 <http://www.spiegel.de/spiegel/print/d-13680018.html> [accessed 1 July 2019]

SMITH, HELENA, 'Shocking Images of Drowned Syrian Boy Show Tragic Plight of Refugees', *The Guardian*, 2 September 2015 <http://www.theguardian.com/world/2015/sep/02/shocking-image-of-drowned-syrian-boy-shows-tragic-plight-of-refugees> [accessed 1 July 2019]

TIMMONS, PATRICK, 'Shocking Photo of Drowned Father and Daughter Highlights Migrants' Border Peril', *The Guardian*, 26 June 2019 <http://www.theguardian.com/us-news/2019/jun/25/photo-drowned-migrant-daughter-rio-grande-us-mexico-border> [accessed 1 July 2019]

TONG, ALLAN, ' "The only place to execute some kind of power was the film set": Agnieszka Holland on her Career' <http://www.filmmakermagazine.com/85231-the-only-place-to-execute-some-kind-of-power-was-the-film-set-agnieszka-holland-on-her-career/> [accessed 1 July 2019]

WALSER, MARTIN, 'Die Banalität des Guten: Erfahrungen beim Verfassen einer Sonntagsrede aus Anlass der Verleihung des Friedenspreises des Deutschen Buchhandels', *Frankfurter Allgemeine Zeitung*, 12 October 1998, p. 15

WEINRAUB, BERNARD, 'The Talk of Hollywood; "Europa" Surfaces in Oscar Angling', *New York Times*, 14 January 1992, p. 11

—— 'German Filmmakers Express Support for "Europa"', *New York Times*, 18 January 1992, p. 11

WOOD, GENEVIÈVE, 'Er war "Hitlerjunge Salomon" und führte ein Doppelleben', *Hamburger Abendblatt*, 27 January 2011 <http://www.abendblatt.de/hamburg/article1769348/Er-war-Hitlerjunge-Salomon-und-fuehrte-ein-Doppelleben.html> [accessed 1 July 2019]

Interviews

DOERRY, MARTIN, and VOLKER HAGE, 'Ich fürchte das Melodramatische' [interview with W. G. Sebald], *Der Spiegel*, 12 March 2001, pp. 228–34

GAFFNEY, ELIZABETH, 'Interview with Günter Grass', *Paris Review*, 124 (1991) <http://www.theparisreview.org/interviews/2191/the-art-of-fiction-no-124-gunter-grass> [accessed 1 July 2019]

Goldschmidt, Georges-Arthur, in conversation with Susanne Wittek, 6 November 2014 <http://www.youtube.com/watch?v=cQLn90VF2YM> [accessed 1 July 2019]

—— 'Ich hoffe, dass Deutschland nicht vergaulandet!', *Die Zeit*, 18 December 2018 <http://www.zeit.de/zeit-magazin/2018/53/georges-arthur-goldschmidt-schriftsteller-flucht-gestapo-rettung> [accessed 1 July 2019]

'Jeder Tag bringt eine kleinere oder größere Provokation' [interview with Martin Walser], *Die Welt*, 6 October 1998 <http://www.welt.de/print-welt/article626366/Jeder-Tag-bringt-eine-kleinere-oder-groessere-Provokation.html> [accessed 1 July 2019]

'Joseph-Breitbach-Preis an Georges-Arthur Goldschmidt', *Frankfurter Allgemeine Zeitung*, 28 July 2005 <http://www.faz.net/aktuell/rhein-main/kultur/auszeichnung-joseph-breitbach-preis-an-georges-arthur-goldschmidt-1255911.html> [accessed 1 July 2019]

KERTÉSZ, IMRE, 'Wichtig ist die Öffentlichkeit: Gespräch mit Sebastian Hefti und Wolfgang Heuer', in *... alias Wilkomirski: Die Holocaust Travestie: Enthüllung und Dokumentation eines literarischen Skandals*, ed. by Daniel Ganzfried and Sebastian Hefti (Berlin: Jüdische Verlagsanstalt, 2002), pp. 207–18

LEWIS, CHRIS, 'Der verkaufte Schatten? Interview mit Günter de Bruyn am 27. September 1996', in *Günter de Bruyn in Perspective*, ed. by Dennis Tate (Amsterdam: Rodopi, 1999), pp. 207–29

MUSALL, BETTINA, UND NIKOLAUS VON FESTENBERG, 'Die Tränen flossen nach innen' [interview with Solomon Perel], *Der Spiegel*, 16 March 1992 <http://www.spiegel.de/spiegel/print/d-9275452.html> [accessed 1 July 2019]

NAJAFI, SINA, 'Picturing Innocence: An Interview with Anne Higonnet' <http://www.cabinetmagazine.org/issues/9/picturing_innocence.php> [accessed 1 July 2019]

ROBERTS, SHEILA, 'Cate Shortland Talks *Lore*' <http://www.collider.com/cate-shortland-lore-interview> [accessed 30 June 2018]

SAUTER, JOSEF-HERMANN, 'Interview mit Bruno Apitz', *Weimarer Beiträge*, 19 (1973), 26–37

SCHOLZ, CHRISTIAN, 'Aber das Geschriebene ist ja kein wahres Dokument: Ein Gespräch mit dem Schriftsteller W. G. Sebald über Literatur und Photographie', *Neue Zürcher Zeitung*, 26 February 2000, p. 77

TASZMAN, JÖRG, '"NaPolA — Elite für den Führer": Gespräch mit dem Regisseur Dennis Gansel' <http://www.deutschlandradio.de/archiv/dlr/sendungen/fazit/338801/index.html> [accessed 1 July 2019]

TEHRANI, BIJAN, 'Cate Shortland Talks about LORE', 13 February 2013 <https://cinemawithoutborders.com/3311-cate-shortland-lore/> [accessed 1 July 2019]

TIBBETTS, JOHN C., 'An Interview with Agnieszka Holland: The Politics of Ambiguity', *Quarterly Review of Film and Video*, 25 (2008), 132–43

WELZER, HARALD, 'Im Gedächtniswohnzimmer: Warum sind Bücher über die eigene Familiengeschichte so erfolgreich? Ein Zeit-Gespräch mit dem Sozialpsychologen Harald Welzer über das private Erinnern', *Die Zeit*, 25 March 2004 <http://www.zeit.de/2004/14/st-welzer> [accessed 1 July 2019]

WITTSTOCK, UWE, 'Interview mit Günter de Bruyn' <http://blog.uwe-wittstock.de/?p=2069> [accessed 1 July 2019]

WOLF, CHRISTA, *The Fourth Dimension: Interviews with Christa Wolf*, trans. by Hilary Pilkington (London: Verso, 1988)

Websites

Hamburger Schulmuseum <http://www.hamburgerschulmuseum.de> [accessed 1 July 2019]

Lumiere database <http://lumiere.obs.coe.int/web/search/> [accessed 1 July 2019]

Secondary Literature

ADORNO, THEODOR W., 'Was bedeutet: Aufarbeitung der Vergangenheit', in Theodor W. Adorno, *Gesammelte Schriften*, ed. by Rolf Tiedemann with Gretel Adorno and others, 2 vols (Frankfurt a.M.: Suhrkamp, 1970–1986), x.2: *Kulturkritik und Gesellschaft II* (1977), 555–73

—— 'What Does Coming to Terms with the Past Mean?', in *Bitburg in Moral and Political Perspective*, ed. by Geoffrey H. Hartman (Bloomington: Indiana University Press, 1986), pp. 114–29

ANDERSON, JON, *Understanding Cultural Geography: Places and Traces*, 2nd edn (London: Routledge, 2015)

ANDERSON, LINDA, *Autobiography* (London: Routledge, 2001)

ANDERSON, MARK M., 'A Childhood in the Allgäu: Wertach, 1944–52', in *Saturn's Moons: W. G. Sebald: A Handbook*, ed. by Jo Catling and Richard Hibbitt (London: Legenda, 2011), pp. 16–42

ANNE FRANK STICHTING, JANRENSE BOONSTRA, and MARIE-JOSÉ RIJNDERS, *Anne Frank House: A Museum with a Story*, trans. by Nancy Forest-Flier (Amsterdam: Anne Frank Stichting, 2000)

ARCHARD, DAVID, *Children: Rights and Childhood* (London: Routledge, 2004)

ASSMANN, ALEIDA, *Der lange Schatten der Vergangenheit: Erinnerungskultur und Geschichtspolitik* (Munich: Beck, 2006)

—— 'Limits of Understanding: Generational Identities in Recent German Memory Literature', in *Victims and Perpetrators: 1933–1945 — Representing the Past in Post-Unification Culture*, ed. by Laurel Cohen-Pfister and Dagmar Weinroeder-Skinner (Berlin: de Gruyter, 2006), pp. 29–48

—— 'Memory, Individual and Collective', in *The Oxford Handbook of Contextual Political Analysis*, ed. by Robert E. Goodin and Charles Tilly (Oxford: Oxford University Press, 2006), pp. 210–27

—— 'On the (In)Compatibility of Guilt and Suffering in German Memory', *German Life and Letters*, 59 (2006), 187–200

—— 'Lichtstrahlen in die Black Box: Bernd Eichingers *Der Untergang*', in *Das Böse im Blick: Die Gegenwart des Nationalsozialismus im Film*, ed. by Margrit Fröhlich, Christian Schneider, and Karsten Visarius (Munich: Text + Kritik, 2007), pp. 45–56

—— *Shadows of Trauma: Memory and the Politics of Postwar Identity*, trans. by Sarah Clift (New York: Fordham University Press, 2016)

ASSMANN, JAN, *Kultur und Gedächtnis* (Frankfurt a.M.: Suhrkamp, 1988)
—— 'Communicative and Cultural Memory', in *A Companion to Cultural Memory Studies*, ed. by Astrid Erll and Ansgar Nünning (Berlin and New York: de Gruyter, 2008), pp. 109–18
BAER, ELIZABETH, 'W. G. Sebald's *Austerlitz*: Adaptation as Restitution', in *Adaptations in Film, the Arts, and Popular Culture: Reworking the German Past*, ed. by Susan G. Figge and Jenifer K. Ward (Rochester, NY: Camden House, 2010), pp. 181–203
BEIER-DE HAAN, ROSMARIE, 'Re-Staging Histories and Identities', in *A Companion to Museum Studies*, ed. by Sharon MacDonald (Oxford: Blackwell, 2010), pp. 186–98
BAIRD, JAY W., 'From Berlin to Neubabelsberg: Nazi Film Propaganda and *Hitlerjunge Quex*', *Journal of Contemporary History*, 18 (1983), 495–515
BAKER, JULIA, '*Fragments* and Beyond: Childhood Trauma in Binjamin Wilkomirski's and Georges-Arthur Goldschmidt's Holocaust Testimonies and Life-Writing', in *Trajectories of Memory: Intergenerational Representations of the Holocaust in History and the Arts*, ed. by Christina Guenther and Beth Griech-Polelle (Newcastle upon Tyne: Cambridge Scholars Publishing, 2008), pp. 279–313
BANGERT, AXEL, *The Nazi Past in Contemporary German Film: Viewing Experiences of Intimacy and Immersion* (Rochester, NY: Camden House, 2014)
BARTH, MECHTHILD, *Mit den Augen des Kindes: Narrative Inszenierungen des kindlichen Blicks im 20. Jahrhundert* (Heidelberg: Winter, 2009)
BARTHES, ROLAND, *Camera Lucida: Reflections on Photography*, trans. by Richard Howard (New York: Hill and Wang, 1993)
BARTHOLEYNS, GIL, 'Representation of the Past in Films: Between Historicity and Authenticity', *Diogenes*, 48 (2000), 31–47
BARTOV, OMER, *The 'Jew' in Cinema: From* The Golem *to* Don't Touch my Holocaust (Bloomington: Indiana University Press, 2005)
BARZILAI, MAYA, 'On Exposure: Photography and Uncanny Memory in W. G. Sebald's *Die Ausgewanderten* and *Austerlitz*', in *W. G. Sebald: History — Memory — Trauma*, ed. by Scott Denham and Mark McCulloh (Berlin: de Gruyter, 2006), pp. 205–19
BAUER, BARBARA, and WALTRAUD STRICKHAUSEN, EDS,'*Für ein Kind war das anders': Traumatische Erfahrungen jüdischer Kinder und Jugendlicher im nationalsozialistischen Deutschland* (Berlin: Metropol, 1999)
BEHRENDT, KATHY, 'Hirsch, Sebald, and the Uses and Limits of Postmemory', in *The Memory Effect: The Remediation of Memory in Literature and Film*, ed. by Russell J. A. Kilbourn and Eleanor Ty (Waterloo: Wilfrid Laurier University Press, 2013), pp. 51–71
BERGEN, DORIS L., 'The Nazi Concept of "Volksdeutsche" and the Exacerbation of Anti-Semitism in Eastern Europe, 1939–45', *Journal of Contemporary History*, 29 (1994), 569–82
BERGER, KARINA, 'Children of the Lebensborn: The Search for Identity in Selected Literary Texts of the Berlin Republic', *Focus on German Studies*, 15 (2008), 105–20
BESSLICH, BARBARA, KATHARINA GRÄTZ, and OLAF HILDEBRAND, eds, *Wende des Erinnerns? Geschichtskonstruktionen in der deutschen Literatur nach 1989* (Berlin: Schmidt, 2006)
BETTELHEIM, BRUNO, *The Uses of Enchantment: The Meaning and Importance of Fairy Tales* (London: Peregrine, 1978)
BLICKLE, PETER, *Heimat: A Critical Theory of the German Idea of Homeland* (Rochester, NY, and Woodbridge: Camden House, 2002)
BLOCH, ERNST, *Das Prinzip Hoffnung* (Frankfurt a.M.: Suhrkamp, 1959)
—— *The Principle of Hope*, trans. by Neville Plaice, Stephen Plaice, and Paul Knight (Cambridge: MIT Press, 1986)
BOA, ELIZABETH, 'Wolf, *Kindheitsmuster*', in *Landmarks of the German Novel (2)*, ed. by Peter Hutchinson and Michael Minden (Oxford: Lang, 2007), 77–93

—— 'Lost Heimat in Generational Novels by Reinhard Jirgl, Christoph Hein, and Angelika Overath', in *Germans as Victims in the Literary Fiction of the Berlin Republic*, ed. by Stuart Taberner and Karina Berger (Rochester, NY: Camden House, 2009), pp. 86–102

BODE, SABINE, *Kriegsenkel: Die Erben der vergessenen Generation* (Stuttgart: Klett-Cotta, 2009)

BOESE, STEFANIE, '"Forever Just Occurring": Postwar Belatedness in W. G. Sebald's *Austerlitz*', *Journal of Modern Literature*, 39.4 (2016), 104–21

BRAZIL, KEVIN, *Art, History, and Postwar Fiction* (Oxford: Oxford University Press, 2018)

BRETTSCHNEIDER, WERNER, *'Kindheitsmuster': Kindheit als Thema autobiographischer Dichtung* (Berlin: Schmidt, 1982)

BREYSACH, BARBARA, 'Verfolgte Kindheit: Überlegungen zu Ilse Aichingers frühem Roman und Georges-Arthur Goldschmidts autobiographischer Prosa', in *Bilder des Holocaust: Literatur — Film — Bildende Kunst*, ed. by Manuel Köppen and Klaus R. Scherpe (Cologne: Böhlau, 1997), pp. 47–63

BROCKMANN, STEPHEN, *Literature and German Reunification* (Cambridge: Cambridge University Press, 1999)

—— 'Martin Walser and the Presence of the German Past', *German Quarterly*, 75 (2002), 127–43

BROOKSHAW, SHARON, 'The Material Culture of Children and Childhood: Understanding Childhood Objects in the Museum Context', *Journal of Material Culture*, 14 (2009), 365–83

BRUNSSEN, FRANK, 'A Moral Authority? Günter Grass as the Conscience of the German Nation', *Journal of Contemporary European Studies*, 15 (2007), 565–84

BUFFINGA, JOHN O., 'Transnational Memory in Michael Haneke's *The White Ribbon* and Cate Shortland's *Lore*', in *The Changing Place of Europe in Global Memory Cultures: Usable Pasts and Futures*, ed. by Christina Kraenzle and Maria Mayr (Cham: Palgrave Macmillan), pp. 103–19

CAMBI, FABRIZIO, ed., *Gedächtnis und Identität: Die deutsche Literatur nach der Vereinigung* (Würzburg: Königshausen & Neumann, 2008)

CAMPT, TINA, *Other Germans: Black Germans and the Politics of Race, Gender, and Memory in the Third Reich* (Ann Arbor: University of Michigan Press, 2004)

CHAMBERS, ROSS, 'Orphaned Memories, Foster-Writing, Phantom Pain: The *Fragments* Affair', in *Extremities: Trauma, Testimony and Community*, ed. by Nancy K. Miller and Jason Tougaw (Urbana: University of Illinois Press, 2002), pp. 92–112

COE, RICHARD N., *When the Grass Was Taller: Autobiography and the Experience of Childhood* (London: Yale University Press, 1984)

COHEN-PFISTER, LAUREL, and DAGMAR WEINROEDER-SKINNER, 'Introduction: History and the Memory of Suffering: Rethinking 1933–1945', in *Victims and Perpetrators: 1933–1945 — Representing the Past in Post-Unification Culture*, ed. by Laurel Cohen-Pfister and Dagmar Weinroeder-Skinner (Berlin: de Gruyter, 2006), pp. 3–29

—— and —— eds, *Victims and Perpetrators: 1933–1945 — Representing the Past in Post-Unification Culture* (Berlin: de Gruyter, 2006)

COVENEY, PETER, *The Image of Childhood: The Individual and Society* (Harmondsworth: Penguin, 1967)

CRAIG-NORTON, JENNIFER, *The Kindertransport: Contesting Memory* (Bloomington: Indiana University Press, 2019)

CROWNSHAW, RICHARD, JANE KILBY, and ANTONY ROWLAND, eds, *The Future of Memory* (New York: Berghahn, 2010)

CUNNINGHAM, HUGH, *Children and Childhood in Western Society since 1500*, 2nd edn (Harlow: Pearson Longman, 2005)

DE WEVER, BRUNO, 'Prologue: Historical Film as Palimpsest', in *Perspectives on European Film and History*, ed. by Leen Engelen and Roel Vande Winkel (Ghent: Academia, 2007), pp. 5–12

DICKMANN, AXEL, *Grimms Märchen von A bis Z: Kleines Lexikon der Märchenmotive* ([n.p.]: Book on Demand, 2014)

DONAHUE, WILLIAM COLLINS, 'Pretty Boys and Nasty Girls: The Holocaust Figured in Two German Films of the 1990s', *New England Review*, 21 (2000), 108–24

DOUGLAS, KATE, *Contesting Childhood: Autobiography, Trauma, and Memory* (New Brunswick: Rutgers University Press, 2010)

DOW ADAMS, TIMOTHY, *Telling Lies in Modern American Autobiography* (Chapel Hill and London: University of North Carolina Press, 1990)

DUTTLINGER, CAROLIN, 'Traumatic Photographs: Remembrance and the Technical Media in W. G. Sebald's *Austerlitz*', in *W. G. Sebald: A Critical Companion*, ed. by J. J. Long and Anne Whitehead (Edinburgh: Edinburgh University Press, 2004), pp. 155–71

—— 'The Ethics of Curiosity: Ruth Klüger, *weiter leben*', in *Curiosity in German Literature and Culture from 1700 to the Present*, ed. by Carolin Duttlinger and Johannes Birgfeld (= special issue of *Oxford German Studies*, 38 (2009)), pp. 218–32

DWORK, DEBÓRAH, *Children with a Star: Jewish Youth in Nazi Europe* (Newhaven and London: Yale University Press, 1991)

EAKIN, PAUL JOHN, 'Breaking Rules: The Consequences of Self-Narration', *Biography*, 24 (2001), 113–27

EICHENBERG, ARIANE, *Familie — Ich — Nation: Narrative Analysen zeitgenössischer Generationenromane* (Göttingen: V&R unipress, 2009)

EIGLER, FRIEDERIKE, 'Engendering Cultural Memory in Selected Post-Wende Literary Texts of the 1990s', *German Quarterly*, 74 (2001), 392–406

—— *Gedächtnis und Geschichte in Generationenromanen seit der Wende* (Berlin: Schmidt, 2005)

EISEN, GEORGE, *Children and Play in the Holocaust: Games among the Shadows* (Amherst: University of Massachusetts Press, 1988)

ERIKSON, ERIK H., *Identity: Youth and Crisis* (New York: Norton, 1968)

ERLL, ASTRID, 'Literature, Film, and the Mediality of Cultural Memory', in *A Companion to Cultural Memory Studies*, ed. by Astrid Erll and Ansgar Nünning (Berlin and New York: de Gruyter, 2010), pp. 389–99

ERLL, ASTRID, and ANN RIGNEY, 'Introduction: Cultural Memory and its Dynamics', in *Mediation, Remediation, and the Dynamics of Cultural Memory*, ed. by Astrid Erll and Ann Rigney (New York: de Gruyter, 2009), pp. 1–15

ESHEL, AMIR, *Futurity: Contemporary Literature and the Quest for the Past* (Chicago: University of Chicago Press, 2013)

EVANS, OWEN, *Ein Training im Ich-Sagen: Personal Authenticity in the Prose Work of Günter de Bruyn* (Berne: Lang, 1996)

—— '"Schlimmeres als geschah, hätte immer geschehen können": Günter de Bruyn and the GDR in *Vierzig Jahre*', in *Günter de Bruyn in Perspective*, ed. by Dennis Tate (Amsterdam: Rodopi, 1999), pp. 171–89

—— *Mapping the Contours of Oppression: Subjectivity, Truth and Fiction in Recent German Autobiographical Treatments of Totalitarianism* (Amsterdam: Rodopi, 2006)

FAST, VERA K., *Children's Exodus: A History of the Kindertransport* (London: I. B. Tauris, 2011)

FEHRENBACH, HEIDE, 'War Orphans and Post-Fascist Families: Kinship and Belonging after 1945', in *Histories of the Aftermath: The Legacies of the Second World War in Europe*, ed. by Frank Biess and Robert G. Moeller (New York and Oxford: Berghahn, 2010), pp. 175–96

FINCH, HELEN, '"Die irdische Erfüllung": Peter Handke's Poetic Landscapes and W. G. Sebald's Metaphysics of History', in *W. G. Sebald and the Writing of History*, ed. by Anne Fuchs and J. J. Long (Würzburg: Königshausen & Neumann, 2007), pp. 179–97

FISCHER, ANDRÉ, *Inszenierte Naivität: Zur ästhetischen Simulation von Geschichte bei Günter Grass, Albert Drach und Walter Kempowski* (Munich: Fink, 1992)

FISCHER, TORBEN, PHILIPP HAMMERMEISTER, and SVEN KRAMER, eds, *Der Nationalsozialismus und die Shoah in der deutschsprachigen Gegenwartsliteratur* (Amsterdam: Rodopi, 2014)

FISHER, JAIMEY, *Disciplining Germany: Youth, Reeducation, and Reconstruction after the Second World War* (Detroit: Wayne State University Press, 2007)

FLYNN, RICHARD, '"Infant Sight": Romanticism, Childhood, and Postmodern Poetry', in *Literature and the Child: Romantic Continuations, Postmodern Contestations*, ed. by James Holt McGavran (Iowa City: University of Iowa Press, 1999), pp. 105–30

FREI, NORBERT, *1945 und wir: Das Dritte Reich im Bewußtsein der Deutschen* (Munich: Beck, 2005)

FRIEDRICHS, AXEL, ed., *Deutschlands Aufstieg zur Großmacht 1936* (Berlin: Junker und Dünnhaupt, 1939)

FUCHS, ANNE, *Die Schmerzensspuren der Geschichte: Zur Poetik der Erinnerung in W. G. Sebalds Prosa* (Cologne: Böhlau, 2004)

—— '"Ehrlich, du lügst wie gedruckt": Günter Grass's Autobiographical Confession and the Changing Territory of Germany's Memory Culture', *German Life and Letters*, 60 (2007), 261–75

—— *Phantoms of War in Contemporary German Literature, Films and Discourse: The Politics of Memory* (Basingstoke: Palgrave Macmillan, 2008)

FUCHS, ANNE, and MARY COSGROVE, 'Introduction', in *German Memory Contests: The Quest for Identity in Literature, Film, and Discourse since 1990*, ed. by Anne Fuchs, Mary Cosgrove, and Georg Grote (Rochester, NY: Camden House, 2006), pp. 1–21

GAFFNEY, PHYLLIS, *Constructions of Childhood and Youth in Old French Narrative* (Farnham and Burlington, VT: Ashgate, 2011)

GANSEL, CARSTEN, *Rhetorik der Erinnerung: Literatur und Gedächtnis in den 'geschlossenen Gesellschaften' des Real-Sozialismus* (Göttingen: V&R unipress, 2009)

GARLOFF, KATJA, 'The Task of the Narrator: Moments of Symbolic Investiture in W. G. Sebald's *Austerlitz*', in *W. G. Sebald: History — Memory — Trauma*, ed. by Scott Denham and Mark McCulloh (Berlin: de Gruyter, 2006), pp. 157–71

GERSTENBERGER, KATHARINA, *Truth to Tell: German Women's Autobiographies and Turn-of-the-Century Culture* (Ann Arbor: University of Michigan Press, 2000)

GIGLIOTTI, SIMONE, *The Train Journey: Transit, Captivity, and Witnessing in the Holocaust* (New York: Berghahn, 2009)

GIGLIOTTI, SIMONE, and MONICA TEMPIAN, eds, *The Young Victims of the Nazi Regime: Migration, the Holocaust and Postwar Displacement* (London: Bloomsbury Academic, 2016)

GREENFELD, HOWARD, *The Hidden Children* (New York: Ticknor & Fields, 1993)

GRUNBERGER, RICHARD, *The 12-Year Reich: A Social History of Nazi Germany, 1933–1945* (New York: Holt, Rinehart and Winston, 1971)

GUENTHER, CHRISTINA, and BETH GRIECH-POLELLE, eds, *Trajectories of Memory: Intergenerational Representations of the Holocaust in History and the Arts* (Newcastle upon Tyne: Cambridge Scholars Publishing, 2008)

GULLESTAD, MARIANNE, 'Modernity, Self, and Childhood in the Analysis of Life Stories', in *Imagined Childhoods: Self and Society in Autobiographical Accounts*, ed. by Marianne Gullestad (Oslo and Oxford: Scandinavian University Press, 1996), pp. 1–41

HALLE, RANDALL, *German Film after Germany* (Urbana: University of Illinois Press, 2008)

HAMMEL, ANDREA, and BEA LEWKOWICZ, eds, *The Kindertransport to Britain 1938/39: New Perspectives* (Amsterdam: Rodopi, 2012)

HANDKE, PETER, 'Vorwort', in Georges-Arthur Goldschmidt, *Die Absonderung* (Zurich: Ammann, 1991), pp. 7–9

HARRIS, STEFANIE, 'The Return of the Dead: Memory and Photography in W. G. Sebald's *Die Ausgewanderten*', *German Quarterly*, 74 (2001), 379–91

HARTH, DIETRICH, 'The Invention of Cultural Memory', in *A Companion to Cultural Memory Studies*, ed. by Astrid Erll and Ansgar Nünning (Berlin and New York: de Gruyter, 2008), pp. 85–96

HEBERER, PATRICIA, *Children during the Holocaust* (Lanham, MD: AltaMira Press in association with the United States Holocaust Memorial Museum, 2011)

—— 'The Nazi "Euthanasia" Program', in *The Routledge History of the Holocaust*, ed. by Jonathan C. Friedman (Abingdon and New York: Routledge, 2011), pp. 137–48

HEIDELBERGER-LEONARD, IRENE, 'Ruth Klüger *weiter leben* — ein Grundstein zu einem neuen Auschwitz-"Kanon"', in *Deutsche Nachkriegsliteratur und der Holocaust*, ed. by Stephan Braese and others (Frankfurt a.M.: Campus, 1998), pp. 157–73

HEINLEIN, MICHAEL, *Die Erfindung der Erinnerung: Deutsche Kriegskindheiten im Gedächtnis der Gegenwart* (Bielefeld: transcript, 2010)

HETZER, TANJA, *Kinderblick auf die Shoah: Formen der Erinnerung bei Ilse Aichinger, Hubert Fichte und Danilo Kiš* (Würzburg: Königshausen & Neumann, 1999)

HEYWOOD, COLIN, *A History of Childhood*, 2nd edn (Cambridge: Polity Press, 2017)

HIEBER, JOCHEN, 'Unversöhnte Lebensläufe: Zur Rhetorik der Verletzung in der Walser-Bubis-Debatte', in *Hinauf und zurück in die herzhelle Zukunft*, ed. by Michael Braun and Birgit H. Lermen (Bonn: Bouvier, 2000), pp. 543–59

HILBERG, RAUL, *The Destruction of the European Jews* (London: Allen, 1961)

HILLMAN, ROGER, 'Europe's Children across the Borders of Memory', in *The Young Victims of the Nazi Regime: Migration, the Holocaust and Postwar Displacement*, ed. by Simone Gigliotti and Monica Tempian (London: Bloomsbury Academic, 2016), pp. 321–36

HIRSCH, MARIANNE, 'Family Pictures: *Maus*, Mourning, and Post-Memory', *Discourse*, 15.2 (1992), 3–29

—— 'Projected Memory: Holocaust Photographs in Personal and Public Fantasy', in *Acts of Memory: Cultural Recall in the Present*, ed. by Mieke Bal, Jonathan V. Crewe, and Leo Spitzer (Hanover: Dartmouth College; Hanover and London: University Press of New England, 1999), pp. 3–24

—— 'Surviving Images: Holocaust Photographs and the Work of Postmemory', *The Yale Journal of Criticism*, 14.1 (2001), 5–37

—— 'The Generation of Postmemory', *Poetics Today*, 29 (2008), 103–28

—— *The Generation of Postmemory: Writing and Visual Culture after the Holocaust* (New York and Chichester: Columbia University Press, 2012)

HOFFMANN, HILMAR, *The Triumph of Propaganda*, trans. by John Broadwin and Volker R. Berghahn (Providence: Berghahn, 1996)

HOFMANN, REGINA, *Der kindliche Ich-Erzähler in der modernen Kinderliteratur: Eine erzähltheoretische Analyse mit Blick auf aktuelle Kinderromane* (Frankfurt a.M.: Lang, 2010)

HOLLAND, PATRICIA, *Picturing Childhood: The Myth of the Child in Popular Imagery* (London: I. B. Tauris, 2006)

HOLLINDALE, PETER, *Signs of Childness in Children's Books* (Stroud: Thimble Press, 1997)

HORSTKOTTE, SILKE, *Nachbilder: Fotografie und Gedächtnis in der deutschen Gegenwartsliteratur* (Cologne: Böhlau, 2009)

HUYSSEN, ANDREAS, *Present Pasts: Urban Palimpsests and the Politics of Memory* (Stanford: Stanford University Press, 2003)

JARON, STEVEN, 'Autobiography and the Holocaust: An Examination of the Liminal Generation in France', *French Studies*, 56 (2002), 207–19

JENKS, CHRIS, *Childhood* (London: Routledge, 2005)

JOHNSON, ERIC, *The Nazi Terror: The Gestapo, Jews, and Ordinary Germans* (London: Murray, 2000)

JONES, SARA, *Complicity, Censorship and Criticism: Negotiating Space in the GDR Literary Sphere* (Berlin and New York: de Gruyter, 2011)

JOPLING, MICHAEL, *Re-Placing the Self: Fictional and Autobiographical Interplay in Modern German Narrative (Elias Canetti, Thomas Bernhard, Peter Weiss, Christa Wolf)* (Stuttgart: Heinz, 2001)
KANE, ROBERT B., *Disobedience and Conspiracy in the German Army 1918–1945* (London: McFarland, 2002)
KAPLAN, MARION, 'The School Lives of Jewish Children and Youth in the Third Reich', *Jewish History*, 11 (1997), 41–52
KATER, MICHAEL H., *Hitler Youth* (London: Harvard University Press, 2004)
KEHILY, MARY JANE, and HEATHER MONTGOMERY, 'Innocence and Experience: A Historical Approach to Childhood and Sexuality', in *An Introduction to Childhood Studies*, ed. by Mary Jane Kehily (New York: Open University Press, 2004), pp. 57–75
KIESEL, HELMUTH 'Zwei Modelle literarischer Erinnerung an die NS-Zeit: *Die Blechtrommel* und *Ein springender Brunnen*', *German Monitor*, 60 (2004), 343–61
KIRSCHNICK, SYLKE, *Anne Frank und die DDR: Politische Deutungen und persönliche Lesarten des berühmten Tagebuchs* (Berlin: Links, 2009)
KITZINGER, JENNY, 'Who Are You Kidding? Children, Power, and the Struggle against Sexual Abuse', in *Constructing and Reconstructing Childhood: Contemporary Issues in the Sociological Study of Childhood*, ed. by Allison James and Alan Prout (London: Falmer, 1997), pp. 165–90
KLEMPERER, VIKTOR, *Kultur: Erwägungen nach dem Zusammenbruch des Nazismus* (Berlin: Neues Leben, 1946)
KLICHE-BEHNKE, DOROTHEA, *Nationalsozialismus und Shoah im autobiographischen Roman: Poetologie des Erinnerns bei Ruth Klüger, Martin Walser, Georg Heller und Günter Grass* (Berlin: de Gruyter, 2016)
KLIGERMAN, ERIC, *Sites of the Uncanny: Paul Celan, Specularity and the Visual Arts* (Berlin: de Gruyter, 2007)
KLINGER, JUDITH, and GERHARD WOLF, eds, *Gedächtnis und kultureller Wandel: Erinnerndes Schreiben, Perspektiven und Kontroversen* (Tübingen: Niemeyer, 2009)
KLÜGER, RUTH, 'Kitsch ist immer plausibel: Was man aus den erfundenen Erinnerungen des Binjamin Wilkomirski lernen kann', in *... alias Wilkomirski: Die Holocaust-Travestie: Enthüllung und Dokumentation eines literarischen Skandals*, ed. by Daniel Ganzfried and Sebastian Hefti (Berlin: Jüdische Verlagsanstalt, 2002), pp. 225–29
—— 'Wanderer zwischen falschen Leben: Über W. G. Sebald', in *W. G. Sebald*, ed. by Heinz Ludwig Arnold (Munich: Text + Kritik, 2003), pp. 95–102
KNOPP, GUIDO, *Die große Flucht: Das Schicksal der Vertriebenen* (Munich: Econ, 2001)
KÖLBEL, MARTIN, 'Nachwort', in *Ein Buch, ein Bekenntnis: Die Debatte um Günter Grass' 'Beim Häuten der Zwiebel'*, ed. by Martin Kölbel (Göttingen: Steidl, 2007), pp. 335–57
KOEPNICK, LUTZ, 'Reframing the Past: Heritage Cinema and Holocaust in the 1990s', *New German Critique*, 87 (2002), 47–82
KOOP, VOLKER, *'Dem Führer ein Kind schenken': Die SS-Organisation Lebensborn e.V.* (Cologne: Böhlau, 2007)
KORFF, GOTTFRIED, and MARTIN ROTH, 'Einleitung', in *Das historische Museum: Labor, Schaubühne, Identitätsfabrik*, ed. by Gottfried Korff and Martin Roth (Frankfurt a.M.: Campus, 1991), pp. 9–41
KOSTA, BARBARA, *Recasting Autobiography: Women's Counterfictions in Contemporary German Literature and Film* (Ithaca: Cornell University Press, 1994)
KOVACH, THOMAS A., 'Commentary', in Thomas A. Kovach and Martin Walser, *The Burden of the Past: Martin Walser on Modern German Identity: Texts, Contexts, Commentary* (Rochester, NY: Camden House, 2008), pp. 96–107
KRELL, ROBERT, 'Child Survivors of the Holocaust: The Elderly Children and their Adult Lives', in *And Life is Changed Forever: Holocaust Childhoods Remembered*, ed. by Martin Ira Glassner and Robert Krell (Michigan: Wayne State University Press, 2006), pp. 1–17

―― 'Elderly Children as Grown Ups: Child Survivors of the Holocaust', *Psychoanalytic Perspectives*, 5 (2007), 13–21

KULLE, DANIEL, ' "Tut so was ein deutscher Junge?": Verantwortung und Mitleid in *Napola — Elite für den Führer*', in *Das Böse im Blick: Die Gegenwart des Nationalsozialismus im Film*, ed. by Margrit Fröhlich, Christian Schneider, and Karsten Visarius (Munich: Text + Kritik, 2007), pp. 219–31

LACAPRA, DOMINICK, *Representing the Holocaust: History, Theory, Trauma* (Ithaca and London: Cornell University Press, 1998)

LANDSBERG, ALISON, *Prosthetic Memory: The Transformation of American Remembrance in the Age of Mass Culture* (New York: Columbia University Press, 2004)

LANDY, MARCIA, 'Introduction', in *The Historical Film: History and Memory in Media*, ed. by Marcia Landy (London: Athlone, 2001), pp. 1–25

LANG, BEREL, *Post-Holocaust: Interpretation, Misinterpretation, and the Claims of History* (Bloomington: Indiana University Press, 2005)

LANGER, LAWRENCE, *The Holocaust and the Literary Imagination* (New Haven and London: Yale University Press, 1975)

―― *Using and Abusing the Holocaust* (Bloomington: Indiana University Press, 2006)

LATHEY, GILLIAN, *The Impossible Legacy: Identity and Purpose in Autobiographical Children's Literature Set in the Third Reich and the Second World War* (Berne and New York: Lang, 1999)

LEEB, JOHANNES, *'Wir waren Hitlers Eliteschüler': Ehemalige Zöglinge der NS-Ausleseschulen brechen ihr Schweigen* (Hamburg: Rasch und Röhring, 1998)

LEFEVERE, ANDRÉ, *Translation, Rewriting, and the Manipulation of Literary Fame* (London and New York: Routledge, 1992)

LEJEUNE, PHILIPPE, *On Autobiography*, ed. by Paul John Eakin, trans. by Katherine Leary (Minneapolis: University of Minnesota Press, 1989)

LEZZI, EVA, *Zerstörte Kindheit: Literarische Autobiografien zur Shoah* (Cologne: Böhlau, 2001)

LLOYD, ALEXANDRA, 'Writing Childhood in Ruth Klüger's *weiter leben: Eine Jugend*', *Forum for Modern Language Studies*, 49 (2013), 175–183.

―― ' "Institutionalized Stories": Childhood and National Socialism in Contemporary German Museum Displays', in *Post-War Literature and Institutions*, ed. by Seán M. Williams and W. Daniel Wilson (= special issue of *Oxford German Studies*, 43 (2014)), pp. 89–105

―― 'Dolls and Play: Material Culture and Memories of Girlhoods in Germany, 1933–1945', in *Deconstructing Dolls: The Many Meanings of Girls' Toys and Play*, ed. by Miriam Forman-Brunell and Jennifer Whitney (New York: Lang, 2015), pp. 37–63

―― 'Songs of Innocence and Experience: Michael Haneke's Cinematic Visions of Childhood', *Modern Language Review*, 111 (2016), 183–207

LOEWY, HANNO, 'Das gerettete Kind: Die "Universalisierung" der Anne Frank', in *Deutsche Nachkriegsliteratur und der Holocaust*, ed. by Stephan Braese and others (Frankfurt a.M.: Campus, 1998), pp. 19–43

LONG, J. J., 'History, Narrative, and Photography in W. G. Sebald's "Die Ausgewanderten" ', *Modern Language Review*, 98 (2003), 117–37

LORENZ, HILKE, *Kriegskinder: Schicksal einer Generation* (Munich: List, 2003)

LUNGSTRUM, JANET, 'Foreskin Fetishism: Jewish Male Difference in *Europa, Europa*', *Screen*, 39 (1998), 53–66

MACARDLE, DOROTHY, *Children of Europe: A Study of the Children of Liberated Countries: Their War-Time Experiences, their Reactions, and their Needs, with a Note on Germany* (London: Gollancz, 1949)

MÄCHLER, STEFAN, *Der Fall Wilkomirski: Über die Wahrheit einer Biographie* (Zurich: Pendo, 2000)

—— *The Wilkomirski Affair: A Study in Biographical Truth*, trans. by John E. Woods (London: Picador, 2001)

MAGUIRE, NORA, *Childness and the Writing of the German Past: Tropes of Childhood in Contemporary German Literature* (Berne: Lang, 2014)

MARSTINE, JANET, 'Introduction', in *New Museum Theory and Practice: An Introduction*, ed. by Janet Marstine (Oxford: Blackwell, 2006), pp. 1–37

MARTIN, ELAINE, *Gender, Patriarchy and Fascism in the Third Reich: The Response of Women Writers* (Detroit: Wayne State University Press, 1993)

MCCULLOH, MARK RICHARD, *Understanding Sebald* (Columbia: University of South Carolina Press, 2003)

MCDOUGALL, ALAN, 'A Duty to Forget? The "Hitler Youth Generation" and the Transition from Nazism to Communism in Postwar East Germany, c. 1945–49', *German History*, 26 (2008), 24–46

MCGAVRAN, JAMES HOLT, ed., *Literature and the Child: Romantic Continuations, Postmodern Contestations* (Iowa City: University of Iowa Press, 1999)

MEEK, MARGARET, and VICTOR WATSON, *Coming of Age in Children's Literature* (London: Continuum, 2003)

MILLER, ALICE, *Am Anfang war Erziehung* (Frankfurt a.M.: Suhrkamp, 1980)

MODLINGER, MARTIN, '"You can't change names and feel the same": The Kindertransport Experience of Susi Bechhöfer in W. G. Sebald's *Austerlitz*', in *The Kindertransport to Britain 1938/39: New Perspectives*, ed. by Andrea Hammel and Bea Lewkowicz (Amsterdam: Rodopi, 2012), pp. 219–32

MOELLER, ROBERT G., *War Stories: The Search for a Usable Past in the Federal Republic of Germany* (Berkeley: University of California Press, 2001)

MOSES, A. DIRK, *German Intellectuals and the Nazi Past* (Cambridge: Cambridge University Press, 2007)

MÜLLER, BEATE, 'Agency, Ethics and Responsibility in Holocaust Fiction: Child Figures as Catalysts in Bruno Apitz's *Nackt unter Wölfen* (1958) and Edgar Hilsenrath's *Nacht* (1964)', *Internationales Archiv für Sozialgeschichte der deutschen Literatur*, 36 (2011), 85–114

MYERS FEINSTEIN, MARGARETE, *Holocaust Survivors in Postwar Germany: 1945–1957* (Cambridge and New York: Cambridge University Press, 2010)

NAFICY, HAMID, *An Accented Cinema: Exilic and Diasporic Filmmaking* (Princeton and Oxford: Princeton University Press, 2001)

NICOLETTI, L. J., 'No Child Left Behind: Anne Frank Exhibits, American Abduction Narratives, and Nazi Bogeymen', in *Visualizing the Holocaust: Documents, Aesthetics, Memory*, ed. by David Bathrick, Brad Prager, and Michael D. Richardson (Rochester, NY: Camden House, 2008), pp. 86–114

NIVEN, BILL, *Facing the Nazi Past: United Germany and the Legacy of the Third Reich* (London: Routledge, 2001)

—— 'Literary Portrayals of National Socialism in Post-Unification German Literature', in *German Culture and the Uncomfortable Past: Representations of National Socialism in Contemporary Germanic Literature*, ed. by Helmut Schmitz (Aldershot: Ashgate, 2001), pp. 11–29

—— *The Buchenwald Child: Truth, Fiction, and Propaganda* (Rochester, NY: Camden House, 2007)

—— 'German Victimhood Discourse in Comparative Perspective', in *Dynamics of Memory and Identity in Contemporary Europe*, ed. by Eric Langenbacher, Bill Niven, and Ruth Wittlinger (New York: Berghahn, 2012), pp. 180–95

—— ed., *Germans as Victims: Remembering the Past in Contemporary Germany* (Basingstoke: Palgrave Macmillan, 2006)

NIVEN, WILLIAM J., 'The Reception of Steven Spielberg's *Schindler's List* in the German Media', *Journal of European Studies*, 25 (1995), 165–89

NORA, PIERRE, 'Between Memory and History: *Les Lieux de Mémoire*', *Representations*, 26 (1989), 7–24

—— *Realms of Memory: Rethinking the French Past*, trans. by Arthur Goldhammer (New York: Columbia University Press, 1996)

OLIN, MARGARET, 'Lanzmann's *Shoah* and the Topography of the Holocaust Film', *Representations*, 57 (1997), 1–23

—— *Touching Photographs* (Chicago: University of Chicago Press, 2012)

O'SULLIVAN, EMER, 'Englishness in German Translations of *Alice in Wonderland*', in *Interconnecting Translation Studies and Imagology*, ed. by Luc van Doorslaer, Peter Flynn, and Joep Leerssen (Amsterdam: Benjamins, 2016), pp. 87–109

ÖZDAMAR, EMINE SEVGI, *Mother Tongue*, trans. by Craig Thomas (Toronto: Coach House Press, 1994)

—— *Mutterzunge: Erzählungen* (Cologne: Kiepenheuer & Witsch, 1998)

PARKES, STUART, 'Günter Grass and his Contemporaries in East and West', in *The Cambridge Companion to Günter Grass*, ed. by Stuart Taberner (Cambridge: Cambridge University Press, 2009), pp. 209–23

PARRY, CHRISTOPH, 'Die Rechtfertigung der Erinnerung vor der Last der Geschichte', in *Grenzen der Fiktionalität und der Erinnerung*, ed. by Christoph Parry and Edgar Platen (Munich: Iudicium, 2007), pp. 98–111

PASCAL, ROY, *Design and Truth in Autobiography* (Cambridge: Cambridge University Press, 1960)

PAVER, CHLOE, '"Ein Stück langweiliger als die Wehrmachtsausstellung, aber dafür repräsentativer": The Exhibition Fotofeldpost as Riposte to the Wehrmacht Exhibition', in *German Memory Contests: The Quest for Identity in Literature, Film, and Discourse since 1990*, ed. by Anne Fuchs, Mary Cosgrove, and Georg Grote (Rochester, NY: Camden House, 2006), pp. 107–25

—— *Refractions of the Third Reich in German and Austrian Fiction and Film* (Oxford: Oxford University Press, 2007)

—— '"You Shall Know Them by their Objects": Material Culture and its Impact in Museum Displays about National Socialism', in *Cultural Impact in the German Context: Models of Transmission, Reception and Influence*, ed. by Rebecca Braun and Lyn Marven (Rochester, NY: Camden House, 2010), pp. 169–87

PEUKERT, DETLEV, *The Weimar Republic: The Crisis of Classical Modernity*, trans. by Richard Deveson (London: Penguin, 1993)

PICKAR, GERTRUD BAUER, 'In Defense of the Past: The Life and Passion of Alfred Dorn in *Die Verteidigung der Kindheit*', in *New Critical Perspectives on Martin Walser*, ed. by Frank Pilipp (Columbia, SC: Camden House, 1994), pp. 134–56

PINE, LISA, 'Creating Conformity: The Training of Girls in the Bund Deutscher Mädel', *European History Quarterly*, 33 (2003), 367–85

—— *Education in Nazi Germany* (Oxford and New York: Berg, 2010)

PINFOLD, DEBBIE, *The Child's View of the Third Reich in German Literature: The Eye among the Blind* (Oxford: Clarendon Press, 2001)

—— 'The Sins of the Fathers: Mark Herman's *The Boy in the Striped Pyjamas* (2008) and Cate Shortland's *Lore* (2012)', in *Childhood in German Film after 1989*, ed. by Alexandra Lloyd and Ute Wölfel (= special issue of *Oxford German Studies*, 44 (2015)), pp. 254–71

PLUNKA, GENE A., *Holocaust Drama: The Theater of Atrocity* (Cambridge: Cambridge University Press, 2009)

PREECE, JULIAN, 'Damaged Lives? (East) German Memoirs and Autobiographies, 1989–1994', in *The New Germany: Literature and Society after Unification*, ed. by Osman Durrani,

Colin Good, and Kevin Hilliard (Sheffield: Sheffield Academic Press, 1995), pp. 349–64
—— *The Life and Work of Günter Grass: Literature, History, Politics* (Basingstoke: Palgrave Macmillan, 2004)
PRESCOTT, ANDREW, 'The Textuality of the Archive', in *What Are Archives? Cultural and Theoretical Perspectives: A Reader*, ed. by Louise Craven (Aldershot: Ashgate, 2008), pp. 31–53
PROSE, FRANCINE, *Anne Frank: The Book, the Life, the Afterlife* (London: Atlantic, 2010)
RADSTONE, SUSANNAH, 'Cinema and Memory', in *Memory: Histories, Theories, Debates*, ed. by Susannah Radstone and Bill Schwarz (New York: Fordham University Press, 2010), pp. 325–43
RECHTIEN, RENATE, 'Gelebtes, erinnertes, erzähltes und erschriebenes Selbst: Günter de Bruyns *Zwischenbilanz* und Christa Wolfs *Kindheitsmuster*', in *Günter de Bruyn in Perspective*, ed. by Dennis Tate (Amsterdam: Rodopi, 1999), pp. 151–70
RECTOR, MARTIN, 'Frühe Absonderung, später Abschied: Adoleszenz und Faschismus in den autobiographischen Erzählungen von Georges-Arthur Goldschmidt und Peter Weiss', *Peter Weiss Jahrbuch*, 4 (1995), 122–39
REECE, JAMES, 'Remembering the GDR: Memory and Evasion in Autobiographical Writing from the Former GDR', in *Textual Responses to German Unification: Processing Historical and Social Change in Literature and Film*, ed. by Carol Anne Costabile-Heming, Rachel J. Halverson, and Kristie A. Foell (Berlin and New York: de Gruyter, 2001), pp. 59–77
REESE, DAGMAR, 'The BDM Generation: A Female Generation in Transition from Dictatorship to Democracy', in *Generations in Conflict: Youth Revolt and Generation Formation in Germany 1770–1968*, ed. by Mark Roseman (Cambridge: Cambridge University Press, 1995), pp. 227–47
REICH-RANICKI, MARCEL, *Über Ruhestörer: Juden in der deutschen Literatur* (Munich: Piper, 1973)
—— 'Vorwort', in *Meine Schulzeit im Dritten Reich: Erinnerungen deutscher Schriftsteller*, ed. by Marcel Reich-Ranicki (Cologne: Kiepenheuer & Witsch, 1982), pp. 9–12
—— ED., *Meine Schulzeit im Dritten Reich: Erinnerungen deutscher Schriftsteller* (Cologne: Kiepenheuer & Witsch, 1982)
REIDY, JULIAN, *Rekonstruktion und Entheroisierung: Paradigmen des 'Generationenromans' in der deutschsprachigen Gegenwartsliteratur* (Bielefeld: Aisthesis, 2013)
—— 'Die Unmöglichkeit der Erinnerung: Arno Geigers "Es geht uns gut" als Persiflage des Generationenromans der Gegenwartsliteratur', *German Studies Review*, 36 (2013), 79–102
REITER, ANDREA, 'Die Funktion der Kinderperspektive in der Darstellung des Holocausts', in *'Für ein Kind war das anders': Traumatische Erfahrungen jüdischer Kinder und Jugendlicher im nationalsozialistischen Deutschland*, ed. by Barbara Bauer and Waltraud Strickhausen (Berlin: Metropol, 1999), pp. 215–29
—— 'Memory and Authenticity: The Case of Binjamin Wilkomirski', in *The Memory of Catastrophe*, ed. by Peter Gray and Kendrick Oliver (Manchester: Manchester University Press, 2004), pp. 132–46
—— ED., *Children of the Holocaust* (London: Vallentine Mitchell, 2006)
RICHTER, GERHARD, 'Acts of Memory and Mourning: Derrida and the Fictions of Anteriority', in *Memory: Histories, Theories, Debates*, ed. by Susannah Radstone and Bill Schwarz (New York: Fordham University Press, 2010), pp. 150–61
ROSEMAN, MARK 'Introduction', in *Generations in Conflict: Youth Revolt and Generation Formation in Germany 1770–1968*, ed. by Mark Roseman (Cambridge: Cambridge University Press, 1995), pp. 1–47

ROSENFELD, ALVIN H., 'Popularization and Memory: The Case of Anne Frank', in *Lessons and Legacies: The Meaning of the Holocaust in a Changing World*, ed. by Peter Hayes (Evanston: Northwestern University Press, 1991), pp. 243–79

RÜTHER, GÜNTER, 'Ein Schriftsteller, der keiner sein will: Einführung in Leben und Werk von Georges-Arthur Goldschmidt' <www.kas.de/wf/doc/kas_7553-544-1-30.pdf?051118133259> [accessed 1 July 2019]

SAEGER, JAMES SCHOFIELD, 'The Mission and Historical Missions: Film and the Writing of History', *The Americas*, 31 (1995), 393–415

SAYNER, JOANNE, *Women without a Past? German Autobiographical Writings and Fascism* (Amsterdam: Rodopi, 2007)

SCHADE, RICHARD E., 'Layers of Meaning, War, Art: Grass's "Beim Häuten der Zwiebel"', *German Quarterly*, 80 (2007), 279–301

SCHAUMANN, CAROLINE, 'From *weiter leben* (1992) to *Still Alive* (2001): Ruth Klüger's Cultural Translation of her "German Book" for an American Audience', *German Quarterly*, 77 (2004), 324–39

—— *Memory Matters: Generational Responses to Germany's Nazi Past in Recent Women's Literature* (Berlin: de Gruyter, 2008)

SCHIRRMACHER, FRANK, *Die Walser-Bubis-Debatte: Eine Dokumentation* (Frankfurt a.M.: Suhrkamp, 1999)

SCHMIDT, NADINE JESSICA, *Konstruktionen literarischer Authentizität in autobiographischem Erzählen* (Göttingen: V&R unipress, 2014)

SCHMITZ, HELMUT, 'Introduction', in *German Culture and the Uncomfortable Past: Representations of National Socialism in Contemporary Germanic Literature*, ed. by Helmut Schmitz (Aldershot: Ashgate, 2001), pp. 1–11

—— 'Soundscapes of the Third Reich: Marcel Beyer's *Flughunde*', in *German Culture and the Uncomfortable Past: Representations of National Socialism in Contemporary Germanic Literature*, ed. by Helmut Schmitz (Aldershot: Ashgate, 2001) pp. 119–41

—— *On their Own Terms: The Legacy of National Socialism in Post-1990 German Fiction* (Birmingham: Birmingham University Press, 2004)

—— 'Introduction', in *A Nation of Victims? Representations of German Wartime Suffering from 1945 to the Present*, ed. by Helmut Schmitz (Amsterdam: Rodopi, 2007), pp. 1–31

—— ED., *German Culture and the Uncomfortable Past: Representations of National Socialism in Contemporary Germanic Literature* (Aldershot: Ashgate, 2001)

—— ED., *A Nation of Victims? Representations of German Wartime Suffering from 1945 to the Present* (Amsterdam: Rodopi, 2007)

SCHNEIDER, CHRISTIAN, 'Sehen, Hören, Glauben: Zur Konstruktion von Authentizität', in *Das Böse im Blick: Die Gegenwart des Nationalsozialismus im Film*, ed. by Margrit Fröhlich, Christian Schneider, and Karsten Visarius (Munich: Text + Kritik, 2007), pp. 15–30

SCHNEIDER, CHRISTIAN, CORDELIA STILLKE, and BERND LEINWEBER, *Das Erbe der Napola: Versuch einer Generationengeschichte des Nationalsozialismus* (Hamburg: Hamburger Edition, 1996)

SCHÖDEL, KATHRIN, *Literarisches versus politisches Gedächtnis? Martin Walsers Friedenspreisrede und sein Roman 'Ein springender Brunnen'* (Würzburg: Königshausen & Neumann, 2010)

—— 'Martin Walser's *Ein springender Brunnen* (*A Gushing Fountain*)', in *The Novel in German since 1990*, ed. by Stuart Taberner (Cambridge: Cambridge University Press, 2011), pp. 108–23

SCHOEPS, KARL-HEINZ, *Literature and Film in the Third Reich* (Rochester, NY: Camden House, 2003)

SCHUBERT, KATJA, *Notwendige Umwege: Gedächtnis und Zeugenschaft in Texten jüdischer Autorinnen in Deutschland und Frankreich nach Auschwitz = Voies de traverse oblige* (Hildesheim: Olms, 2001)

SCHUCHALTER, JERRY, *Poetry and Truth: Variations on Holocaust Testimony* (Oxford: Lang, 2009)
SCHULTE-SASSE, LINDA, '"Living On" in the American Press: Ruth Klüger's "Still Alive" and its Challenge to a Cherished Holocaust Paradigm', *German Studies Review*, 27 (2004), 469–75
SHAVIT, ZOHAR, *A Past without a Shadow: Constructing the Past in German Books for Children* (London: Routledge, 2005)
SIMINE, SILKE ARNOLD-DE, *Memory Traces: 1989 and the Question of German Cultural Identity* (Oxford and New York: Lang, 2005)
SINYARD, NEIL, *Children in the Movies* (London: Batsford, 1992)
SOKOLOFF, NAOMI, 'Childhood Lost: Children's Voices in Holocaust Literature', in *Infant Tongues: The Voice of the Child in Literature*, ed. by Elizabeth Goodenough, Mark A. Heberle, and Naomi Sokoloff (Michigan: Wayne State University Press, 1994), pp. 259–75
SPIELMANN, MONIKA, *Aus den Augen des Kindes: Die Kinderperspektive in deutschsprachigen Romanen seit 1945* (Innsbruck: Universität Innsbruck, 2002)
STAHL, JOHN DANIEL, 'Moral Despair and the Child as Symbol of Hope in Pre-World War II Berlin', *Children's Literature*, 14 (1986), 83–104
STARGARDT, NICHOLAS, *Witnesses of War: Children's Lives under the Nazis* (London: Cape, 2005)
STEEDMAN, CAROLYN, *Strange Dislocations: Childhood and the Idea of Human Interiority, 1780–1930* (London: Virago, 1995)
STEINLEIN, RÜDIGER, '*Sternkinder* und *Tote Engel* — Bilder des Holocaust in der Kinder- und Jugendliteratur zwischen pädagogisch-moralischer Wiedergutmachung und dokumentarisch-katastrophischer Wirkungsästhethik', in *Bilder des Holocaust: Literatur — Film — Bildende Kunst*, ed. by Manuel Köppen and Klaus R. Scherpe (Cologne: Böhlau, 1997), pp. 63–97
STERN, FRITZ, *Five Germanys I Have Known: A History & Memoir* (New York: Farrar Straus Giroux, 2006)
STONE, KATHERINE, *Women and National Socialism in Postwar German Literature: Gender, Memory, and Subjectivity* (Rochester, NY: Camden House, 2017)
STRAUS, NINA PELIKAN, 'Sebald, Wittgenstein, and the Ethics of Memory', *Comparative Literature*, 61 (2009), 43–53
STROBL, INGRID, ed., *Das kleine Mädchen, das ich war: Schriftstellerinnen erzählen ihre Kindheit* (Munich: dtv, 1984)
SULEIMAN, SUSAN R., 'Problems of Memory and Factuality in Recent Holocaust Memoirs: Wilkomirski/Wiesel', *Poetics Today*, 21 (2000), 543–59
—— 'The 1.5 Generation: Thinking about Child Survivors and the Holocaust', *American Imago*, 59 (2002), 277–95
—— 'Do Facts Matter in Holocaust Memoirs? Wilkomirski/Wiesel', in *Obliged by Memory: Literature, Religion, Ethics*, ed. by Steven T. Katz and Alan Rosen (Syracuse: Syracuse University Press, 2006), pp. 21–43
TABERNER, STUART, 'A Manifesto for Germany's "New Right"? Martin Walser, the Past, Transcendence, Aesthetics, and *Ein springender Brunnen*', *German Life and Letters*, 53.1 (2000), 126–41
—— '"Deutsche Geschichte darf auch einmal gutgehen": Martin Walser, Auschwitz, and the "German Question" from *Ehen in Philippsburg* to *Ein springender Brunnen*', in *German Culture and the Uncomfortable Past: Representations of National Socialism in Contemporary Germanic Literature*, ed. by Helmut Schmitz (Aldershot: Ashgate, 2001), pp. 45–65
—— *German Literature of the 1990s and Beyond: Normalization and the Berlin Republic* (Rochester, NY, and Woodbridge: Camden House, 2005)
—— 'Private Failings and Public Virtues: Günter Grass's *Beim Häuten der Zwiebel* and the Exemplary Use of Authorial Biography', *Modern Language Review*, 103 (2008), 144–54

—— 'Günter Grass's *Peeling the Onion*', in *The Cambridge Companion to Günter Grass*, ed. by Stuart Taberner (Cambridge: Cambridge University Press, 2009), pp. 139–51
—— *Aging and Old-Age Style in Günter Grass, Ruth Klüger, Christa Wolf, and Martin Walser* (Rochester, NY: Camden House, 2013)
TABERNER, STUART, and KARINA BERGER, eds, *Germans as Victims in the Literary Fiction of the Berlin Republic* (Rochester, NY: Camden House, 2009)
TABERNER, STUART, and PAUL COOKE, 'Introduction', in *German Culture, Politics, and Literature into the Twenty-First Century: Beyond Normalization*, ed. by Stuart Taberner and Paul Cooke (Rochester, NY, and Woodbridge: Camden House, 2006), pp. 1–17
TATE, DENNIS, 'Changing Perspectives on Günter de Bruyn: An Introduction', in *Günter de Bruyn in Perspective*, ed. by Dennis Tate (Amsterdam: Rodopi, 1999), pp. 1–9
—— *Shifting Perspectives: East German Autobiographical Narratives before and after the End of the GDR* (Rochester, NY: Camden House, 2007)
TAYLOR, JENNIFER, 'Ruth Klüger's *weiter leben: Eine Jugend*: A Jewish Woman's Letter to her Mother', in *Out from the Shadows: Essays on Contemporary Austrian Women Writers and Filmmakers*, ed. by Margarete Lamb-Faffelberger (Riverside, CA: Ariadne Press, 1997), pp. 77–88
TEBBUTT, SUSAN, *Gudrun Pausewang in Context: Socially Critical 'Jugendliteratur'* (Frankfurt a.M.: Lang, 1994)
—— 'Journey to an Unknown Destination: Gudrun Pausewang's Transgressive Teenage Novel *Reise im August*', in *German Culture and the Uncomfortable Past: Representations of National Socialism in Contemporary Germanic Literature*, ed. by Helmut Schmitz (Aldershot: Ashgate, 2001), pp. 165–83
THESZ, NICOLE A., *The Communicative Event in the Works of Günter Grass: Stages of Speech, 1959–2015* (Rochester, NY: Camden House, 2018)
TONKIN, KATI, 'From "Sudetendeutsche" to "Adlergebirgler": Gudrun Pausewang's *Rosinkawiese* Trilogy', in *Coming Home to Germany? The Integration of Ethnic Germans from Central and Eastern Europe in the Federal Republic*, ed. by David Rock and Stefan Wolff (New York: Berghahn, 2002), pp. 119–213
TURNER, VICTOR, *The Ritual Process: Structure and Anti-Structure* (London: Routledge & Kegan Paul, 1969)
—— *Dramas, Fields, and Metaphors: Symbolic Action in Human Society* (Ithaca and London: Cornell University Press, 1974)
USTORF, ANNE-EV, *Wir Kinder der Kriegskinder: Die Generation im Schatten des Zweiten Weltkriegs* (Freiburg: Herder, 2008)
VAN GENNEP, ARNOLD, *The Rites of Passage*, trans. by Monika B. Vizedom and Gabrielle L. Caffee (London: Routledge and Kegan Paul, 1977)
VEES-GULANI, SUSANNE, *Trauma and Guilt: Literature of Wartime Bombing in Germany* (Berlin: de Gruyter, 2003)
VICE, SUE, *Children Writing the Holocaust* (Basingstoke: Palgrave Macmillan, 2004)
VOLAVKOVÁ, HANA, ed., *I Never Saw Another Butterfly: Children's Drawings and Poems from Terezin Concentration Camp 1942–1944* (New York: McGraw-Hill, 1964)
VON GLASENAPP, GABRIELE, and HANS HEINO EWERS, *Kriegs- and Nachkriegskindheiten: Studien zur literarischen Erinnerungskultur für junge Leser* (Frankfurt a.M.: Lang, 2008)
VON HELLFELD, MATTHIAS, and ARNO KLÖNNE, *Die betrogene Generation: Jugend im Faschismus* (Cologne: Pahl-Rugenstein, 1985)
WARD, ELIZABETH M., 'Dismantling the Third Reich in Cate Shortland's *Lore* (2012)', *Film & History: An Interdisciplinary Journal*, 47.1 (2017), 18–27
WASMEIER, MARIE LOUISE, 'The Past in the Making: Invented Images and Fabricated Family History in Marcel Beyer's *Spione*', in *New German Literature: Life-Writing and*

Dialogue with the Arts, ed. by Julian Preece, Frank Finlay, and Ruth J. Owen (Berne and Oxford: Lang, 2007), pp. 343–58

WEISS-WENDT, ANTON, ed., The Nazi Genocide of the Roma: Reassessment and Commemoration (New York: Berghahn, 2013)

WELZER, HARALD, 'Schön unscharf: Über die Konjunktur der Familien- und Generationenromane', Mittelweg, 36 (2004), 53–64

WELZER, HARALD, SABINE MOLLER, and KAROLINE TSCHUGGNALL, Opa war kein Nazi: Nationalsozialismus und Holocaust im Familiengedächtnis (Frankfurt a.M.: Fischer, 2010)

WEST, NANCY MARTHA, Kodak and the Lens of Nostalgia (London: University Press of Virginia, 2000)

WILKES, GEORGE, 'Changing Attitudes to the "European-ness" of the Holocaust and of its Victims', in Remembering for the Future: The Holocaust in an Age of Genocide, ed. by John K. Roth and Elisabeth Maxwell, 3 vols (New York: Palgrave, 2001), I: History, pp. 130–55

WILLER, STEFAN, 'Being Translated: Exile, Childhood, and Multilingualism in G.-A. Goldschmidt and W. G. Sebald', in German Memory Contests: The Quest for Identity in Literature, Film, and Discourse since 1990, ed. by Anne Fuchs, Mary Cosgrove, and Georg Grote (Rochester, NY: Camden House, 2006), pp. 87–107

WHITEHEAD, ANNE, 'Telling Tales: Trauma and Testimony in Binjamin Wilkomirski's Fragments', Discourse, 25 (2003), 119–37

WIESEL, ELIE, 'Art and Culture after the Holocaust', in Auschwitz: Beginning of a New Era? Reflections on the Holocaust, ed. by Eva Fleischner (New York: KTAV, 1977), pp. 403–15

WINTERBERG, YURY, and SONYA WINTERBERG, Kriegskinder: Erinnerungen einer Generation (Berlin: Rotbuch, 2009)

WOLF, CHRISTA, 'Eine Diskussion über Kindheitsmuster', German Quarterly, 57 (1984), 91–95

WOOLF, VIRGINIA, 'Lewis Carroll', in Aspects of Alice: Lewis Carroll's Dreamchild as Seen through the Critics' Looking-Glasses, 1865–1971, ed. by Robert Philips (London: Gollancz, 1972), pp. 47–50

ZEHFUSS, MAJA, Wounds of Memory: The Politics of War in Germany (Cambridge: Cambridge University Press, 2007)

ZEILLINGER, GERHARD, Kindheit und Schreiben: Zur Biographie und Poetik des Schriftstellers Julian Schutting (Stuttgart: Heinz, 1995)

ZEMPELIN, HANS GÜNTHER, Des Teufels Kadett: Napola-Schüler von 1936 bis 1943: Gespräch mit einem Freund (Frankfurt a.M.: Fischer, 2000)

ZIMMERMAN, BARRY J., and TIMOTHY J. CLEARY, 'Adolescents' Development of Personal Agency: The Role of Self-Efficacy Beliefs and Self-Regulatory Skill', in Self-Efficacy Beliefs of Adolescents, ed. by Frank Pajares and Timothy C. Urdan (Greenwich, CT: IAP, 2006), pp. 45–71

ZIPES, JACK DAVID, 'Introduction', in Fairy Tales and Fables from Weimar Days, ed. and trans. by Jack David Zipes (Hanover and London: University Press of New England, 1989), pp. 3–31

—— 'The Contemporary German Fascination for Things Jewish: Toward a Minor Jewish Culture', in Reemerging Jewish Culture in Germany: Life and Literature since 1989, ed. by Sander L. Gilman and Karen Remmler (New York and London: New York University Press, 1994), pp. 15–46

—— The Brothers Grimm: From Enchanted Forests to the Modern World (Basingstoke: Palgrave Macmillan, 2002)

ZUR NIEDEN, SUSANNE, '"... stärker als der Tod" — Bruno Apitz' Roman Nackt unter Wölfen und die Holocaust-Rezeption in der DDR', in Bilder des Holocaust: Literatur — Film — Bildende Kunst, ed. by Manuel Köppen and Klaus R. Scherpe (Cologne: Böhlau, 1997), pp. 97–109

INDEX

adolescence 33, 113, 128–29, 143–44
    and liminality 33, 149–50
Assmann, Aleida 3, 20–21, 22–23, 162
authenticity 27–28, 125, 132–34, 174–75
    and autobiographical writing 31–32, 48–50
    and cinema 153–58, 162
    and film/photography 32, 48, 118, 132, 140
autobiography 90–91, 103
    and the Hitler Youth generation 42–43
    and truth 68–69, 119–21, 125–26

Benedict XVI [Joseph Ratzinger] 2, 3, 64–65
Buchenwaldkind [Buchenwald child] 79–80, 81, 87–88, 175

childhood:
    and agency 31, 149, 175
    and authenticity 31–32, 116–17, 123, 163–64
    and autobiography 44–45, 60–61, 116–17, 120–21
    and difference 28, 83–85
    and innocence 11, 28–29, 30, 33, 46, 48, 51, 56, 57, 81, 84, 93, 99, 103, 127–28, 132, 134, 147–48, 149, 151, 161, 173
child's perspective 10, 122–23, 127
cinema after reunification 139, 158, 162, 173–74
curiosity 43, 62–63, 83, 98, 122–23, 127, 133, 172

de Bruyn, Günter 4–5, 43–44, 45, 57, 58, 66, 67, 68, 164
    Das erzählte Ich [The Narrated Self] 47, 48, 49–50, 68–69
    Zwischenbilanz [Taking Stock] 45–52, 62, 68, 98, 100, 173, 177
defamiliarization 10, 55, 83, 171

education, school 16–17, 25–26, 92–93, 113, 117, 143, 145–47, 148, 149, 156

fairy tales 55–56, 73 n. 74, 88–89, 117, 129, 149–51, 159–60, 161
Fest, Joachim 54–55
Frank, Anne 80–82 87, 175
Freud, Sigmund 28, 57–58, 83, 91, 107 n. 60, 135 n. 8, 153

Gansel, Dennis, 145–52, 153, 156, 164–65

gefühlte Geschichte [emotionally experienced history] 23–24, 147, 162
German wartime suffering 20–21
Goldschmidt, Georges-Arthur 5, 10
    Die Absonderung [Seclusion] 78, 79, 90–96, 102–04, 112, 132–33, 172, 173, 175, 177
Grass, Günter 2, 4–5, 164
    Beim Häuten der Zwiebel [Peeling the Onion] 5, 43–44, 45, 59–66, 67, 68, 69–70, 99, 172, 173, 174, 177
    Die Blechtrommel [The Tin Drum] 60, 61–62, 63–64, 70, 168 n. 91

Heimat 56, 94–95, 161
Hirsch, Marianne 24, 116, 132, 134
Hitlerjunge Quex [Hitler Youth Quex] (dir. Steinhoff) 141, 146–47
Hitlerjunge Salomon [Europa Europa] (dir. Holland) 101, 140–45, 147–48, 164
Hitler Youth 15–16, 146
Holland, Agnieszka 141–42, 155–56

identity 101, 115–16, 143

Jewish children 16–17, 18–19, 77–78, 79–82

Kindertransports 17, 77, 78, 112, 118
Klüger, Ruth 5, 8, 59, 122
    weiter leben: Eine Jugend [Still Alive: A Holocaust Girlhood Remembered] 78–79, 82–90, 91, 96, 98, 102–04, 127, 174, 175
    Dichter und Historiker: Fakten und Fiktionen [Poets and Historians: Facts and Fictions] 103
Kunert, Günter 5, 79, 96–102, 103, 103–04
    Erwachsenenspiele [Games for Grown-Ups] 79, 96–102, 103–04, 172, 173, 175, 177

Lebensborn [Fountain of Life] programme 16, 19, 144
Lore (dir. Shortland) 158–62, 163–65

memorials 77–78
memory:
    communicative 22
    cultural 22–23
    lieux de mémoire [sites of memory] 25
    memory contests 2, 3

postmemory 24, 25
prosthetic memory 24–25
museums and exhibitions 21, 25–27, 29–31, 54–55, 123, 155

NaPolA: Elite für den Führer [Before the Fall] (dir. Gansel) 140, 145–52, 159, 164–65, 172
national identity 176–77
National Socialism:
  and persecution 16–17, 78, 108 n. 73
  and youth 15–16

Parzival 63, 149, 172
Pausewang, Gudrun 18, 111–12
  Reise im August [The Final Journey] 5–6, 111–12, 126–30, 133, 172, 173, 174, 175, 178
Perel, Solomon [Sally Perel] 141, 164
photography, photographs 114–18, 121, 131–32, 134, 155

remembrance, *see* memory
Reich-Ranicki, Marcel 60
  Meine Schulzeit im Dritten Reich [My Schooldays in the Third Reich] 1, 66–67, 164, 171

Sebald, W.G. 131–32
  Austerlitz 112–19, 155, 172–73, 175
  Die Ausgewanderten [The Emigrants] 114–15
Second World War, *see* World War II

sex, sexual development 29, 46, 65, 81, 83, 92–93, 94, 100–01, 143–44, 147–48, 172–73
Shortland, Cate 140, 158–62, 164

Third Reich, *see* National Socialism
toys 30–31, 64, 93–94
trauma 13 n. 36, 19, 20, 24, 25, 42, 78, 86, 92–93, 95, 104, 112, 114–15, 123–24, 132

Walser, Martin 4–5, 43–44, 57–58, 100, 120, 125, 142, 164, 173, 177
  and the 'Friedenspreisrede' [Peace Prize Speech] 2, 174
  Die Verteidigung der Kindheit [Defending Childhood] 53–54
  Ein springender Brunnen [A Gushing Fountain] 52–59, 65, 97, 167 n. 49
  Ohne einander [Without Each Other] 142
  Über Deutschland reden [Speaking of Germany] 53, 57, 58–59
Wilkomirski, Binjamin [Bruno Doesseker] 95, 131, 174
  Bruchstücke [Fragments] 5, 8, 75 n. 128, 111, 119–26, 127, 131, 132, 133, 134, 173, 174, 175, 178
Wolf, Christa 2, 8, 41–42, 58
  Kindheitsmuster [Patterns of Childhood] 41–42, 51, 66, 178
World War II 2, 8–9, 19–20, 43, 47, 65, 97, 176

Zeller, Eva 43, 44–45, 75 n. 121

www.ingramcontent.com/pod-product-compliance
Lightning Source LLC
Chambersburg PA
CBHW050453110426
42743CB00017B/3350